The Science
Basic L-Rod Dowsing

The Science of Basic L-Rod Dowsing
An Investigation

Richard Warburton

McFarland & Company, Inc., Publishers
Jefferson, North Carolina

LIBRARY OF CONGRESS CATALOGING-IN-PUBLICATION DATA

Names: Warburton, Richard, 1964– author.
Title: The science of basic L-rod dowsing : an investigation / Richard Warburton.
Description: Jefferson, North Carolina : McFarland & Company, Inc., Publishers, 2025 | Includes bibliographical references and index.
Identifiers: LCCN 2024013749 | ISBN 9781476694016 (paperback : acid free paper) ∞
ISBN 9781476651699 (ebook)
Subjects: LCSH: Dowsing. | BISAC: BODY, MIND & SPIRIT / Divination / General
Classification: LCC BF1628 .W36 2024 | DDC 133.3/23—dc23/eng/20241011
LC record available at https://lccn.loc.gov/2024013749

ISBN (print) 978-1-4766-9401-6
ISBN (ebook) 978-1-4766-5169-9

© 2025 Richard Warburton. All rights reserved

No part of this book may be reproduced or transmitted in any form or by any means, electronic or mechanical, including photocopying or recording, or by any information storage and retrieval system, without permission in writing from the publisher.

Front cover images © Hluboki Dzianis/Shutterstock;
© franciscodiazpagador/iStock

Printed in the United States of America

McFarland & Company, Inc., Publishers
Box 611, Jefferson, North Carolina 28640
www.mcfarlandpub.com

Table of Contents

Acknowledgments — vii
Symbols and Abbreviations Used in This Book — ix
Preface — 1

1. Introduction — 3
2. General Observations of the Dowsing Signal — 10
3. Preliminary Observations and Requirements for the Dowsing Effect — 17
4. The Psychology of Dowsing — 22
5. Radioactivity and Subatomic Particles — 33
6. Gravity — 37
7. Parallel Bands and Fields Produced by Rotating Objects — 39
8. Nuclear Magnetic Resonance — 46
9. Sound — 49
10. Electric Fields and Static Electricity — 51
11. Telluric Magnetism and Currents — 59
12. Nature of the Dowsing Response — 66
13. Location of Dowsing Sense Organ — 82
14. Magnetism and Magnetic Fields — 88
15. Electromagnetic Fields and Dowsing — 100
16. Dowsing Frequency Band — 112
17. Source of Electromagnetic Radiation — 124
18. Resolution of Dowsing Signal — 131
19. Memory Effects — 152
20. Depth — 170
21. Measuring the Dowsing Response Instrumentally — 191
22. Dowsing in Three Dimensions — 206
23. Mechanisms for Detection of Magnetic Fields in Animals — 210

Table of Contents

24. Interaction of Electromagnetic Fields with Biological Systems	218
25. Remaining Mysteries and Interesting Reports	235
26. Conclusions	243
Final Words	247
Appendix: Properties of Waves	249
Annex: Instrumentation Used	261
Chapter Notes	265
Selected Bibliography	290
Index	291

Acknowledgments

I would like to thank my wife Jenny Warburton, my son Andrew Warburton, M.D., daughter Lia Warburton and friend John Wayt for their helpful discussions, extraordinary patience and invaluable assistance with this project.

Symbols and Abbreviations Used in This Book

Symbols

A_G	Antenna gain
a	Height (opposite) of right angled triangle, aperture, aperture (m)
B	Magnetic flux density (T)
B_F	Spectral radiance based (W.s/steridan/m²)
B_λ	Spectral radiance (W/steridan/m)
c	Speed of light, 3×10^8 m/s
C	Capacitance (F)
C_H	Heat capacity (J/K)
d	Piezoelectric coefficient, diameter, width, distance (m)
D	Depth (m)
e	Exponential constant (~2.718)
E	Energy (J), Heat (J)
E_f	Electric field (V/m)
E_k	Kinetic energy (J)
E^o	Standard electrode potential (V)
E_p	Potential energy (J)
f	Force (N)
F	Frequency (Hz)
F_c	Faraday constant (9.648×10^{-4} C/mol)
G	Gravitational constant, (6.674×10^{-11} m³kg⁻¹s⁻²)
g	Acceleration due to gravity (9.8 m/s² at sea level)
h	Planck's constant, (6.626×10^{-34} m² kg/s)
H	Magnetic field strength (A/m)
i	Current (Amperes [A])
I	Intensity (W/m²)
J	Average saturation magnetism (T)
k_B	Boltzmann constant (1.381×10^{-23} m² kgs⁻² K⁻¹)
ke	Coulomb's constant (8.99×10^9 Nm²C⁻²)
L	Length (m)
l	Inductance (H)
m	Mass (kg)
M	Magnetic moment (J/T)
n	Number of electrons, integer, refractive index
P	Penetration depth (m)
P_p	Piezoelectric polarization (C/m²)
Φ	Magnetic flux
Q	Charge (C)
R	Resistance (Ohms)
R_c	Gas constant (8.314 JK⁻¹mol⁻¹)
R_m	Magnetic saturation remanence
r	Radius or distance (m)
S	Conductance (Siemens or $^{Ohm-1}$), strain (no units)
T	Temperature (K)
T_c	Critical temperature for superconductivity (K)
t	Time (s)
V	Potential difference, Electromotive force or Voltage (V), Volume (m³)
v	Velocity or speed (m/s)
w	Width (m)
β	Volume (m₃)
γ	Gyromagnetic ratio (rad s–1T–1)
Δx	Change in x
δ	Diameter (m)
δ_p	Penetration depth (m)
ε_0	Permittivity of free space ($8.854187813 \times 10^{-12}$ Fm⁻¹)
ε_r	Relative permittivity (vs vacuum)
θ	Angle (radians or degrees)
θ_c	Critical angle (radians or degrees)
λ	Wavelength (m)
μ	Magnetic permeability (H/m)
μ_o	Permeability of free space (vacuum) (12.57×10^{-7} H/m)
μ_r	Relative magnetic permeability
ρ	Resistivity (^{Oh}m⁻¹cm⁻¹)
σ	Conductivity (Ohm.cm)
σ_{TC}	Thermal conductivity (W/K),
τ	Time constant or characteristic response time (s), Molecular relaxation time (s)
Φ	Magnetic flux (T/m²)
ϕ	Phase angle (degrees or radians)
ϕ_H	Thermal flux (W)

ω   Angular frequency (radians/s)
[i] Concentration of species i.

Abbreviations

ADP	Adenosine diphosphate
AM	Amplitude modulation
AMSU unit	Advanced microwave sounding
ATP	Adenosine triphosphate
CERN	Conseil Européen pour la Recherche Nucléaire
DC	Direct current
DNA	Deoxyribonucleic acid
ECG	Electrocardiogram
EEG	Electroencephalogram
EHF	Extremely high frequency
EM	Electromagnetic
EMG	Electromyography
ESP	Extra sensory perception
FBI	Federal Bureau of Investigation
FCC	U.S. Federal Communications Commission
FDA	U.S. Food and Drug Administration
FM	Frequency modulation
GPR	Ground penetrating radar
GWUP	Gesellschaft zur wissenschaftlichen Untersuchung von Parawissenschaften
IARC	International Agency for Research on Cancer
IEEE	Institute of Electrical and Electronics Engineers
LASER	Light amplification and stimulated emission of radiation
LED	Light emitting diode
LNB	Low noise block
MASER	Microwave amplification and stimulated emission of radiation
MHD	Magnetohydrodynamic
MRI	Magnetic resonance imaging
NASA	U.S. National Aeronautics and Space Administration
NMR	Nuclear magnetic resonance
POES	Polar Operational Environmental Satellites
PVC	Polyvinyl chloride
RF	Radio frequency
RNA	Ribonucleic acid
RPS	Revolutions per second
SDR	Software-defined radio
TNS	Transcranial magnetic stimulation
TV	Television
UHF	Ultra-high frequency
USB	Universal Serial Bus
UV	Ultraviolet (light)
WHO	World Health Organization

Preface

> *In science it often happens that scientists say, "You know that's a really good argument; my position is mistaken," and then they would actually change their minds and you never hear that old view from them again. They really do it. It doesn't happen as often as it should, because scientists are human and change is sometimes painful. But it happens every day. I cannot recall the last time something like that happened in politics or religion.*
> —Carl Sagan (1987)[1]

Dowsing has been known since at least the Middle Ages, and there is some evidence, open to interpretation, that it has been known for millennia. For example, the Roman architect and engineer Vitruvius is reported to have described how he dowsed a site for water,[2] though his actual comments are less clear. This book is not a detailed history of dowsing, since that has been done elsewhere,[3] nor is it a how-to manual on how to dowse, since there are many books available that cover that perspective. For as long as people have been dowsing, debates have raged as to how it works. The theories range from it being the work of the Devil (Martin Luther) and occult forces,[4] to being based on various physical phenomena, to a basis in psychic effects like extrasensory perception (ESP). This book attempts to provide an explanation for how basic L-rod dowsing works, treating it as a physiological response to a physical phenomenon. Unfortunately, I have no personal experience of ESP (or occult forces for that matter), and so ESP effects are only briefly mentioned for completeness, and attributing unexplained phenomena to occult forces is not likely to be very helpful for figuring out the mechanisms at work.

The first part of the book introduces dowsing and critically reviews the major physical theories presented to date to explain it. Most of these theories fall into two suspect camps. In the first camp are the those who argue, but with minimal evidential support, that dowsing is most likely caused by gravitation fluctuations or magnet field distortions or other scientific phenomena. In the second are those who insist that dowsing is a strange phenomenon (true enough), and therefore it must either be the result of a new force of nature, a mysterious dowsing field, or strange elusive particles not commonly observed. There have been several prior scientific studies into the mechanism behind dowsing, and most of them offer insight but do not tell the complete story. The second half of the book builds on these prior studies, develops the evidence and presents a theory for the physical component of dowsing based on known physics and known biology. Alas, presented here are no new forces or new energy fields previously unknown to science, which some might argue shows a lack of creativity on my part, and also ruins my chances of getting a Nobel Prize.

Requirements for a Comprehensive Theory of Dowsing

A comprehensive theory for dowsing must explain the following:

- The source of the dowsing signal.
- How this dowsing signal can be affected by objects/materials buried beneath the surface.
- How this signal can reach the surface.
- Why dowsers can detect a wide range of very different materials, including water, metals, metallic minerals, empty plastic pipes, and graves.
- How this signal is detected by the dowser's body.
- How this signal, once detected, can cause the rods to move.
- How the detection of the signal is spatially determined so that the rods only cross when the dowser is standing over the object.

This book is intended for two types of readers. First, the general reader who has an interest in dowsing and who seeks a general understanding of the subject but does not want to get bogged down in the details; second, the more technical reader who wants greater mathematical detail and more technically persuasive arguments. I have therefore added more detailed background information as well as calculations, etc., in sidebars that are easily identifiable to those readers who prefer to skip over them. Even so, some chapters may go into more depth than all readers will desire. To serve as guideposts to the content, I have included a very brief summary at the start of each chapter with the key take-home message of the chapter.

1

Introduction

> Peasants have believed in dowsing, and scientists used to believe that dowsing was only a belief of peasants. Now there are so many scientists who believe in dowsing that the suspicion comes to me that it may only be a myth after all.
> —Charles Fort[5]

Chapter summary: Dowsing has been around for at least half a millennium and is practiced in many forms, some with an apparently physical basis, others appearing to be more clairvoyant. Basic L-rod dowsing—done while walking with two rods in one's hands—is the simplest form of dowsing that most people can do after brief instruction. This book describes an investigation into the physical basis behind basic L-rod dowsing.

The traditional form of dowsing was (and still is) performed using a Y-shaped stick, held between the hands, which is reported to move in a way that signifies the presence of water and other objects under the ground. Intuitively, it defies common sense that a stick would provide information about objects below the ground's surface (poking the surface with the stick excepted). The general scientific consensus is that dowsing is nonsense, mere wishful thinking, and any actual movements of the stick are caused by the ideomotor effect (a psychological phenomenon wherein a person makes motions unconsciously).

Types of Dowsing

Dowsing remains a controversial area, since it defies common sense, but its adherents honestly believe in the effect. Muddling the issue further are the many different types of dowsing, with many different methods, seeking a wide assortment of information. Dowsing varies from the purely physical to the apparently purely psychic, as illustrated in Figure 1.1.

Most field dowsers believe there is some physical basis to the practice, at least in part, but they are not sure what it is. Field dowsing is what most people have in mind when thinking about dowsers, people with L-rods or forked branches traipsing through fields looking for water. The very basic dowsing which most people can do appears to be a physiological response to a physical stimulus, as, for example, in finding pipes beneath the ground, and basic dowsing is the subject of this book. More advanced dowsers,

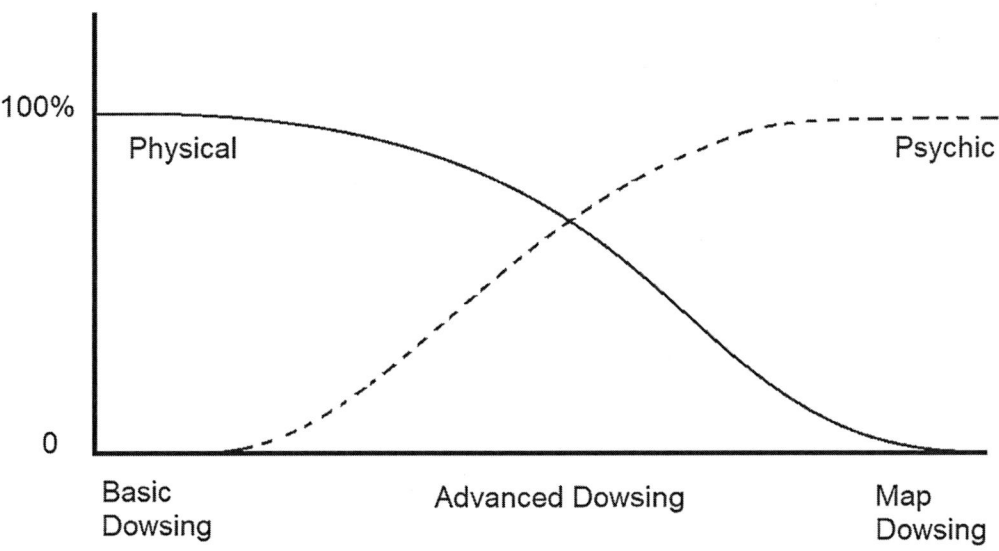

Figure 1.1. Physical vs. psychic dowsing.

for example, people who can identify their target from a distance or at greater depths, appear to use a combination of physical and psychic detection. For a good account of various well-known advanced dowsers and their methods, the book by Henri Mager is a great resource.[6]

Even the methods that some practitioners use for L-rod field dowsing sound like they are not relying on entirely physical phenomena. For example, some people will use rods to find a specific mineral and do so by placing a small amount of that mineral on the rods so as to "tune" them to that target. Again, these non-physical methods are outside the scope of this book. For those who are interested in understanding some of these less physical methods and aspects of dowsing, I recommend Elizabeth Brown's book *Dowsing: The Ultimate Guide for the 21st Century*,[7] Dennis Wheatley's *The Essential Dowsing Guide*[8] and Richard Webster's *Dowsing for Beginners*.[9]

Information dowsing is a very broad subject area of which there are many interesting accounts. For example, there is a report from 1692 that after a wine seller and his wife were murdered, French dowser Jacques Aymar offered to help with the investigation. His dowsing rod became violently agitated at the scene of the crime and led him, like a bloodhound, on the trail of the murderers over several days. One of the murderers, who later confessed, was discovered in a prison but his two accomplices escaped from France.[10] Over three hundred years later, it is hard to assess whether there is any truth to this story, but to the extent it is true, it would fall under the category of information dowsing. Dennis Wheatley[11] describes many cases where he has performed information dowsing that make Aymar's accomplishments seem a little less extraordinary.

Pendulum dowsing is another common form of dowsing, where the dowser holds a pendulum and observes whether it twists or rocks side to side/front to back in response to questions. If the pendulum is held over a map of an area, the pendulum may indicate where water or other resources are to be found. With the dowser looking at the map, they can be a great distance away from the actual location, thousands of miles in some cases. In contrast to field dowsing, map dowsing and information dowsing do not appear to involve any physical process, and so to the extent that they work, they are probably using clairvoyance or psi methods similar to remote viewing. Many other devices can and have been used for dowsing, and dowsing devices vary with region; so, for example, in India, some dowsers are reported to use coconuts.[12] The main point is that the world of dowsing is very large and varied and basic L-rod dowsing is only a small part of it, but it is the part of dowsing that appears to have a physical basis.

Traditionally, dowsing has been used to find water, but it has also been used to locate minerals and other objects. L-rod dowsing works well for locating pipes and it can be used to find water pipes, plastic gas mains, graves, and drainage pipes made of PVC, concrete, plastic and metal. With the introduction of plastic gas lines, metal detectors no longer work, but L-rods do (acoustic methods, ground penetrating radar and electronic transmission methods are also available[13]). This simple technique can locate an incredibly wide range of materials. Many utility companies use dowsing to find buried cables and pipes because it is considered to be a dependable method.[14] However, utility companies tend to keep it low key, since some companies have experienced the adverse effects of publicity about public companies wasting funds using scientifically bogus methods.[15] Similarly oil and mineral exploration companies often successfully use dowsers.[16] The most widely known use of dowsing is for searching for water, and dowsing is still widely used for that purpose. A friend of mine was having a well drilled and the driller from the well company pulled out a couple of L-rods and searched for the best place to drill the well. He commented that in western Pennsylvania, dowsing is the main method used to decide where to sink wells. The main approach appears to be to identify dowsing lines and drill where they intersect in the hope that this spot indicates where fault lines cross and so the best location to find water. On its face, to the extent that dowsing can identify fault lines, the logic appears reasonable, and the driller did find some water, but not as much as was needed.

A Brief History of Dowsing

Lloyd Youngblood wrote an article that reviewed various ancient artifacts that may offer evidence of dowsing, including 8,000-year-old cave paintings from the Tassili Caves in Algeria, a 5,000-year-old etching of the Chinese emperor Yu the Great (大禹) (c. 2123–2025 BC) and 4,000-year-old temple wall etchings from Egypt, and accounts in the Old Testament of Moses striking a rock with his rod to release water roughly 3,400 years ago.[17] However, it is difficult to be certain about the actual meaning of these images and accounts and whether they involve dowsing at all. The image in Figure 1.2 is a woodcut from Georgius Agricola's *De Re Metallica* (pub. 1556) which unambiguously shows men using divining rods to locate mineral veins. Though Agricola did not believe that dowsing was helpful, his book shows that these methods were in use at that time.

Dowsing has been used widely since the 16th century, but progress in understanding how it works has progressed surprisingly little since then. These days the most common form of dowsing is probably L-rod dowsing, performed with two metal rods, each bent into an L-shape, approximately 10 cm (4 inches) on one leg and

A—Twig.   B—Trench.

Figure 1.2. Woodcut from Georgius Agricola, *De Re Metallica* (publ. 1556). Translated from the First Latin Edition of 1556, by Herbert Clark Hoover and Lou Henry Hoover (Project Gutenberg EBook, Release Date: November 14, 2011, http://www.gutenberg.org/files/38015/38015-h/38015-h.htm, accessed July 19, 2020).

30 cm (12 inches) on the long leg. The shorter ends are held loosely in the hand with an open fist, so that the rods can rotate, or alternatively a holder can be used such that the rods can turn in the holder. These holders can be simple tubes, and the tubes from the cheap ballpoint pens work well. The dowser holds the rods roughly horizontal in front of them, with arms bent ~ 90 degrees at the elbow, so that the upper arms are vertical, and the forearms are horizontal, as illustrated in Figure 1.3. Most people walk along with the rods steadily, but I remember one gentleman who kept his rods swinging back and forth. I am not sure how he did it, but he and I found the same spots.

If one looks on Amazon, eBay and other online purveyors, there are many variations of the rods available, but there is no need to purchase these special L-rods, a simple but effective pair of rods can easily be made from a wire coat hanger. For improved performance, Michael Fercik describes how to make very low-friction dowsing rods using bearings made from bicycle wheel spokes,[18] which sound very good, though I have not tried them.

The Study of Dowsing

Dowsing has impressed many scientists and scholars over the years. Robert Boyle (1627–91), best known for his work studying the properties of gases, wrote in 1663:[19]

> A forked hazel twig is held by its horns, one in each hand, the holder walking with it over places where mineral lodes may be suspected, and it is said that the fork by dipping down will discover the place where the ore is to be found. Many eminent authors, amongst others our distinguished countryman Gabriel Plat, ascribe much to this detecting wand, and others, far from credulous or ignorant, have as eye-witnesses spoken of its value. When visiting the lead-mines of Somersetshire I saw its use, and one gentleman who employed it declared that it moved without his will, and I saw it bend so strongly as to break in his hand. It will only succeed in some men's hands, and those who have seen it may much more readily believe than those who have not.

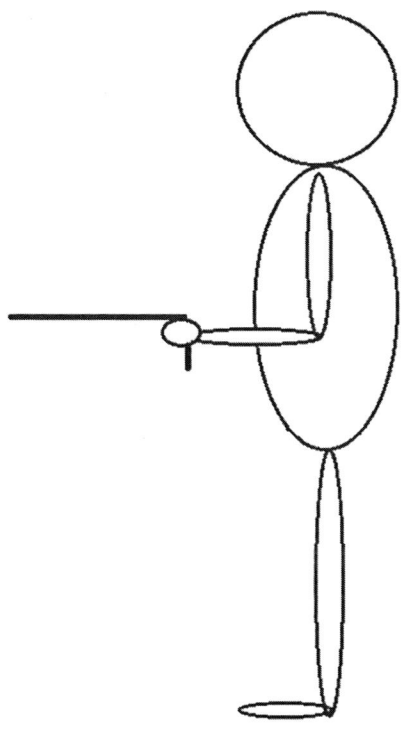

Figure 1.3. L-rods are typically held in front with the arms relaxed at one's side, with the elbows bent about 90 degrees.

Roger Jennison, Emeritus Professor of physical electronics and radio astronomy, University of Kent (UK), wrote, "There are many aspects of physics associated with dowsing which merit serious investigation."[20]

Perhaps the most remarkable aspect of dowsing is that it has been investigated by many respected scientists,[21] but so far no one has presented a comprehensive explanation. One of the more notable investigations was performed by Sir William Barrett, F.R.S, and published in the book *The Divining Rod*.[22] The investigations were primarily performed by Barrett (1844–1925), a well-respected physicist, and the book was compiled 43 years after his death by well-known author Theodore Besterman. The book is written in beautiful prose and is a pleasure to read. It provides a detailed history of dowsing and many detailed accounts of dowsers besting geologists and other experts to locate wells. While the authors provided good evidence for the reality and efficacy of dowsing, primarily searching for water, they were unable to give a good explanation for how it works. Their book concludes, "We do not believe that the accumulation of further masses of evidence [for dowsing], though of course this is not undesirable, will make the argument for these contentions any stronger. All that is required is the discovery of some fruitful generalisation which will permit the orthodox scientist to incorporate cryptesthesia into the canon of accepted and indisputable scientific knowledge. We believe that the first movement of thought in this direction will occur from the impossibility of finding any normal explanation of the phenomena of dowsing."

Those who have studied it in detail tend to conclude that the effect is real, but the mechanism remains elusive. Even Albert Einstein commented, "I know very well that many scientists consider dowsing as they do astrology, as a type of ancient superstition. According to my conviction this is, however, unjustified. The dowsing rod is a simple instrument which shows the reaction of the human nervous system to certain factors which are unknown to us at this time."[23]

Leslie Shepard wrote very well about the challenge of understanding dowsing: "The dowsing reaction certainly has a physical basis in as much as there is a chain of events which begins with a physical fact and ends with a physical indication, but the estimation of depth and yield of springs, or of the nature and quantity of metals, undoubtedly involves a more intuitive factor. ... When dowsing includes occult divination the whole subject becomes clouded by accusations of superstition, delusion and fraud. Modern dowsing is still uneasily poised between science and magic—yet it works."[24]

There have been several detailed investigations into the dowsing effect. One of the most thorough was Cecil Maby and Bedford Franklin's in their book *The Physics of the Divining Rod*.[25] They made many detailed observations and were the first authors that I have seen who actually proposed a quantitative physical explanation for how dowsing works. With the advantage of hindsight of over 60 years since their book was written, I believe that some of their basic assumptions were flawed, and so their theory is incorrect; but it is an impressive work, and their observations are referenced frequently throughout the present book. Another investigator was Solco Tromp, who also made many useful observations, but was not able to combine them into a good explanation.[26] There have been several good reviews of dowsing, including ones by John Wilcox,[27] George Hansen,[28] and Anne Miller.[29]

Nandkumar Dharmadhikari et al. reported that dowsing results matched vertical ground resistivity, presumably due to water filling fault lines.[30] Similarly, Duane Chadwick and Larry Jensen tested over 150 people independently over several tracks for their dowsing ability and found that all but one person could get a dowsing response.[31] They also compared the positions of the dowsing response by having participants drop a wood block whenever the rods crossed. The authors found that the responses of the participants were correlated. They also used a magnetometer to measure the magnetic field over the courses and found a weak statistical correlation (i.e., may or may not be relevant). One of the issues that investigators face is that even if they find a correlation between ground resistivity or any other physical effect and the dowsing response, it does not mean that the effect is the cause. For example, an underground fault line could show a change in resistivity, ground currents, local gravitation field, local magnetic field, etc., etc., all of which may show some correlation to the dowsing signal, but not necessarily be the physical basis for it.

Though Y-stick and L-rod dowsing have been known at least since the Middle Ages and have been studied by a number of very eminent people, it is surprising that there is no consensus on how dowsing works. People generally fall into three camps. The first camp includes the advocates, who use L-rods for dowsing because it works, even though they are not sure how it works.[32] The second camp includes those who believe that all forms of dowsing are scientifically impossible and therefore any discussion is just fanciful and a waste of time. The largest group is comprised of those people who do not have an opinion because they have probably not tried it, or if they did successfully try it, thought it was odd and moved on to more important things.

Who Can Dowse?

It appears that most people who try L-rod dowsing are successful. Webster wrote that most people can do L-rod dowsing with minimal training,[33] Z. V. Harvalik estimated 80 percent of people can dowse with L-rods,[34] and Wheatley believed that anyone could dowse, and went on to say that in his many years as a professional dowser teaching dowsing classes, he had never met a person who could not dowse.[35] I.N. Hume found by testing that 9 out of 10 men could dowse with L-rods but only 3 out of 10 women,[36] whereas Thomas Fiddick found that there was no difference in dowsing ability between the sexes.[37] Barney Turner, the head of the Nor Cal Dowsers, claimed that 98 percent of people can dowse.[38] The general consensus appears to be that most (90+%) people can dowse, and this high percentage indicates that L-rod dowsing is not a special ability, but is probably a natural response to some stimulus, comparable in frequency to the percentage of people who are right-handed (~90%).[39] Dowsing is clearly a special ability, but as is often said, everyone is special. In summary, dowsing is something that most people can do, it appears to work, but no one knows how it works. As John Wilcox said in his excellent review of dowsing, "What is now required is the development of a general theory which will permit scientists to incorporate the biolocation mechanism into scientific knowledge."[40]

2

General Observations of the Dowsing Signal

> The fact of the turning down of the stick when above water veins or metals is uncontestably true. Recent experiments have established it as wholly correct. Precise measures have been taken in great number, and the phenomenon, which is as certain as all chemical and physical logical phenomena, cannot be denied.
> —Charles Richet[41]

Chapter summary: Many people have studied dowsing, some achieving fame if not fortune. There have been many studies of dowsers from simple to elaborate, with some showing success by the dowsers, whereas others have concluded that dowsing is no more than self-delusion.

Some Famous Dowsers

As mentioned above, most people can dowse if they try, and there have been many reports of dowsers obtaining information that would otherwise be inaccessible. There have been examples where dowsing made the difference between life and death. During the Gallipoli campaign of World War I, in August 1915 the British Expeditionary force camped in Suvla Bay, and the Turks were confident that the British would not be able to maintain a large military force there, because the Gallipoli peninsula lacked any freshwater sources. The British planned to bring in water by barges from Malta, but there were technical glitches and the water was not forthcoming. Sapper Stephen Kelly from the Australian Light Horse Brigade was summoned, and with a short piece of copper wire found a spring within 100 yards of the divisional headquarters that produced over 2,000 gallons of fresh water per hour. Within a week, Kelly had located more than 32 other well sites which provided a gallon of water a day for over 100,000 men.[42] Afterwards the British Army continued to use dowsers, but with some reluctance as the following passage by Gordon Rattray Taylor indicates. "If there is one subject which lies precisely on the borderline between the scientifically acceptable and superstition, it is the art of the dowser—the man who finds water and sometimes iron objects with a divining rod. For many centuries his skills have been widely accepted as valid, and the British Army has long employed dowsers to find water for troops in desert regions. Yet, in the absence of any plausible scientific explanation and because the results obtained vary so much in consistency, science has remained sceptical."[43]

One of the most famous dowsers was Alexis-Timothée Bouly, from France, who was born on December 11, 1865, ordained in 1890 and is best known as Abbé Bouly.[44] He discovered he had a talent for dowsing, and found water supplies, and then broadened his investigations to metals, cavities, and microbes. He explained his talents, saying, "Each body, animal, plant, mineral, is only an accumulation of energy whose vibrations are spread throughout the universe, it is possible to grasp and identify these radiations with a dowsing rod." He became well known for his dowsing ability:

- He found several sources of fresh water in the Canary Islands necessary for the expansion of crops, in particular bananas, essential to the local economy.
- In Lens, he identified rubble-filled cavities during the restoration of the Saint-Léger church which would not have supported the foundations initially planned, preventing a disaster.
- After the First World War, the War Department employed his services to detect unexploded ordnance on the Champagne battlefields of the Aisne and Artois, etc. It was reported that he could even distinguish between German and Allied ammunition.[45] The French government awarded him with the Legion of Honor in 1950 for services rendered to the nation.

Another well-known dowser was Henry Gross (1895–1979), who was a game warden in Biddeford, Maine, and showed remarkable dowsing ability, as documented by his friend, the novelist Kenneth Roberts. According to Roberts, Gross's ability developed over time from being able to find water veins below his feet, to finding them elsewhere on a property, to finding them remotely just looking at map. In addition, Gross could ask his rods any question on almost any topic (e.g., about which team will win a sports event) and get answers. Gross's forte, though, was finding water, and he could tell the depth of the stream, the flow and flow direction and the rocks above it. He did less well in controlled studies of water versus sand in hidden jars, which Roberts felt were poorly designed and improperly carried out "indicating only the stupidity of the scientist and his closed mind in refusing to believe the incontrovertible facts." The overall account suggests that Gross was an exceptional dowser, though the account is written through somewhat rose-colored glasses.[46] There are many other accounts of dowsers finding water, and pipes and metal objects, for example, Latimer gives a detailed account of his use of dowsing for all of these items.[47] Even modern-day celebrities such as television presenter Jeremy Clarkson (best known for the BBC show *Top Gear*) found Victorian pipes on his land through dowsing.[48]

Brief Review of Dowsing Studies

The first question to address is whether dowsing is a real physical phenomenon or whether it is a product of the collective imagination of its proponents. There have been several tests where investigators have shown results with dowsing which were significantly better than random guessing; and other tests where the results were not so good for the dowsers. A selection of these studies is summarized below.

- HRB Singer Inc. ran some preliminary trials with four dowsers and found good agreement between them mapping out underground caves (without a surface entrance) and locating a septic tank on property unknown to the dowsers.[49]

- John Wilcox similarly mapped out unknown underground caverns in limestone rock using dowsing and then confirmed them with divers.[50] While these tests were not statistical, and were not tightly controlled, they claimed to demonstrate that dowsing can provide information not previously known to the dowser.
- The University of Calgary ran some double-blind tests and found that experienced dowsers performed significantly better than random.[51]
- Geologist Peter Blythe found that six opal miners in South Africa indicated the same spot by dowsing when independently tested. When subsequently examined, this spot corresponded to a vertical fracture in the limestone rock.[52]
- Hans-Dieter Betz performed a series of double-blind tests, finding a movable pipe beneath a platform, and also the location of underground rivers later verified using other methods such as geological surveys and ground penetrating radar. Betz found a wide variability between subjects. Some subjects performed close to what would be expected based on random chance, but other subjects performed far better than would be expected from random chance alone.[53] It should be noted, however, that not everyone agrees with Betz's conclusion, including J. T. Enright, who reanalyzed the data and came to the opposite conclusion.[54]
- John Greenwood from the Nottingham Trent University described a site survey course in which Robert Price, a Partner with Castle Rock Geotech, Nottingham, UK, demonstrated his dowsing ability by tracking a service duct away from a manhole. The 15 attendees then tried and found that two-thirds of them also experienced a similar response with dowsing rods at the same location. The same group then walked along a 15 meter tape that had been laid along the ground and recorded any responses they observed. Those people who had a response did so at a similar location to Price.[55]
- N. P. Dharmadhikari et al. tested dowsing against physical methods to locate a groundwater vein and determine its width and depth. The methods included near-surface geophysical methods such as Semiconductor LASER Light Box and Proton Precession Magnetometer coupled with Vertical Electrical Soundings and the authors found very good agreement between these methods and L-rod dowsing.[56]

Carl Weschcke and Joe Slate[57] reported three remarkable tests with dowsing.

- They tested eight college students (five male, three female) with no dowsing experience, with copper L-rods tipped with quartz crystals who had to identify which one of five identical black plastic gallon containers contained water in double—blind testing. The dowsers had a few practice runs at the start and then were tested for two sessions a week over four weeks. All participants improved their performance record over the test period, with the success rate more than doubling, though with considerable variations in rates of improvement between individuals, suggesting that dowsing skills can be learned or at least innate skills can be improved through practice.
- In the second double-blind study, Weschcke and Slate had 20 college students using L-rods tipped with quartz crystals identify which of nine identical black plastic gallon containers filled with water was contaminated with a pesticide. Half of the students had previously been trained in the use of L-rods in a

parapsychology course, and all ten were correct, compared to only two of other students who had no training.
- In the third test 14 college students using quartz-tipped copper L-rods tested
  (a) three steel samples, each 2" × 5" × ¼", that were identical in appearance, but one contained a small internal fissure, and
  (b) three plastic specimens of the same size, of identical appearance, but one contained an air bubble that had been previously detected using a non-destructive test method.

The dowsers were tasked with finding the defective sample without touching the samples. Eight of the students correctly identified the defective steel sample and nine of them correctly identified the defective plastic sample, with six students being correct both times, and two wrong both times.

Conversely, there have been many other studies of dowsers, where the dowsers have failed to perform better than random chance.

- Michael Martin, a professor at Boston University, tested a well-known dowser during a class on the Philosophy of Science and the Occult to find which of four pipes had running water through it. Alas, the dowser failed to perform as well as he had hoped.[58]
- John John Yeosock[59] conducted laboratory tests using divining rods to detect an assortment of military weapons. Heart rate, skin resistance and skin temperature measurements were made to determine if these physiological parameters could be used to predict whether a target detection, false alarm, correct rejection or missed target would be reported. The resulting data indicated the success rate was not better than random.
- In 1971 R. A. Foulkes ran a series of tests with dowsers with support from the British Army and Ministry of Defence to determine if buried mines could be located by either map or field dowsing.[60]
  - For the map dowsing tests, 20 inert mines were buried along several military roads. Seven dowsers were asked to locate the mines and given maps of the roads. Only chance results were obtained.
  - For the field dowsing, a grid was established with each square being 20 feet (6.1 meters) on a side. Five different types of objects (80 of each type) were buried randomly. Tests were conducted with 22 dowsers to determine whether they could identify the objects. Again only chance results were obtained.
  - Lastly, an experienced dowser was asked to determine whether water was flowing in a plastic pipe. The water was randomly turned on or off for 50 trials. However, the results were not significantly different from random.
- Maby also claimed to be able to detect unexploded bombs by dowsing, but the results of testing were not nearly as good as he had hoped for and meant that he lost his funding from the British Admiralty, War Office and Air Ministry.[61]
- Two tests were conducted in 1989–1990, under the auspices of the German skeptic's society Gesellschaft zur wissenschaftlichen Untersuchung von Parawissenschaften (GWUP; Society for the Scientific Examination of Parasciences).[62]
  - In the first test, the dowsers were located in a tent and two pipes, one under the tent and one around the tent, were buried 20 inches below the surface. The

two pipes were connected to a pump and a valve that switched between them. With a $10,000 prize incentive, the dowsers had to determine whether the pipe under their tent had flowing water or stationary water. The selection of which pipe was connected to the pump was random and performed out of sight of the dowsers. Unfortunately for the dowsers, they did no better than would be expected if they simply guessed the answer at random.

Note: A similar test was performed with dowsers in Australia, with similar results.[63]

- ○ The second test by the GWUP involved the dowser identifying which of ten opaque plastic boxes in a row contained a randomly positioned object compared to the other nine boxes. The dowser could choose one of the following materials to go into the box: iron, coal, gold, silver, copper, or a magnet. However, again, the dowsers did no better than random chance. These Kassel Dowsing Experiments are now taught at Berkeley as part of a statistics course about the using a null hypothesis.[64]
- The FBI ran a test to determine if two groups of volunteers could detect which of nine graves contained nonhuman bones, the first group by visual clues and the second using dowsing rods. The volunteers with the dowsing rods did no better than the other group or random chance.[65]

The results of all these studies are confusing. There is evidence that we all have some innate ability to dowse, and as is true with most aspects of life, some people are better endowed than others and dowsing skills can be improved through training and experience. Some tests show that dowsers can provide information not otherwise available, indicating that dowsing is a real phenomenon; but at other times even experienced dowsers sometimes fail during what appears to be simple testing. Dowsing is a subtle effect and so is influenced not only by the physiological response to the dowsing signal, but also by psychological effects, such as stress, personal beliefs, etc. These topics are discussed in more detail in the later chapters. Dowsers who fail the tests often complain that the tests were not fair because the tests are asking the dowser to detect things that they normally would not do. People often claim that dowsers can read the lay of the land and determine what lies beneath the surface. However, to be able to do that better than non-dowsers implies that dowsers have a different special ability, just not dowsing. Below is a simple test protocol that should be fair to both the dowser and the tester.

Proposed Dowsing Test

The following is a test that I believe is fair to the dowser and fair to the tester. It is fair to the dowser, because it measures what dowsers typically detect and which can be measured independently. The test involves mapping the utilities to a property, water pipes, sewer, surface drainage, etc. However, if identifying underground objects is not what the dowser normally does, then the test should be modified in advance as needed until all parties agree it is fair.

There are three main characters involved. The tester is a neutral character who supervises the test. The dowser is the person being tested, and the control is a person with non-relevant background to assess what information can be determined by

2. General Observations of the Dowsing Signal

simple observation. Additional representatives and assistants may also be involved as needed.

Step 1. The tester should select a property that has several underground utilities on it. The property can for example be a car park next to a building. The dowser should not know the identity or location of the property in advance and neither the control, nor the dowser, should visit the property beforehand. A sketch of the site should be provided showing the lot, and position of buildings and the area of the test marked on the sketch. This area should be at least 2,000 sq. meters (0.5 acres).

Step 2. The tester should select someone to act as a control. The control should be someone with average skills and abilities in locating underground utility lines, so a civil engineer or someone who spent most of their career working for utility companies locating and repairing broken lines probably has above average skill and would not be a good control.

The control should attempt to map out the underground utilities based on what is visible to the best of his or her ability, but without any special equipment. For example, if there is a gas valve at the curb and a gas meter going into the building, then there is probably a gas line in between. The course of drains from downspouts can often be seen by changes in the shade of green of the lawn.

There are of course rules:

- ° Manholes and other covers cannot be lifted, covers cannot be removed, downspouts cannot be taken apart to see the directions pipes go, etc.
- ° Holes cannot be dug, and the property cannot be damaged.
- ° No instrumentation or equipment can be used by either the control or the dowser, except that the dowser may use his or her dowsing apparatus.

Step 3. With the tester present but control absent, the dowser should now attempt to map out the utilities of the property and mark up a copy of the sketch of the site to show the presence of all pipes and underground utilities that he or she can identify. There should be no time pressure and the dowser should be able to use whatever technique he or she prefers so long as it follows the rules above (no lifting manholes, etc.).

Step 4. With the tester present the control should mark up the sketch of the site to show the presence of all pipes and underground utilities that he or she can identify. The dowser should not be present while the control is surveying the land, but a representative of the dowser can be present to check that the rules are followed. This representative must not convey any site information to the control. He or she is merely there to ensure the rules are followed.

Step 5. After both the dowser and control have created their sketches, the tester should contact the local utility companies and have them map out the property, identifying all power lines, drains, water and gas mains, cable TV lines etc. Alternatively, hire a ground survey company that uses technologies such as ground penetrating radar and have them map out the underground utilities. The people mapping are welcome to lift covers and manholes etc. as needed.

Step 6. Compare the sketch produced by the dowser to the examiner and to the utility companies and see if the dowser was able to find any more information than the control.

A score should be developed. For each line that the utility company identifies give the control and the dowser a 0 to 5 score. A score of 5 is a perfect match and 0 is totally missed. A line that is detected but off a couple of feet may only get a 4, if the line starts OK and then wanders off in the wrong direction, perhaps it only gets a 2 or 3. Add up the scores for all the utility lines. The same scoring scheme should be used for the control and the dowser, and the two scores are then compared.

Dowsing is not an exact science and so some mistakes and omissions will occur. In addition, the dowser may detect signals from objects that are not on the utility company maps (disused pipes, for example), or old foundations from long-gone structures. For scoring purposes, these other underground signals should be ignored, unless they can be independently verified.

The dowser's effectiveness can be estimated using the following calculation:

Dowser Effectiveness = (Dowser Score—Control Score)/(Control Score)

If the dowser scores the same as the control, i.e., they both saw the same visual clues, then dowser's effectiveness will be zero. If the dowser scores less than the control, then his or her effectiveness will be negative and if the dowser scores more than the control then his or her effectiveness will be greater than zero. If the dowser scores twice as much as the control, then the dowser effectiveness is 1.

It would be better if more than one dowser were being tested with more than one control. The same scoring system can be used with the same control or the average of multiple controls. The overall effectiveness of the dowsers would be the median of their respective dowser effectiveness scores. Of course other metrics can be developed and probably have merit, but the dowser effectiveness is both simple to calculate and simple to interpret.

3

Preliminary Observations and Requirements for the Dowsing Effect

It [dowsing] is a form of science and is only as good as the practitioner using it. All life forms have energy or a wave length. The dowser just tunes into the specific energy or wave length that he is looking for. Like a radio or TV wave length. You turn to the channel you are looking for.
—Carol Gader[66]

Chapter summary: Many people have looked into dowsing and have proposed theories for the underlying mechanism. From the observations are some basic conclusions about the nature of the dowsing, the nature of the dowsing signal and where it comes from, as well as the dowsing response and the role of the dowsing rods.

I started this project after reading an article saying that dowsing was simply due to the ideomotor response. In other words dowsing is not real and instead it is merely a figment of the subconscious mind. There were several reasons why I didn't believe this explanation based on my personal experience:

- Dowsing provides information that I did not have before.
- Experiments often gave results contrary to what I was expecting. If it were all in my mind, I would at least expect the results to follow my expectations.
- Dowsing fits with physical reality. For example, I have traced an unknown dowsing line, and later found the same line with a metal detector. In this particular case, I still do not know what the source was (perhaps an electrical conduit), but the metal detector indicates that the response was real. Similarly, I have traced a pipe from a visible water valve by the road to the side of a neighbor's house and had them confirm that location as the point where the water line enters their house.

It seemed to me that dowsing must have a physical basis, and so I set out to identify the science behind basic L-rod dowsing.

Dowsing Rod Material

There has been some debate about whether the material the L-rods or forked branch are made of is important. For example, in 1680 Nicholas Jena wrote[67]:

I draw this conclusion that this virtue or power is not attached to the wood, nor to the instrument one uses, but rather to the efficiency of blood of him who uses it. It is the blood which causes the wood to turn by the impression it communicates to it at the moment the man takes it with his two hands, so that this instrument, whatever its quality, is only a signal of which the man makes use to indicate to him the movement of his blood upon what there is hidden. A mark of this truth is that the dry wood, of whatever nature it may be, turns as easily as the green, and not only the wood, but also iron, silver, brass, wire, whalebone, and other supple and solid matters, excepting in the cases which we will name afterwards.

Similarly, Solco Tromp stated that the material the rod is made out of makes no difference, as verified by electrocardiogram (ECG) data.[68] Others claim the material is important, Vincent Reddish,[69] for example, claimed that aluminum rods gave very different results from other metals, but Z. V. Harvalik used aluminum rods successfully.[70]

I performed some quick tests with rods to determine if the material made any difference. Unless stated otherwise all of my tests described below were performed using steel rods made from wire coat hangers. Each coat hanger is cut to make two rods. The wire is a convenient thickness and stiffness, and of course the price is right.

- I made rods from aluminum wire and they performed similarly to the steel ones, though they were less responsive. It is likely that the response is balance between gravity causing the rods to move and friction at the handles preventing their movement. The aluminum wires were thinner than the steel wires and aluminum has a lower density than steel (2.7 g/cm^3 and 7.9 g/cm^3, respectively) giving a weaker response.
- I took some 12 gauge Romex[71] cable (for residential wiring) and pulled out the two copper conductors and the ground wire and bent them to form rods. The two insulated conductors worked fine with their insulation on, so electrical connection to the hands is not necessary.
- I tested the bare copper ground wire, paired with a steel coat-hanger rod, one in each hand, and the pair worked the same as if they were both premium coat-hanger rods.
- I also repeated the test with a partially broken wooden doweling rod (~ 3mm diameter) and found that it worked too, though not as well (probably too much friction for the low mass). Wood works, but of course wooden Y sticks are the traditional tool of the dowser.

It appears that the rods can be made from a wide variety of materials. There is a small effect on the material type, such that low-density rods tend to be less responsive than higher density rods, consistent with the rods' movement under gravity, opposed by friction.

Brown and Harrison wrote, "The most popular divining rods are made of brass, steel or twigs. Dowsers who prefer brass or steel insist that metal rods are far more sensitive to the magnetic field of their targets [odd comment since brass is diamagnetic], and they wrap a non-conductive material around the rods handle to keep the dowsers known electromagnetic energy from interfering with the signals. But those who prefer twigs argue that only natural divining rods can adequately respond to the natural elements that are usually the objects of the search."[72]

I am not sure what the electromagnetic (EM) energy is that dowsers risk losing to their non-insulated rods, and as mentioned above, I saw no difference between insulated and non-insulated rods. The conclusion therefore is that the material is not too important, and indeed there are reports that dowsing can be performed by some sensitive individuals, such as Evelyn Penrose, without any rods at all, relying only on a sensation in their hands and arms.[73]

The most plausible explanation for such reports is that the rods are merely indicators of processes within the dowser's body. It is generally believed that the dowsing physiological response manifests as slight involuntary muscle movements in the shoulders, and the rods simply give a clear visual indication of slight involuntary muscle movements. The elbows lift slightly, the wrists turn in and the lightly balanced rods rotate towards the center and cross. Since the rods only provide an easy way to see when the muscles twitch, the material they are made of has very little bearing on the result, except for the reasons outlined above. Y-stick dowsing probably works the same way, but I did not test them.

Source of Dowsing Signal

Even without knowing the cause of the dowsing effect we can identify its source. Since the dowsing signal contains information about what is beneath the surface of the ground, the signal must be coming from the ground. The signal is presumably some kind of wave, particle or field, a description which really does not narrow the possible options down much, since the description includes almost everything in the known universe.

The signal could potentially originate from the ground, or it could originate from the sun or universe and be reflected back from objects in the ground, just as the light that we see for vision during the day comes from the sun and is reflected off objects, enabling us to see them. We may think of the ground as opaque, but whether an object is opaque or not depends on the wavelength of the light. Glass, for example, is transparent in the visible wavelengths, but is opaque in the ultraviolet.

Outside our house there are some underground pipes which give a good dowsing signal. I tested the response at night in the dark and the dowsing response was still strong. Therefore, it is unlikely that the dowsing response is coming from the sun, unless the signal which causes it can pass through the Earth. If this signal was able to pass through the Earth, then it is unlikely that the signal would have enough interaction with matter to create a dowsing response from an empty PVC pipe beneath my feet. The signal could potentially come from the sky and be reflected back, but that does not explain why a small pipe 10 m (~30 ft) deep can give a signal. Therefore, on balance, it appears that the dowsing signal is not coming from the sky but is coming from the ground. Highcock also reported that the dowsing effect was the same day or night,[74] but curiously, Reddish found that the dowsing effect does depend on light.[75]

Dowsing—Requirements for Detection?

The next question is whether dowsing is an active or passive detection system. A metal detector, for example, generates an oscillating magnetic field and then detects changes in that magnetic field caused by the induction of currents in the metal target. Metal detectors are a form of active measurement. In contrast a microphone is a passive device, merely taking in an external signal without affecting the environment it is in. The difference between a passive and active detection system is similar to someone looking at an object in natural light during the day, versus looking at the same object at night under the light from a torch or flashlight. The former is a passive system relying on detecting a change in the local environment (pattern of light intensity and color), whereas the latter is an active system, the torch/flight light is lighting the object, and we are observing the reflected light with our eyes. In dowsing, as far as we are aware, neither the dowser nor the L-rods are emitting a dowsing signal that can be reflected back; rather, dowsing appears to be a passive process, detecting changes in the local environment. By defining the parameters needed for a dowsing signal it should be possible to eliminate some potential sources and better recognize likely ones. This dowsing signal must have the following properties to be suitable for dowsing.

- Naturally occurring and not dependent on a man-made radiation, such as radio transmitters, since dowsing was known long before radio waves were discovered or used.
- People dowse around the world in a wide range of environments, indoors and outside and so the dowsing field or radiation must be present globally in all or at least in a wide range of environments.
- The signal must be able to penetrate rock to a depth of at least several meters and it must come through the ground and up to the dowser in order for him or her to detect something in the ground.
- The signal is probably created in the ground. If the dowsing radiation from a small plastic pipe is strong enough to give a signal, then it is unlikely to be radiation which passes through the entire Earth or is reflected from space.
- The signal must interact with water, plastic pipes, voids, metal objects, etc., so the dowser has something to detect.
- The signal must interact with the human body so that the signal can be detected. The detection process is not known, and it is possible that the detection process is entirely novel, but it should be expected that any detection mechanism will not violate too many of the known laws of physics and medicine.
- Dowsers walk along and detect a signal on the second time scale, and so the interaction of the dowser with the dowsing signal must have a response time of seconds or faster.
- Dowsers can detect objects that are a few inches across, and so the dowsing field must be able to resolve dimensions of this magnitude. For example, a signal with a wavelength of several meters is unlikely to resolve an object that is only 5 cm (2 inches) across.
- The dowsing signal can't be excessively harmful to humans and animals, since we live in the same environment. For example, cosmic radiation is very high energy, ionizing radiation that we are fortunately protected from by the Earth's magnetic field. If cosmic radiation were considered as a source of the dowsing effect, then to get enough radiation to be able to distinguish between turf and turf with a plastic pipe buried a meter below in a few seconds might require more radiation than would be good for us. Fortunately, only about eight cosmic rays and their daughter products reach the Earth's surface per square meter second,[76] which is not enough to resolve an underground pipe.

3. Preliminary Observations and Requirements for the Dowsing Effect

- Lastly, many writers on dowsers are quick to assert that there is a new type of field or energy or radiation, usually with minimal supporting evidence. While, again, it is possible that the dowsing effect arises because of a completely new field, force or radiation, an explanation based on the application or extrapolation of known science is much preferred. A new fundamental force of nature would require rewriting all the physics textbooks and the evidence needed to support such a change in the current paradigm would have to be overwhelming for it to be accepted.
- Dowsers can detect the location of an underground object directly under their feet to a few cm (inches); and so any proposed mechanism also needs to explain this spatial selectivity. The distance from the dowser to a pipe a meter below his or her feet is not very different from the distance to another pipe that is a meter below and 50 cm to the front. However, the latter is detected, and the former must wait for the dowser to take a couple more steps.

Many mechanisms have been proposed to explain the dowsing effect, and the next few chapters will examine a few of these against the criteria above and supporting evidence to determine if they are plausible.

4

The Psychology of Dowsing

> I was particularly interested in your remarks about psychologists, because it has always been astonishing to me how little interest, among most scientific men, can be aroused in connection with new phenomena, no matter how much factual material is available, until some progress has been made toward setting up a plausible theory. It is almost as if they said, "If I don't understand how it works, it isn't true."
> —Letter from Dan Comstock to Kenneth Roberts (1948)[77]

Chapter summary: A common view is that dowsing is caused by the ideomotor effect and is therefore a form of self-delusion. While the ideomotor effect is undoubtably real, and can influence dowsers, the ideomotor effect fails to explain how dowsing can provide information not otherwise known. Interestingly, many dowsers state of mind is important to their success.

Needless to say, not everyone who has encountered dowsing believes that dowsing works, and in many instances these critics are correct. This chapter discusses some of the common arguments against dowsing and the psychological aspects of dowsing, including the role of clairvoyance.

Dowsing Is Not Real

The simplest explanation was given by William E. Whittaker, who suggested that when the dowser focuses on something, he or she leans forward and that is why rods cross.[78] Another theory explaining dowsing states that successful dowsers are good at reading the local environment or have a thorough knowledge of the local geology rather than any special ability.[79] However, since most people are unable to read the environment that well, the proponents of this idea are just substituting one special ability with another.

M. A. Wadsworth proposed a purely mechanical theory of dowsing in 1898 to explain dowsing with a forked stick.[80]

> The process is exceedingly simple. Take any forked twig of a reasonably tough fibre in the clenched hands with the palms upward. The ends of the limbs forming the twig fork should enter the closed fists on the exterior side of each fist, i.e., on the two sides of the clenched hands furthest from each other. When a twig is grasped in this position it will remain stationary if held loosely, or with only a moderately firm grasp; but the moment the grasp is tightened, the pressure on the branches will force the end of the twig to bend downwards. The harder the grip the more it must curve. The curvature of the twig is mechanically caused by

the pressure of the hands forcing the limbs to assume a bent and twisted position, or the force that causes the forked limb to turn downwards is furnished by muscles of the hands, and not from any other cause. The whole secret of the "divining-rod" seems to reside in its position in the hands of the operator, and in his voluntarily or involuntarily increasing the closeness of his grasp on the two ends of the branches forming the fork. If the above conditions are fulfilled the twig will always bend downwards—water or no water, mineral or no mineral; anyone can be an operator, and any material can be used for the instrument, provided the limbs forming the fork are sufficiently tough and flexible. It can be easily understood how an ignorant operator may deceive himself, and be perfectly honest in supposing that some occult force, and not his hands, causes the fork to curve downwards.

The last sentence from over a century ago describes the prevailing scientific explanation for the dowsing effect, which is that dowsing relies on the ideomotor effect. This effect is well known in psychology and has been discussed in many articles, and is the non-paranormal explanation for the movements of a Ouija board and table turning, the latter of which was debunked by Michael Faraday in 1853.[81] John Jackson wrote about the ideomotor effect being behind the dowsing response of people using L-rods: "A complete novice who is told that water is beneath the ground at a certain point will find that as they cross the point, their dowsing rods will deflect or cross. This is because they know where the point is and they subconsciously move their hands slightly, which crosses the rods. The important point to stress is that this is done unconsciously. The person who is crossing the rods does not realise that they are themselves doing it; in fact, it feels as if some external force is acting upon the rods, which makes the experience even more powerful."[82]

The ideomotor effect can be demonstrated as illustrated in an article from Tom Stafford in 2013.[83] Stafford directed that a pendulum should be set up from a piece of string about 30 cm (12 in) long with a small weight on the end. The subject should then hold the pendulum at arm's length in front of them and ask a question, saying that that weight will rotate one way (clockwise or anticlockwise) for yes and the reverse for no. After a short while, the pendulum will start to rotate, providing an answer to the question. Stafford goes on to explain, "There's no supernatural force at work, just tiny movements you are making without realising. The string allows these movements to be exaggerated, the inertia of the weight allows them to be conserved and built on until they form a regular swinging motion. The effect is known as Chevreul's Pendulum, after the 19th Century French scientist who investigated it."

James Randi, a former magician and leading dowsing skeptic, has described dowsing as follows: "This is the world's most popular and pervasive delusion.... Yes, it is very convincing because you feel the sticks twisting in your hands and you seem to think it is from an outside power. There is not an outside power at all."[84]

Randi also demonstrated the power of the ideomotor effect, writing, "I showed a reporter how strongly a large magnet would attract a bent iron wire even through a cardboard box, He held the wire—and noted the strong attraction, until I pointed out to him that I had secretly removed the magnet from the box. He had been allowing his expectation to convince him of the magnetic pull that was not there. His bent wire dowsing device had been swinging very positively towards the box, repeatedly, but ceased when he knew the truth."[85]

Randi commented that dowsers are generally very honest people who believe that what they are doing is real, but one's success at finding wells is not sufficient evidence of the dowsing ability because 90 percent of the world's surface has reachable water beneath. He went on to say that it would be more challenging to find a dry spot within 100 meters of a well the dowser found.[86] William Whittaker, Iowa state archaeologist, said something similar based on his experience with dowsers who search for lost graves: "None of them [dowsers] are intentionally deceptive; to the contrary, dowsers are a very earnest group, providing what seems to be a vital service to people who desperately need answers. The problem is that the answers provided by dowsing are very often wrong, and this can lead to legal and financial problems for everyone involved. If a burial is missed by dowsing and the plot is sold to a family that then damages the existing grave while digging a new one, the cemetery officials who approved the sale on the basis of dowsing could be held liable by either family."[87]

It is likely that the ideomotor effect plays a significant effect in dowsing, but it is not the whole story, since dowsing provides information which was not otherwise known. The ideomotor effect is an underappreciated challenge that dowsers face, and unfortunately, many dowsers' performances are not as good as they would like to believe. I know from my own testing that it is easy to have a conclusion already in one's mind, and then, when the rods move, it provides confirmation, especially if it is something that I can see. I try to remind myself that I am often wrong and tell myself that I need to watch the rods, since they may do something unexpected. I hope that this questioning approach helps at least in part to counter the ideomotor effect in the various tests that are described in this book. There have also been many instances where I had an expectation for what would happen, but the result was completely different, and my initial expectations were subsequently proved wrong. So while the ideomotor effect is a factor that dowsers should keep in mind, there is more to dowsing than the ideomotor effect.

State of Mind

Many experienced dowsers claim that dowsing needs or is best performed with a specific mental state. Greg Storozuk, a professional dowser from Edgewater, Colorado,[88] described the mental state needed to dowse, saying "Anyone can do this. The key is you have to want to. There is a mental attitude that is essential. … You have to know exactly what you are looking for, and you have to ask the right questions. Either something exists or it does not."

Retired chemist Duane Kniebes, who has spent several years dowsing unmarked burials for the Colorado Council of Genealogical Societies' cemetery mapping project, commented for the *Denver Post* that "conventional science does not explain dowsing, but amazingly enough, it works. … I have become convinced that the rods work on what you are thinking about. It doesn't have to be just water or bones or whatever. It has some sort of connection with your conscience."[89] The dowser's state of mind does appear to be very important for the dowser's success. Many dowsers claim to be sensitive to moving water, but not stationary water.[90] Dennis Wheatley discussed comments from well-known dowser Guy Underwood: "Guy believed the dowsing reaction is associated with underground streams where the water is in motion in its natural channel, such as rock fissures, subject to friction, under pressure, and connecting ultimately with the sea. In support of his belief, he pointed out that a skilled water diviner, faced with ten lidded containers with only one filled with water, would not achieve better than 'chance' odds in attempting to find the container holding the water."[91] It is interesting that Underwood is using the lack of results in systematic tests to illustrate his idea, though a skeptic would use the same statistics to argue that dowsing is not real. Thomas Fiddick wrote about dowsing, deception, and state of mind in 1913, saying, "It was, however, quite possible for persons, by exercise of their will, to cause the rod to turn in the absence of both mineral and water and thus appear to be able to divine. Ignorance of those facts, not only to the public, but often by dowsers, must undoubtedly be connected with many of the disappointments attached to this practice. These experiments showed how easy it was to deceive and be deceived. In genuine dowsing a man willingly surrendered his conscious mind to the dowsing influence and simply registered the result."[92]

This explanation does provide an explanation for the dowsers' failure in the GWUP tests mentioned earlier. For what it is worth, in my own testing, I could distinguish between an empty hose pipe and one full of water, but I was not able to distinguish between a hose pipe full of water and a hosepipe with water flowing in it. To what extent the ideomotor effect was at play I can't say, since the hose was lying on the ground in front of me, and I was the one who turned the water on and off. Wheatley also commented on the need to visualize the target, writing, "In the dowsing discipline, the first law is, simply, 'You will not detect that which you cannot visualize.'" In other words, if you do not know what you seek, you will never find it. There is a vital need to visualize a dowsing target to the best of one's ability. … In visualizing any target, it is important to hold this visualization in mind to the exclusion of everything else. "In this one-pointed visualization, you are completely 'tuning in' to the target and 'tuning out' the rest of the universe. Nothing but the target must exist for you."[93]

These advanced methods are far beyond what I can do, and perhaps my limited ability is in part due to my mental state. I have to admit that I have never asked the rods a question; rather, I tend to watch them the same way that I would watch an instrument such as a multi-meter or hand-held infrared thermometer (i.e., run an experiment and observe what the rods do).

I have noticed that if I am very nervous, then my dowsing ability weakens significantly. Recently, I had to pressure wash the side of my house, which meant climbing a ladder about 6–7 m (20 feet) in the air, which was a challenge for me, since I do not like heights. Just before going up the ladder, I grabbed a pair of rods and tested them on a known dowsing line. I had almost no response. I suspect that my stress levels were so high that neither my muscles nor any other part of me were relaxed, and this blocked the dowsing response. Therefore, it seems safe to conclude that state of mind is important to successful dowsing.

It is interesting that Underwood commented about failing to identify which of several containers contained water. Similarly, even Henry Gross failed tests involving finding which of six mason jars in paper bags held sand versus water, or which of several small boxes contained a coin.[94] Dowsing requires the dowser to be relaxed, and perhaps one of the reasons for the low success rate under test conditions is test anxiety. Many people in school flunk examinations because the anxiety of the test causes them to forget what they have studied. After the test is over, it of course all comes back again.

Dowsing appears to be one of those activities where the harder one tries, the worse the outcome. It is perhaps like board breaking in martial arts. Many of the karate-style martial arts break wooden boards to show the progress of the students. Typically a board is held by other people and a punch or kick converts it into firewood. Speed breaking is a more advanced form of board breaking, where the board is loosely suspended or sitting on a surface. Whereas the held boards can be broken with enough force (big guys have a clear advantage here), speed breaking requires speed not blunt force, and speed requires that one be very relaxed and one's muscles loose. If one tries too hard, one's muscle tense, and the board will just fall back when hit. Breaking the board requires the sudden speed change of a high-speed strike. Perhaps dowsing is similar, in that the harder one tries, the more tense the muscles become and the less successful the outcome will be. One web page commented that certain drugs can have a negative impact on the dowsing results, especially drugs for mental problems, pain relievers and sedatives, and in particular all drugs which disturb driving. Alcohol is included,[95] though a small amount of whiskey is reported to calm the nerves and actually help dowsing.[96] I have not verified these statements.

Clairvoyance

The *Nevada Daily Mail* had an interesting story about a dowser called Bernard Daniel who used to dowse for graves. "Daniel even says he can tell if the bodies in the graves are male or female remains. 'You have to drop your sticks a certain way to determine if a grave contains a male or female body,' he said, a method called 'clearing the sticks.'"[97]

Neal Du Shane has been very successful identifying graves and described his method of identifying the gender of the deceased: "Standing over the center of the grave, balance the handle of one rod on your index finger, holding the rod straight down. The rod will begin making a circular motion. It will rotate clockwise for a male and counterclockwise for a female."[98]

However, he added that the movement of rods varies in different places and with different dowsers. I have also found graves under the floor of an old church; however, I always assumed that the grave was detected because of the void it presents rather than the presence of the interred individual. It is also possible that the signal arises because the ground has been changed by digging the soil out and packing it back in again sufficiently to give a dowsing signal. However, Daniel's "clearing the sticks" method is clearly taking the detection of graves to another level, and I have no explanation, though there is some corroborating evidence. Carol Brooks and Norma Dennis, reporters from the *Jamestown News*, tested dowsing for graves, writing, "[They] first went to Deep River Friends Cemetery. They walked among the graves and the rods crossed over known burials. Brooks did not look at the grave markers so she would not be influenced as to the sex. Every reading was correct. The length of the body of a child's grave also rang true. Part of this cemetery is known to have many unmarked graves, several of which were found during the test."[99]

Leroy Bull has been dowsing since he was 12, and in addition to siting wells, he has been called to find dinosaur bones, bodies lost in lakes, lost pets, missing stones from engagement rings, and holes in pipes creating underground leaks. For Bull, dowsing is a spiritual technique, and he explained his abilities by saying that we are surrounded by a primordial soup of frequencies and dowsing involves separating out the frequency wanted.[100] Bull believes that asking the right question, concentrating on the target you want, is critical to dowsing success, and his use of this approach has resulted in an approximately 95 percent success rate. He described one time he was looking for a location to dig a well: "You see in your mind's eye the answer. ... You can ask the pertinent question and see which way the pendulum is swinging. All of the land was going uphill away from me. I could see it all at the same time. I saw little gold lines running through the grass. I realized they were underground water veins. In the upper-right-hand corner of the lot was a place where they cross, and in my mind's eye it was going beep beep beep. I quote 'saw' that intuitively without using the stick. It becomes automatic, like power steering."[101]

Bull's spiritual technique invokes spirit guides; for example, he described how he dowses using a pendulum.[102] As part of his dowsing he calls on spirit guides who bring him knowledge from the spiritual world and help him find his dowsing target. Steve Herbert is another dowser who invokes spiritual entities to get answers to his searches. As described by Dan Schwartz, "Its [the other side's] beings are agents of Mother Earth who facilitate the workings of our natural world. They are the gnomes that live beneath the soil in rocks and ores and roots, the undines that float through water and flit through mist, the fire spirits that bask in heat and light, the sylphs that seek dry air. There are others, but these are the ones he calls upon most, for they, like any good custodian, know where to find this world's things."[103]

Robert Humphries claimed that he could find anything with dowsing, including water, whether it will rain here today, whether the Steelers will beat the Colts, and whether his wife is home from work yet.[104] Humphries went on to say, "One theory is that dowsing is linked to what Carl Jung called the collective subconscious, where all knowledge resides. ... Dowsing is a way to unlock it. The subconscious then sends the message by electrochemical impulse to the hands, which transfer it to the divining rod. All this is done without conscious knowledge.... Sometimes, even sophisticated scientific testing devices are unable to pick it up. ... The body doesn't lend itself to empirical testing."

Bull, Herbert and Humphries's claims and the mechanisms they propose are far outside current physical science and well beyond the scope of the physical. For each, their mechanism is a form of clairvoyance, and many of the better dowsers apparently have a similar ability. Map dowsing is performed by the dowser holding a pendulum over a map and searching for water, oil, missing people, etc., and it is clearly not a physical effect. Tromp[105] investigated map dowsing and was convinced as to its effectiveness, as was Maby.[106] Montague Keen commented that "dowsers commonly assert that their power is linked with, if not fulfilled by, wishes. Any attempt to examine this evidence, let alone suggest mechanisms to account for its diverse operations, would doubtless have pushed Dr Betz and his collaborators into the pariah region. Yet no serious study of dowsing, if made with a view to testing a hypothesis, can be limited simply to experiments for the location of water or buried pipes."[107]

I would like to think that this book is a serious study even if it *is* largely limited to experiments for the location of buried pipes, because we have to start somewhere. Even though Keen dismisses such experiments as too simple, there is currently no good theory for how buried pipes are detected by dowsing.

Some people use dowsing to speak to spirits,[108] find past lives[109] and for other mystical activities which are also far outside the scope of this book. Some field dowsers claim to be able to distinguish between water, metals and minerals beneath the ground. Part of a letter from Harry Sangster (Brownville, KY), a dowser of fifty years, to Charles Latimer (Cleveland, OH), May 10, 1876, explains the method used.[110]

What you wish to know is, after the substance is shown to exist beneath a certain point, whether it be mineral, metal or water, and the kind, character and description of each. As you are aware of the fact, the simple "forked rod" will indicate the presence of either of these. Now, to tell which of these it is, and the character of the same; if it be water, the kind of water. This is my method of testing the same, whether it be water, mineral or metal: It is on the principle of affinity—the attraction that like substances have for each other. After the rod indicates the particular spot, I take a sponge and saturate it with ordinary drinking water, either from spring or well, and put it on the top of the rod, and test it with this. If the substance beneath be water is the same kind of that in the sponge, it will turn much stronger, and the demonstration be more active and powerful. But, if the rod should not turn at all, it will be some other substance, either mineral or metal. To test the kind of water, after I am satisfied that it is water—to discover, for instance, whether it be sulphur water, I dip my sponge in that kind of water, and test as above. If the movement of the rod be active and strong when this is done, the water below will be that species of water. If salt water, dip the sponge in that kind of water, and the result will be similar; and so on through the whole catalogue of waters.

In regard to the metals. The tests are made in a similar manner. After I discover by proper tests that it is a metal, which are as follows: If it be metal or mineral, after the sponge is saturated with water, the rod will not act at all. I then put a piece of metal on the top of the rod; first, a small bit of iron. If there is no movement of the rod at the spot already indicated, it is safe to conclude that the substance is not of that nature; so I continue the experiment with different kinds of metal—lead, silver, copper, tin, gold, etc., until I find some one of these that will cause the rod to turn and operate in a manner sufficiently strong and satisfactory. The same method pertains to the minerals. Of course, a great deal of the practical operations of these various tests, will depend upon one's discretion and judgment at the time they are made, which it is impossible to put upon paper. This is but a general outline of the system.

Latimer described his actions on receipt of this letter.[111]

Immediately after receiving this letter, I made some experiments as follows: I took a green, forked twig, and found that over iron water-pipe, gas-pipe, and over a cistern of water, it turned down vigorously. I then took a wet rag and fastened it on top of the twig or rod. As Mr. Sangster testifies, I found it powerless over the iron water-pipe and over the gas-pipe, but it turned rapidly over the cistern. I put a key on the end of the rod over the wet rag; then the rod turned over both iron pipes promptly. Again, I took off the rag and put the key on the rod, and walking to the cistern, found that there was no movement. I took off the key and the rod turned instantly. I have no doubt but that he is correct as regards other metals.

Sangster and then Latimer seem to be achieving a remarkable capability. These more sensitive forms of dowsing appear to be a form of psychic phenomenon, similar to telepathy or remote viewing.[112] In such cases, success is attributed to the so-called psi field, or tapping the ethereal world or other non-physical process. Unfortunately, I have never experienced anything remotely ethereal in dowsing and cannot vouch for or against it, but I am including reports of such phenomena in this book for the sake of completeness.

Psychological Aspects of Dowsing

There appear to be three parts to dowsing, the relative influence of the three depending on the dowser and circumstances. The three parts are physical, clairvoyance and mental. The physical is the focus of this book, and to the extent it works, clairvoyance is the dominant effect in map dowsing, but some more "intuitive" dowsers appear to use it in field dowsing too. The mental part is the psychological, ideomotor effect and confirmation bias that the dowsing community prefers not to consider and which many skeptics only consider. There is quite a wide variation in how dowsers operate, and what they are able to do, and much of this variance probably depends on the relative influence of these three parts. As dowsers, I think we have to recognize that these psychological influences are real, and significant, but I hope this book also helps some of the skeptics understand that there is a real physical effect here too.

Another area of difficulty is the inherently subjective nature of the measurement, which gives rise to a number of problems:

- Ideomotor response—yes, as discussed above, people's subconscious minds may influence their bodies without their consciously deciding to take action. It happens all the time in our everyday lives and there is no reason to believe it is not at work in dowsing too. Even small actions such as changing one's stance or leaning in can affect the rods, so that what appears automatic may not actually be so. By repeating the test, and changing variables to give results that are not immediately obvious, it is possible to reduce the effects of ideomotor response, but perhaps not eliminate it completely.
- State of mind. Dowsing requires the dowser to be calm and relaxed and for some people very focused. Unlike many athletic performances, dowsing does not benefit from adrenaline or stress.
- Confirmational bias—definitely an issue. I found it especially hard to reduce confirmational bias when testing the theories outlined in this book, since I often had a strong idea as to what the result "should be," and so even a small signal was confirmation of the idea. To try to compensate, I would repeat the test multiple times, from different directions, and remind myself that I am frequently wrong, but it remains a challenge to overcome.
- Interpretation of visual cues. As people go about dowsing, of course they see the world around them, and interpret it accordingly. If one is looking for a water pipe, and there is a water valve in the ground, it does not take a genius to say that the water pipe probably connects to the valve. However, often it works the other way too. One follows a dowsing line and ends up at the water valve, and now can identify the dowsing line as a water pipe.
- Interpretation of results. Absent the clairvoyance that some people apparently have, the rest of us receive little information from the rods—position of crossing and strength of crossing. At least in my experience, there is no difference in signal between a PVC pipe underground and a steel gas main. In my experience, the dowsing rods are rather like a cheap (non-discriminating) metal detector, which says that there is metal there, but cannot distinguish between a pot of gold and a rusty piece of iron. The main approach is to follow the signal (e.g., placing yellow pieces of tape or flags on the ground marking where the rods crossed) until it comes to something identifiable, such as a gas valve or a drain, which thus identifies what the dowsing signal was from. However, even this method is not always useful.

I did a survey of our house and the space between our houses and our neighbors. There was a dowsing line that went straight from a downspout on our house to a downspout on theirs, and then a PVC pipe from their downspout emptied in the woods behind our houses. Based on the dowsing response, I assumed that our downspout connected to theirs, but I was wrong. When I put the hose down our spout, the water ran through a pipe along the side of our house and out to the street. (I could hear it running). I don't know what the dowsing line between our downspout and our neighbor's is, but it is always there; but it is not a PVC pipe connecting our downspouts. This error served to demonstrate, to me at least, how dependent we are on outside facts to make our interpretation of the information we get from the dowsing rods. It is easy to jump to assumptions that may or, in my case, may not be correct.

In summary, dowsing appears to be a real phenomenon, because it provides information that we did not previously have and which is not apparent from simple observation of the environment. However, dowsing is fraught with psychological issues such as the ideomotor effect, confirmation bias, reading visual clues and errors in assumptions and analysis. The goal of this book is to try to answer the question of what the physical basis of dowsing is, while recognizing that these other psychological issues add "noise" to the measurements. The dowser's state of mind appears to be important element for many, and many dowsers use questions to direct the rods to find their desired goal. Some of the claims made by dowsers are not readily describable by physical mechanisms and if verified would appear to support clairvoyance of some kind, but that discussion is beyond the scope of this book.

Another psychological aspect to dowsing concerns how people view dowsing. There are the devotes who believe strongly that dowsing is effective, the skeptics who believe that it is pseudo-science and cannot possibly be real and a large number of people who are unsure. Dowsing has been frequently used in archaeology and has been described as a useful technique in the popular book by Ivor Hume,[113] the director of the Department of Archaeology at Colonial Williamsburg, a major center for the preservation and interpretation of American colonial history. Hume wrote, "There is no denying that one feels a little idiotic walking across a field intently watching two pieces of coat hanger. Nevertheless, they serve a useful purpose and are included in every Williamsburg archaeologist's box of tricks. Like the elaborate metal detectors, 'angle rods' are a means of finding objects and not of locating sites. Their principal application is in tracing utility lines, which must be avoided by excavators, but they also enable one to locate possible fragile metal objects as the excavation proceeds, thus providing a warning that one should proceed with increased caution."

Another archaeologist, Kathryn Denning did a survey of faculty and students in the Archaeology Department at the University of Sheffield.[114] She found that half of the 24 respondents had tried dowsing, of which nine found it helpful. There were eight cases where dowsing had been used by archaeologists to find underground features, seven of which were successful, but 19 of the 24 surveyed did not believe that map dowsing was possible, with the other five noncommittal. The survey also showed that while many archaeologists were willing to consider dowsing as a method, they would not accept dowsing results without further proof. I suspect that the lack of an apparent physical explanation for the method, unlike technological methods such as ground penetrating radar, ground resistivity or magnetometer surveys, always places a question mark over dowsing. The subjective nature of dowsing and the variability from person to person is another factor that reduces the trust in the method by both dowsers and non-dowsers alike.

Quackery and Fraud

Dowsing is a poorly understood method with few established procedures, and in addition to the ideomotor effect, suggestion, and self-deception, there is ample room for those who wish to practice simple fraud.

Some devices give dowsing a bad name. For example, Sniffex, which later became Homeland Safety International, claimed their device, which the *New York Times* described as dowsing rods, was able to detect explosives. Testing by the U.S. military showed that it performed no better than random chance.[115] The patent for the device[116] claims the device emits a frequency between 10 MHz and 1.3 GHz, at the corresponding resonance frequency of the target and detects the resulting interference response. However, disassembly of the device by the U.S. Navy showed there was no battery, no transmitter and only three magnets at the end of a brass cylinder. The Securities and Exchange Commission charged the company with fraud,[117] though according to the *New York Times*,[118] Sniffex and others went on to sell large numbers of these devices to the Iraqi security forces to search for explosives. According to the newspaper, it is likely that lives were lost because the security forces relied on these devices.

Similarly, Global Technical Ltd, a UK company, persuaded Thailand, Saudi Arabia, Hong Kong, Indonesia, and Mexico to buy large numbers of their GT200 device to detect explosives, narcotics and other illicit materials. Doubts were cast when the devices failed to detect several car bombs and several people were killed, and in 2010 the UK government issued a warning that these devices were wholly ineffective.[119] The National Institute for Justice, Part of the U.S. Department of Justice, issued guidance for the selection of explosive detectors,[120] including a warning about dowsing-based explosives detectors:

> 7. WARNING: DO NOT BUY BOGUS EXPLOSIVES DETECTION EQUIPMENT
>
> From time to time, there are new devices that enter the market. Most companies make reasonable claims, and their products are based on solid scientific principles. Claims for some other devices may seem unreasonable or may not appear to be based on solid scientific principles. … Although there may be other types of non operational devices around, dowsing devices for explosives detection have emerged during the past couple of years.
>
> There is a rather large community of people around the world that believes in dowsing: the ancient practice of using forked sticks, swinging rods, and pendulums to look for underground water and other materials. These people believe that many types of materials can be located using a variety of dowsing methods. Dowsers claim that the dowsing device will respond to any buried anomalies, and years of practice are needed to use the device with discrimination (the ability to cause the device to respond to only those materials being sought). Modern dowsers have been developing various new methods to add discrimination to their devices [Blame all dowsers as a group]. These new methods include molecular frequency discrimination (MFD) and harmonic induction discrimination (HID). MFD has taken the form of everything from placing a xerox copy of a Polaroid photograph of the desired material into the handle of the device, to using dowsing rods in conjunction with frequency generation electronics (function generators). None of these attempts to create devices that can detect specific materials such as explosives (or any materials for that matter) have been proven successful in controlled double-blind scientific tests. In fact, all testing of these inventions has shown these devices to perform no better than random chance.….
>
> Things to look for when dealing with "new technologies" that may well be a dowsing device are words like molecular frequency discrimination, harmonic induction discrimination, and claims of detecting small objects at large distances. Many of these devices require no power

to operate (most real technology requires power). Suspect any device that uses a swinging rod that is held nearly level, pivots freely and "indicates" the material being sought by pointing at it. Any device that uses a pendulum that swings in different shaped paths to indicate its response should also arouse suspicion. Advertisements that feature several testimonials by "satisfied users," and statements about pending tests by scientific and regulatory agencies (but have just not happened yet) may be indications that the device has not been proven to work. Statements that the device must be held by a human to operate usually indicate dowsing devices. Statements that the device requires extensive training by the factory, the device is difficult to use, and not everyone can use the device, are often made to allow the manufacturer a way of blaming the operator for the device's failure to work. Another often used diversion is that scientists and engineers cannot understand the operation of the device or the device operates on principles that have been lost or forgotten by the scientific community.

The sales of these types of charlatan devices damage the already strained reputation of dowsing as a technique. These devices have almost nothing to do with dowsing, and a lot to do with people making a quick dollar over the gullibility of others. While there is a physical basis to dowsing (as this book argues) and the effect is real, there is no shortage of quackery that goes along with it, so it is not surprising that most people do not hold dowsing and dowsers in high regard.

The next few chapters review some of the physical explanations that have been put forward by other investigators into the mechanism of dowsing. Some of these are the result of serious study, some less so. Many theories have been proposed to explain the dowsing effect, including clairvoyance,[121] psi power, local variations in gravity,[122] magnetic fields caused by flowing water, abnormalities in the Earth's magnetic field,[123] interaction of the dowser's electric field with that of the ground/atmospheric electric field,[124] EM fields, EM radiation or some unspecified type or combinations of them. For the most part, the majority of people who have looked into dowsing hold that while they don't know how it works, they just know it does work.

5

Radioactivity and Subatomic Particles

> It was necessary at this point to find a new term to define this new property of matter manifested by the elements of uranium and thorium. I proposed the word radioactivity which has since become generally adopted; the radioactive elements have been called radio elements.
> —Marie Curie[125]

Chapter summary: Radioactivity and various subatomic particles have been proposed as the basis for the dowsing signal. This chapter reviews the types of radiation occurring in nature and compares them to what would be required of a dowsing signal. The conclusion is that dowsing is not caused by radioactivity.

Radioactivity has been suggested as the physical basis for the dowsing response by several investigators,[126] and studies have been conducted to look at the effect of radiation on dowsing. For example, Maby and Franklin wrote, "(1) A small tube of radium was sometimes placed under a covering box and at other times removed without the dowser's knowledge. The more skilled dowser gave the right answer (rods reacted to the radium present) ten times out of ten, while the less skilled dowser, who had only used a rod a few times before the tests, got nine successes out of twelve trials. (2) Tests with lead screening of the radium showed that gamma-rays still caused reactions, though the latter were appreciably weakened by the exclusion of the alpha and beta particles."[127]

These are impressive results; however, it is not at all clear how or why this type of radiation would give a dowsing response to underground objects and materials. As discussed earlier, in order for a radiation to give a dowsing response it must be able to pass through at least several meters/yards of soil and rock and then it must interact with the dowser sufficiently strongly to give a response. The most common forms of radioactivity do not meet these criteria and so radioactivity is unlikely to be the basis of the dowsing effect.

Fiddick found that his dowsing cone stopped rotating over pitchblende, suggesting that the radioactivity somehow suppressed the dowsing effect.[128] Pitchblende, now usually called uraninite, is an ore of uranium oxides comprised mainly of UO_2 and U_3O_8. Uranium oxides tend to be semiconductors[129] and so it is likely that the pitchblende was detected because of the effect of its conductivity on the dowsing signal (discussed below) rather than because of its radioactivity. However, this conclusion does not explain Maby and Franklin's results with vials of radium.

Atoms and Radioactivity

To understand radioactivity, one must understand the composition of matter and its terminology. Matter is made of atoms and atoms consist of a nucleus containing protons and neutrons, surrounded by a cloud of electrons. Protons have a positive charge, electrons an equal but opposite negative charge and neutrons, as the name suggests, have no charge. A typical atom is about 0.2 nm across, so very small, but the nucleus is a thousand times smaller, buried deep inside the atom. When atoms interact with other atoms, it is the electron clouds of one atom affecting its neighbors. These electron clouds essentially control all of chemistry, most of physics and determine most of the physical structures that we see in the world around us. Apart from maintaining charge balance (and the weak force), the nucleus plays little role in the world of chemistry.

Radioactivity on the other hand is a nuclear process; the role of the electron clouds is largely incidental. Before I explain this statement, here are some atomic definitions that will be helpful here and later in the in book.

- The number of protons in an atom defines the element; for example, oxygen atoms with eight protons are different from carbon with six protons per atom.
- The number of protons is the atomic number, and the number of protons plus neutrons is the atomic mass.
- The number of electrons in a neutral atom is the same as the number of protons to maintain charge neutrality and the mass of electrons is so much smaller than protons and neutrons that it can usually be ignored.
- Different isotopes of the same element have the same number of protons, but different numbers of neutrons. Isotopes can be defined by the atomic weight; for example, uranium (atomic number 92) has two main naturally occurring isotopes (Uranium 235 and uranium 238), where the number following the name represents the atomic mass, so uranium 235 has 92 protons and (235–92 =) 143 neutrons.

Some isotopes are stable and others unstable. Unstable isotopes break apart (decay); the unstable nuclei may give off various types of particles and radiation when they decay and are called radioactive. Unstable nuclei undergo radioactive decay, during which they typically change a neutron into a proton by releasing a beta particle (electron) or give off a couple of protons and neutrons (alpha particle), often also releasing energy in the form of gamma radiation. Often the products of radioactive decay are themselves radioactive, so for example the decay of uranium 238 goes via multiple steps until it eventually reaches a stable isotope (lead 206).[1] Part of this sequence is shown in Table 5.1.

Table 5.1. Part of the Sequence of Radioactive Decay of Uranium 238

Starting Isotope	Ending Isotope	Emitted Particle
Uranium 238	Thorium 234	Beta
Thorium 234	Protactinium 234	Beta
Protactinium 234	Uranium 234	Beta
Uranium 234	Thorium 230	Alpha
Thorium 230	Radium 226	Alpha
Radium 226	Radon 222	Alpha
Radon 226	Polonium 218	Alpha

---

1. "Uranium Its Uses And Hazards," Institute for Energy and Environmental Research," https://ieer.org/resource/factsheets/uranium-its-uses-and-hazards/#:~:text=Uranium%2D238%20decays%20by%20alpha,series%20starting%20at%20uranium%2D238., accessed September 1, 2020.

Types of Radioactivity

There are several types of radiation, each with different abilities to penetrate materials. The first type is alpha particles (helium nuclei), which can penetrate only a few centimeters of air and are unable to penetrate a sheet of paper or skin. Many radioactive elements, such as uranium, thorium, and radium, are alpha emitters, and they present a severe hazard because the alpha particles of the radioactive material can be breathed in as a dust and then the alpha particles are emitted in the lungs, and do not have to go far before they cause damage. Even if the dowsing signal were somehow encoded in alpha particles, they could not be physiologically detected because they cannot penetrate the skin. Similarly, alpha particles cannot penetrate several meters of rock. It is therefore clear that the dowsing response is not from alpha particles.

The second type of radiation is beta particles (electrons), which are emitted by elements such as strontium 90. These have a penetration of about a meter or two in air, and while they can penetrate the body about 1 to 2 cm, beta particles are unable to penetrate through a thin sheet of metal, plastic, wood or concrete. A related radiation is the positron, the positive antimatter version of the electron. It too can only travel in air for a short distance and cannot travel through significant thicknesses of rock, whereas dowsers can detect objects several meters (yards) down, and so beta particles are not the basis of the dowsing signal. In addition, the concentration of beta particles in normal air is quite low, below that needed to convey the dowsing signal.

Another type of radiation consists of neutrons, which are high-energy particles that have an exceptional ability to penetrate other material because they have no charge and so are barely affected by the electrons in atoms. Neutrons can travel long distances in air and require extensive hydrogen-containing materials, e.g., water and water-containing material to block them. However, neutron radiation is rarely found outside of a nuclear reactor and therefore neutrons are unlikely to be behind dowsing.

Gamma rays are a very energetic form of EM radiation, having higher energy and higher frequency than even x-rays. When gamma rays are absorbed, they are such high energy photons that they may ionize the molecules that absorb them, or break molecular bonds, causing very fast reactions.[130] The penetration of gamma rays though water or soft tissue is about four inches or ten cm for the intensity to reduce to 50 percent (half value thickness).[131] While they can readily penetrate air, several feet of concrete or a few inches of dense material (such as lead) is enough to block gamma rays. The amount of radiation from two meters (~ 6.5 feet) below the surface will be greatly reduced (~ one millionth) by the time it reaches the surface. Gamma rays are produced by some nuclear decay processes, but outside of a few nuclear waste dumps, there are not enough radioactive isotopes around us and in the soil beneath our feet to give enough radiation to be able to detect the things that dowsing does. For example, dowsing can detect a thin sheet of aluminum foil on the ground, but such a sheet would have little impact on gamma rays. Similarly, dowsing can detect a PVC pipe buried in the ground, but again, PVC pipe will have minimal impact on gamma radiation. The conclusion is that gamma rays are also unlikely to be the source of the dowsing signal. There are other particles emitted too during radioactive decay, but these are much rarer and again unlikely to constitute the dowsing signal. In conclusion, though often mentioned as a possible basis for the dowsing reaction, radioactivity is unlikely to be the mechanism.

It has been suggested that radioactivity is produced by flowing water, and that somehow this radioactivity interacts with the body.[132] However, radioactivity comes from the presence of unstable radio isotopes, not the movement of fluids. There is no evidence that flowing water would cause radioactivity and such an occurrence would be completely counter to our understanding of how radioactivity and fluids operate. On the experimental front, Maby found that photographic plates placed inside first floor rooms over streams where the dowsing fields were normally very strong fogged very slowly but not differently from those in other locations,[133] confirming that radioactivity is not the mechanism behind dowsing.

One suggestion that has been made is that the dowsing response is due to neutrinos, with no supporting evidence.[134] For example, one online commentator going by the name of Angel_09 wrote, "Since atoms are constantly vibrating and emitting radiation, a low frequency is developed and radiates in the infrared region. Neutrino bombardment from the sun increases the amplitude of this frequency and resonates with the frequency of the amplified atom from the dowsing rod. These two frequencies having the same wavelength are interacting like 'transmitter and receiver' where the manifestation is the movement of the rod."[135]

Neutrinos are almost mass-less particles ($< 2.14 \times 10^{-37}$ kg)[136] that are produced in large numbers during nuclear fusion reactions, such as the processes which power the sun. However, they have no charge and have almost no interaction with regular matter. We are constantly radiated with neutrinos from the sun which pass directly through us and the earth with almost no absorption, with about 100 billion solar neutrinos passing through your thumbnail every second.[137] It is true that objects at room temperature emit infrared radiation (see discussion on Planck radiation in Chapter 7), but since neutrinos have almost no interaction with matter, they are not going to increase the amplitude of this radiation. The very low interaction between neutrinos and the ground and us, means neutrinos are very unlikely to be the basis of the dowsing reaction. The rest of Angel_09's description is unsupported by evidence or conventional science. Interestingly though, it has been suggested that one day neutrinos could be used for oil and gas exploration,[138] if a way can be found to detect them with sufficient sensitivity and accuracy.

The dowsing response is also believed by some people to be due to the result of a tachyon beam normally striking the Earth, that tachyons can be detected by dowsing[139] or that we are surrounded by a tachyon field.[140] Tachyons have been suggested to be subatomic particles that travel faster than light. However, there is no evidence to support their existence and some strong theoretical reasons, such as Einstein's theory of special relativity, suggesting that they do not exist.[141] Consequently, it seems highly unlikely that tachyons form the basis of the dowsing response. Sometimes it seems that each time a new subatomic particle is discovered, it is rapidly attributed by some as a potential basis of dowsing, such as occurred with the Higgs boson,[142] discovered in 2012 by the Large Hadron Collider at CERN. It is ironic how as new subatomic particles are discovered or theorized they come under scrutiny as the basis for the ancient art of dowsing.

6

Gravity

Dowsing is in the same category as gravity and quantum mechanics in that science cannot explain how it works, but that it works is irrefutable.
—Rev. Martin J. Smith, Wilmslow, Cheshire[143]

Chapter summary: Another common theory for dowsing is that the dowser is responding to gravitational anomalies, caused by underground water and objects. This chapter discusses the theory of gravity and compares the properties of gravity to the requirements of a dowsing signal. The conclusion is that dowsing is not caused by gravitational anomalies.

Gravity Variances

Gravitational variances have also been suggested as a possible cause of the dowsing effect.[144]

For example, Larry Marshall CEO of Australia's Commonwealth Scientific and Industrial Research Organisation, told the Australian Broadcasting Corporation in a radio interview, "I've seen people do this [dowsing] with close to 80% accuracy, and I've no idea how they do it. ... When I see that, as a scientist, it makes me question, 'Is there instrumentality that we could create that would enable a machine to find that water?' ... I've always wondered whether there is something in the EM field, or gravitational anomaly."[145] He later commented that "the largest detectable sources of changing gravitational anomalies are bodies of water and ice."

The Earth's gravitational field is fairly uniform, but there are variations due to the different densities of rocks, heights of rock (mountains vs. valleys). Gravity surveys are used by civil engineers, archaeologists and geologists to locate underground features such as aquifers.[146] A quantum gradient gravity device has been developed by the University of Birmingham (UK) which detected an underground utility tunnel 2-m by 2-m internal cross section and a reinforced concrete wall of approximately 0.2-m thickness that ran under a road. The instrument was able to determine the center to ±0.19 meters horizontally and the center depth as (1.89 −0.59/+2.3) meters.[147] However, the variations in the local gravity are so small that it is highly unlikely that gravity can explain the dowsing response. Also, gravity does not explain how thin aluminum foil can block the dowsing response from something below or gives its own dowsing response. The conclusion therefore is that the dowsing response is not in response to local variances in gravity from the presence of underground objects or masses.

Force of Gravity

Gravity is a long-range force and every particle with mass in the universe is attracted to every other particle. The law of gravity was developed by Sir Isaac Newton, and it states that the force between two objects of mass m_1 and m_2 respectively is proportional to their masses, and inversely proportional to the square of the distance r between them.

$$\text{Force} = Gm_1m_2/r^2$$

where G is the gravitational constant (6.674×10^{-11} m^3 kg^{-1} s^{-2}). The gravitational constant is very small, so the gravitational attraction between two small objects is usually negligible. Suppose there were two masses, one the dowser, about 100 kg (220 lb), and the other, a body of water, about 1000 kg (2,200 lb, 264 US gallons), separated by a distance of 10m (33 ft), the gravitational force between them is about 6.7×10^{-8} kgm/s^2 (1.5×10^{-8} poundforce). For comparison, the weight of a fruit fly is about 10 µN,[1] or 100 times greater, so if a small insect or a piece of dust landed on the dowser, it would completely overwhelm the dowsing response.[2] Gravity is a very weak force between small objects.

In the example above, the force on the person from that 1000 kg of water would be as calculated above, but the gravitational abnormality would be less because the abnormality would be the difference between having the water there and not having the water there, i.e., the difference between having rock there and water there. Additionally, if the detection sense organ was much smaller, a nerve perhaps or a small part of the brain with a mass of 1 gram, the force would be 100,000 times smaller than for an entire body.

Gravity links every particle in the universe to every other particle and so it is very nonspecific. There is not, for example, a gravitational force that is indicative of water and a different force indicative of rock. If gravity is the basis for dowsing, then there would be no difference between water and a rock type of similar density. There is also no known material that can block gravity, the force depends on mass and distance. A heavy mass 10 m below the surface may cause a gravitational anomaly, but there would be little difference between the gravitational force on the dowser standing directly above it or 1 meter away. The dowsing signal is highly collimated (discussed below), and so again change in the local gravitational field is unlikely to be the basis of the dowsing signal.

1. MH Dickinson and KG Götz, "The Wake Dynamics and Flight Forces of the Fruit Fly *Drosophila Melanogaster*," *J Exp Biol*. vol. 199 (pt. 9) (September 1996), 2085–104, doi: 10.1242/jeb.199.9.2085. PMID: 8831148.
2. *Ibid.*

7

Parallel Bands and Fields Produced by Rotating Objects

Everything is determined, the beginning as well as the end, by forces over which we have no control. It is determined for the insect, as well as for the star. Human beings, vegetables, or cosmic dust, we all dance to a mysterious tune, intoned in the distance by an invisible piper.
—Albert Einstein

Chapter summary: One of the more interesting explanations of dowsing is that it is caused by a response to torsion fields, fields theorized to be generated by rotating objects. While torsion fields are outside the realm of standard physics, the evidence and theory are reviewed in relation to dowsing, but at least in this author's opinion, they were unconvincing.

Vincent C. Reddish, former Regius Professor of Astronomy at the University of Edinburgh, proposed in his 2010 book that the dowsing effect was caused by an unknown field created by rotating bodies, and that some dowsing lines are caused by interference between the fields created by the rotation of the sun and the Earth.[148] He called this new field a torsion field and the radiation torsion radiation. Below are some of the observations made by Reddish and my comments:

- The first observation is that parallel pairs of horizontal linear structures above ground produce a dowsing response of equally spaced lines, which Reddish believed was an interference pattern. He also found that water has a major effect on this pattern and that different handholds on the rods detect different interference patterns.

  I do not know what Reddish was observing, but I doubt it was an interference pattern since in order to see an interference pattern, it helps to have monochromatic (single frequency) waves (or harmonics). The characteristic peaks and valleys that one sees in an interference pattern are caused because where two waves pass through each other, they can either add together if in phase, or subtract from each other if out of phase (see the superposition and reflection section in the Appendix). If the waves are not monochromatic, they will still interfere with each other, but the resulting pattern will not be clear peaks and valleys. It seems a great coincidence that these mysterious waves are not only monochromatic, but just the right wavelength needed to create the dowsing pattern, especially if formed by the motion of the Earth and sun.

I tried to observe the effects that Reddish described by dowsing towards and away perpendicular to various structures which have horizontal linear sections, including a wooden fence with three parallel bars, a steel handrail with two parallel bars and a steel shopping cart rack with four parallel rails. However, I did not observe any interference pattern or any response from the rods from about 5 paces away up to the structure itself, let alone any interference pattern.

- Reddish also found that linear structures on the ground give a dowsing response. He directed: "Lay a hose pipe on the ground, the dowsing rods will respond to its linear structure, fill with water and the dowsing rods will also respond. Stand stationary over the hose and have someone turn on the water, so the water is moving, and the dowsing rods will respond. Have a hose coil, stand in the middle with dowsing rods, and have someone else turn on and off the water and the dowsing rods will respond to the flowing water."

    When I tried this suggestion I found a weak effect from an empty hose-pipe on the ground, moderately strong signal when hose pipe was full of water, and stronger when coiled into a three hose-pipe width coil of about 1.5 m diameter, such that rods fully crossed. Walking across the coil circle caused the initially parallel rods to cross over the first side of the circle, partially uncross across the middle, re-cross on crossing the second diameter and back to parallel again outside the circle. Having water flowing through the pipe gave the same result as having the hose full of static water.

- Reddish also stated that the dowsing effect is caused by a transverse wave that is not electromagnetic (EM). Reddish's book did not go into details about how he determined that the wave was transverse.

    However, I agree with him that the dowsing signal is transverse, since it is polarized (see later) and only transverse waves can be polarized. I also do not know how he determined that the dowsing signal is not EM. I found it was EM, but again, I am getting ahead of myself and risk spoiling the story for the rest of the book.

- Reddish also claimed that dowsing rods made of aluminum, silver, gold and tin behave differently from other materials such as copper, steel, wood and PVC because aluminum reflects the dowsing wave whereas the other materials transmit it.

    I have observed no significant difference between rods made of aluminum, copper or steel. I have even found that wood rods work, so the material is not critical. The rods appear to provide a visual indication of small movements of the arms, and so do not detect the dowsing signal themselves. For a given arm movement, the speed and extent of response from the rods will depend on a balance between mass (the rods fall under gravity) and friction against the skin or rod holder. Therefore there will be some differences between rods of different materials in terms of how they indicate the dowsing response, but not the dowsing response (arm movement) itself.

- Reddish said that overhead cables caused the rods to rotate when standing directly beneath them.

    This result makes sense; see the later chapter on dowsing as a three-dimensional effect.

- Reddish found that aluminum foil and tin plate on the soles of the feet block the dowsing response.

7. Parallel Bands and Fields Produced by Rotating Objects

I have observed that aluminum foil blocks the dowsing response, as have other people,[149] although foil on the feet had only a limited impact, whereas foil under the chin had a major effect on the dowsing signal (see discussion later). I am unclear how aluminum foil blocking the dowsing signal supports Reddish's proposed mechanism, but the effect of aluminum is explained by the mechanism proposed later in this book.

- Reddish also found that aluminum foil can reflect the dowsing waves and polarize them on reflection.

  If the dowsing response is caused by a transverse wave, then it makes sense that it would be polarized on reflection, though I have not confirmed this experimentally. The observation that aluminum foil can block and reflect the dowsing signal is consistent with the signal being EM, despite Reddish's conclusions to the contrary. This observation is also consistent with the mechanism proposed in this book. He also reported that stretched polyethylene film polarizes torsion radiation, but having been unable to detect torsion waves, I have not tested this observation.

- Reddish also noted that wood, cardboard and hardboard are transparent to the dowsing waves.

  I also found that cardboard appears to be transparent to the dowsing waves. Placing cardboard on the ground does not appear to affect the dowsing response.

- Reddish observed that parallel pairs of horizontal linear structures aboveground produce a dowsing response of equally spaced lines. The spacing between the patterns flipped twice a year and, more remarkably, the spacing using a similar apparatus in New Zealand flipped at about the same time as that observed in Scotland.

  This result suggests that they are observing some global phenomenon, and not just a local effect, which obviously elevates the significance of their observation. My suspicion is that Reddish and Co. were very good experimentalists and ran the experiment outside, at the same time of day in both locations. As discussed later in the chapter on dowsing in three dimensions, the sun emits EM radiation that can cause a dowsing response, and I suspect their response changed depending on whether it was light or dark outside. Since New Zealand and Scotland are almost opposite each other on the Earth (The longitude and latitude for Edinburgh are 55.95° N and 3.2° W; and for Wellington the longitude and latitude are 41.3° S, 174.8° E), the response pattern would switch twice a year, around the same time and in the opposite direction, as reported.

- Reddish reported that dowsers can detect a wide range of linear objects, such as pipes, drains, cables, edges of old roads, whether or not there is water in them.

  Many dowsers would agree with this observation; however, I don't believe the response is limited to linear objects.

- The structures can be copper, steel, PVC etc., and so the dowsing effect is not EM. Reddish believed this conclusion was confirmed because he still saw the dowsing effect in an EM shielded lab (courtesy of BAE).

  I agree that dowsing can detect copper, steel, PVC, etc., but this observation does not mean that the dowsing effect is not EM. A shielded room (Faraday cage) would be expected to block the dowsing signal if the dowsing signal is comprised of external thermal radio waves and microwaves. However (SPOILER

ALERT), if the object they were detecting was inside the room, then the thermal radiation from the room itself may be enough to detect it. This observation is potentially very important for the theory of dowsing, but the experimental details of this experiment are unclear.

- Reddish found that a rotating mass (bench grinder) created a dowsing wave which could be reflected by aluminum foil.

  I tried to reproduce this experiment. Unfortunately I do not have an angle grinder, so I took an electric drill (Dewalt DW505 Hammer VSR Hammer Action Drill, 120V, 7.2 A) set to hammer off, drill (not screw), clockwise rotation, and inserted a small grindstone (7.6 cm/3 inches diameter, 1 cm/0.5 inch thick). The drill was mounted 1.4 m (54 inches) above ground level, and it was tested using dowsing rods by walking in front of the grindstone, with the grindstone front surface about 12 inches from the bottom of my sternum. There was no dowsing signal with the drill off or on. So unfortunately, I was not able to reproduce the effect. Reddish found that the waves from torsion wave generators (bench grinders) were proportional to the rotation rate and mass rotated, but independent of the material being rotated. Again, I was unable to recreate the effect of moving bodies, but I suspect the effect that Reddish observed may have been EM, because the higher the rotation rate of the electric motors, the higher the current draw.

- Reddish discussed that dowsing does not work in the dark, citing a conversation with C. M. Humphries.

  In my tests, dowsing worked the same in the dark as in the light, during the day and night and the same with my eyes open or closed. Latimer also reported that dowsing worked for him whether he was blindfolded or not.[150] The dowsing effect therefore does not depend on either the presence of light or the light being seen.

If Reddish's torsion is caused by or modified by celestial objects, then presumably it can be transmitted through a vacuum, which groups it with EM radiation and gravity waves. Most other waves (sound, water, etc.) need a medium to transmit through. As described, this torsion radiation is different from other types of radiation known to science. Considerably more data will be required before theories of torsion radition become generally accepted.

Many dowsers have found so-called parallel bands, dowsing lines that run parallel to a stream, pipe or other source of the dowsing signal. For example, Anne Miller wrote[151]:

> The situation [Novice dowsers detecting many different responses] is confused for the novice by the tendency of buried structures (e.g., a pipeline) to create a series of parallel dowsing lines, similar, though not identical, to diffraction pattern. However, with experience the dowser learns to "focus on the question" and can then get a reaction only at the centre line, without being confused by the parallels. Interestingly, the spacing of these parallels oscillates with the diurnal cycle, reaching a maximum at about 1500h local time, thus suggesting a possible link with the normal daily variation of earth's magnetic field which reaches a minimum at about 13–1400h.

Maby and Franklin wrote their book *The Physics of the Divining Rod*[152] almost entirely about these parallel bands and developed a theory about their origin. They found that a linear structure such as a pipe had a succession of parallel bands (dowsing responses) which run parallel to the pipe, with peaks and troughs of intensity, with the peaks about 15 feet apart. They proposed that the pipe was emitting Hertzian waves (radio waves), and its first harmonic and these frequencies combined setting up standing waves, with a wavelength around 15 ft. They believed that the pipe was emitting radio waves because it was being excited by cosmic radiation.

There are a number of issues with this explanation including the fact that the cosmic radiation intensity is too low to cause such an effect; only about eight cosmic particles reach each square meter of the Earth's surface a second.[153] Furthermore, even if a pipe were bombarded with cosmic radiation, there is no reason to believe it would emit radio waves. Lastly, to create standing waves would require a particular frequency to be reflected back on itself, and no clear mechanism is described. However, theories aside, the observations are very interesting. There were a number of remarkable features about these parallel bands that Maby and Franklin noted.

- The bands were found parallel to any linear "conductor," such as metal pipes and streams, and around circular "conductors" such as trees or poles.

  I did not find any bands within 40 ft of an underground gas line passing under a trail made from a former railway bed, though I had a very clear response from the gas line itself.

  I did find a band next to a small stream that was passing underground through a pipe for about 50 yards. The band was an irregular distance from the pipe. The pipe had been laid in the valley (large ditch) and soil filled in over and around it so as to enlarge an area for a baseball field; and the irregular band was probably the interface between the original stream bank and the fill material.

- In addition to detecting these bands using dowsing rods (Y type), Maby and Franklin also detected the bands with changes in position by a magnetized needle magnetometer, and with a neon discharge tube under voltage.

  Using the magnetometer in my cell phone, I saw no significant difference (< +/- ~2 µT) in the magnetic field in the x, y or z directions nor the total magnetic field (~52 µT) on or off dowsing lines caused by underground pipes, so unfortunately, I was unable to reproduce this key finding of Maby that the parallel bands could be measured using a magnetometer. I suspect a magnetized needle magnetometer is much less sensitive and more prone to error than the magnetometers built into modern cell phones. If they were seeing these bands with a magnetometer, then these bands indicate differences in local magnetic field. I don't know what would cause that, but perhaps there were other structures or material differences underground near their target, such as an iron or water pipe that ran parallel the stream, or other structures that could change the local magnetic field.

- These bands changed with time, sometimes flipping maxima and minima, apparently in response to changes in the Earth's magnetic field.

  I am not sure what they were observing. However, they may have been seeing changes that occurred at certain times of the day that coincidentally corresponded to changes in the Earth's magnetic field, such as tidal effects (discussed below).

- Every conductor in air appears to be surrounded by a very local field of ionizing particles which can be detected by a dowser.

This statement appears to be unlikely. It takes a high electric field or some other energetic energy source to ionize the air; for example, the breakdown voltage of air is about 30 kV/cm.[154] However, Maby and Franklin believed that the dowsing response was caused by ionization by cosmic rays, and so their statement may be interpreted to say that a dowsing signal was observed near large metallic objects. I have observed that the rods cross when approaching large steel objects, such as shipping containers, which is discussed later.

- Vertical conductors exhibit four cardinal rays at right angles which can be detected by a dowser.

  I have not been able to reproduce this effect, and I am not sure what Maby and Franklin were observing. However, I did find that a vertical steel pole gives a dowsing response in the shadow of the sun. Since the shadow moves with the sun's position through the day, the dowsing line will move throughout the day too. The explanation behind this observation is given in Chapter 22, "Dowsing in Three Dimensions." If the connection was not made with the movement of the sun, then the dowsing response would appear to move with time.

- Points of reaction were found along the length of conductors, corresponding to standing waves in the conductor.

  I don't know what they were observing.

- A moving conductor, such as a stream exhibits a flow field due to its motion through the primary magnetic field.

  A stream might have a small effect on the local magnetic field due to its different magnetic permittivity from the surrounding rock, but since there is no net charge flow in a stream, the stream is unlikely to create a magnetic field.

- The intensity of all dowsing phenomena shows a very strong correlation with other phenomena such as wireless fading, magnetic storms, auroras, etc., which depend on the electrical state of the ionosphere.

  Their observations may or may not be correct, but the explanation is probably not. I have not observed a difference between day and night, but the dowsing response was less during heavy rain.

- The above fields can be verified by means of an ionization counter, a metal filing coherer.

  Maby's ionization counter was a neon bulb operated at a potential just below that needed to trigger the arc. This device may detect ionization, but it would also respond to EM fields. The metal filing coherer was a glass tube with metal filings that was used as an early radio detector. When a radio frequency signal is applied to the device, the metal particles would cling together or "cohere," reducing the initial high resistance of the device, thereby allowing a much greater direct current to flow through it.[155] It is not clear what Maby was detecting with this device.

I think it is clear from their description that Maby and Franklin were studying a real physical phenomenon. The dowsing responses observed by Maby and Franklin in their parallel bands were repeatable, and they claimed they could be measured by other physical methods, but it is unclear what exactly they were observing. These parallel bands varied with the time of day and were reported to be correlated with changes in the Earth's magnetic field.

7. Parallel Bands and Fields Produced by Rotating Objects

I went to a local stream which was about 6 m (20 ft) wide and ~ 15 cm (6 in) deep and had a water speed in the middle of about 8 cm/s, or 1 meter in 5 seconds. The stream ran next to a grassy area with a slight slope down to the water. I searched for any parallel bands, and to my surprise I found two parallel bands, one that ran along the length of the stream and the other which was more intermittent. However, the distance from the water's edge to the bands, and from band to band varied greatly from 7 feet to about 20 feet. This variation suggests that the bands are not due to Maby and Franklin's standing waves which would be expected to form a more consistent spacing.

I don't know what caused the bands, but I suspect that they reflect differences in the adjacent soil. If there is a stream, then presumably the ground is waterlogged for some distance away from the stream, which may vary with the different rock strata. If the stream is in a valley, then the stream bed may have meandered around over the last few million years and created old, now buried stream banks, and if the original stream ran down a fault, perhaps there are other parallel fault lines. Even if the stream is now running inside a pipe, the adjacent underground geological features will remain. The extent of water saturation into the ground may well vary over time, and with local weather, which in turn may depend on the lunar cycles, etc. It is well known that the moon's tidal forces can cause diurnal shifts in ground water,[156] and the moon can even weakly affect rainfall.[157] Other factors such as atmospheric pressure can also contribute to the diurnal changes in the water table.[158] It appears plausible that such diurnal changes in the water table gave rise to the shifting parallel bands observed by Maby and Franklin. There are many similarities between the parallel bands of Reddish and of Maby and Franklin. It is likely that both investigations were looking at the same or related phenomena, though exactly what it was that they observed and what its origin was, is less clear.

8

Nuclear Magnetic Resonance

I have not yet lost a feeling of wonder, and of delight, that this delicate motion should reside in all the things around us, revealing itself only to him who looks for it. I remember, in the winter of our first experiments, just seven years ago, looking on snow with new eyes. There the snow lay around my doorstep—great heaps of protons quietly precessing in the earth's magnetic field. To see the world for a moment as something rich and strange is the private reward of many a discovery.
    —Edward Mills Purcell, Nobel lecture (11 December 1952)[159]

Chapter summary: Nuclear magnetic resonance (NMR) is a fascinating topic involving the quantum spin states of certain atomic nuclei in a magnetic field, and an ingenious theory for the physics of dowsing. However, the differences in spin energies due to the Earth's magnetic field are so small that they are negligible and so it is unlikely that NMR is the basis for dowsing.

Nuclear Magnetic Resonance

Quantization of EM radiation

EM radiation (light, radio waves, microwaves etc.) is quantized, meaning that light comes in discrete units called photons. This quantization can be illustrated using a rather poor analogy, that of someone firing a shotgun at a target. The overall effect is that the target is hit by the shotgun blast, and at close range it may look like a single shot, but in fact, the damage is caused by hundreds of small discrete particles (pellets) hitting the target. In an analogous way, we may see a light beam, but it is comprised of a large number of light photons, each streaming towards the target.

Each photon of EM radiation has a fixed amount of energy, and the energy of the photon is given by the Planck equation:

$$E = hF$$

where h is the Planck's constant (6.626×10^{-34} joule second), and F is the frequency. Thus a radio wave has relatively low energy per photon, but a gamma photon has much higher energy. If the intensity of a light beam doubles, then the number of photons per second doubles, but the energy of each photon remains the same for the same frequency. Using the shotgun again, the cartridge can have small pellets, bird shot (radio waves) that do little damage, or a few large pellets, buckshot (gamma rays) that do a lot of damage.

One very imaginative proposal for the dowsing effect, by Yves Rocard, professor of physics at the École Normale Supérieure in Paris, the university with the largest number of Nobel Prize winners among its alumni of any school in the world,[160] was nuclear magnetic resonance. He argued that hydrogen nuclei in the earth's magnetic field would process at 2000 rps for a proton. Precession is the slow rotation of a rotating body about the axis of rotation; for example, a spinning gyroscope will precess.[161] If the dowser is in a non-uniform field, some of the protons in his body will have a speed of

---

Nuclear Magnetic Resonance

Atomic and subatomic particles have various quantized properties, such as mass and charge, and spin. Spin is quantized, which means that it is restricted to certain values. For protons (hydrogen ions [H^+]), the spin is +/- one half, and if there is a magnetic field, the spin will either align with the field (−1/2) or against the field (+1/2). Aligning with the field is slightly lower energy than aligning against the magnetic field.

If a proton's spin is aligned with an external magnetic field, then if the proton can absorb the exact energy between the two states, then the spin can be flipped. It has to be the exact energy. Combining several photons of lower energy will not work, nor will a photon with too much energy. If the protons are exposed to EM radiation (photons) with just the right frequency (energy), then the proton can absorb a photon and switch the alignment. The exact energy needed depends on the chemical environment the proton finds itself in, and proton NMR is widely used in organic chemistry to study the structure of organic compounds. There are also carbon 13 NMR as well as NMR for several other elements whose nuclei have spin (most elements do not have a net spin). The difference in energy between the proton spin states is proportional to the strength of the magnetic field. A typical proton NMR spectrometer with a 1.5 Tesla magnetic field uses radio waves at 64 MHz to excite spins.[1] For comparison, the Earth's magnetic field is about 50 µT, and so the energy needed is only 2×10^{-29} J. This energy corresponds to a radio frequency around 2 kHz.

The protons' spins do not align exactly with the magnetic field, but rather they precess around the magnetic field at an angle, analogous to the rotation of a gyroscope. The protons' spins precess around the external field axis with an angular frequency known as the Larmor frequency,

$$\omega = -\gamma B$$

where ω is the angular frequency, and B is the magnetic flux density, i.e., the magnitude of the applied magnetic field, and where γ is called the gyromagnetic ratio.[2]

The gyromagnetic ratio varies with the nucleus and for the proton its value is 2.675×10^8 s^{-1}T^{-1}.[3]

At room temperature (25°C, 298K), $3k_B T/2$ is about 6×10^{-21} m^2 kg s^{-2}. The average thermal energy of rotation of a gas is much greater than the difference in energy of a photon in the Earth's magnetic field. This means that in the Earth's weak magnetic field, the populations of spins aligned with the field will be similar to the population aligned against the field. While the gas is rotating, water and biological molecules at room temperature are vibrating and rotating so it is unlikely that NMR would have any significant effect on the rate of movement of protons in different parts of the dowser's body, since it is so much lower energy than background thermal energy. Thus the dowsing mechanism proposed by Rocard involving NMR, while very creative, is probably not the correct explanation.

---

1. "NMR," http://electron6.phys.utk.edu/phys250/modules/module%203/nmr.htm, accessed August 28, 2020.
2. "G-factor (physics)," Wikipedia, https://en.wikipedia.org/wiki/G-factor_(physics), accessed December 29, 2020.
3. Daniel J. Bell, "Gyromagnetic Ratio," *Radiopaedia*, last revised on November 30, 2019, https://radiopaedia.org/articles/gyromagnetic-ratio?lang=us, accessed January 7, 2023.

2000 rps, and others may be 2001, corresponding to a variation of 0.25 mOe (=0.02A/m or 25 nT). These two frequencies will interact to give beats, which in turn may give rise to changes in muscle tone.[162] This theory would also explain the reported sensitivity of dowsers to magnetic field gradients. There is, unfortunately, no record of any experimental work being done to test this hypothesis. The problem with this theory of dowsing is that the energy needed for precession of protons in the terrestrial magnetic field is very small, and is much less than the thermal noise, and so the beats are unlikely to have any effect on muscle tone. In addition, it would not explain why aluminum foil can block the dowsing signal.

NMR is a standard technique in most university chemistry departments, but the magnetic fields employed are much higher to separate the energy levels of the proton spins (typically 1 to 10 Tesla or higher[163]), so that they can be determined using radio waves (60 to 900 MHz typically).

Interestingly, NMR-related phenomena have been used to search for water underground. A 1999 report from Iris Instruments in France claimed to have been able to map underground water to a depth of over 80 meters. The device uses the Earth's magnetic field and pulsing with radiofrequency radiation and monitoring the reflected signal. By applying a series of pulses of varying lengths of time, the imaging system receives responses from the protons in the water. The field strength of the pulses decays with depth, and protons exposed to weaker fields respond best to longer pulses and the reflected signal is detected using a 100 m diameter wire loop laid out on the surface. Unlike the mechanism proposed by Rocard, the Iris system is not causing the interaction with the protons to affect muscle tone, rather it is measuring radio frequency absorption and emission. Analysis of the signal shows the amount of water as a function of depth.[164] This equipment is available commercially and a more detailed description of the instrument is available on the manufacturer's website.[165] While this instrument shows that NMR-type equipment can be used to detect water at depth, it is applying radio frequency pulses to detect the water. People in general and dowsers, specifically, do not normally emit pulse radio frequency radiation, so this mechanism is probably not applicable to understanding the dowsing effect.

9

Sound

The most beautiful thing we can experience is the mysterious. It is the source of all true art and all science. He to whom this emotion is a stranger, who can no longer pause to wonder and stand rapt in awe, is as good as dead: his eyes are closed.

—Albert Einstein[166]

Chapter summary: Sound has many characteristics needed to be the basis of dowsing: it travels through rock, it is affected by changes in density and it is used to measure underground objects and rock strata. Though sound is very promising, it does not check all the boxes and the conclusion is that sound is not the basis of dowsing.

The suggestion that sound is the basis of dowsing appears very reasonable based on the criteria listed in Chapter 3. Sound passes through rock, water, air and people readily, and it interacts with subsurface structures to give information. It is after all the way that bats navigate the air, dolphins navigate the waters, and geologists map rock strata.

Joseph Wűst, a German physical chemist, reported that some dowsers working in mines could only locate mineral lodes accurately when mining machinery was active and suggested the dowsers might have been sensing small vibrations or sound waves passing through the rock.[167] Sound waves are modulated by the geology of the rock they pass through, and so vary with different sediments and rock fractures. These seismic studies can be done from earthquakes, or from sudden sounds (a sledgehammer hitting metal plate is a common method[168]), but background noise and vibrations will also have an effect and have been shown to vary on the presence of faults, etc. It has been suggested that dowsers are able to tune into the small differences in the background sound vibrations in the ground, and some tests have shown a correlation between differences in the background sound level with dowsers' responses.[169]

To clearly differentiate objects on the size of 10 cm to 1 m, the wavelength of a sound wave must be similar or smaller. If the speed of sound through a soil is 3,000 m/s, then a wavelength of 10 cm corresponds to a frequency of 30,000 Hz and a wavelength of 1 m corresponds to a frequency of 3 kHz, a frequency that most people would hear. People can hear from about 20 Hz up to about 20,000 Hz, the top range falling as we get older. If the dowsing effect was in this range, we would hear it, but we don't. Furthermore, higher sound frequencies, ultrasound, seems unlikely, since the attenuation of sound increases with frequency.[170] There is no obvious source of ultrasound in the environment and so without an apparent source, and rapid attenuation, ultrasound seems an unlikely basis for the dowsing effect.

Another possibility is lower frequency sound, or infrasound.[171] Infrasound is used by large animals such as elephants because it travels a long distance.[172] Infrasound is generally inaudible, with a frequency of <20 Hz, but we can still sometimes sense it. Perception of low-frequency sound in the range 2 to 100 Hz is comprised of both hearing and tactile sensations. At low intensities infrasound may be easily missed, High intensity infrasound levels may induce resonance responses in body cavities. There are other physiological effects of infrasound in humans, including changes in blood pressure, respiratory rate, and balance for exposures to infrasound at levels generally above 110 dB. Physical damage to the ear or some loss of hearing has been found in humans and/or animals at levels above 140 dB,[173] but these intensities are not relevant to dowsing.

At lower intensities, the primary effect of infrasound in humans at lower levels is annoyance, with lower frequencies being more effective in this regard than with higher frequencies. Workers exposed to simulated industrial infrasound of 5 and 10 Hz and levels of 100 and 135 dB for 15 minutes reported feelings of fatigue, apathy, and depression, pressure in the ears, loss of concentration, drowsiness, and the vibration of internal organs. This observation indicates that there is a physiological response to infrasound, even at low levels, which makes infrasound more plausible as the basis for dowsing.

There are also natural sources of infrasound. According to the *Encyclopædia Britannica* seismic waves vary from a high frequency above 20 Hz down to an oscillation of the entire planet with a period of 54 minutes, but in small to moderate earthquakes the dominant frequencies in surface waves tend to be in the range of 1 to 0.1 hertz.[174] Most of the low frequency part of the spectrum (below 1 Hz) is due to natural causes, especially ocean waves. Most of the noise above 1 Hz, seismic noise, is produced by human activities such as road traffic and industrial work; but there are also natural noise sources, like rivers. Around 1 Hz, wind and other atmospheric phenomena are also a major source of ground vibrations.[175] In summary, there are natural sources of infrasound, and these frequencies can have physiological effects, and so infrasound remains a potential candidate for the dowsing sense.

There are some obstacles to the infrasound explanation. Seismic stations continuously record low-frequency vibrations, and if there were a large continuous infrasound signal, it would be very noticeable to them, but it has not been reported. However, the biggest challenge to the infrasound theory is that the dowsing effect is blocked by metal foil being laid on the ground. Sound passes easily through metals, and aluminum foil would not be much of a barrier. Though sound has many of the physical properties needed for the dowsing effect, it is unlikely that sound is the basis for it.

10

Electric Fields and Static Electricity

The concepts most familiar to us are often the most mysterious.
—Étienne Klein[176]

Chapter summary: Static electric fields are often claimed to be the basis of dowsing. We are familiar with static charges, such as the small zap on a door handle after walking across a synthetic carpet. There is an electric field in the atmosphere, but the ground is much more conductive than the air, and so static electricity also fails to explain the dowsing effect.

Static electricity is common to all of us who have received a small zap from a door handle on a winter's day when the humidity is low. As we walk across a carpet, we pick up some static charge and we can end up several thousand volts different from ground. When we touch a grounded metal object, such as a switch, the accumulated charge discharges to ground via a spark. The voltages may be high, but currents are usually very small.

Static electricity has been used to explain the dowsing effect, as illustrated by this passage from the American Society of Dowsers: "The divining rods are charged with static electricity from the dowser's own body. This static electricity can be seen quite adequately with a simple millivolt meter. This voltage is measured between the hands of the dowser, to measure this voltage accurately a diff amp should be used at the input to the voltmeter, to help eliminate stray signals which are common to both hands. The amount of voltage will vary depending on the person. A good dowser will have a high reading, 'above 100 mV' while a poor dowser may read as low as '0 mV.'"[177]

I tested myself using a multimeter with the leads between the base of my fingers and saw no difference in mV DC, mV AC, mA AC, or frequency, over active dowsing points versus non-active points. It appears therefore according to the above criteria that I must be a poor dowser. Another report[178] reads as follows: "If you place a 250k ohm potentiometer between the dowser's hands as he is dowsing. You will see a decrease in his dowsing ability as this resistance is decreased to zero ohms. In testing this I have also found it to be valid."

If this report is true, then connecting a wire between the hands should reduce the dowsing effect, since it is equivalent to a potentiometer with the resistance adjusted down to zero. I clipped a wire with crocodile clips between the skin on my forearms, about three to four inches from my elbows and tight enough to hurt a little. However, I saw no difference in dowsing response with and without the shorting wire. These

Atoms, Charges, Forces, Fields and Terminology

Of the four fundamental forces, the second best known after gravity is the EM force, which commonly manifests as electric and magnetic fields. One of the fundamental properties of subatomic particles, and hence larger objects made of these particles, is charge. The structure of atoms was discussed earlier in Chapter 5.

In a neutral atom the number of negatively charged electrons equals the number of positively charged protons. If an electron is lost, then the atom is no longer neutral and has a positive charge and is called a positive ion (aka a cation), and if an electron is gained, then the atom has a negative charge and becomes a negative ion (aka an anion). For electrical charges, the old saying that opposites attract and similars repel is true. Electrons and negative ions will be repelled by negative charges and protons are repelled by positive charges, so energy will have to be supplied to push similar charges together and energy will be released as opposite charges move towards each other. The effect of one charge on another at a distance is called the electric field and the voltage is a measure of this change in energy per unit charge (J/C). The electric field (E_f) is the voltage divided by the distance, i.e., the larger the separation, the smaller the field and the lower the attractive or repulsive forces between the charges.

$$E_f = V/r$$

If we have two parallel plates, 1 cm apart, and apply a 100 V potential difference (V) to them, the electric field (E_f) between the plates is 10,000 V/m (Figure 10.1). Anytime there is a separation of charge, there will be an electric field. Conversely, to get an electric field, one needs separation of charge.

Magnetic fields are also part of the EM system. While electric fields are caused by difference in electrical charge, magnetic fields are caused by moving charges. An electric current (i) is the net movement of charge, such as electrons down a wire, or ions moving in solution. The magnetic field created by the electric current passing down a wire is described by the following equation, which is a form of Amperes' law.

$$B = \mu_o i/(2\pi r)$$

Where B is the magnetic flux, at distance r from a long wire carrying current i and μ_o is the permeability of free space. Moving charge creates a magnetic field, and if a current passes through a wire coil, the magnetic field from each turn combines to give a stronger magnetic field, which is the basis for electromagnets. If a coil is near a magnetic field, it will be attracted or repulsed, depending on their relative polarity (north attracts south and repels another north), and this is the basis for electric motors. Conversely a changing magnetic field, or a conductor moving in a static magnetic field, induces electric fields and hence currents in conductors. This effect is the basis for electrical generators.

This rather long introduction to electromagnetism is included because electric fields, magnetic fields and other aspects of electromagnetism are frequently cited as the basis for the dowsing response. If someone says that the dowsing response is due to the presence of an electric or magnetic field, they are stating something very specific with a precise meaning. Often much of the terminology that people use to describe the mechanism of dowsing is not as precise as may be desired.

results suggest that electric fields and static electricity are not the basis for the dowsing response.

One argument in favor of electric fields is that many animals can detect electric fields to find prey or warn of predators. Fish and amphibians for example, can detect electric fields using electroreceptors in their mechanosensory lateral line organs. Even

> ## Static Electricity and the Triboelectric Effect
>
> One way to look at how static charges form is to consider that when two things touch, some chemical bonds form between them. If the two things are the same material, then when they separate, there should be no net gain of charge on one or the other. However, if the materials of the two things are different, then the electrons in the bond may prefer to remain on one surface or the other, and the formerly neutral surface now with the more electrons becomes negative and the other surface is now positive. If the object is an insulator, then these charges remain where they formed, on the surface, but if the object is a conductor, like a human (our bodies are about 0.4 percent sodium chloride,[1] so our body fluids are reasonably conductive), then the charges can move around. If the separation process is repeated, additional charge separation can occur until the potential (voltage) increases negative on the surface receiving electrons until no more electrons can make the jump, or positive on the other surface until no more electrons are given up.
>
> Then after one walks across the carpet, and a finger touches the switch, all the charge built up discharges at once with a small spark. Whether a material gains or loses charge depends on its composition relative to the other material. An electrostatic scale (triboelectric series) has been developed, and the further apart on the scale, the greater the tendency to get a separation of charges.
>
> ### Triboelectric Series—Most Positive to Most Negative
>
> **Most positive**
>
> - Rabbit fur
> - Glass
> - Human hair
> - Nylon
> - Silk
> - Aluminum
> - Paper
> - Cotton
> - Steel
> - Copper
> - Rayon
> - Polyester
> - Teflon (PTFE)
>
> **Most negative**
>
> ---
>
> 1. Len Fisher, "How Much Salt Is In A Human Body?," BBC Science Focus, https://www.sciencefocus.com/the-human-body/how-much-salt-is-in-a-human-body/, accessed January 8, 2023.

some mammals can detect electric fields, including monotremes such as the duck billed platypus[179] and dolphins, which are capable of electroreception as low as 4.8 μV/cm, sufficient to detect small fish. Dolphins have comparable sensitivity to the electroreceptors in the platypus.[180] However, all of these creatures live in the water and there are no known land animals which detect static electric fields on land.

Electric fields have been suggested as the mechanism of dowsing, with the rods aligning themselves with the various electrostatic fields present around underground features.[181] Other experimenters claim that dowsers respond to anomalous electric fields in their vicinity, which they say affects their blood pressure and their pulse rates.[182] I am not aware of any systematic studies to confirm or deny this, but as is discussed later, my pulse rate (by ECG) did not change on going over a known dowsing line.

Many people have claimed that dowsers respond to the electric fields created by running water, and if this is the mechanism, then the triboelectric effect is a potential candidate. When non-conductive fluids are passed through non-conductive pipes (e.g., fuels through a PVC pipe), then static electricity can build up, and the resulting sparks can ignite the fuel and cause an explosion. For example, the U.S. Occupational Safety and Health

---

Kelvin Water Dropper Experiment

In the Kelvin water dropper experiment a pipe of flowing water is divided into two and each flow then passes through a metal ring. The water then continues to a sprayer where it is turned it into droplets which collect in a metal bucket below as shown in Figure 10.1.

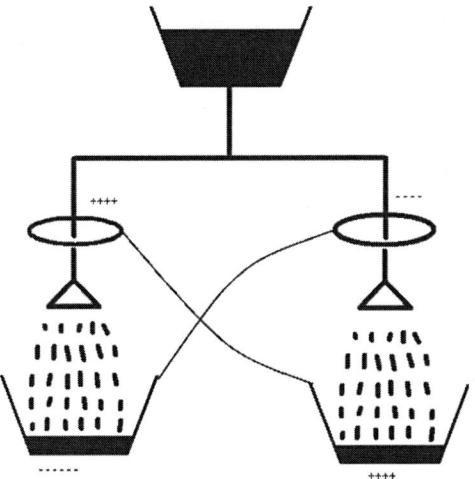

Figure 10.1. Kelvin water dropper experiment.

The bucket for each flow is connected by wire to the opposite ring. If there is any random charge imbalance between the rings, then the negative ring will attract the positive ions and repel the negative ions and so the water falling into the bucket below will have a slight positive charge. Conversely on the other side, since the buckets are connected to the opposite rings the very small charge imbalance on the rings is now magnified by the charged water, and the charge separation becomes much more effective. Since the water forms droplets, it is prevented from conducting and neutralizing the charge. High voltages can rapidly build up and sparks will fly if the metal pieces from both sides are close to each other. There are several very good videos of the Kelvin water dropper experiment on YouTube[1] that are worth watching.

---

1. Derek Muller (Veritasium), "Sparks from Falling Water: Kelvin's Thunderstorm," https://www.youtube.com/watch?v=rv4MjaF_wow, accessed August 28, 2020; Steven Dufresne (RimstarOrg), "Kelvin Water Dropper and How it Works/Lord Kelvin's Thunderstorm," https://www.youtube.com/watch?v=sArNxGnYhNU, accessed August 28, 2020.

Administration offers a warning against using plastic pipe to transport flammable gases for this reason.[183] However, pure water is slightly conductive and water with dissolved minerals can be very conductive depending on the concentration of minerals dissolved in the water. Most natural waters have some conductivity. If there were a charge separation, then a current could easily flow through the conductive water dissipating the charge, and a high potential would never build up. It therefore seems unlikely that electrics fields caused by the triboelectric effect (static electricity) are responsible for the dowsing effect.

Flowing water can be made to create a charge, using the ingenious setup developed by Lord Kelvin, but its principle is electrostatic induction rather than the triboelectric effect and this effect has also been suggested to be the source of the dowsing effect.[184] Even though the Kelvin water drop experiment is a dramatic example of static charge being created by flowing water, it is unlikely to occur in water flowing underground, since the conductivity of the water and the rocks would cause any charge formed to dissipate. It is therefore unlikely that static electricity caused by moving water is the cause of the dowsing effect.

In addition, it would not explain how dowsers can detect empty PVC pipes, graves or underground metal bars, neither of which would generate static electricity, since nothing is moving in or against them (at least we hope not in the graves). Lastly, even if an electric field were generated, it would be small after traveling though the overlying soil compared to the high voltages of other static electricity. If static electricity was the basis behind dowsing, then walking across a polyester carpet would be very problematic for dowsers.

Piezoelectric Effect

Bo Nordell proposed a novel theory for the dowsing effect, specifically that it was caused by the piezoelectric properties of bones,[185] and Arpad Vass, an instructor at the National Forensic Academy in Oak Ridge, Tennessee, has used the same explanation for how he and others have been able to find buried human remains.[186] Many crystals are piezoelectric such that if squeezed they create an electrical potential, and if an electrical potential is applied to them, they will move. Piezoelectric materials are found in devices ranging from microphones to gas lighters. High voltages can be produced by the distortion of piezoelectric rocks (e.g., quartz). Animal sensitivity to the resulting electric fields has been suggested as an explanation for the apparent foresight that some animals have about earthquakes[187] and glows, lightning and other earthquake lights that have been reported during seismic activity.[188] The most common, and one of the best, piezoelectric materials is quartz, but bone is also somewhat piezoelectric.[189] Nordell found that knocking on the end of a pig forearm bone generated 1–2 V across between the sides with the side that is becoming more convex on flexing becoming positive and the concave side becoming negative.[190]

The reverse is also true, the so-called inverse piezoelectric effect, whereby if a voltage is applied to piezoelectric materials, the dimensions of the materials will lengthen or contract. Nordell's proposal is that dowsers sense changes in the EM field, which causes potential differences across the bones. These potential differences in turn cause movement of the arms due to the piezoelectric effect of the bones, and the rods move. This explanation has a couple of drawbacks. The bones in a living person or creature are surrounded by the conductive physiological medium, and so any electric potentials formed across the bone due to external electric fields will be very small, too small for the piezoelectric behavior to be significant. Secondly, the movement resulting from plausible electric fields is insignificant. Therefore, though Nordell's proposal is certainly interesting, it is unlikely to be the basis of the dowsing effect.

Estimate of the Inverse Piezoelectric Response[1]

If an electric field E_f is applied to a piezoelectric material a strain is created which is known as the inverse or converse piezoelectric effect. The strain can be calculated using the following equation, where d is the piezoelectric coefficient.

$$\text{Strain} = E_f d$$

The strain is the ratio of deformation in the direction of the stress, compared to the initial dimensions. The opposite occurs if a stress (=force/area) is applied to a piezoelectric material creating a potential.

The basic equation of piezoelectricity is

$$P_p = df/A$$

where P_p is the polarization (pC/m^2), f is the force and A is the area. The polarization is the charge formed per unit area and the voltage V can be calculated from the capacitance C of the piezoelectric material V = Q/C where Q is the charge. Rearranging these two equations and substituting the equation for capacitance $C = \epsilon_0 \epsilon_r A/L$, the voltage created can be found:

$$V = dLF/(\epsilon_0 \epsilon_r A)$$

where L is the length of the piezoelectric material and ϵ_0 and ϵ_r are the permittivity and the relative permittivity, respectively, of free space.

The piezoelectric constant d is approximately 3×10^{-12} m/V for quartz[2] and for bone the value is about 0.2×10^{-14} and 2.0×10^{-14} m/V for hydrated and dry bones respectively.[3] Assume a dry bone is 1 cm width and thickness, then to get a compression of 2 μm (strain = 2μm/1cm = 2×10^{-4}), the electric field needed = strain/d = $2 \times 10^{-4}/2.0 \times 10^{-14} = 1 \times 10^{10}$ V/m. The voltage (across the width of the bone) to create this electric field is 1×10^{10} V/m × 1cm = 1×10^8 V.

This number indicates that to get a motion of a micrometer would require an applied voltage of about a 100 million volts. It is very unlikely that only 2 micrometer of movement would give any noticeable response of the hands. One hundred million volts, on the other hand, is similar to the voltage of a lightning strike (~300 million volts),[4] and those high voltages are very unlikely to be induced by very weak external EM fields. If such voltages were induced, it is likely there would be more severe consequences than a microscopic movement of the arm.

---

1. "Piezo Electricity," Libre Texts Engineering, https://eng.libretexts.org/Bookshelves/Materials_Science/Supplemental_Modules_(Materials_Science)/Electronic_Properties/Piezoelectricity, accessed August 4, 2021.

2. "Piezoelectric coefficient," *Encyclopedia Britannica*, https://www.britannica.com/science/piezoelectric-coefficient, accessed December 20, 2020; Electric properties of matter, Piezoelectricity, Encyclopedia Britannica, https://www.britannica.com/science/electricity/Electric-properties-of-matter#ref307225, accessed December 20, 2020.

3. Thomaz Ghilardi Netto and Robert Lee Zimmerman, "Effect of Water on Piezoelectricity in Bone and Collagen," *Biophysical Journal* vol. 15 (1975), 573.

4. "How Powerful Is Lightning?" National Weather Service, https://www.weather.gov/safety/lightning-power, accessed December 20, 2020.

Earth's Electric Field

Another theory proposed to explain dowsing is that it is a response to the Earth's electric field. We are all familiar with natural electric sparks in the form of lightning that either jumps between clouds or between a cloud and the ground. The ground is relatively conductive, but the air is in most cases insulating until altitudes of greater than about 50 km (20 miles). The conductivity of air depends on the presence of ions in the air, which varies with altitude. At high altitude ions can arise from the effects of cosmic radiation. At low altitude ions can be formed from thunderclouds,[191] radiation (radon)[192] and pollution.[193] The air at ground level has a very small conductivity, about 10 pA/m², and the atmosphere has a positive charge and the ground a negative charge. There is an electric field through the non-conductive lower regions of the atmosphere, which is about 100 V/m at ground level. The charge difference between the ground and the upper atmosphere is caused by thunderclouds, which generate massive potentials between the top and bottom as ice particles rise up through them like giant Van de Graaff generators. A typical thundercloud may generate a potential difference around a giga volt.[194] Lightning strikes to the surface impart negative charge to the ground, and the 40,000 lightning strikes a day around the globe are enough to maintain the Earth's electric field.[195]

The proposed explanation for dowsing is that water in the ground, buried pipes or metal objects, etc., causes changes to the local electric field and these changes are detected by the dowser. One of the keenest proponents of this theory was Anthony Hopwood, who conducted a set of tests with an overhead wire that was connected to ground via a resistance, or a high-voltage source.[196] Hopwood found that the resistance

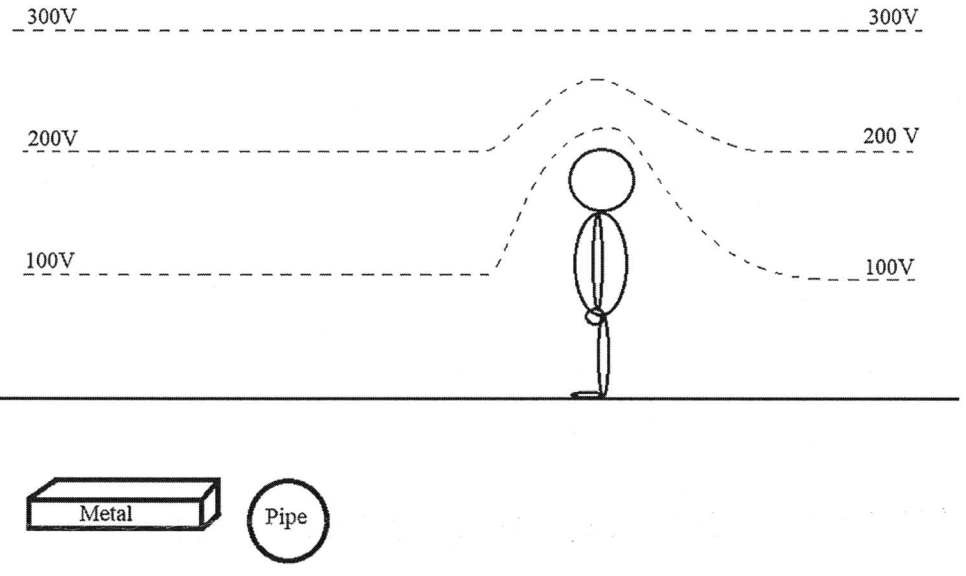

Figure 10.2. Sketch showing the lack of distortion of the atmospheric electric field above buried objects and the field distorting around a person.

to ground made little difference, and there was a small difference between grounded and insulated wire, which may or may not have been significant, since he also reported large variations depending on whether the sun was shining or behind clouds. When he applied a voltage to the wire, he saw no effect with negative voltages until −800 V when the rods swung outwards, and a smooth decrease in response as the voltage increased from 400 to 1,300 V until there was no response at 1,600 V. It is unclear what effect Hopwood was observing, and it appears that he only conducted the test once, so it is difficult to judge the potential experimental error in his measurements. His description of the test method was also very limited.

There are several challenges to the idea that dowsers detect underground objects by their effect on the local electric field. Consider a PVC pipe and metal block both buried underground. Both would give a dowsing response, but the atmospheric electric field idea does not explain the dowsing response. The ground is normally very conductive compared to the air, and even though the PVC pipe is insulating and the metal highly conductive, they will have essentially no effect on the atmospheric electric field, since the ground above them is conductive and at ground potential. Additionally, compared to the air, dowsers themselves are highly conductive, and so they will distort the electric field around them (see Figure 10.2), unlike the objects buried beneath the ground. Thus our dowser is not going to experience a change of electric field across his or her body because of the buried metal or PVC pipes. Therefore, it seems unlikely that the atmospheric electric field is the cause of the dowsing effect.

11

Telluric Magnetism and Currents

A ley line is what might be called a field of force, a trail of telluric energy. There are hundreds of them, perhaps thousands, all over Britain, and they've been around since the Stone Age.
—Stephen R. Lawhead[197]

Chapter summary: Telluric (Earth) currents and magnetism are another suggestion that has been made several times for the basis of dowsing. These currents flow through the ground as the Earth rotates; the voltage varies with the composition of the ground and the flowing current generates a magnetic field that interacts with the Earth's magnetic field. Despite all this great science, telluric currents are not the secret to dowsing.

Telluric Currents[198]

John Janks ran a series of dowsing experiments which are summarized below and concluded that the dowsing effect was most likely caused by telluric currents,[199] or changes in the ground resistance caused by the presence of conductors.[200] Telluric currents have been known for over a century and are currents induced by changes in the Earth's magnetic field primarily due to solar activity causing particle interactions in the ionosphere. The changes in the magnetic field are small, about one fifty-millionth of the steady magnetic field. Though small, these changes induce significant currents in the Earth's surface, so called telluric currents. These currents in turn create their own magnetic fields, which can be measured. Telluric currents and their associated magnetic fields can provide indications of changes in the electrical conductivity of rocks, such as commonly occur at basement, at shale-limestone interfaces, at faults, etc., down to the upper mantle. These currents are present all around the world and contain all frequencies from cycles per day to cycles per second.

Telluric currents can be detected by placing two electrodes in the ground separated by a distance of about 300 meters (1,000 feet) or more and measuring the potential difference between them. The potentials measured are usually a few tenths of millivolts, up to a few hundred millivolts in some cases. The U.S. Geological Survey has published an excellent guide to telluric current methods for anyone looking for additional information,[201] and a more mathematically rigorous analysis is also available for those people interested.[202]

The search for water is the most common application of dowsing, and the

Resistance, Resistivity, Conductance and Conductivity

Anyone who has studied electronics is familiar with Ohm's law, which says that the current flowing through a resistance is proportional to the applied voltage.

$$V = iR$$

Ohm's law is often written as

$$i = V/R \text{ or } R = V/i$$

where V is the voltage, i is the current and R is the resistance. The resistance of a conductor such as metal has been found to increase with length and decrease with surface area, and so to compare different materials the resistivity (ρ) is used which is independent of the dimensions of the material. The resistance can be found using the following equation:

$$R = \rho L/A$$

where L is the length and A is the area. The resistivity has units of $Ohm^{-1}cm^{-1}$. Sometimes it is better to define Ohm's law in terms of the conductance S.

$$I = VS$$

The conductance is the inverse of the resistance (S = 1/R) and has units of ohm^{-1}, also sometimes written as Siemens (S). Similarly, the conductivity σ is defined as the inverse of the resistivity ($\sigma = 1/\rho$).

It is common practice to speak of the resistance of solids but the conductance of liquids, although the units are convertible. However, there is a difference in the way they are measured. Resistance is usually measured by applying a small DC voltage and measuring the resulting current, for example, with a multimeter. Most conduction in liquids is ionic conduction, such as salt water (mercury is an obvious exception). If one applies a dc voltage to an ionic solution there will be a charge buildup at the electrodes, the electrodes will polarize, or there may even be oxidation/reduction reactions at the electrode/solution interfaces. These effects make the measurement of the resistance unstable, and the resistance will change over time. To prevent electrode polarization, an ac signal is often used with conductivity measurements using a conductivity meter.

---

electrical properties of most rocks in the upper part of the Earth's crust are dependent primarily upon the amount of water in the rock, the salinity of the water, and the distribution of the water in the rock. Water-saturated rocks have lower resistivities than unsaturated and dry rocks. The higher the porosity of the water-saturated rock, the lower its resistivity; and the higher the salinity of the saturating fluids, the lower the resistivity.

Measurements of the amplitude variations in the telluric electric field E, and the associated magnetic field H, are used in magneto-telluric studies to determine the resistivity of the ground. Lower frequencies can penetrate the Earth better than higher frequencies, and by measuring the response at different frequencies, information is obtained from depths of a few hundred meters to depths of hundreds of kilometers.[203]

Janks found the following results in his tests:

- Dowsing rods can detect metals, ceramics, or plastic objects.
    I agree with this comment,

Resistivity and Rocks

The resistivities of rocks vary greatly, from almost perfect insulator (Quartz) to conductive (graphite or elemental copper). There is no other physical property of rocks which varies over such a wide range, and so resistivity is a very useful method for characterizing the sub-surface structure.

Table 11.1. Resistivity of Some Rocks[1]

Material	Approximate Resistivity (ohm.m)
Graphite	10^{-6}
Saline saturated clays	< 1
Clays	~ 10
Fresh water–saturated sand and gravel	15 to 600
Dry basalt flows, dry sand, and gravel	1,000
Limestone	10,000
Quartzite rocks	10^{12}

1. A.A.R. Zohdy, "Electrical Methods," in *Techniques of Water-Resources, Investigations of the United States Geological Survey,* A.A.R. Zohdy, G.P. Eaton, and D.R. Mabey, Chapter Dl, "Application of Surface Geophysics to Ground-Water Investigations, Book 2 Collection of Environmental Data," https://pubs.usgs.gov/twri/twri2-d1/pdf/twri_2-D1_b.pdf, accessed December 31, 2022; "Geophysics Foundations: Physical Properties, Electrical Resistivity of Geologic Materials," https://www.eoas.ubc.ca/courses/eosc350/content/foundations/properties/resistivity.htm, accessed December 31, 2022.

- Water, above or below ground had no influence on rod movement.

  Dowsing is widely used to find water, and so this statement would not be supported by most dowers. If I walk up to the edge of a stream, I see a strong dowsing response.
- Dowsing rods are highly successful at locating linear features (e.g., trip wires) above or below ground.

  Dowsing can certainly be used use to find linear structures, but I do not believe it is limited to linear. A trip wire is usually very thin and may not give a dowsing response.
- The human body, for whatever reason, is an essential part of dowsing rod use.

  Most investigators agree that the rods are just pieces of wire or sticks held in the hands of a dowser, and the sticks or rods merely amplify small movements from the dowser's body into an easy to visualize signal.
- Rod behavior is dictated by the size, shape and nearness to other buried objects.

  In general these statements appear reasonable.
- The rod held furthest from the source always moves the most.

  I have not experienced this directionality of the rods.
- Dowsing rods respond to (low-flying) aircraft.

  Seems unlikely, unless they were VERY low and then only if they were casting a shadow.
- Garbage such as used tires, aluminum cans and vegetation do not affect rod behavior.

Based on the explanation in this book, I would not expect much response from used tires (without rims), and vegetation but I would expect a response if standing on top of a can, though not if the can was off to the side.

- If two buried objects are close to each other, dowsing rods can detect their presence 60+ meters along the line they define.

  I have not experienced this level of sensitivity or discrimination in dowsing. If the rods will respond to objects within 60 feet of the dowser, then there will be simultaneous responses from many potential sources all around, and it will make dowsing difficult.

- Rods can trace and locate buried cord and objects that are connected to the cord.

  I have not tried this experiment.

Many of Janks's results are similar to those of others, but some are significantly different. In particular, the lack of impact of water, the specificity of search at a distance (e.g., finding a buried can at 60m), and detecting low flying aircraft. He also described how if walking parallel to a hidden can, the rod further away would point in the direction of the can. I don't have an explanation for Janks's report, but several of Janks's descriptions are somewhat similar to those of dowsers who claim results that would require a significant degree of clairvoyance.

While telluric currents may not explain Janks's observations, telluric currents do meet many of the criteria needed for the physical basis of dowsing as described in Chapter 3, and so are worth considering. However, there are a couple of reasons why telluric currents are probably not the physical mechanism behind dowsing. The first is their directionality. Telluric currents tend to follow the sun flowing from east to west as the sun's solar wind hits the ionosphere. However, there is no apparent directionality to dowsing. The rods work equally well whether one is facing north, south, east or west or walking round in a large circle. If dowsing were dependent upon the telluric currents, then we would expect that they would work better, or at least differently, with the current rather than against it or perpendicular to it. Telluric currents vary with the time of day because they are formed by the diurnal changes in the Earth's magnetic field, and most dowsing signals from underground objects do not appear to change with the time of day, so dowsing can be performed at night in the dark.

The second reason why telluric currents are probably not behind the dowsing effect is that the potentials measured are very small, a few millivolts over hundreds of meters. The electric field strengths are thus tiny ($\mu V/m$). For comparison, a rusty nail and an aluminum drink can placed in the soil can develop about a volt potential difference between them because of the difference in electrode potentials between the two metals, comparable to an alkaline battery (~1.3 volts).

Electrochemical Potentials

Some rocks contain materials that can be oxidized, and others contain materials which can either be reduced or which can reduce oxygen from the air. Combined, these rocks can generate an electrochemical potential similar to a naturally occurring battery. For example, sulfide minerals (such as iron pyrites [CuS]) can be oxidized by oxygen dissolved in water percolating down from the surface. The resulting electric current flows through the ore body and back through the surrounding groundwater, which acts as the electrolyte. This electrochemical process can give up to 50–400 millivolts and provides a means to identify the location of continuous metallic sulfide bodies that lie astride the water table.[204] The half-cell reactions are probably more complex than the ones shown in Figure 11.1, but these equations illustrate the concept. Presumably if there is a sulfide mineral mass, then the reduction of the oxygen will occur near the top, where the oxygen first makes contact, and the oxidation of the sulfide will occur lower down, making the lower part of the sulfide mineral mass the cathode (i.e., the negative terminal of this natural battery) and the upper part the positive terminal or anode.

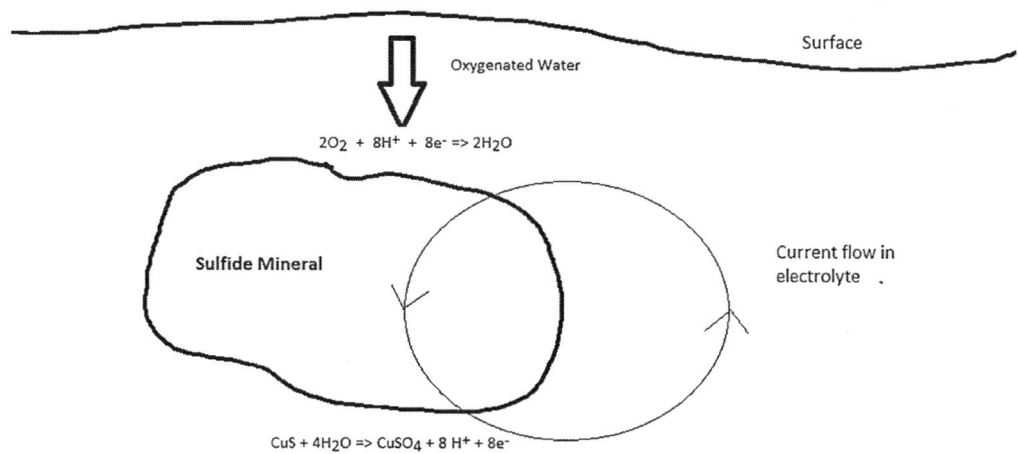

Figure 11.1. Underground electric currents due to oxidation of sulfide minerals.

Sulfide minerals often have variable stoichiometry (ratio of copper to sulfur) and conductivity. For example, the conductivity of $Cu_{2-x}S$ varies from 0.07 ohm^{-1} to 2400 ohm^{-1} as the stoichiometry increases from x = 0 to x = 0.2.[205] So the electric current flow through the sulfide mineral mass may involve both electron conduction (as in a metal) and ion flow in the ground water electrolyte. However, the voltages produced are small (< 0.5V) compared to those produced by static electricity and so are unlikely to be detected by a dowser.

Electrochemical processes such as these are very common, and the tendency of a mineral to oxidize or be reduced/reduce oxygen is described by the electrode potential. The electrode potentials of various minerals have been catalogued.[206] Electrochemical processes appear unlikely to be the source of the dowsing response. If they were, then a small rusty nail would throw off the dowsing response just as that same nail can give a false signal to a metal detector that can't discriminate against ferrous metal targets. Electrochemical processes also do not explain how non-conductors such as empty PVC pipes or plastic gas pipes can be detected, since neither will give an electrochemical response.

Earth (Schumann) Resonances

Jong Doo Lee offered an explanation for dowsing, writing in a couple of patent applications:

> In general, a water vein is a stream body of water flowing at the depth of approximately 10–40 m below the ground or under a rock mass. From the water vein, an EM wave is generated which is called a water-vein wave having a frequency near approximately 7.8 Hz, the frequency of the earth's magnetic field. It has been known that the influence of the water-vein wave reaches up to the upper floors of a high rise building.[207]
>
> Locating Yang (masculine) energies in nature and ideal spots, and more particularly, to such a Yang energy and ideal spot detector which can precisely detect whether or not there are positive charges collected on the earth's surface by influences of underground veins of water, Yang energies, i.e., the masculine or positive element in nature, and the like.[208]

There seem to be several ideas here that are intermixed. The Schumann resonances are EM resonances of the atmosphere. It is unclear exactly what Lee is saying and how the Schumann resonances relate to underground water veins or "Yang energy." These Schumann frequencies correspond to the resonant frequency of the cavity formed between the Earth's surface and the ionosphere, not the frequency of a sub-surface water vein. For a water vein to have a resonance of this frequency, it would have to have dimensions close to the wavelength. The wavelength of an EM wave with frequency 7.8 Hz is about 21,000 miles (or 38,500 km), comparable to the circumference of the Earth, which is ~ 25,000 miles.[209] It seems therefore unlikely that Schumann resonances are responsible for the dowsing signal.

Schumann Resonances

At any time, there are over 1,000 thunderstorms rolling over the Earth, producing some 50 flashes of lightning every second, which produce broad spectrum pulses of EM radiation (from radio waves to ultraviolet and sometimes even gamma radiation).[1] The conductivity of the air near the surface is low, but at higher altitudes the ionosphere becomes conductive. The ionosphere and the ground's surface form a cavity and radio wave portions are reflected between the top and bottom of the cavity. Resonance will occur when the distances involved correspond to a multiple of the wavelength, analogous to sound waves of a particular frequency resonating when one blows over the end of a pipe. One can imagine standing waves circling the globe in the cavity between the ground and the ionosphere with a primary frequency and higher harmonics. These resonances are known as Schumann resonances. They occur at several frequencies, specifically 7.8, 14, 20, 26, 33, 39 and 45 Hertz, with a daily variation of about +/- 0.5 Hertz.[2] As mentioned above 7.8 Hz corresponds to a resonance with a wavelength approximately the diameter of the Earth, and 14 Hz corresponds to a resonance with a wavelength a quarter of the diameter of the Earth.

1. Elizabeth Gibney, "Mystery Gamma Rays Could Help Solve Age-Old Lightning Puzzle," *Nature, News Feature*, February 17, 2021, https://www.nature.com/articles/d41586-021-00395-3.
2. "Schumann Resonance," NASA, https://www.nasa.gov/mission_pages/sunearth/news/gallery/-schumann-resonance.html, accessed December 31, 2020; "What is a Schumann Resonance?" https://image.gsfc.nasa.gov/poetry/ask/q768.html, accessed December 31, 2020.

Brain Waves

Electroencephalograms (EEGs) of the brain show characteristic frequency bands depending on the subject's state of consciousness and what they are doing.[210] These wave forms can be briefly summarized, to the irritation of neurologists everywhere, as follows:

- Delta (less than 4 Hz)
  Sleeping.
- Theta (4–8 Hz)
  Daydreaming, long distance running, calming showers—often a time when creative ideas are formed. Some dowsers claim that theta waves are important for dowsing, for example, Geoff Brooks, a psychologist and dowser, has reported measurements showing an increase in his *theta* waves while dowsing.[211]
- Alpha (8–12 Hz)
  Quiet resting relaxed state, meditation, peaceful walk to get away from work.
- Beta (13–30Hz)
  Actively engaged brain, such as conversation, or making a presentation.
- Gamma greater than 30(Hz)
  Peak concentration.

Much has been written about the similarities between the theta wave frequency and the lowest Schumann resonance[212] and the influence of the Schumann resonances on dowsing.[213] For example, Krinkler and Pismenny proposed that Schumann resonances interact with the water in our bodies to create electrical potentials which trigger the nerves leading to the dowsing response.[214] However, there is little supporting evidence for this or any other theory that the Schumann resonances have any effect on dowsing.

Russian engineer Yu. P. Kravchenko (Ufa Aviation Engineering University) is reported to have built a device that can detect the dowsing effect called the indicator of geophysical anomalies (IGA-1). The IGA-1 description says that it measures the resonance of EM waves at low frequency (1 to 15 kHz) and very low signal strength (1–100 × 10^{-12} V). The measured parameter is a phase shift of the receiving frequency, whose value changes on the borders of objects and structures in the ground (e.g., caverns, pipes, and voids).[215] Unfortunately, there appears to be little published information about this device, at least in English, and so I can't comment about the functionality of the device, except to point out that the wavelength at 1 and 15 kHz is about 300,000 m and 20,000 m, respectively, and so the likelihood that this signal could resolve objects on the order of centimeters is very unlikely.

12

Nature of the Dowsing Response

I maintain, therefore, that there is nothing in the movement of the rod that physical causes cannot attain (or explain), and if one will penetrate them without prejudice or a preformed opinion, without seeing its consequences, or without sheltering oneself under favour of a little knowledge of supernatural causes, we shall discover three things.
—Nicholas Jean (1680)[216]

Chapter summary: The last few chapters have explored what dowsing isn't. This chapter reviews work performed by various investigators trying to identify the nature of the dowsing response, including the effects of magnetism, flowing water and the nature of the physiological dowsing response. This chapter shows that the dowsing response is electromagnetic.

Experiments with Dowsing Rods

The goal of this chapter is to examine the dowsing response to identify the cause. The traditional Y-shaped sticks are wood, and functional dowsing L-rods can be made of plastic, steel, copper, etc., so the material is not important. The general consensus is that the rods or stick do not detect the dowsing signal; rather, the rods provide a simple visual indication of small involuntary muscle movements that cause the wrists to rotate slightly. Thus the dowser is the detector of the dowsing signal, not the rods. Many people have noted that the rods move because of the involuntary movement of muscles. Maby and Franklin found that dowsing fields cause muscles to lose tension, so the dowsing fields cause muscles to relax.[217] Maby and Franklin found that they were able to get a dowsing response in a subject by passing electric current through certain muscles, or exposing them to UV rays, X-rays, beta and gamma rays, or shortwave radio but not ordinary light. They also found that a dowser could detect when he or she walked through a shortwave wireless beam and that when two short-wave transmitters were used at slightly different frequencies the dowser could detect the locations where the two radiations were in phase and so additive. Shortwave radio has a wavelength band of 10 to 80 m (33 to 262 feet) and frequencies of approximately 29.7 to 3.5 MHz.,[218] so the maxima and minima separation of beats would have similar magnitude as the wavelength and a separation of about 10 m is plausible.

For my studies I mainly used underground pipes as the dowsing target. The advantage of pipes is that they are well defined, since they are of known geometry (almost always circular), usually at known depth, of known material and usually with a known

12. Nature of the Dowsing Response

fill material, be it air, water, gas, or whatever. In contrast, water veins, fault lines, etc., are much less well defined.

When I walked along a paved road, parallel to an empty underground pipe for draining surface water there was no dowsing response (except where other lines cross), and if I stood directly over the pipe and walked along the road directly over the pipe there was no response. However, if I step off the pipe, or walk across the pipe, then there is a strong response. This result shows that the dowsing effect is a response to a change in the dowsing signal, not the absolute value of the dowsing signal. From a practical point of view, it makes sense too. The dowser will normally balance his or her rods at the start and the later crossing of the rods indicates a change in the dowsing signal. A point of clarification here: The dowser responds to a change in the dowsing signal, but not necessarily to a rate of change of the signal (difference vs. differential response). In other words, moving slowly does not give less of a response than moving fast, but instead the rods move as the change in signal occurs. Moving fast can weaken the signal, because the rods do not have as much time to react.

A sheet of cardboard ~ 3 ft × 4 ft (~1 × 1.3 m) covered both sides with aluminum foil was placed on the road over the pipe and the dowsing signal was lost. A sheet of bare cardboard had no effect. Thus it appeared that the foil blocked the dowsing response, but cardboard is transparent to the dowsing signal. The observation that aluminum foil and other metals can block the dowsing response has been reported by many people.[219] The fact that the dowsing signal is blocked by aluminum foil suggests the dowsing response may be due to an EM wave. Metallic conductors are known to block EM radiation across much of the spectrum. EM radiation covers radio waves, microwaves, infrared light, visible light, ultraviolet light, x-rays and gamma rays in ascending frequency. As the name suggests, light and other forms of EM radiation have oscillating electric and magnetic fields. While magnetic fields cannot be readily shielded, electric fields cannot pass through a conductor such as a metal and so the EM waves are reflected from metal surfaces. Aluminum foil can block EM radiation down through the visible to the ultraviolet (which is why the foil looks shiny in the visible part of the spectrum). Cardboard is transparent to EM in the radio and microwave regions of the spectrum and the x-ray and gamma regions of the spectrum, but it is opaque in the infrared, visible, and ultraviolet. X-rays and gamma rays are very high energy and are not commonly found in everyday life here on the Earth, except under extreme conditions (thunder clouds can sometimes produce gamma rays[220]), and therefore these simple observations suggest that the dowsing signal may be in the radio or microwave region of the EM spectrum.

Many people have come to the conclusion that the dowsing effect is a physiological response to EM radiation, for example, Evelyn Penrose wrote in 1951, "The explanation of modern scientists who are investigating water-divining from a purely scientific standpoint, that water, minerals and oil give off electro-magnetic waves and fields of force, and that water-diviners are merely human radio-sets who are tuned in to these wave-lengths and can pick them up, certainly knocks the romance and mystery out of the art of divining; but it is, without doubt, the logical and correct explanation of the previously incomprehensible phenomenon."[221]

As Penrose indicated, one of the most common explanations given for the dowsing effect is that it is caused by EM radiation, and several mechanisms have been proposed to explain how EM radiation results in the dowsing effect. For example, Saunders wrote, "The nervous system can pick up a range of magnetic and EM fields, and the experienced dowser has learnt to associate certain responses with physical materials or structures."[222]

This explanation appears on its surface to be plausible, and the interaction of EM radiation with nerves is discussed in more detail below.

Electromyography

A study at the University of Calgary tested some dowsers[223] and found that changes in muscle activity of the arm monitored by electromyography (EMG) associated with walking from a neutral to an active site showed significant decrease in EMG signal. This result shows that the arm muscles are being triggered by moving over an area that gives a dowsing response, but it does not address the detection mechanism.

> **Electromyography (EMG)**
>
> The activation of our muscles is via the nerves and nerves stimulate the muscles with small changes in electrical potential. This electrical activity of the muscles can be measured and the results plotted over time, which is the technique of electromyography. The technique involves placing electrodes on the skin over the middle and end of the muscle and measuring the potential difference versus a third electrode away from the muscle. For medical tests small needles are often inserted through the skin to get a better electrical connection. When the muscle is activated, the result is a cascade of electrical impulses. A weak muscle action, such as maintaining a static position with no load, generates a small signal as only some of the muscle fibers need to activate. Whereas if flexing the muscle or lifting weights or other activities requiring a strong muscle action, then many more muscle fibers activate and the response is much larger.

I tried the EMG technique using a MyoWare Muscle Sensor (AT-04-001) connected to the skin using 3M red dot electrodes. The output from the Myoware sensor was

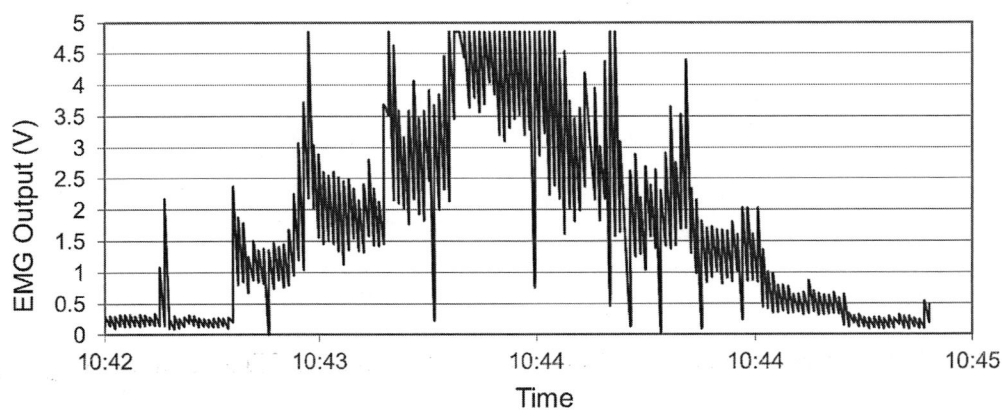

Figure 12.1. EMG of left deltoid muscle lifting straight arm in steps from vertical to horizontal and back again.

monitored by an Arduino Uno sampling at 100 points a second and writing the output to a Windows 10 tablet, where it was saved as a text file.

Note: the EMG voltage is the output voltage from the Myoware sensor, not the magnitude of the signals triggering the muscles, which is in the microvolt/low millivolt range.

Figure 12.1 shows the EMG of my left deltoid muscle (shoulder) lifting the arm out to the side in steps from vertical to horizontal and back. The higher the arm, the greater load and so the greater the steady state activation of the muscles needed to maintain that position. On each movement there is a greater pulse of electrical activity.

Changing the angle of the arm from zero (arm hanging down) to 90 degrees (arm straight out to side) the steady state voltage increases as the torque on the muscles increases (torque = force × length × sin[angle]). Plotting the voltage (y) versus the angle (x) gave a straight line as shown in Figure 12.2.

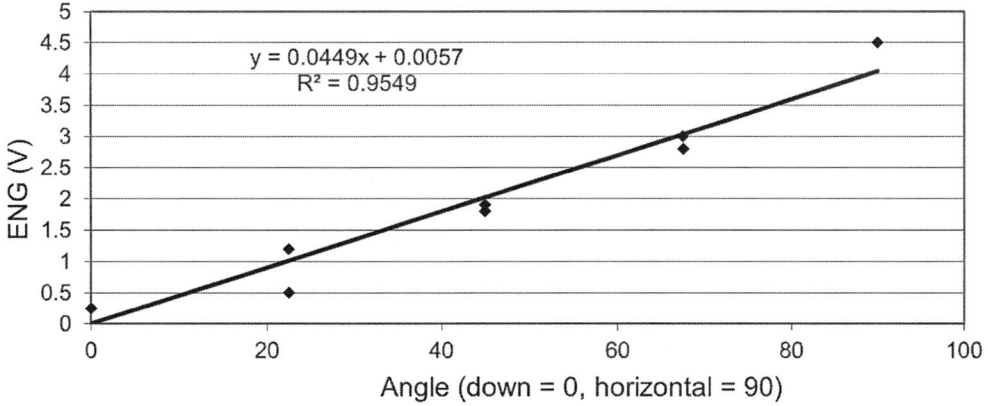

Figure 12.2. EMG steady state signal vs. arm angle.

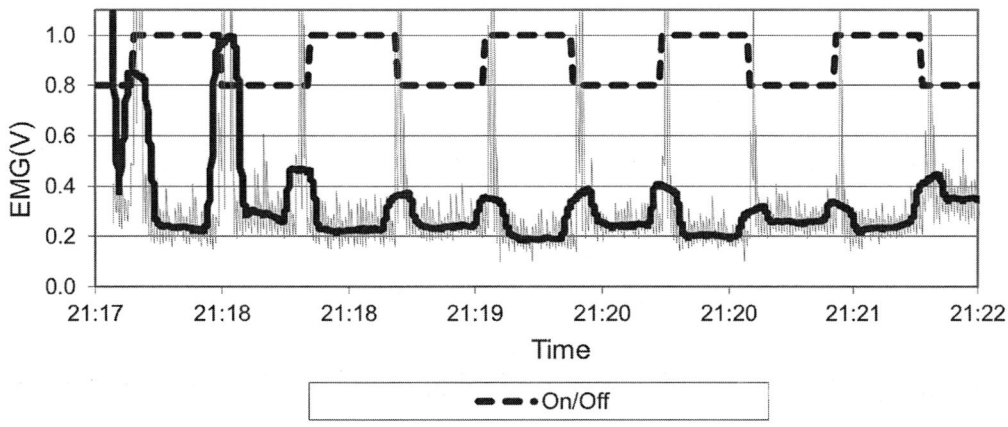

Figure 12.3. EMG of left deltoid muscle, holding a dowsing rod at ~ 90 degrees, stepping on and off a sewer line under a concrete floor every 30s. Data was recorded at 10 points/second, and the dark line shows the 10s running average.

With the left arm down, held at 90 degrees, rod in hand, the EMG was recorded stepping on and off a dowsing line due over the sewer pipe under the basement floor. The results shown in Figure 12.3 were obtained.

When moving, even a simple step, the whole body reacts and so there are spikes associated with each movement on and off. However, when dowsing, the rods move smoothly and stay in position if one stops moving, and so from a dowsing perspective the steady state is more interesting. Looking at the 10s running average of the output voltage, there is a systematic difference between stepping on and stepping off the dowsing line. This difference is about 0.03 V. From the slope of the EMG voltage vs. angle graph above, 0.03 V corresponds to (0.03/0.0449) about 0.7 degrees, an essentially imperceptible change.

The test was repeated with the left bicep muscle, again with the arm down, elbow at 90 degrees, holding a rod. The results are shown in Figure 12.4.

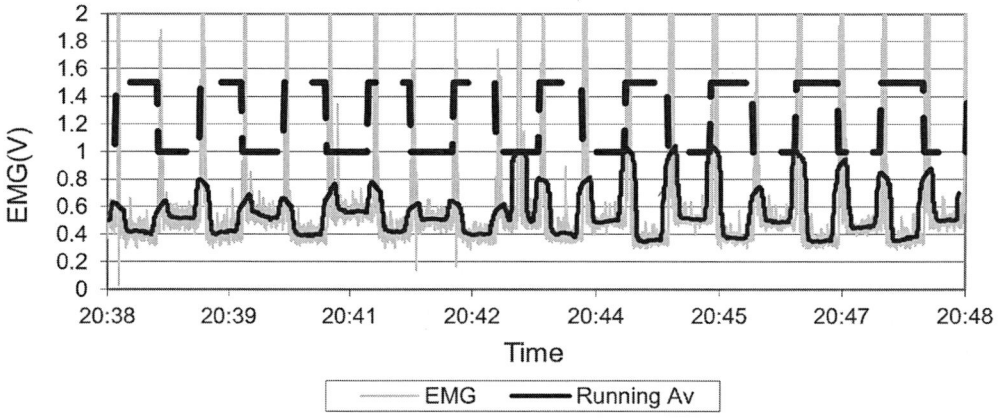

Figure 12.4. EMG of left bicep while holding a dowsing rod and stepping on and off a sewer line under concrete floor every 30s. Data collected at 10 pts/s, and 10s running average.

As with that of the deltoid muscle, the steady state EMG of the left bicep also shows a distinct difference between on and off the dowsing line. The difference between on and off is about 0.1 to 0.2 V. The results are consistent with dowsing signals causing the elbows to rise and the forearms to turn slightly, enough to cause the rods to rotate. These results show that the muscles are activating in response to the dowsing signal. However, the peak in voltage prior to each movement indicates a coordinated process, and therefore most likely under central nervous system control.

Dowsing Static and Moving Water

Dowsing in many people's minds is about finding water, and to locate water for wells is one the most common applications for dowsing. However, it may be noted that the U.S. Geological Survey,[224] echoing the statements of waterworks engineer Thomas M. Riddick from over 50 years earlier,[225] dismissed the utility of dowsing for finding water on the basis that the water table extends under much of the ground and so there is

12. Nature of the Dowsing Response

a good chance of hitting water wherever one digs. However, there is a difference between hitting the water table and finding a good supply of water for a well.

Tromp reported that "very wet soil or wet snow cover usually decreases considerably the sensitivity of the dowser; the dowsing reactions above places where normally strong turnings of the rod are observed might even be completely lacking."[226] To test this idea, I went outside during a rainstorm with an umbrella. It had been raining on and off for several hours. The dowsing signal was noticeably weaker for a sewer pipe in the ground and for electrical cable buried under grass than it is in dry weather. The signal for the surface water drainage pipe in the middle of our paved road was little changed, probably because the rain was running off the road and not penetrating it. These results are consistent with waterlogged soil absorbing the dowsing signal and so damping it.

Other investigators have reported that a pipe radiates dowsing-responsive lines when water is flowing through it.[227] These investigators went on to say that this pattern was modified by an electrical conductor placed parallel to the pipe to an extent dependent on the electrical current through the pipe, presumably from the magnetic field produced by the conductor, which they estimated was about one-tenth of the Earth's magnetic field. It is unclear what the investigators were measuring, whether it was due to a magnetic field from the steel pipe or something else entirely, and the description was too brief to be sure exactly how the experiment was conducted. They interpreted their results to say that the lines produced by the flowing water in the pipe were some form of magnetic field and that the dowsing effect was therefore also a response to this magnetic field. However, without more detail about their experiment, their conclusion that dowsing is a response to a magnetic field remains questionable.

It seems unlikely that flowing water would create significant magnetic fields. Magnetic fields are formed by the movement of net charge and water is electrically neutral. There may be ions dissolved in the water, from dissolved salts such as sodium chloride, which has positive ions (sodium Na^+) and negative ions (chloride Cl^-), but overall the water solution will be electrically neutral. Since the water is electrically neutral, there is no net movement of charge if the water is moving and so no magnetic field is expected. In addition, electronically, water (H_2O) has no unpaired electrons (18 electrons around the oxygen, four or which are shared with the two hydrogens), and so it is diamagnetic.[228] Diamagnetic materials are weakly repelled by magnetic fields, and so pure water is not going to generate a significant magnetic field, flowing or not.

Another proposed theory is that described by Saunders: "Water flowing through pipes is believed by some to create electro-magnetic vibrations, and these frequencies are similar with those of the brain and so experience a resonance with the flow of water."[229] This idea would be stronger if there was evidence that flowing water does indeed create EM radiation, especially if the frequency of the EM radiation matched those of brain waves. The frequencies observed in the brain are typically less than 50 Hz (see the section on EEG and brains waves in the last chapter), which indicates that the wavelength of the EM radiation would be 6000 km, or similar to the very low-frequency band militaries use to communicate with their submarines.[230] This wavelength is used because its absorption by water is very low and so the signal can reach a submerged submarine. It is unlikely that such a long wavelength would have much interaction with a human. If these low frequencies were to be the basis for dowsing, then a means is needed both for the flowing water to emit these frequencies and for the dowser to somehow receive them.

Magnetic Properties of Materials

Most people are familiar with magnets, but various different types of materials respond differently to magnetic fields. The most common types of magnetic materials are listed below. The magnetic properties of a material depend on its electronic structure and in particular the number of unpaired electrons. Electrons have a quantum property called spin, which can be oriented up or down, with nothing in between. Pairs of electrons have spins in opposite directions, and so the spins cancel out. It is the net spin which determines the magnetic properties of the material. Spin was discussed earlier in the discussion about nuclear magnetic resonance.

Diamagnetism

Diamagnetic materials have no inherent magnetism, but they will weakly repel magnetic fields. Most stable compounds have an even number of electrons that are paired off in atomic or molecular orbitals, with two electrons in each orbital, one with spin up and one with spin down. Since all the electrons are paired off, there are no free electrons and no net spin. These materials are diamagnetic.

Note: If the material is a metal (such as copper, zinc, aluminum or brass), changing magnetic fields can induce electric currents which in turn can generate opposing magnetic fields.

Paramagnetism

Some molecules have an odd number of electrons, and so there is an unpaired electron. Some molecules have an even number of electrons, but have two unpaired electrons, of which oxygen (O_2) is the best known example. These unpaired spins will align with a magnetic field and be attracted to a magnet. Such materials are paramagnetic. One of the common types of oxygen sensor uses an electromagnet and then measures the change in the magnetic field in the presence of oxygen as compared to no oxygen.

Ferromagnetism

As mentioned above, electron spins underlay magnetism. If the electron spins of adjacent atoms in a metal crystal, for example, can interact with each other, such that if there is a magnetic field the spins will line up and when the external magnetic field is removed the spins may continue to be lined up, resulting in a permanent magnet. All permanent magnets have a Curie temperature, the temperature at which thermal vibrations are sufficient to overcome these spins and the magnet loses its magnetism. Most common metallic permanent magnets are ferromagnetic, including those made of iron, nickel, cobalt, their alloys, and some rare-earth alloys.

Ferrimagnetism

Ferrimagnetism is similar to ferromagnetism, except that instead of all the spins aligning in the same direction, they align in alternate directions. These materials can still be magnetized (e.g., loadstone is a naturally magnetized piece of the mineral magnetite), but they form weak magnets.

There are some other forms of magnetism, but they are much less common.

Additionally, we have lot of water flowing in our everyday lives, rivers, streams, water in pipes, and as far as I am aware flowing water does not emit low-frequency EM radiation. In addition, it is unclear how this mechanism would explain how dowsers can detect empty pipes underground.

The UK Groundwater Forum proposed the following mechanism, writing, "One theory for this [dowsing] is that the muscles in the body react to some EM effect caused by the presence of the metal or the water flowing through the pipe; the rods then amplify this effect so that the searcher becomes aware of them."[231]

This mechanism presupposes that the "EM effect" created by the presence of metal or flowing water creates EM radiation of sufficient intensity to cause the muscles to respond and give the dowsing response. While frequencies between 1Hz and 10MHz (low-frequency radio waves) can affect nervous system function, causing muscle twitches and spasms, and users of high power radio equipment are warned to limit their exposure,[232] the power levels where these effects are observed are not normally encountered in everyday life and so muscle movement caused by direct interaction of EM radiation with the muscles does not appear to be behind the dowsing effect. A related possibility is that the EM radiation is not interacting with the muscle but with the nervous system that controls the muscles. This idea is explored in more detail later in the book.

In another report, Harry Joel, an electrical engineer, commented, "I noticed on my portable AM radio, that running water changes the reception and superimposes some strange sound on the rf signal. The earth's electro-magnetic field definitely is deformed by underground water (or metal) objects. Have not found any scientific treaties that explore this phenomenon in any detail. You know of any? I have also worked for years in the oil well logging field. So I was doubly curious about the dowsing experience."[233]

I have no idea why running water should affect an AM radio more than static water and I have not been able to find any similar reports. It is possible that something else is affecting Joel's radio that he ascribes to the running water, but without more details of what he observed it is difficult to say.

Dowsing from Vehicles

Huttunen et al. reported that dowsing even works in a car writing "Test subjects walked or were sitting in a slow-moving car, with the windows covered, and a dowsing rod in their hands was recorded. The correlations between the reaction points by test subjects in the moving car and the points by walking along the same path were highly significant. The correlation was not seen in all test locations."[234] Michael Fercik also reported that the dowsing signal in a moving vehicle was much stronger than that found walking on land, and he could detect dowsing targets up to 10 miles away.[235]

I tried to replicate this experiment by dowsing (sitting in the front passenger seat) in a car for several miles along a highway at speeds from 40 to 65 mph, crossing over bridges over valleys below, going under steel bridges and even passing through a tunnel—however, no response. I also tried it at lower speeds around 25 to 40 for several miles along main roads with the same result. Lastly, I tried it on local roads with speeds of 15 to 25 mph and later below 5 mph, passing over water drainage pipes, manholes and other objects known to give a dowsing response, but again with no response. I should add a clarification; no response means no dowsing response. The rods were very sensitive detectors to vibration from bumps in the road surface, to changes in speed and especially to changes in direction (corners etc.) which caused the rods to move. These tests were performed using steel dowsing rods (ex–coat hanger) and significant

The Science of Basic L-Rod Dowsing

inertia, and the movements from the car resulted in a lot of non-dowsing movement as would be expected under these circumstances. In summary, I was not able to replicate the dowsing response obtained by others in a moving car.

Response Time of the Dowsing Response

The response time for muscles to respond to an external stimulus is on the order of 0.1 to 0.3 seconds;[236] so any input on a shorter time scale is not going to have an impact. If the dowsing line is a meter (yard) across and the vehicle is traveling at 10 km/hr (~6 mph) = 2.8 m/s (9.1 ft/s), then the time over which the dowser can potentially get a response is about 0.3 second. If the car is moving at 10 km/s the most a dowser will get for a 1 m dowsing line is perhaps a slight twitch. If the vehicle is going faster, no response is expected because by the time the muscles respond the stimulus is far behind the car.

Although 0.3 seconds is the time for the muscles to start reacting, the rods also need time to react. The rods are believed to move because the dowsing signal causes the elbows to move out slightly and hands to tilt in, causing the rods to move under gravity. Consider a dowser holding two rods in tubes as shown in Figure 12.5. If there is a dowsing response, then the tubes will tilt. The rods are pivoted on the rim and held in place by a force of the handle end of the rod against the inside of the tube.

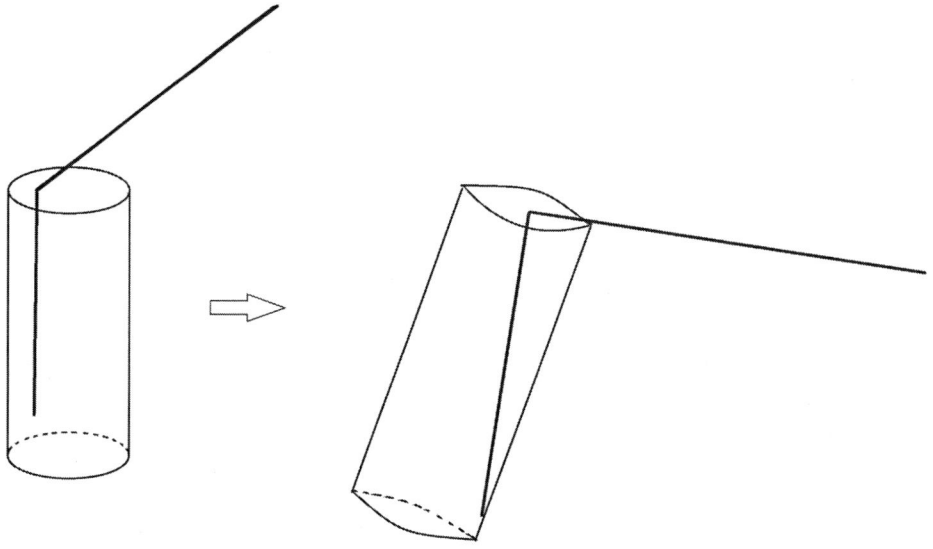

Figure 12.5. Sketch of dowsing rod in holder. When the holder is tilted the dowsing rod will swing around, sliding down the now sloped rim of the holder.

The friction of this interaction will slow down the motion of the rod, so the estimate below will be on the fast side. The same argument applies if the dowser is holding the rods in his or her hands without the tubes.

If the tube tilts, then the rods will slide down the slope. Again, ignoring friction,

12. Nature of the Dowsing Response

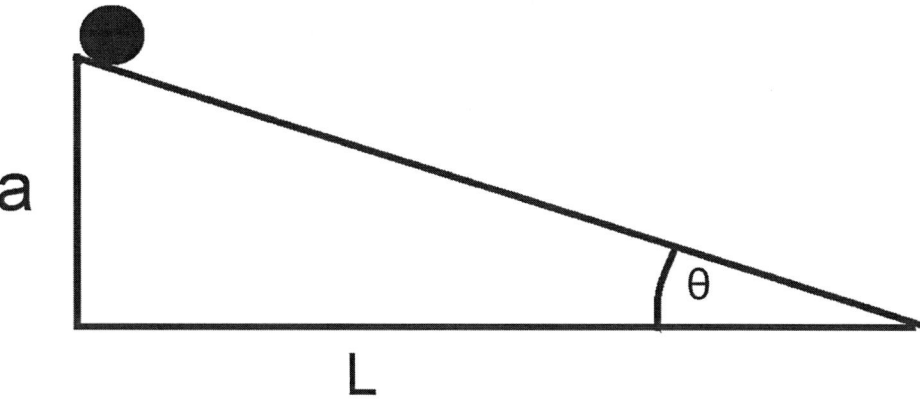

Figure 12.6. The movement of the rod can be represented by a mass sliding down a slope.

the acceleration of the rods can be estimated from the slope. A small deviation is perhaps 10 degrees (θ in Figure 12.6).

The rods have a mass m, and length L. (A typical dowsing L-rod made from half a wire coat hanger is about 11 cm on the short side and 35 cm on the long side [total length 46 cm], with a mass of about 12g.) The midpoint is L/2 and the end of the rods drop a distance a, where a, L and the slope form a right-angled triangle. Assuming the center of mass is the midpoint, then the change in potential energy (E_p) from gravity is

$$E_p = mga/2$$

If there is no friction, then this potential energy gets converted to kinetic energy (E_k). Any friction will lower the kinetic energy and the wasted potential energy becomes heat. The kinetic energy of a moving system is given by the well-known equation

$$E_k = \tfrac{1}{2} mv^2$$

Ignoring friction the change in potential energy is equal to the kinetic energy.

$$\tfrac{1}{2}mga = \tfrac{1}{2} mv^2$$

where v is the velocity. Rearranging this equation gives

$$v^2 = ga \text{ or } v = (ga)^{1/2}$$

For constant acceleration, the average velocity is

$$v_{av} = (v_1 + v_2)/2$$

where v_1 is the starting velocity (assume = zero) and v_2 is the final velocity and therefore the average velocity.

$$v_{av} = v_2/2$$

v_2 is the velocity from drop in the rods and so:

$$v_{av} = (ga)^{1/2}/2$$

Since velocity is distance traveled over time ($\Delta x/\Delta t$), the time for the object to move down the slope Δt can be calculated as:

$$t = a/v_{av}$$

Substituting for v_{av}

$$t = 2a/(ga)^{1/2} = 2(a/g)^{1/2}$$

Since the drop $a = L \sin(\theta)$, then substituting for a

$$t = 2(L\sin[\theta]/g)^{1/2}$$

The angle θ is probably quite small, perhaps 20 degrees, then $\sin(\theta)$ is 0.34, the time is

$$t = 2*(0.35m*0.34/9.8m/s^2) = 0.22 \text{ s}$$

The response time of a dowsing rod is therefore about 0.2 to 0.3 seconds for the reaction time of the nerves and about 0.2 seconds for the rods to move, or about half a second.

Dowsing Theories and Observations

John Janks proposed that dowsing rods detect EM radiation by acting as a dipole antenna, generating a voltage between the dowser's hands which provides the signal causing the movement of the rods.[237] He measured voltages on the order of fractions of a millivolt with a regular multimeter. Physicist Reinhard Schneider also believed that dowsing rods function as a dipole antenna, tunable to EM wavelengths, and he designed a device called the H3 Antenna, which was later manufactured in Switzerland by HPC Corp.[238] However, the dipole theory has some challenges. In particular, dowsing still works if the rods are insulated from the dowser's hands, or even if the rods are made of wood or other non-conductive material, which would preclude them from functioning as a dipole antenna. Also, for most low-end multimeters fractions of a millivolt will be close to the resolution of the multimeter and probably in the range of the noise. While the dipole theory appears lacking, the majority of the evidence does point towards EM radiation being behind the dowsing response, as will be discussed later.

Quick Posture, Pose and Aluminum Foil Tests

I tried some simple tests over the sewer pipe under the basement concrete floor to better understand the dowsing response. This location was chosen not only for convenience, but also for consistency of response over time, since the environment is indoors and thus controlled. The following quick tests were conducted:

- Hold the rods in the normal way and get the normal response. The normal way is standing, with the upper arms relaxed at one's side, and the forearms held horizontally in front, the hands into a loose open fist, with the rods sitting in the fist, initially facing forward and free to rotate. This position is the normal dowsing position for L-rods. This position serves as the base of comparison for later tests.
- If the wrists are consciously locked into position, by tensing the fist, the dowsing response still works, and so the forearms are not involved in the dowsing response.

- If the elbows are consciously locked by pressing them against the side of the body, the dowsing response stops. The dowsing response needs the flexibility that comes from the loose bent arms. Interestingly, Tromp described a contrary observation: "It was found that the more the arm muscles are strained, the more sensitive the dowser becomes. … In this connection it is interesting to mention the observation of Prof. Sommer, a psychologist of the University of Giesen (Germany), who studied the changes in muscular tone of dowsers during a Dowsing Congress at Nauheim (Germany). The changes always occurred before the rod started to turn indicating that the changes in muscular tones is the cause of the rotation of the rod and not a consequence of the turning."[239]
- With arms held straight in front the response does not work. Again, it needs the flexibility that comes from the loose bent elbows and wrists.
- If the arms are lifted out to the side so that the forearms are continuation of shoulders, but with the arms still bent at the elbows, dowsing works but not well. It appears that flexibility around both the shoulders and elbows is important to detect the dowsing signal.
- The dowsing response works if the dowser is walking or being pushed in a chair (with wheels). Therefore, the legs are only involved to the extent of providing locomotion.
- If the sitting test is repeated, but the elbows are resting on something (I used a large pack of toilet rolls on my lap), there is no response. The dowsing response requires the elbows to be mobile.
- Dowsing sideways, i.e., with the rods out front, but stepping sideways across a known dowsing line, gave a response (rods crossed), and shuffling slowly with the feet together showed that the response began from near the outside of the foot (moving to either left or right). With the feet apart, knees bent, the response was roughly head width, evenly centered.
- Wearing aluminum foil soles on my feet (foot shape cutout held in place with masking tape) reduced but did not eliminate the dowsing signal. While the signal must be coming out of the ground, the signal is not exclusively channeled up the legs.
- Wearing foil shorts did stop the dowsing response. The signal is coming up through the body or very close to it. Another reason for doing the testing in my basement is to avoid the questions that would be raised by wearing foil shorts in public.

Some investigators have reported that one has to be able to see the dowsing rods for them to move. Dudley Wheeler, for example, reported that the rods do not move in the dark, or if his eyes are closed. He went on to say that if the left eye is closed, then only the right rod responds and vice versa with the right eye.[240] Personally, I have not observed this effect, and my experience is that the L-rods respond regardless of whether the lights are on or if my eyes are open or closed. Wheeler also reported that walking through a light beam caused the dowsing effect.[241] I have been unable to reproduce this response using an LED-based flashlight producing a horizontal white light beam at hip, waist, chest, shoulder and head heights. However, sunlight obstructed by a metal object can cause a dowsing effect, and this property is discussed later in the book in Chapter 22, on dowsing in three dimensions.

Some dowsers experience a range of symptoms when dowsing. Latimer included the story of the French peasant Bléton, a very sensitive dowser with a reputation for finding underground streams, but who suffered some apparently fairly extreme physical effects from dowsing. The account was recorded by French physician M. Thouvenel in his memoirs.[242]

> Whenever this man was in a place where there existed subterraneous waters, he was immediately sensible of a lively impression, referable to the diaphragm, which he called his *"commotion."* This was followed by a sense of oppression in the upper part of the chest; at the same time he felt a shock, with general tremor and chilliness, staggering of the legs, stiffness of the wrists, with twitchings, a concentrated pulse, which gradually diminished. All these symptoms were more or less strong, according to the volume and depth of the water, and they were more sensibly felt when Bleton *went in a direction against* the subterranean current than when he *followed its course.* Stagnant water under ground did not affect him; nor did open sheets of water, ponds, lakes or rivers affect him. The nervous system of this man must have been susceptible, since he was more sensibly affected by change of weather and variations in the atmosphere than other persons; otherwise he appeared healthy.

It sounds as if Bléton had a very unpleasant experience each time he drowsed, and whenever the weather changed, but exactly what was going on is hard to say. There have been many reports about the influence of the weather on people's health, but the jury is still out on many of them.[243]

Maby also wrote that many dowsers have been known to vomit, faint or suffer from hallucinations, and that he reported that he had felt most of these symptoms to a slight degree and he observed staggering and convulsions in another dowser. Many dowsers report tingling in the arms and other mild symptoms.[244] These results are interesting in that they suggest that the entire body is affected by the dowsing effect, and not just those muscles/nerves needed to move the rods.

Well-known dowser Evelyn Penrose described how tiring dowsing was and how sometimes she was violently ill especially after finding large quantities of water and especially when finding oil or minerals.[245] She also described what it was like for her to detect oil, saying, "The first indication I get … is a violent stab through the soles of my feet like a red-hot knife. When over the oil itself, the action of the rod is so violent that I am turned and twisted about like a doll on the end of a string.… On the strongest dome of the main oil field the shock from the oil was so great that I crumpled up and collapsed being unable to open my left hand or straighten my left side for what seemed a long time, although it was probably only minutes if not seconds."[246]

Apparently, she experienced different sensations with different targets, even when map dowsing. Silver for example also gave her a sharp pain like being stabbed with a red-hot knife. She wrote in her autobiography, "While she was water-divining in British Columbia, a mining man brought her a map of an area near a big silver mine, which he wanted her to survey for gold. While talking to him, she unthinkingly perched on the table and sat on the corner of the map where the silver mine was. The sudden stab of pain made her leap up with a yell. The next day she mentioned this to a friend, who remarked, 'But, my dear, how very convenient to be able to work at both ends!'"[247] Personally, I have never had any adverse sensations or strong physiological reactions. I suspect these symptoms only happen to the very sensitive.

Several investigators have noticed correlations in skin conductivity. For example, Tromp noted that dowsers had lower conductivity (< 50 ohms) between their palms

12. Nature of the Dowsing Response

than non-dowsers (typically 500k to 3Mohms), measured using 4.5V DC and 3 mm electrodes.

Curiously Tromp also found that good and not-so good dowsers could improve their performance by wetting their hands with an electrolyte.[248]

I measured the conductivity between my palms by clipping crocodile clips to my skin, with a YSI model 32 conductivity meter. It hurt, but should have made a good electrical contact, and left a mark for some time afterwards to prove the point. The conductance was 30 µohm^{-1}, which is equivalent to 33 kohm resistance. I obtained the same value pressing the crocodile clips into both palms. When I repeated the test with a digital multimeter, the crocodile clips gave 10.3 Mohm resistance, and pressing the clips into the palms gave a resistance of about 470 to 500 kohms. Therefore, according to Tromp's criteria I am non-sensitive as far as dowsing is concerned.

Rocard similarly noted that the electrical resistance between palms of the hands for a 'good' dowser is a quarter to a third that of a "poor" dowser, but this effect is lessened if his or her hands are moist.[249] The lower electrical resistance if the hands are moist makes sense, since added water will probably decrease the electrical resistance of good dowser and non-dowser alike. However, dowsing rods work if the rods are held in plastic tubes, electrically isolated from the hands, so electrical conductivity between the rods and the skin is not a factor, and skin conductivity does not correlate with any apparent mechanism. If the skin conductivity of dowsers is confirmed to be higher than other people, then skin conductivity is probably a correlation rather than cause and effect of dowsing ability. Also, since internally we are fluid filled (the average conductivity of blood lies between 10^{-20} mΩ^{-1}cm^{-1}),[250] the resistance of our hands is primarily the resistance of the outer skin. As discussed above, some people have profound physiological effects when crossing a dowsing line and perhaps some of these effects make them sweat more and so increases the conductivity of their skin. It would be interesting to know if these dowsers also experience these effects when they happen to cross a dowsing line when they are going about their normal business and not dowsing. If so then the dowsing sense may be more of a curse than a blessing for them, since there are underground pipes and structures throughout our modern world.

In 1952 a team of electrical engineers tested the famous dowser Henry Gross and found that his skin potential changed by up to 200mV over subterranean water, compared with a change of 10mV for non-dowsers.[251] It is unclear in this reference where the potential difference was measured. Assuming it was between his hands, this result is somewhat surprising, since we humans are somewhat conductive and so are unlikely to maintain a dc potential between our limbs. Interestingly, Tromp also reported that "experiments with the strong galvanometer indicate that in this case no permanent changes in the skin potential."[252] It is unclear what he meant here, since a galvanometer is used to measure small currents, not potentials. However, if there is no potential between the hands, then there will be no current.

An electrocardiogram (ECG) measures small potentials on the skin produced by the heart. Tromp ran several experiments with dowsers hooked up to an ECG machine with and without their rods.[253] The ECG machine had a single channel machine connected between the hands. Tromp found that the ECG signal dropped about 20 mV when the subject stepped across a dowsing line, rapidly for an experienced dowser and more gently for a non-dowser. This potential shift was rationalized as a change in the electrical potential between the hands. If this experiment could be verified, it would provide an important insight into the mechanism of dowsing in the body.

To try to reproduce this effect, I used an Emay model EMG-10, which is also a single channel ECG. I held the device so as to measure the potential between my hands with no rods, and to measure the potential between my right hand and chest, a couple of inches below the left nipple, with a rod in my left hand. When I crossed the dowsing line, the rod in my left hand crossed. The protocol was to count heartbeats, 10 before the line, 10 on the line and the remainder up to 30 seconds stepping beyond the line. The same actions were performed a couple of meters away, where there was no dowsing line as a control. The dowsing line used was again the sewer line that runs under our concrete basement floor. There was some movement in the ECG, with the movement and random noise, but I saw no systematic change in the ECG stepping onto or off the dowsing line. The trace shown in Figure 12.7 is an example of one of the EGC traces upon stepping across the line.

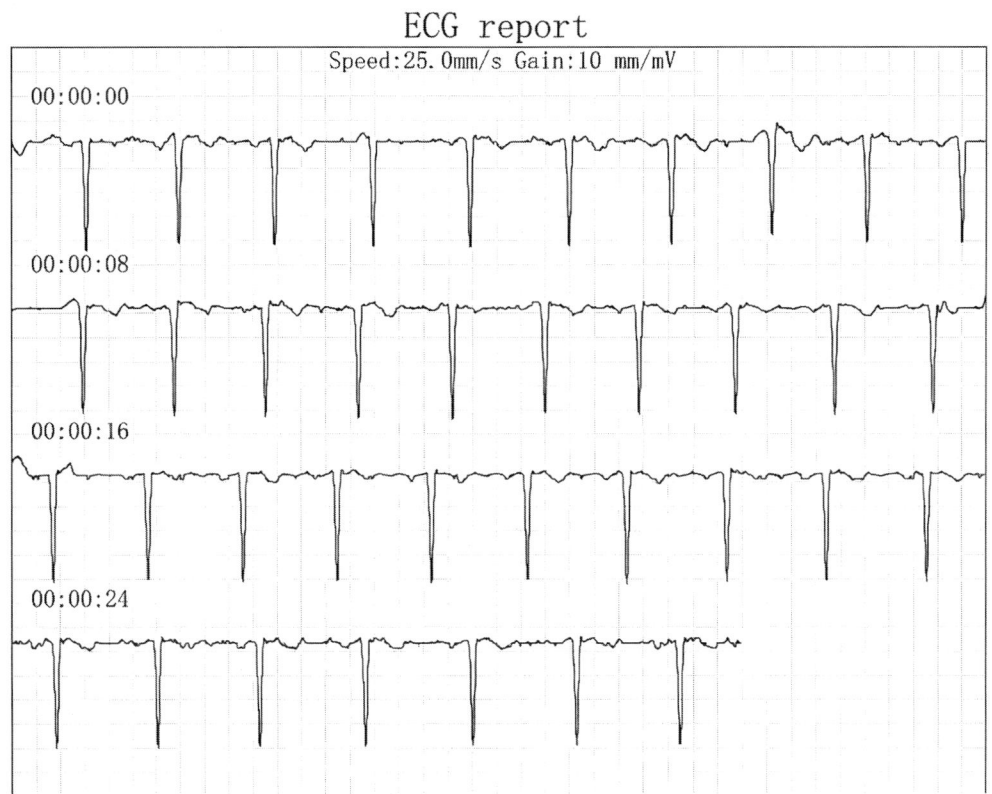

Figure 12.7. ECG (10 mm/mV, 25 mV/s) while holding rod in left hand, measuring potential between chest and right hand. Ten beats before the dowsing line, step, 10 beats on dowsing line, step, remaining beats off dowsing line.

In another test, I connected a multimeter set to DC voltage connected with crocodile clips clipped on to my skin (yes, it hurt a little, which probably meant I had a good connection), and walked across the same dowsing line. There was almost no potential

12. Nature of the Dowsing Response

difference between my wrists and no change in potential on crossing the sewer pipe dowsing line. The conclusion is that I was unable to reproduce Tromp's results of a change in potential between the wrists when the rods respond either by direct measurement using a multimeter or by ECG.

Tromp also found that connecting a thin copper wire to one of the sides of the rod and to the earth usually prevents the turning.[254] The rods are usually sitting at a balance point, so that very small responses cause the rods to move, so I suspect that if there was a trailing wire, even a thin one, its mass or applied tension might be enough to stop the rod from turning.

Tromp found that the dowsing sensitivity usually increased with the better the insulation qualities of the dowser's footwear (e.g., thick rubber soles); walking without shoes usually decreased the sensitivity.[255] The opposite effect was observed by Latimer, who found that he lost the ability to find underground water when his shoes were insulated from the ground with glass ink bottles attached to his sandals, and so concluded that dowsing was caused by electricity.[256] I tested an outdoor location that gave a strong dowsing line, and walked in bare feet across the grass to ensure an electrical connection to the ground and saw a strong response. I repeated the test wearing Crocs, a rubber sandal made of polyethylene-vinyl acetate closed-cell foam,[257] a good insulator. There was no significant difference in the dowsing signal. Therefore, electrical connection to ground does not appear to be necessary for dowsing. Perhaps Latimer's ink bottles partially blocked the dowsing signal similar to foil soles in the shoes, or made him change his stance.

Tromp also found that the faster the dowser walks the stronger the reaction, but he commented that in order to find the exact location of the dowsing response the dowser had to repeat the test slowly.[258] In my experience, walking faster does not increase the dowsing signal, but reduces it. It takes time for the rods to move, perhaps half a second to a couple of seconds, and so if one crosses a dowsing line quickly the rods may move, but do not have time to move fully. I don't think it is a response time as such to the dowsing signal (i.e., how quickly the force is applied to the rods), but rather just the inertia of the rods themselves. Generally, I have found that moving slowly increases sensitivity because it allows time for the rods to respond and so even a weak signal becomes visible, and walking quickly does the opposite. If speed was important, then if one walks to a location where the rods cross and then stop, the rods should uncross, since one's speed would be zero. I have found that the rods stay crossed, so movement of the dowser does not appear to be a requirement for a dowsing response.

13

Location of Dowsing Sense Organ

Think you of the fact that a deaf person cannot hear. Then, what deafness may we not all possess? What senses do we lack that we cannot see and cannot hear another world all around us?

—Frank Herbert[259]

Chapter summary: If dowsing is a response to physical stimulus, is there a dowsing sense organ at a specific location or is it a general bodily response? Prior studies have shown that there is a localized dowsing sense, near the bottom of the brain, though other reports have placed it in the neck, back and even near the adrenal glands/kidneys. This result supports the idea that dowsing may be a sense.

One interesting question is whether the dowsing response is a sense or an irrelevant physiological response. The latter would, for example, be a muscle twitch on applying a voltage to someone's arm. We are all the products of millions of years of evolution, and nature is not going to develop a complex system unless it is useful in some way that gives an advantage to the organism. For example, knowing something of the rock densities or the presence of tree roots in the soil ahead or around a burrowing animal, like a mole, while digging might offer it such an advantage. However, the dowsing sense does not appear to provide significant advantages for larger mammals, including humans. Another possibility is that dowsing is detected using a sense organ intended for a different purpose, or perhaps it is the remnant of the magnetic field sense, a sense which occurs in many animals. The magnetic field sense has been detected subconsciously in humans, though the sensor organ and its physiological mechanism remain to be elucidated.[260] A sense tends to have a sense organ and has evolved for the specific purpose to provide information of the external world to the animal (including humans), such as hearing, smell, temperature, sight. For each of these well-known senses, there is a sense organ and specific receptors within it to detect the external stimulus. Temperature, for example, is measured by the skin, and there are specific neural receptors such as the TRMP8 that respond to low temperatures[261] and the TRPV1 which respond to higher temperatures.[262]

Dowsing in Animals?

If there is a dowsing sense organ, then it is likely that many animals will have similar organs and abilities. This assumption directly raises the question of whether animals are able to dowse. Some animals can perform dowsing-like effects.[263] For example, elephants are known to walk for miles across dusty terrain, stop and then pound the ground and find water below. How they do that is not known; perhaps they can sense the water using the dowsing effect, perhaps they notice a difference in the solidity of the ground, or perhaps they remembered that was the location where water was found previously.[264] In summary, elephants are remarkable creatures with many abilities and we don't know how they find water.

Donkeys (burros) also have an uncanny ability to find water and they are known to dig wells up to 1 meter deep to find water in the Arizona desert to such an extent that they are changing the landscape by providing a water source for other animals.[265] Again it is not known how the donkeys know where to dig, whether it is by smell or some other sense (dowsing or otherwise). Some animals in the Ruaha National Park in Tanzania also dig wells, but they usually do so close to contaminated water holes and riverbeds in the dry season, so deciding where to dig may be just from experience from watching other animals.[266] J. B. Rhine, the famous parapsychologist, found that German shepherd dogs could find land mines better than expected, and wrote "Two German shepherd dogs and their trainer, as a team, attempted to locate empty land mine cases that were buried in a straight line, 4 in. deep in sand under 6–12 in. of water. ... All surface signs except section and unit locations were removed by raking. The dog ... indicated a location by sitting. ... Steady crosswinds, surface ripples, and strong side currents in the water gave good assurance against olfactory cues. On 203 underwater trials there were 38.9% hits where only 20% was expected ($p < .001$)."[267]

It seems to me that without more information this reference provides little support for a dowsing sense organ in animals. The sense of smell in dogs is remarkable and often underappreciated. If dogs can track where someone walked an hour before across open land, then mild crosswinds are not going to stop German Shepherds from detecting land mines. Tromp wrote in 1949 that some animals appear to be responsive to dowsing lines; however, he emphasized that the reports needed to be verified before they could be considered reliable.[268]

- Animals (need to be substantiated)
    - "Mice placed in long cages which were crossed by a dowsing zone always seem to concentrate in the part outside the zone."
    - "Horses and cattle do not seem to graze in those parts of a meadow which are crossed by strong dowsing zones. However, if the grass is cut in these places and given to them in the stables they enjoy eating it."
    - "Chicken seem to sleep only in places free of dowsing zones if a poultry house is crossed by such zones."
    - "It has been reported that bees produce more honey if the beehive is placed in a strong dowsing zone."

While it is known that many animals can detect magnetic fields, and some appear able to detect water, the evidence that animals can dowse remains unconvincing, and therefore, animal behavior does not support the existence of a specific dowsing sense.

Search for the Dowsing Sense Organ

The location in the body where the dowsing response is sensed has been investigated several times in the past. Jeffrey Keen conducted some simple but very elegant tests involving placing a dowsing source (quartz crystal) at various heights and measuring the minimum distance needed to detect it. The height that gave the maximum distance corresponded to the height in the body of the dowsing sense organ, and the location to be the back of the brain.[269] I have to admit, I don't understand why a quartz crystal is a dowsing source but it was still a very elegant experiment.

Harvalik found that dowsers respond to EM radiation in the 48 MHz to 6 GHz range and wrapped metal foil as a shield around parts of the body of the test subjects to identify the location of the "detector" to a narrow EM beam from a generator. The first detector was found in the kidney/adrenal glands area and a second one in the brain near the pineal gland. Harvalik also found that most subjects were sensitive to radiation power in the mW range, but one experienced dowser gave a response in μW power range.

MuMETAL[1]

Manufactured by the Magnetic Shield Corporation, Bensenville, IL, MuMETAL is an iron-nickel alloy with a typical composition of 77 percent nickel, 16 percent iron, 5 percent copper, and 2 percent chromium or molybdenum, which is magnetically soft (easily magnetized, but does not retain the magnetism after the external field is removed). MuMETAL has a very high relative permeability, usually between 80,000 and 100,000 compared to other steels such as carbon steel (100) and ferritic stainless steel (1000–1800).[2] The high permeability allows MuMETAL to be used to shield against magnetic fields, not by blocking them, but by providing a path for the magnetic field lines around the object being shielded. Alloys similar to MuMETAL are available from several other suppliers too.

1. "Mu-Metal," Wikipedia, https://en.wikipedia.org/wiki/Mu-metal, accessed August 7, 2021.
2. "Permeability," Engineering Tool Box, https://www.engineeringtoolbox.com/permeability-d_1923.html, accessed August 7, 2021.

Higgins repeated Harvalik's work and identified two zones by lower or null dowsing signal using shielding with MuMETAL. The zones were the dorsal neck–upper back region and the crown region. Shelley partially replicated Harvalik's left and right kidneys as "dowsing zones" but contrary to Harvalik found that covering the forehead region increased rather than diminished the dowser response measurements. For one dowser the neck area was examined in more detail, and it was found that the dowsing zone covered an approximate two square inch area from the seventh cervical vertebra (C7) to the third thoracic vertebra (T3), so if any part of this area was covered with MuMETAL the dowsing effect was blocked.[270] Jennison used aluminum foil to identify the location of the dowsing sense and concluded that it was in the spinal column, probably at the base of the skull.[271] Keen found that the source of the dowsing response was the back of the brain.[272] Anne Miller,[273] working with Harry Lovegrove, made a 3 mm slit between two sheets of steel lying on the ground so as to generate a beam, and reflected this beam using a 300 mm square mirror at 45° on a height stand. By moving the mirror up and down the stand she could direct the beam up and down Lovegrove's back in a way that he was unable to see. Lovegrove reported that he could sense the beam when it was pointed between his T2 and T4 vertebrae. Miller estimated that the wavelength of the radiation was between 0.1 and 0.3 mm (3 to 1 THz).

13. Location of Dowsing Sense Organ

It is unclear what the precision of Miller's measurements were, and whether there is a significant difference between the shoulder blades and the base of the brain, depending on how far back the mirror was from Lovegrove and the angle of the mirror needed to get a dowsing response. There is more variation in the dowsing sense location reported by the various investigators than is desired, but all of these studies suggest that there is an organ responsible for the detection of the dowsing signal in the upper-back/head area as opposed to a general response from nerves twitching across the entire body.

I did some quick experiments to identify the location of the dowsing sense. The first attempt was to change the orientation of my head, standing bent over at about 90 degrees, and I found that it is still possible to dowse, though it is not the most comfortable position (Figure 13.1).

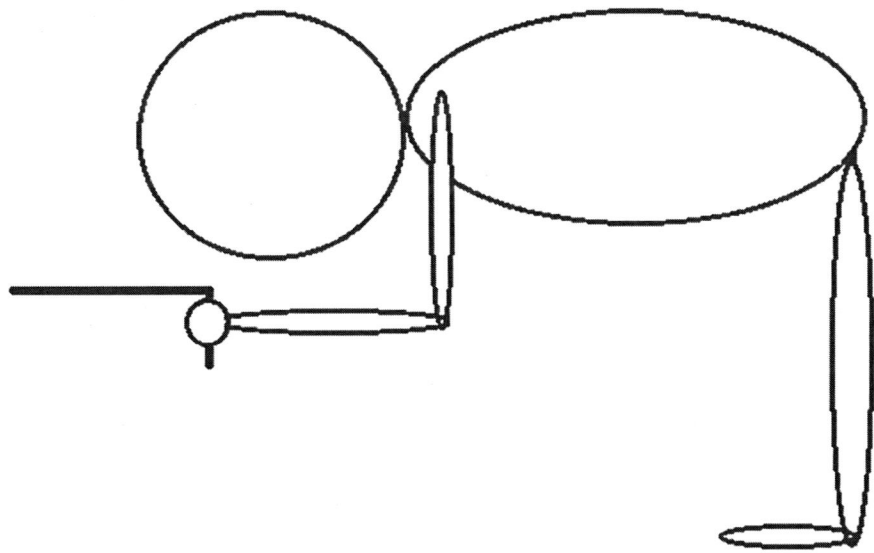

Figure 13.1. Dowsing bent over.

The advantage of this posture is that the head is now forward of the abdomen, which is forward of the hips, as compared to the posture of all in a line for normal dowsing. I did not find a detection zone in the abdomen (wrapping the abdomen and chest in aluminum foil had no effect), nor did wrapping foil around the chest, shoulders and neck. Wrapping foil around the head below the tip of the nose while bent over made no difference, but placing foil at the bridge of the nose blocked the signal. Therefore, the detection center is vertically in front of the ears, and horizontally at eye level, as illustrated in Figure 13.2 below.

This result contrasts with that of Harvalik discussed above, in that foil around the abdomen would have blocked any detection by the kidneys. One major difference is that Harvalik was measuring the response to generated EM fields, not a dowsing signal, but it is unclear if this is significant.

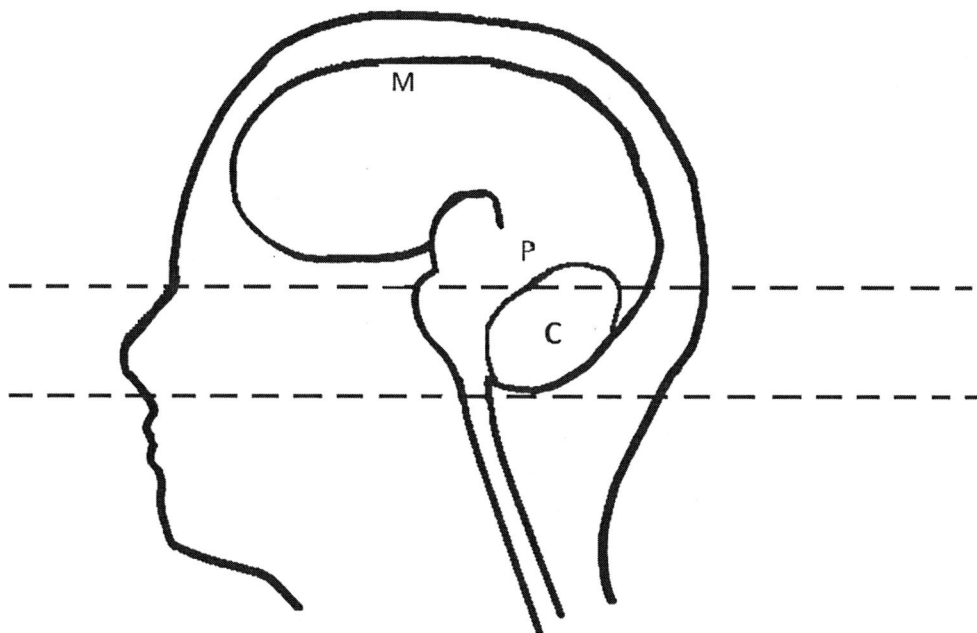

Figure 13.2. Sketch of brain in skull, showing planes that were blocked with aluminum foil. P marks the approximate location of the pineal gland.

While my results are consistent with Harvalik's conclusion that the detection center is by the pineal gland, my results do not have the precision needed to confirm this exact location. The pineal gland's main function is as part of the endocrine system, especially the production of melatonin, which modulates sleep patterns in both circadian and seasonal cycles, and so it is unlikely itself to be a dowsing sense organ. A more likely detection site would be a part of the brain that controls motor functions, since the dowsing response manifests as a slight lifting of the elbows. The motor cortex is located far above the pineal at the top of the brain (M), but a more likely detector candidate is the cerebellum, marked C in Figure 13.2, which is below and behind the pineal. One of the main functions of the cerebellum is to control motion and muscle movement. It typically does not initiate motion, which is the function of the motor cortex, but the cerebellum coordinates muscles, allowing complex movements to occur. The pianist's motor complex may initiate playing Beethoven's Fifth, but it is the cerebellum that knows how to play the piano. Another possible candidate for the dowsing sense organ is the brain stem, the most ancient part of the brain that controls many autonomic functions like breathing. Incidentally, Wu and Dickman found that the magnetic sense center of the brain was located in the brain stem,[274] and as discussed later, one of the theories of dowsing is that it is related to the magnetic field sense.

Looking at posture again, I found that looking down at the ground (normal posture) gave the normal response, but keeping my back straight and looking forward stopped or significantly reduced the response, as illustrated in Figure 13.3. The dowsing sense organ is in the head, such that it is exposed to the dowsing signal when looking down and not when standing erect looking forward. This result suggests that the dowsing signal is lost it if passes through the body. If the dowsing signal is EM radiation and it has to travel through the body to reach the sense organ, then some attrition may be expected, since adult men and women are 60 percent and 55 percent water, respectively.[275] An alternative explanation is that the dowsing sense organ is in the head, but it is sensitive to orientation. The next test involved walking with normal posture, but placing aluminum foil under the lower jaw, and doing so completely stopped the dowsing response. The location of the dowsing sense organ therefore is in the head and the dowsing signal enters the head around the lower jaw. This result suggests that the dowsing signal travels up the front of the person via their lower jaw/neck to reach their head rather than traveling through the length of their body.

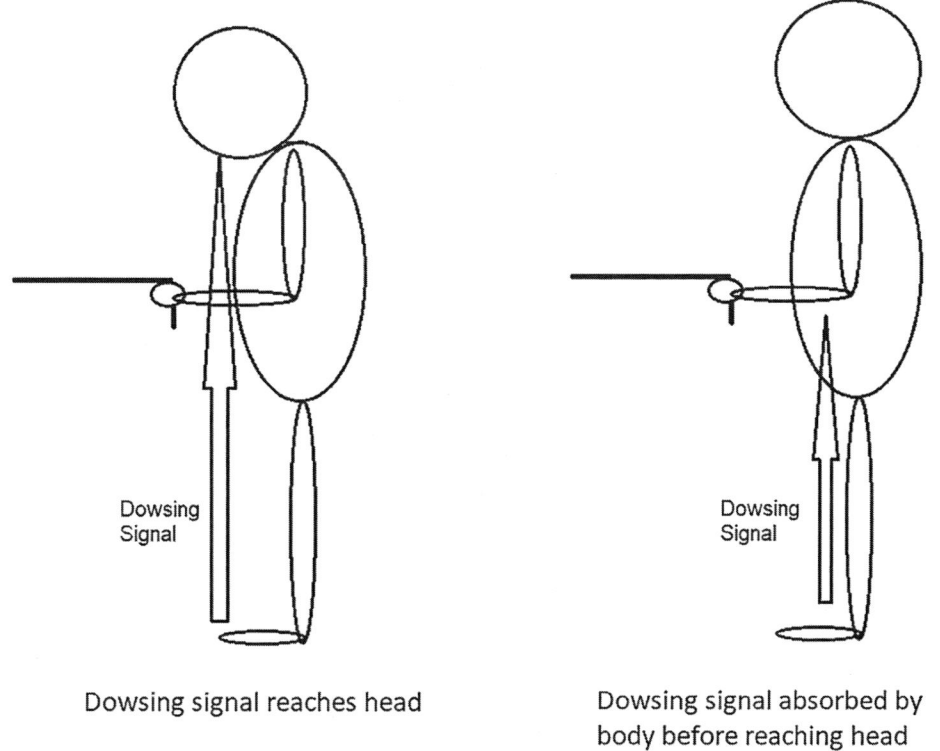

Figure 13.3. Effect of posture on dowsing response.

The observation that standing up straight stops the dowsing response may explain the numerical similarity between the approximately 85 percent of people who can do L-rod dowsing with little or no training[276] and the 90 percent of people in the U.S. who slouch when walking, i.e., lean forward with their heads.[277] It would be an interesting survey to see if the slouchers of the world are better at dowsing than those with better posture. From the literature examples described above, there appears to be a consensus that the dowsing sense organ is at a particular location, rather than a general nervous response. The presence of a single organ suggests that dowsing is using a sense, rather than a coincidental physical effect. The dowsing sense organ is located in the head or close to it.

14

Magnetism and Magnetic Fields

Magnetism: "For what phenomenon is more astonishing? Where has nature shown greater audacity?"
— Pliny the Elder[278]

Chapter summary: Many people have suggested that differences in the local magnetic field are the basis for dowsing, and some prior investigators found that at least some dowsers respond to magnetic fields. Magnetism and magnetic fields appear to be related to the dowsing response, but the dowsing response is not based on variations in static magnetic fields.

One of the explanations proposed for the dowsing effect assumes that dowsers are unusually sensitive to small variations in the Earth's magnetic field and can pick up very small changes caused by water or metal underground.[279] For example, Tom Williamson wrote, "Serious dowsing claims such as those made by Soviet geologists, which are difficult to account for in terms of the reception of normal sensory cues, may be explained by postulating human sensitivity to small magnetic field gradient changes. The theory is supported by a series of tests involving 150 subjects. The magnetic theory predicts that dowsers can achieve above-chance results only if the features they claim to detect are associated with magnetic gradients of at least one nanotesla per metre."[280]

A related theory that has been proposed is that the detection of the magnetic anomaly results in a signal to the dowser's muscles, which experience a small contraction, causing the lightly held dowsing rod to deflect.[281]

Harvalik ran a series of tests looking at the response of his dowsing subjects to magnetic fields. He found that 80 percent of his test subjects with L-rods responded to a magnetic field created by passing a DC or AC current between two electrodes implanted in the ground 20 feet apart but did not respond absent the magnetic field.[282] Harvalik also reported that exceptional dowsers (1%) could detect magnetic fields of 0.0007 gamma[283] (1 gamma = 1 nT), and the Earth's magnetic field is about 50 µT or 50,000 gamma. As discussed above, the magnetotelluric fields are ~ 1/50 millionth of the Earth's magnetic field, so about 0.001 nT, or 0.001 gamma. These differences in magnetic field are in the range that Harvalik measured for the most sensitive dowsers.

There are a couple of criticisms of this study. The first is that by passing the current through the ground, the current path is uncontrolled, and the current and hence magnetic field will vary depending on the lowest conduction path, which in turn depends on the distribution of minerals in the ground, making the field measurements difficult to ascertain. The second criticism is that the magnetic field discrimination seems incredibly small. In my kitchen the magnetic field was about 52 μT according to my cell phone magnetometer app,[284] which dropped to about 47 μT next to the refrigerator, ~60 μT by some lights and down near 40 μT near a TV (turned off). These changes are perhaps typical of the variations of the local magnetic field strength in our modern environment. The magnetic field discrimination that Harvalik measured in some of the individuals is over a million times more sensitive than typical background variations. His papers did not go into great detail about screening outside interferences, but the sensitivities are well below what one would expect for the background noise. Humans can sometimes detect small signals against a large background, like a conductor hearing that one of the violins in an orchestra is slightly out of tune, but such a small signal/noise ratio does raise doubts concerning these results, and Kirschvink commented similarly.[285]

Rocard found that dowsers can respond to changes in magnetic field created by passing current through a square coil to create a 0.4 μT field at the middle from a meter away, and dowsers could detect changes in the magnetic field of 0.1μT/m. Foulkes, however, was unable to get the same results on repeating the test.[286] These results support the idea that the dowsing sense is related to the magnetic sense, but they also suggest that there is a wide variability either in the experimental methods and/or between the dowsers.

Tromp conducted a series of tests on dowsers to determine if they would respond to magnetic fields. The results are summarized as follows:[287]

- Dowsers could detect changes in the strength of an EM field (for instance, by walking through an area with a varying field strength, by switching current on or off, or by changing the direction of the field) but could not detect the field strength itself.
- Sensitive dowsers could detect gradients of less than 0.1 gauss per meter (10 μT/m).
- After 20 trials the dowsers became fatigued and could not respond accurately, but for the first 20 trials, those dowsers who Tromp found were sensitive responded correctly 80 percent of the time.
- Dowsers were able to detect changes in a magnetic field generated by a current through a 1 m (~39 inches) vertical wire loop. Neither the dowser nor the person recording the response knew when the current was changed. Magnetic field gradients of less than 0.001 Gauss/cm (0.1 μT/m) could be detected by sensitive dowsers.
- Dowsers who were not sensitive to the artificial fields when using a loop shaped rod were sensitive when using the pendulum; and the latter, in contrast to findings with the rod, could detect differences in field strength.

Note: While the person recording the responses was not aware if the current was on or off, the experimenter controlling the switch was in the same room as the dowser, so the tests were not double blind. The numbers of subjects, trials, and successes were again omitted.[288]

These results from Tromp provide support for the idea that the dowsing signal is magnetic or at least that the dowsing response is somehow related to sensing magnetic fields. I tried a simple experiment, placing a copper wire coil of about a meter diameter on the floor and connecting it to a DC power supply via some power resistors (to provide some control of the current). The current was then increased, and the magnetic field was measured using the iPhone magnetometer. I increased the current until the field was about 30 µT about 30 cm off the ground, at which point the power resistors became so hot, they burnt a hole in the carpet. However, even at that magnetic field I did not get any dowsing response. This result does not negate Tromp's data, since as he noted, some people are more responsive than others, but at least as far as sensitivity to magnetic fields goes, I appear to be at the low end of the spectrum.

---

iPhone Magnetometer

Modern-day cell phones are wonders of technology and are packed with sensors; for example, the iPhone has a built-in magnetometer, which provides data to the compass application. I added a magnetometer app by Vieyra Software,[1] which provides the magnetic field for all three axes (x, y and z) and the total magnetic field in µT and plots a graph of all four values over time. The total magnetic field is calculated from the square root of the sum of the square of each of the x, y and z components.

I do not have the means to calibrate the cell phone magnetometer app, but in Pennsylvania the Earth's magnetic field has a field strength is about 50 µT.[2] If I stand on my front lawn, I get a total magnetic field of 52 µT, so the magnetometer app appears to be in reasonable agreement with the expected value.

The iPhone coordinates for the magnetometer or motion sensors are Cartesian such that if one is holding the iPhone horizontal, screen up, then the x-axis is left right parallel to screen, the y-axis is up down parallel to the screen and the z-axis is into and out of the screen, i.e., perpendicular to the plane of the screen.[3]

---

1. The magnetometer is part of the Physics Toolbox Apps from *Vieyra Software* (the Apple Store) July 2020.
2. "Intensity Of the Earth's Magnetic Field," J&J Magnetics Inc., https://www.kjmagnetics.com/globe.asp, accessed August 19, 2020.
3. "Intro to 3D Coordinates in Motion," https://support.apple.com/guide/motion/intro-to-3d-coordinates-motn17c66fd6/mac, accessed December 11, 2021.

The above experiment had the magnetic field perpendicular to the floor. A similar experiment was performed with the magnetic field parallel to the floor and perpendicular to the direction of travel. I took a cardboard box (38 × 30 × 30 cm or 15" × 12" × 12") and wound copper wire around the box for ten turns. The wire then connected to a 9V battery via an on/off toggle switch. With the switch closed, the potential across the battery's terminals was about 6.5V and the resistance of the wire was 15.1 ohms. Therefore, the current was about 430 mA. The magnetic field, as measured on my cell phone app from 45 cm (18") from the coil, directly in front of the box with the switch open, was x = 9.2 µT, y = 14.4 µT and z = 45.0 µT. The iPhone was positioned horizontally, with the screen up and home button away from the coils (field along Y axis). When the switch closed the magnetic field was x = 9.2 µT, y = 15.1 µT and z = 45.0 µT, so only the Y component of the magnetic field changed (Δ_y = 0.7 µT). The switch was opened and closed several times to ensure that the readings varied with the switch position. When the phone was placed in the middle of the coils in the box, the magnetic field was

Switch open: x = 13.1 µT, y = 16.0 µT and z = -46.6 µT
Switch closed: x = 12.4 µT, y = 28 µT and z = -47.6 µT, (Δ_y = 12 µT)

The switch was opened and closed several times to ensure that the readings varied with the switch position. I tested the box by placing it on a stand around 1.5 m (59") from the center of the coils and walking in front of the box with dowsing rods. There was no response with the switch open or the switch closed. The box was raised so that the center of the coil was about 175 cm (~69") off the ground, approximately ear height, and again tested with the dowsing rods. There was no dowsing response with the switch open or closed. The distance from the coils to the center of my head was about 45 cm (18").

Estimate of Magnetic Field Strength in Box Coil

The magnetic flux density at the center of a rectangular coil of length L and width d, carrying current I, is given by[1]

$$B = 2\mu_o i(L^2 + d^2)^{1/2}/(\pi L d)$$

For a coil with 10 turns, the magnetic field will be ten times as much.

$$B = 20\mu_o i(L^2 + d^2)^{1/2}/(\pi L d)$$

For μ_o = 12.57×10−7 H/m, i = 0.43 A, L = 0.38 m, d = 0.3 m, B = 14.6 µT, which is close to the (28−16 = 12 µT) measured on the cell phone magnetometer y axis.

1. David Halliday and Robert Resnick, *Physics Parts 1 and 2*, 3rd Ed (Wiley, 1978), 768.

The effect of very strong static magnetic fields on humans and other biological systems is fairly well known. For example, it is known that when the static magnetic field exceeds roughly 2 Tesla, movement in the magnetic field can induce electric fields in the head which can result in vertigo, nausea, visual sensations, a metallic taste in the mouth, and sometimes acute neuro-cognitive effects, with subtle changes in attention, concentration and visuo-spatial orientation. The peripheral nervous system is less affected for normal movements, the threshold for peripheral nerve stimulation is around 8 T.[289] These effects are unlikely to be encountered in normal life, since most people will not be exposed to such intense magnetic fields. For comparison, the Earth's magnetic field is around 50 µT, so about 100,000 times smaller.

Many animals can navigate using the Earth's magnetic field, and there is some evidence that humans can sense magnetic fields. In the 1970s, University of Manchester zoologist Robin Baker[290] took blindfolded students on bus journeys, each wearing a helmet, some of which contained magnets. The students were then asked to get out of the bus and point in the direction of home. Baker concluded that there was "no question that humans have a magnetic sense." However, scientists in both Sheffield (UK) and in the United States were unable to replicate these results.[291] Some people have suggested that the large number of AM radio stations in that area may have nulled the effect of the magnets,[292] but this explanation seems somewhat unconvincing.

To determine if the dowsing signal was a change in the local magnetic field, the iPhone magnetometer was held over a known dowsing line, a water pipe under asphalt, but no apparent change was seen in the value of the total magnetic field, nor for the magnetic field for the individual axes between on and off the dowsing line. If there were any changes, then they were too small to observe, and much smaller than the random

> ## Magnetic Field Units
>
> Magnetic fields are generated by moving charges (electric currents) and are described by two vector quantities: the magnetic field strength H and the magnetic flux density B. Magnetic field strength reflects the magnetic field generated by an electric current. For example, the magnetic field around a long wire carrying current i is described by the following equation.
>
> $$H = i/(2\pi r)$$
>
> Where r is the distance from the wire. However, the measured magnetic field also depends on the material it is in, and so the magnetic flux density includes the permeability µ of the material.
>
> $$B = \mu H = i\mu/(2\pi r)$$
>
> If the magnetic field is measured in a vacuum, then the permeability is the permeability of free space μ_o which is equal to $4\pi \times 10^{-7}$ H/m ~ 12.57×10^{-7} H/m. There are various units for B and H, some of which are listed below.
>
> ### Table 14.1. Units for H and B
>
> | H Units | B Units | Unit System |
> |---|---|---|
> | Amps per meter | Tesla | SI Units |
> | Oersteds | Gauss | CGS |
>
> Another unit that is used is the Weber, which is a measure of magnetic flux. The magnetic flux per square meter is the Tesla (1 T = 1 Wb/m²).
>
> To convert from SI to CGS units the following multipliers are used.
>
> **H:** 1 Oe = 79.58 A/m
> **B:** 1 Tesla = 10000 G
>
> Another unit that is sometimes used is the gamma, which is equivalent to a nanotesla (10^{-9} T) or as 10^{-5} gauss, thus 1 Tesla = 1,000,000,000 (or 10^9) γ (gamma), = 10,000 (or 10^4) G (*Gauss*)
>
> For comparison, the Earth's field ranges between approximately 25 and 65 µT (0.25–0.65 G). By comparison, a strong refrigerator magnet has a field of about 10 milliTeslas (100 G).[1]
>
> ---
> 1. "Earth's Magnetic Field," https://en.wikipedia.org/wiki/Earth%27s_magnetic_field, accessed December 31, 2022.

variation that came from general movement and other noise. If the dowsing effect was based on a static magnetic field, then changes in the magnetic field would need to be above the noise threshold. The conclusion therefore is that the dowsing effect does not appear to be caused by changes in the local static magnetic field, at least to the resolution of the iPhone magnetometer (< 1 µT).

The response of humans to weak changes in magnetic field has been described as the dowser's reflex, and Rocard reported that the dowsing response was triggered when someone passes through a changing magnetic field of at least 0.01 µT/s.[293] Not everyone's tests were successful. Foulkes attempted to replicate Rocard's work with artificial magnetic fields.[294] A single dowser, after a short series of learning trials in which he knew whether the current was on or off, was tested with three runs of 25 trials with no indication given to the dowser whether the current was on or off. Only chance results were obtained. Balanovski and Taylor tested dowsers' sensitivities to magnetic fields of around 100 gauss (0.01 T) and saw no response.[295] Whitton and Cook also attempted to determine whether subjects could detect the presence of weak magnetic fields. In the first test, 27 individuals, including two self-reported dowsers, were asked to determine whether an alternating current was flowing through a coil similar to Rocard's. Each person was allowed a preliminary learning trial conducted without the use of dowsing instruments, although the subjects were allowed to move around. They simply stated verbally whether the current was on or off. Only chance results were obtained. In a second experiment, eleven subjects, none of them professional dowsers, were asked to determine whether current was flowing through the coil of wire when it was placed in a known horizontal position beneath the floor of the room. In this case direct current was used. The subjects were given L-rods to use. Again, based on verbal reports from the subjects, only chance results were obtained.[296]

It is interesting that some researchers like Rocard and Harvalik found that dowsers respond to very low-intensity magnetic fields, whereas others found no effect. The fact that some people responded to very low level magnetic fields in both Harvalik's and Rocard's experiments suggests that we humans are able to detect magnetic fields, though some people can obviously detect them better than others. This person-to-person difference is typical with most physical activities. Track athletes these days routinely run a mile in less than four minutes, but I know that I never shall. There may also be important, if subtle, differences in the way the tests were conducted.

Dowsers can find PVC pipes in the ground, graves, underground streams and other objects which will not have an appreciable effect on the local magnetic field. In addition, as discussed previously the dowsing signal is blocked by aluminum foil, which is not expected to have any effect on a static magnetic field. Therefore, it seems likely that while the sensitivity to low magnetic fields is related to the dowsing effect, magnetic fields are not the primary physical basis for dowsing.

Effect of Geomagnetic Field on Water

Dowsing is best known for finding water, and many suggestions have been made that underground water can somehow affect the local magnetic field, and this change in the magnetic field is sensed by the dowser. Rocard spent some time looking at this question and based on his observations estimated the energy of interaction between a water molecule and the geomagnetic field and found the energy to be very small compared to the energy associated with thermal motion,[297] and so the interaction will be lost in the noise and be insignificant.

Chadwick and Jensen argued that the magnetic permeability of water will cause a disturbance in the magnetic field, and even estimated the impact of water on the local magnetic field.[298] However the magnetic permeability of water is not very different from that of many common rocks, as shown in Table 14.2 below, with the exception of those materials which are known to be magnetic (i.e., the iron and the magnetite).

> **Molecular Energy**
>
> A single gas atom can move in any of three dimensions, and so it is said to have three degrees of freedom. From the theory of ideal gases, the motion of gas molecules can be described, and the energy of motion is found to be proportional to the absolute temperature (in Kelvin). As atoms and molecules get hotter, they move more vigorously, and the temperature can be viewed as the average microscopic random kinetic energy in a system. Theoretical models predict that the energy of each degree of freedom on average is equal to $½k_BT$, where k_B is a constant known as the Boltzmann constant (1.381×10^{-23} m² kg s⁻² K⁻¹) and T is the temperature in Kelvin (room temperature is about 70°F, 25°C, or 298 K). For a simple atomic gas, there are three degrees of freedom and so the average energy at temperature T is $3/2k_BT$. This energy is therefore the random energy of an ideal gas, and so any energy input less than this amount will not be noticeable above the random thermal movement. The theory becomes much more complex with more complicated molecules, which have internal vibrations and so more degrees of freedom. However, the Boltzmann limit is often used to determine if an energy change is significant. Since Rocard found that the interaction of a water molecule and the Earth's magnetic field was less than k_BT, then any interaction would be negligible compared to random thermal movement.

Table 14.2. Magnetic Permeabilities of Some Common Materials[299]

Material	Magnetic Permeability (N.A⁻²)	Relative Permeability
Water	1.256627×10^{-6}	0.999992
Vacuum	$4\pi \times 10^{-7} \sim 1.25664 \times 10^{-6}$	1
Quartz	1.25662×10^{-6}	0.999985 to 0.999988
Calcite	1.25663×10^{-6}	0.999988 to 0.999994
Magnetite	7.36092×10^{-6}	2.5 to 16
Iron	0.25	200,000

For a 1 m wide aquifer of pure water surrounded by quartz or calcite, Chadwick and Jensen estimated that the magnetic flux density (B) at 10 m will be 99.5 percent of the field without the aquifer. This model assumed that the aquifer was pure water, but most aquifers are porous rock with water in the pore structure, in which case the difference would be much smaller. Since diamagnetic effects are usually smaller than paramagnetic effects and much smaller than ferro and ferri magnetic effects, this small effect of the water is unlikely to be significant. The authors also calculated the magnitude of some other EM effects, such as streaming potentials of flowing water, but found that all these effects were also too small to be significant.

Effect of Flowing Water on Local Magnetic Field

Many people have reported that they are more sensitive to flowing water than to static water, and one of the common proposals is that flowing water creates magnetic fields which the dowser then detects. Rocard observed that dowsers could not detect static water in ponds or flowing water in streams, but could detect water filtering through porous media, in permeable layers adjacent to beds of clay.

Note: In contrast to Rocard, I found the same response from moving and static water and found a strong dowsing response from flowing water in streams.

Rocard considered whether a dowser, a conductor (blood contains a lot of dissolved electrolytes[300]), walking in the terrestrial magnetic field will generate a potential across their body. He estimated the induced electromotive force in the chest of a dowser to be less than 1μV. This value is too small to be significant and so voltage induction is unlikely to the mechanism of detecting the dowsing signal.[301] Maby and Franklin also made a similar comment.[302] Furthermore, the dowsing response is the same walking forward or backward across a dowsing line, which is also contrary to the idea of dowsing being due to an induced EMF by moving in the Earth's magnetic field, since the EMF if generated would presumably change direction with the direction of motion.

Flowing water is a conductor moving through the Earth's magnetic field, and so there is the possibility of magnetohydrodynamic (MHD) effects[303] occurring. The fundamental concept behind MHD effects is that magnetic fields can induce a voltage and hence a current in the fluid, which creates its own magnetic field opposing the original one. Under this idea, flowing water modifies the local magnetic field, and this change would be the signal detected by dowsers. However, the Earth's magnetic field is very

---

Magnetic Induction

Magnetic induction is the basis for electrical generators, inductors and many electrical motors. Magnetic induction is described by Faraday's law, which states: *The electromotive force around a closed path is equal to the negative of the time rate of change of the magnetic flux enclosed by the path.*

If there is a loop of wire in a magnetic field with flux density B, then the magnetic flux Φ through the coil will be proportional to the flux density, the area of the coil (A) and the angle between them θ.

$$\Phi = AB\cos(\theta)$$

If the coil has n turns, each of area A moving, then the flux is given by

$$\Phi = nAB\cos(\theta)$$

The electromotive force (EMF) (V) is proportional to the rate of change of the magnetic flux Φ

$$V = d\Phi/dt$$

This EMF is produced perpendicular to the plane of the coil and the magnetic field, as described by the so-called left-hand induction rule. With the fingers of the left hand closed and the thumb sticking up in the direction of the changing magnetic field, then the current will flow in the direction formed by the fingers. An induced current will create its own magnetic field, and so this current must flow in a way that creates a magnetic field which opposes the applied magnetic field (Lenz's law). If the current went the other way, then the new field would build up the original field, which in turn would increase the current, the process would run out of control, and we would soon be violating the conservation of energy and mass law. If, instead of a wire coil, a flat sheet of metal is used, then currents will still be induced in it in similar manner. These currents are known as eddy currents.

small and so the movement of an underground stream is unlikely to produce enough current to make a significant difference to the local magnetic field.

EM Fields Caused by Flowing Water

One of the more commonly cited theories is that dowsers respond to the electrical current from underground water. Physics professor Philip Jennings of Perth's Murdoch University suggested that water could send out weak EM fields if it contained dissolved salts of chemicals such as sodium chloride or calcium carbonate.[304] There will be thermal emissions (see discussion of blackbody radiators later in the book), but these emissions do not depend on the water flowing rather than being stationary. Otherwise, there are no obvious sources of EM radiation from underground streams.

Permanent Magnets and Dowsing

To test whether static magnetic fields created a dowsing response, I obtained over 20 approximately 3 cm (1¼") diameter neodymium magnetic disks, each about 3mm (⅛" in) thick. These were first marked north or south (using a permanent marker and a compass needle) and then the magnets were laid out across the floor in a row about 5 cm (~ 2 in) apart. The distance was just enough that the magnets did not pull together. Before the test, the floor area was found to be free of dowsing signals. On walking towards the magnets (perpendicular to the row), there was a dowsing response over the magnets, suggesting that perhaps magnets do give a dowsing response.

Every other magnet was then turned over, so that along the line, the magnets were North, South, North, South, etc. This arrangement should completely change the magnetic field pattern and weaken the measured magnetic field away from the magnets. On testing, the same dowsing response was obtained with half of the magnets reversed. The conclusion is that dowsing rods are responding to the magnets, but not because of their magnetic field. The magnets were replaced by U.S. quarter dollar coins, as a simple non-magnetic metal disk and tested for their dowsing response.

Note: U.S. quarters have a diameter of 24.26 mm (0.955 in.), comprised of cupro-nickel 8.33 percent Ni, Balance Cu, mass 5.670g.[305]

   a.) The quarters were set up in a row, each touching in a straight row—moderate dowsing response.
   b.) Adding a second layer, touching the first—stronger signal
   c.) Adding a third layer—Strong signal
   d.) Back to single row—moderate response again
   e.) Removed every other quarter—weak response
   f.) Removed every other quarter (so only 1 in 4 left of the single row)—weaker response
   g.) Removed every other quarter (so only 1 in 8 left)—very weak response
   h.) One quarter—no significant response above baseline
   i.) No quarters—no significant response.

The conclusion is that metal disks on the floor in aggregate can cause the dowsing response, and the more there are, the stronger the dowsing signal. The response from the neodymium disk magnets therefore was not because they were magnetic, but because they were metal disks laid out on the floor. It should be noted that even though these neodymium magnets were strong magnets, the magnetic fields as measured by the iPhone magnetometer did not extend very far. Holding the iPhone above a magnet and lowering it slowly down, a deviation from background was only observed about 20 to 30 cm (8 to 12 in) away from the magnet.

Superconductivity as the Basis of the Dowsing Response

As has been already discussed there have been many possible mechanisms suggested as the physical basis behind the dowsing effect. One of the most unusual and creative suggestions was that the dowsing sense may arise from biological superconductive

---

Superconductors and Josephson Junctions

Electricity arises from the movement of electrical charge. Electrical charge is one of the fundamental properties of sub-atomic particles (positive, negative or neutral). Opposites attract and similars repel, so an electron with a negative charge will be attracted to a positive ion or electrode and repelled by a negative ion or electrode. Metals are generally electrically conductive, and the resistance decreases as the temperature drops.

[Note: Resistance = 1/conductance, so the conductance of metals increases as the temperature decreases.]

For some metals at very low temperature, it was found that the resistance suddenly dropped to zero below a critical temperature (T_c) that depended on the material. With zero resistance the metal becomes a superconductor, earning the discoverer, Heike Kamerlingh Onnes, the Nobel Prize for physics in 1913.[1] For mercury, T_c is 4K, (−452°F) and for most metals that show superconductivity, the critical temperatures are near absolute zero (0K).

Superconductors have many interesting properties, not the least of which is that once a current starts flowing, it continues, since there is no electrical resistance to impede it. Superconductors will repel magnets, and if two superconductors are separated by a very thin insulating junction, the electrons from one superconductor will quantum mechanically tunnel across the junction to the other, forming a so-called Josephson junction.[2] These Josephson junctions have useful applications, especially as very sensitive detectors for electrical currents and magnetic fields.

Some people have speculated that the brain operates using superconductivity in its operation.[3] This theory has some modeling, but very little physical evidence behind it. Some of the limited evidence comes from Mikheenko, including experiments using pig brains treated with graphene (a form of carbon).[4] Nerves function using chemical potentials related to ion concentrations inside versus outside cells, and there is little if any electrical conduction. The graphs presented by Mikheenko et al which they interpreted as the apparent onset of superconductivity in the pig brains look to me more like the onset of some redox process, of which there are many in the brain, and such processes are fairly well understood. Another theory is that biological superconductivity is the mechanism of nonthermal effects of microwaves,[5] but there is also similarly limited evidence to support this theory too.

---

1. "Heike Kamerlingh Onnes, Biographical," https://www.nobelprize.org/prizes/physics/1913/onnes/biographical/, accessed September 25, 2020.

2. Richard Newrock, "What Are Josephson Junctions? How Do They Work?" *Scientific American*, November 24, 1997, https://www.scientificamerican.com/article/what-are-josephson-juncti/.

3. E.H. Halpern and A.A. Wolf, "Speculations of Superconductivity in Biological and Organic Systems," in *Advances in Cryogenic Engineering* vol. 17, K.D. Timmerhaus, ed. (Springer, 1972), https://link.springer.com/chapter/10.1007/978-1-4684-7826-6_11.

4. P. Mikheenko, "Possible Superconductivity In Brain," *J Supercond Nov Magn* 32 (December 13, 2018), 1121–1134, https://arxiv.org/ftp/arxiv/papers/1812/1812.05602.pdf, accessed August 31, 2020.

5. Freeman W. Cope, "Superconductivity—A Possible Mechanism for Non-Thermal Biological Effects of Microwaves," *Journal of Microwave Power* 11, no. 3 (1976), 267–269, https://www.tandfonline.com/doi/abs/10.1080/00222739.1976.11689004.

Josephson junctions.[306] However, to date there is no experimental evidence to support the existence of biological Josephson junctions and so Josephson junctions seem a very unlikely explanation for the dowsing effect. Josephson junctions are only formed with superconductors at very low temperatures (< –100°C, –150°F).

Changing Magnetic Fields

When it comes to magnetic induction, the relative movement of a conductor with respect to the magnetic field is important. It does not matter if the conductor moves in a stationary magnetic field, or if the magnetic field changes around a static conductor. It is well known that changing-intensity magnetic fields can have a physiological effect, and so the open question is whether changing-intensity magnetic fields could be the mechanism behind dowsing. For high magnetic field strengths, if the magnitude of the change is large enough, then currents can be induced in the body and in the nerves, causing peripheral nerve stimulation. For example, many people have noticed tingling near high-voltage power lines.[307]

The effect is more than perceptive. For example, Kholodov found that applying/removing static magnetic fields in the range of 1 to 800 Oe (0.01 to 0.01 to 8 Tesla) to a neuronally isolated strip of cerebral cortex in a non-anesthetized rabbit increased the amplitude of the EEG potentials coming from it.[308] These field strengths are obviously many orders of magnitude greater than the terrestrial magnetic field but they do indicate that mammalian brains do respond to changes in high-strength magnetic fields.

Medical scans such as MRI also use strong magnetic fields, and in rare cases tingling, muscle twitching, or painful sensations may also sometimes occur during scanning.[309] The Duke-UNC Brain Imaging and Analysis Center advises patients not to clasp their hands together during scanning, since doing so can cause a conductive loop that may worsen the effects experienced from the changing magnetic field. The magnets used for MRI imaging are very strong and though they are normally operated with a static field, there is a varying field as the field turns on, 40 mT/min over about 0.1 ms. Currents induced in the body can cause peripheral nerve or muscle stimulation, which may result in a slight tingling sensation or a brief muscle twitch. At higher rates of magnetic field change this sensation may escalate to unpleasant or painful experiences.[310] The FDA guidance[311] sets the maximum rate of magnetic field change at 20 T/s, i.e., much greater than is typical for an MRI machine,[312] ~ 0.7 mT/s. The changing magnetic fields used in MRI applications are an extreme condition that is orders of magnitude greater than anything normally encountered in everyday life.

Much lower changing magnetic fields can also have an influence on the body. Transcranial magnetic stimulation (TMS) is a method that is used to actively stimulate neurons. A TMS coil is placed over a region of interest on the skull. When a changing current flows through the coil, a changing EM field is created which induces an electric field in the brain that can stimulate cortical neurons. The effects of TMS are often measured by behavioral observation, for example, involuntary, brief movement of the hand following stimulation over the motor cortex. Commercial magnetic stimulators use coils with an outer diameter of 50–150 mm and produce magnetic fields of 1–2.5 Tesla with a field rise time of 50–200 μsec. Despite its having been used for many years, the mechanistic details of how TMS stimulates neurons is still being worked out.[313] However, this method does demonstrate that varying magnetic fields can stimulate neurons and cause muscle movements if the appropriate part of the brain is stimulated, though the changing magnetic fields are orders of magnitude higher than those expected in dowsing.

Many people have studied the effect of alternating signal on the human body over the last hundred years or so in relation to dowsing. Maby, for example, examined the relationship between dowsing and alternating EM fields.[314] Maby found during some tests that a sensitive dowser could tell using his rods when strong AC electromagnets were turned on or off with almost 100 percent success. Maby also found that the dowser's muscles were significantly stronger than normal when oriented parallel to the magnetic field but weaker when oriented perpendicular to the magnetic field. Moving the electromagnet closer to the dowser's pectoral, forearm, and biceps muscles saw the dowsing response increase, but there was no effect when the electromagnet was moved near the dowser's leg muscles. Maby wrote, "So that it may safely be concluded that *normal dowsing reactions are not due to a generalized conscious or unconscious sensitivity of the nervous system, but are purely reflex, and due to direct electrical excitation of such neuro-muscular groups as control the chosen indicators and reaction-meters*" (emphasis in original).

Maby also found that wrapping an insulated lead from a high-voltage induction coil around the arm caused weakness and a dowsing response. In contrast, Tromp[315] reported that alternating currents of high frequency (100,000–1,000,000 Hz) did not cause any physiological stimulation even with the highest current intensity. The difference is probably due to differences in experimental details, such as the power, frequency and method of exposure. If Maby's power source to the induction coil was utility mains power, then the frequency was 50 Hz, well below the minimum frequency that Tromp was using.

There has not been much work on the effects of alternating magnetic fields on dowsing responses. The effect of EM radiation on the body varies greatly with frequency and this is discussed later in the book. In summary, many people have found that dowsers respond to changes in magnetic fields over distance, but not the rate of change. This result has important implications in understanding how the magnetic sense operates in humans. While very low magnetic fields were detected by some dowsers, others gave no response to much larger fields. The dowsing signal itself does not appear to be due to changes in the local magnetic field, but it appears that the dowsing response is somehow related to the magnetic field sense.

15

Electromagnetic Fields and Dowsing

Nothing is too wonderful to be true, if it be consistent with the laws of nature.

—Michael Faraday[316]

Chapter summary: Earlier chapters have shown that the dowsing signal is electromagnetic and in this chapter the evidence is presented showing that the dowsing signal is microwave radiation in the low GHz frequency range and that a dowsing response can be obtained using a microwave signal generator.

EM radiation and fields are one of the most commonly discussed causes of the dowsing signal, but the discussions tend to be rather thin on the mechanistic details. The evidence is reviewed in this chapter.

EM Radiation in Dowsing Overview

EM radiation occurs all around us from both human and natural sources. It is known that exposure to very high-intensity EM radiation across the spectrum can have adverse effects, but the debate is to what extent low-intensity EM radiation can have an adverse effect. In 1996 the World Health Organization (WHO) launched a large, multidisciplinary research effort to try to answer this question, along with many other researchers. In the last 30 years approximately 25,000 articles have been published concerning the biological effects and medical applications of non-ionizing radiation . Based on this literature, the WHO concluded, "Current evidence does not confirm the existence of any health consequences from exposure to low level EM fields. However, some gaps in knowledge about biological effects exist and need further research."[317]

As discussed earlier, EM radiation spans from low energy, long wavelength radio waves to microwaves, infrared, visible, ultraviolet, x-rays and high energy, short wavelength gamma rays. Of these only ultraviolet, x-rays and gamma rays have enough energy per photon to ionize (kick out an electron from) molecules or atoms. If these molecules are part of a biological system, and they are exposed to UV light, then this ionization can lead to a range of issues (e.g., UV exposure can cause sunburn).

As discussed earlier, we can narrow down the part of the EM spectrum which is relevant to dowsing. From simple experiments we know that aluminum foil can block the dowsing signal, but cardboard is transparent to it. Radio waves and microwaves can pass through cardboard, but infrared, visible, and UV do not. X-rays are only formed under high energy processes (sparks, lightning, or x-ray guns in medical x-ray machines), so they are unlikely to be relevant to dowsing. Similarly, gamma rays are generally associated with radioactive decay and are occasionally formed in lightning storms, but otherwise are not commonly found at sufficiently high concentration to carry dowsing information (see earlier chapter on radioactivity). That leaves radio waves and microwaves, which are EM radiation in the frequency ranges 3 kilohertz (RHz)–300 Megahertz (MHz), and 300 MHz–300 gigahertz (GHz), respectively.[318]

Several researchers have examined the effect of radio wave and microwave radiation on dowsers. Harvalik et al. found that one very sensitive dowser (Mr. De Boer) responded to radio waves between 1 Hz and 1 MHz, with no strong frequency dependence, as discussed above.[319] While most people do not have this sensitivity, the fact that one dowser does suggests that EM radiation might be behind the dowsing effect. The lack of frequency dependence is surprising. The wavelength for EM radiation at 1 MHz is 30 m, so much larger than the dimensions of the dowser, and of course the wavelength at 1 Hz is a million times larger. Therefore, the detection of the radiation is probably not based on a resonance effect.

Taylor and Balanovski also tested a number of people, including dowsers, for sensitivity to high-frequency, low power level EM fields. The subjects sat close to an antenna while the power was randomly switched on or off. Between 10 and 60 trials per subject were conducted but the subjects were unable to tell whether the power was on or off.[320] The differences between the results may have arisen because of differences in experiment design and because Taylor and Balanoyvski did not have the remarkable Mr. De Boer in their lab.

Dowsing Response to Microwaves

I found that when I placed my iPhone on the ground with Wi-Fi, cellular and Bluetooth turned off, there was a weak dowsing response on walking directly over it, presumably because of all the metal components inside. However, when the Wi-Fi was turned on, there was a strong dowsing response. Similarly, when the iPhone was used to call a telephone number, there was also a strong dowsing response. My cellular provider is Verizon Wireless, which operates at 2.4 GHz,[321] so the dowsing response is triggered by 2.4 GHz radiation (12.5 cm wavelength). The Wi-Fi in the iPhone[322] meets the IEEE 802.11ac standards, which use 2.4 GHz and 5 GHz. My router uses both, and the same dowsing response was obtained with the 2.4 GHz channel and the 5 GHz channel. These results show that 2.4 and 5 GHz signals can trigger the dowsing response. Even though the Wi-Fi and cellular signals are modulated, it is unlikely that the modulation is relevant to the dowsing signal. Signal amplitude is probably more important.

A series of tests were performed to determine if microwaves could produce a dowsing response and determine the characteristics of this response. These tests involved a microwave signal generator, various antennas and a microwave power meter.

Characterization of the Signal Generator

Microwaves were generated as a continuous stream, without modulation using a Gigatronics model 900 signal generator. The output power of the signal generator with zero attenuation was approximately 1 mW over the frequency range 0.5 to 12.5 GHz. Lower power signals were obtained using the built-in attenuation function on the signal generator (0 to −99 dB) and/or an Agilent 30 dB attenuator (model 11708A). Microwave power was measured using a HP 473B power meter, with HP 8481D power sensor.

Characterization of the Antennas

The antennas used were 8.5 cm monopole antennas, 10W 1.4-20.5 GHz UWB antenna from Oumefar (Shenzhen, China), model Oumefarr9dvzky7cu and log-periodic antennas from Kent Electronics, model WA5VJB. The Oumefar and log-periodic antennas were fabricated with active elements on a printed circuit board. Except where stated otherwise, the results presented are for the Oumefar antenna, though similar results were also obtained for the log-periodic antenna.

The first step was to characterize the antennas by measuring the transmission of microwaves between two identical antennas 30 cm apart over frequency. The monopole antennas were mounted vertically (see Figure 15.1), and the other two were mounted in the same plane and facing tip to tip.

Cardboard is essentially transparent to microwaves and if the cardboard did absorb any, it would only be power radiated away and not headed to the other antenna. The power transmitted between two monopole antennas as a function of frequency is shown in Figure 15.2. A similar graph for a pair of Oumefar (solid line) and the log-periodic (dashed line) antennas is shown in Figure 15.3.

Log-periodic antennas are commonly used where a wide frequency response is needed, but the Oumefar antenna not only had a wider frequency response, but also much greater power transmission. Using pairs of antenna makes the analysis easier than using different antenna, since with the latter any peaks or valleys could

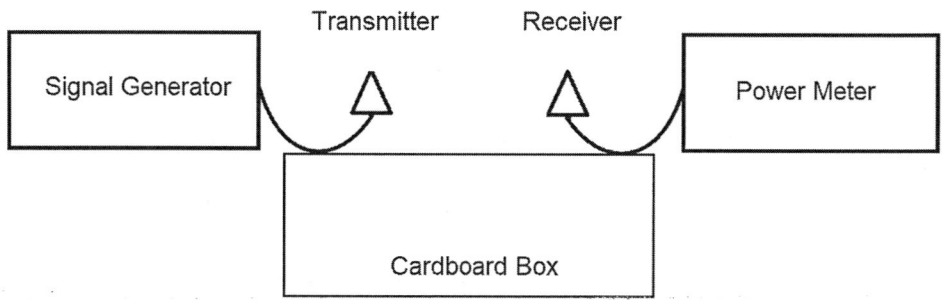

Figure 15.1. Set-up to measure frequency dependence of identical antennas, mounted 30 cm apart on a cardboard box, one antenna connected to the signal generator and the other to the power meter.

15. Electromagnetic Fields and Dowsing

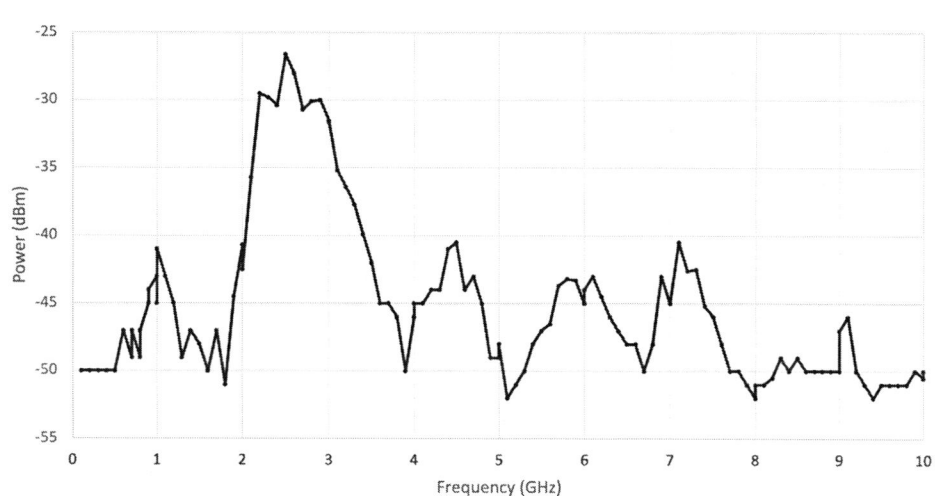

Figure 15.2. Characterization of two 8.5 cm monopole antennas, one as transmitter, the other as receiver.

be due to either the transmitter or antenna. The power transmitted depends on both the ability of the antenna to transmit the radiation, and the ability to receive it. The theory of reciprocity in antenna theory equates the two parameters, and so looking at the transmit/receive pair gives a direct measure of the antenna behavior (see Figure 15.1).

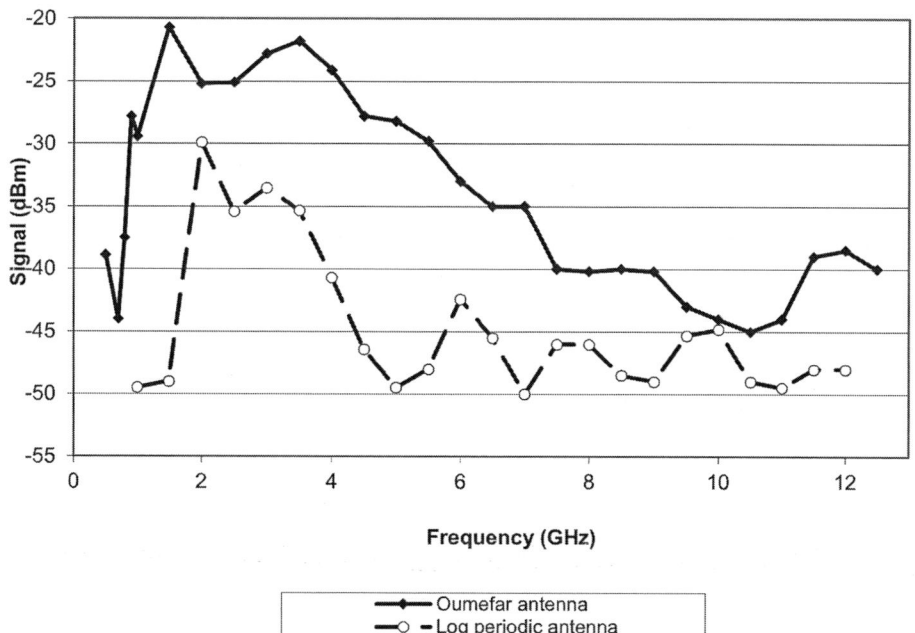

Figure 15.3. Frequency dependence of power between pairs of antennas.

The effect of antenna separation was also determined as shown in Figure 15.4A and B. As expected, the greater the distance between the antennas, the lower the power, and a plot of power (mW) versus 1/distance was a straight line passing through the origin.

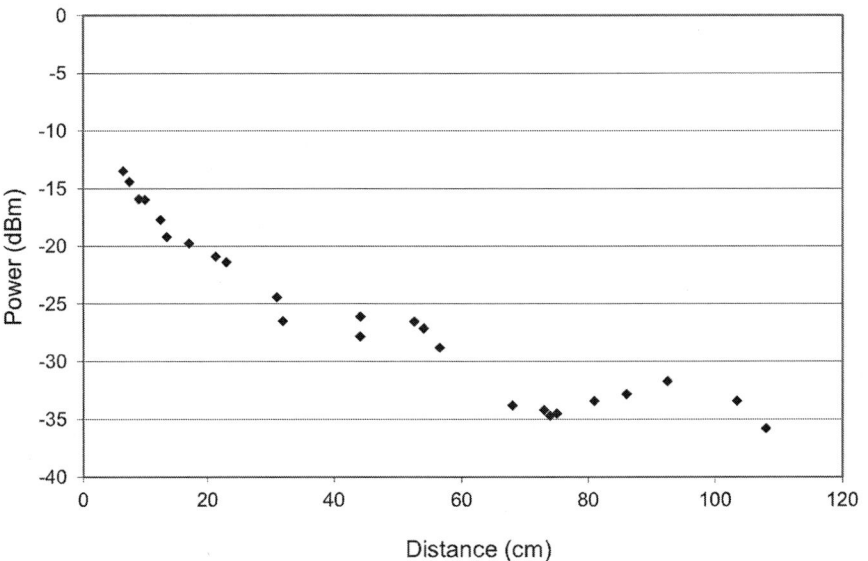

Figures 15.4A (above) and 15.4B (below). Graphs showing the effect of power (dBm) with distance for the Oumefar antenna (A) and the power (mW) plotted against inverse distance (B).

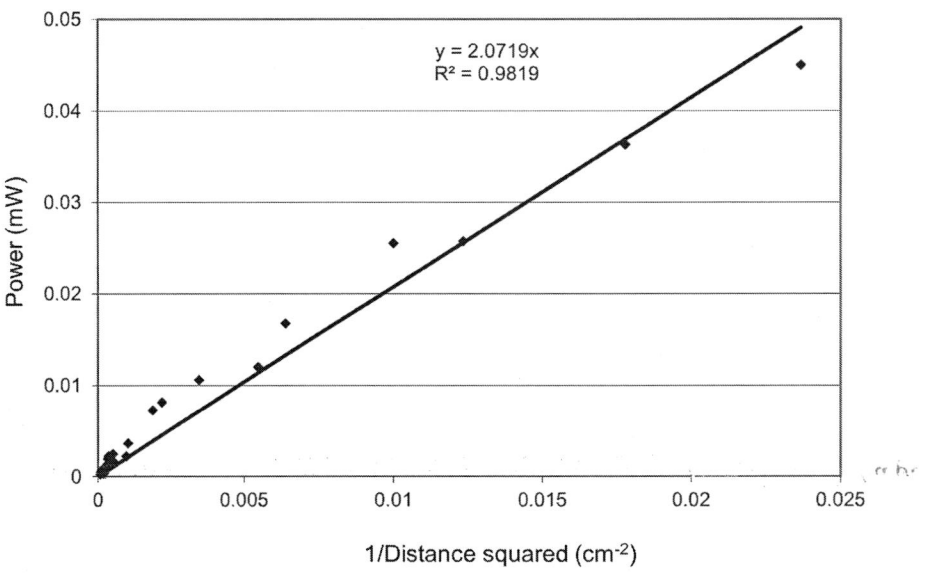

15. Electromagnetic Fields and Dowsing

The angular dependence was also measured, using the same apparatus, but rotating the receiving antenna at fixed distance to the transmitted, such that the receiver is always pointing at the transmitter. The results are shown in Figure 15.5.

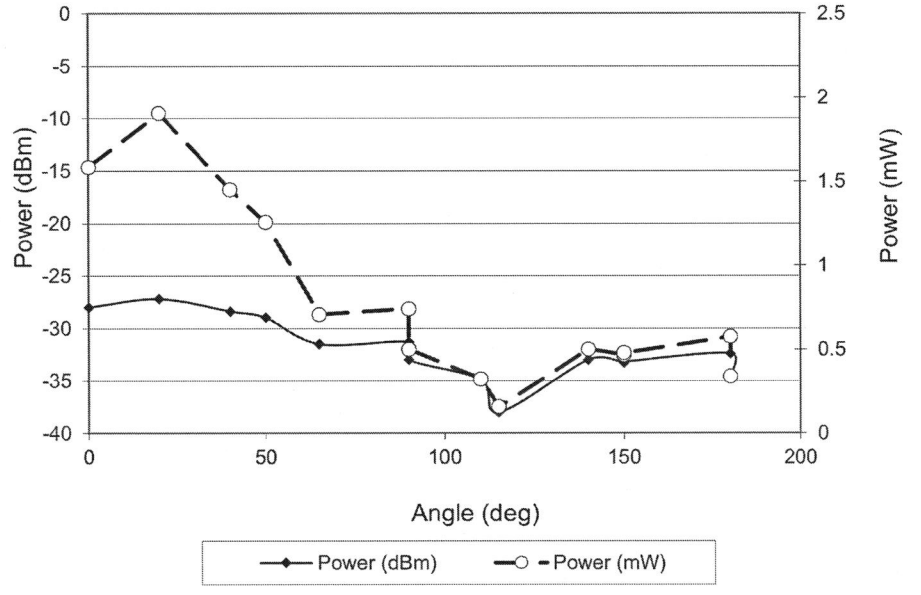

Figure 15.5. Effect of angle on power between two Oumefar antennas, 30 cm apart.

It may be seen that the log-periodic antennas showed a strong angular dependence, whereas the angular dependence of the Oumefar antennas was much less.

The following section of the book describes some experiments that gave unexpected results and which are somewhat complex. However, it is an important section for understanding dowsing and how it works. The data is presented below, warts and all, and I hope it encourages others to repeat these experiments and test the ideas presented.

To measure the dowsing response from the microwaves, the signal generator was connected to an antenna, with the antenna placed on the floor pointed vertically up. The antenna was comprised of planar traces on a flat circuit board, and so the emitted radiation was polarized, and polarization was easily apparent based on the orientation of the plane of the antenna's circuit board. The tip of the antenna was about 10 cm off the floor so that one could easily step over it while holding dowsing rods, as shown in Figure 15.6.

The response was measured using dowsing rods balanced to straight forward about a meter away from the antenna, and then I walked forward, directly over the antenna, and noted the response, if any, from the rods. On stepping away, the frequency would be changed to the next value, and the test repeated. The test was performed with the plane of the antenna parallel to the direction of walking as well as perpendicular to the direction of walking. The power to the antenna was changed by changing the attenuation using the attenuation function built into the signal generator. The extent of the response

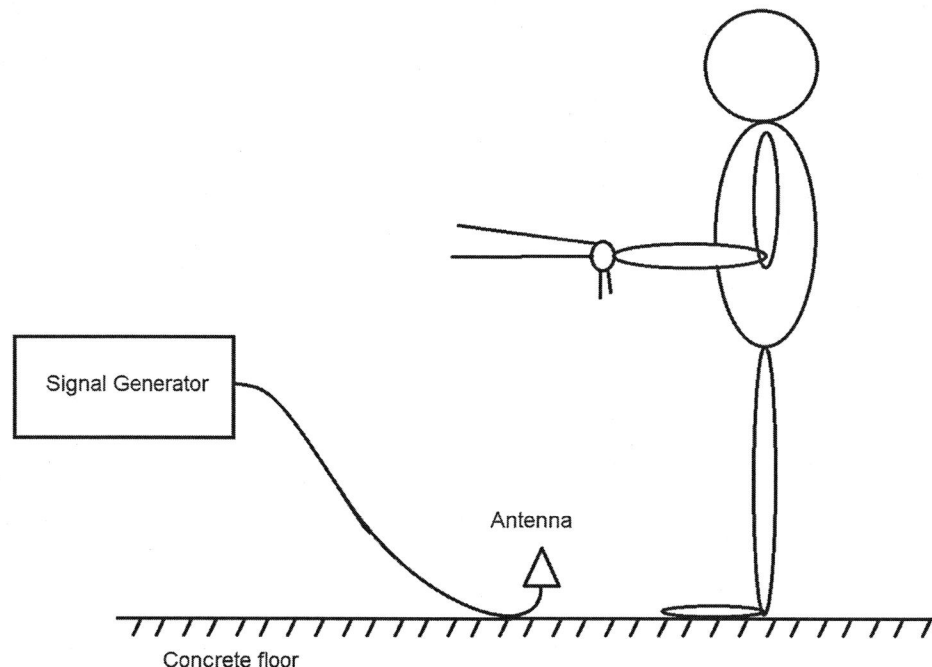

Figure 15.6. Measuring dowsing response to microwaves.

judged by how much the rods crossed and the angle was estimated by eye (those geometry classes in school are at last paying off). Zero indicates the rods are straight ahead and 90 degrees indicates the rods are completely crossed. Since the angle was estimated by eye, the accuracy of the angle measurement is no better than ten degrees.

Walking over the antenna holding the rods with the signal generator power off gave no response. The dowsing response to various frequencies between 0.5 and 12.5 GHz was measured with the plane of the antenna parallel to the direction of walking over the antenna, with no signal generator attenuation. When the signal generator was on at certain frequencies, the rods crossed and subjectively, the response to the microwaves felt similar to a normal dowsing response, a slight involuntary tensing of the muscles in the back and shoulders. The results using a log-periodic antenna are shown in Figure 15.7. Superimposed on this graph is the power transmission curve for this antenna. There does not appear to be much correlation between the dowsing response and the power output of the antenna.

The same experiment was repeated but with the plane of the antenna perpendicular to the direction of walking. The frequency dependence of walking parallel to the plane of the antenna compared to walking over the antenna perpendicular to its place is shown in Figure 15.8. Not only do the dowsing responses not appear to be related to the power transmission and reception properties of the antennas, but the parallel and perpendicular curves are different too.

These results, however, are not as simple as they appear because while there were strong responses at various bands in the spectrum, the response faded away in a short time until there was no response to the microwaves. When the direction was changed,

15. Electromagnetic Fields and Dowsing

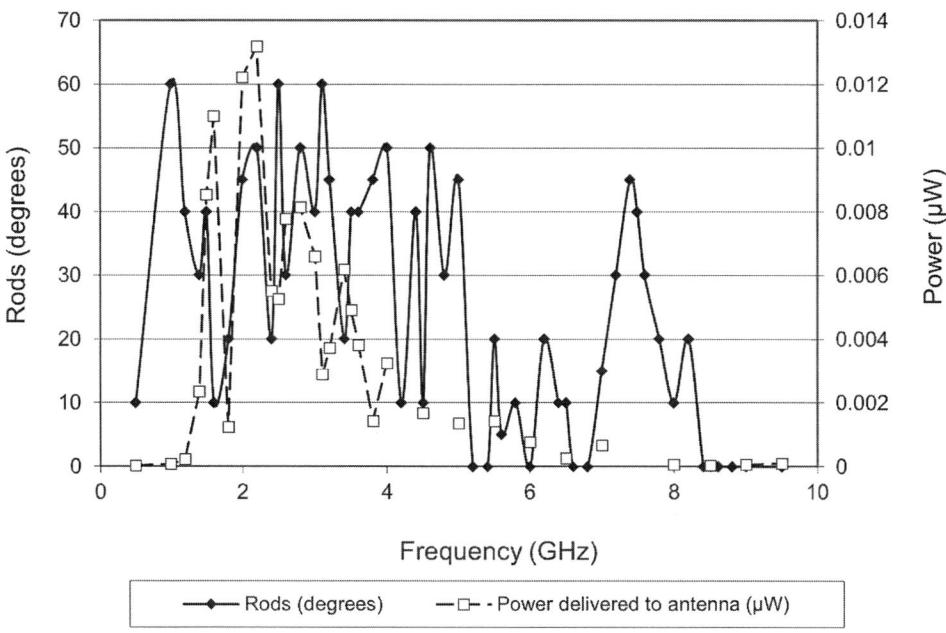

Figure 15.7. Dowsing response to microwaves with antenna parallel to the direction of walking, attenuation = –99 dB.

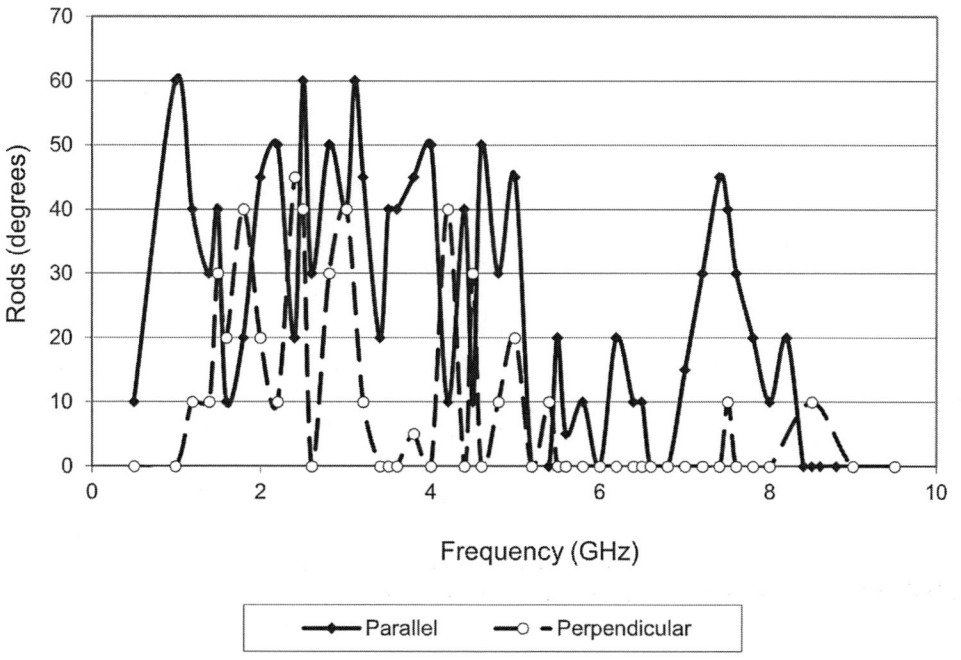

Figure 15.8. Dowsing response to microwaves with antenna plane parallel or perpendicular to direction of walking, -99 dB attenuation (see caution below).

to walking over the antenna perpendicular to the plane of the antenna, the dowsing response came back, but also soon faded to zero. The test area was the basement of my house, with a concrete floor at ground level, with no lower floor.

In one location under the concrete there is the dowsing line from the PVC sewer line. It was found that after the dowsing response had faded after exposure to microwaves with the plane of the antenna parallel to the direction of walking, there was no longer a dowsing response to the sewer line. However, the dowsing response over the sewer was close to normal after exposure to the microwaves with the plane of the antenna perpendicular to the direction of walking to the extent that there was no further response to the microwaves. Furthermore, after exposure to the microwaves parallel to the direction of walking such that the response to both the microwaves and the dowsing signal has been suppressed, walking over the sewer pipe sideways gave a dowsing signal. These results indicate that the dowsing response to the sewer pipe is polarized and furthermore that the physiological detector of microwaves and dowsing is also polarized, and the "detector" can detect both polarizations separately.

The signal generator output from the signal generator was attenuated by ~-129 dB (-99 dB internal and -30 dB external) and there was still a dowsing response. Prolonged exposure caused the dowsing response to fade away, even at this very low power. Reducing the attenuation (i.e., increasing the microwaves' signal strength) brought back the dowsing response to the microwaves for a short time until the signal again faded away. This process could be repeated several times, each time reducing the attenuation until there was no attenuation (max power ~ 1 mW delivered to the antenna). The dowsing response thus occurs in a remarkably wide power range of -129 dB, and perhaps the fading response corresponds to saturation of the "detector." This wide range can be compared, for example, to hearing, which ranges from 20 µPa (defined as 0 dB), the hearing threshold for a young healthy individual, to the pain threshold at 20 Pa, or a range of ~120 dB for the frequency range of 3–4 kHz.[323]

This fading effect from microwave exposure was studied at 2.4, 3, 5 and 11 GHz on different days, and the response faded quicker at higher frequency than at low. For example, in a test at 2.4 GHz, with attenuation of -129 dB, for repeated 30s exposures, there was no loss in signal for the first two exposures, then over the next two exposures the response decreased, until there was no response. At 11.5 GHz, the response starts to fade within a few seconds of exposure.

Physiological effects at 2.4 GHz are of concern because this frequency is commonly used for Wi-Fi, Bluetooth, cellular and other communications. So far, apart from losing the ability to dowse after exposure to the microwaves, no other effects have been observed. The ability to dowse returns over several hours; for example, after the test at 2.4 GHz, there was no improvement for the first hour, but the response steadily improved after that, returning to normal after about four hours.

Since the response to microwaves fades over time, the frequency dependence of the microwave response, shown in Figure 15.9, was collected over many days, to allow the dowsing response to recover between measurements. The response was measured at a reference value (e.g., 7 GHz), then at several other frequencies, then at the reference value. If the reference value was the same, then the responses at the other frequencies were included; otherwise, they were not. At the low end of the spectrum about 6 to 9 measurements could be performed, but at around 11 to 12 GHz, only a single measurement could be taken between reference measurements before waiting another 10 to 12 hours recovery time before the next attempt. It is clear that the dowsing response to microwaves occurs over the entire spectral range tested and the line of best fit is almost horizontal. The standard deviation for these measurements is 12 degrees/GHz, so there is quite a lot of scatter.

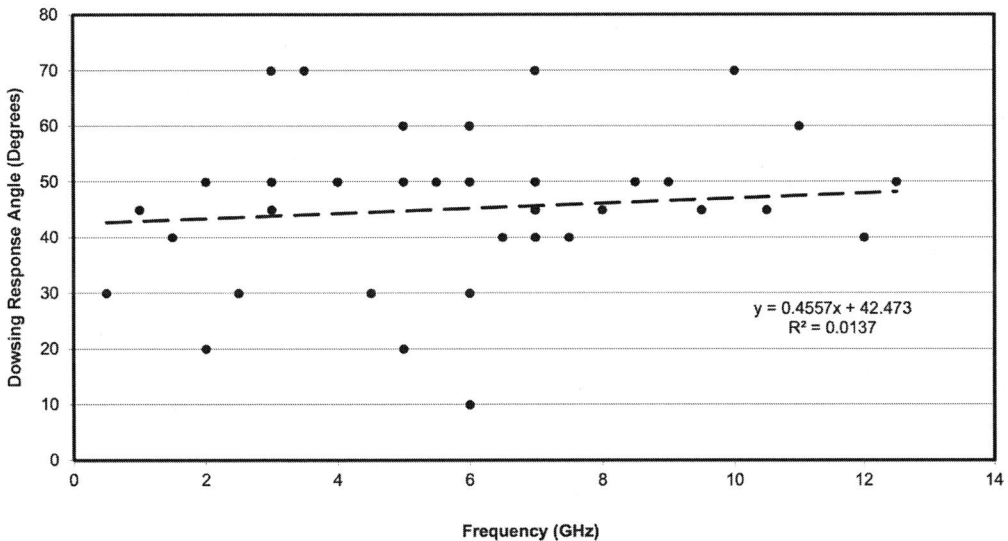

Figure 15.9. Dowsing response to microwaves as a function of frequency.

The microwave power over this frequency range varies with the efficiency of the antenna, but since the dowsing method has such a wide dynamic range, it does not appear to make a large difference under these test conditions. Since the dowsing response to the microwaves occurs over such a large dynamic range, it is likely that exposure to steady state will produce a similar responses with the rods, even if short-term measurements show more peaks and valleys, as described above. Therefore, the results in Figures 15.7 and 15.8 should be viewed with caution. These results were obtained by rapidly stepping up the frequency in one run, and some of the peaks may be lower intensity because the fading has already occurred, whereas the data in Figure 15.9 was collected over about a week.

The detection limit for the dowsing response to microwaves was determined using the log-periodic antenna, which had a lower output than the Oumefar antenna (see Figure 15.3). The minimum microwave power needed to get a response was determined by setting the attenuation at 3 GHz to its maximum (−99 dBm), at which there was no response, and then reducing the attenuation until there was a response. The first response was around -90 dBm, which corresponds to a power of about 1 pW being delivered to the antenna. The results presented here show that there are interactions with microwaves that do have a physiological effect at much lower levels than previously discussed. While no adverse effects are apparent, other than temporarily losing the ability to dowse, future research may reveal more subtle adverse effects. Dowsing rods, as used herein, provide a means to detect the interaction with microwaves at powers much lower than normally perceptible. It is unclear what the mechanism of the fading is, but it is reminiscent of olfactory fatigue, whereby we lose our sense of smell after prolonged exposure. Some gases, such as hydrogen sulphide, are notorious for having very low olfactory detection limits, but this sense of smell fades quickly as the concentration of hydrogen sulphide increases.[324] Perhaps there are a range of "detectors" that operate over different intensities, higher-intensity detectors requiring a higher intensity microwave to knock them out.

The dowsing sense organ is reported to be located near the base of the brain.[325] The dowsing response to the microwaves occurs when the antenna is just in front of one's feet, by about 15 to 20 cm. This suggests that the microwave may be passing in front of the torso. I folded some aluminum foil so that it fit under my chin, covering the chin, neck and chest down to the top of the sternum, and slightly wider than the head width. The following three-step test was used:

   i. Measure the response the microwaves with the L-rods with an attenuation of –129 dB and the Oumefar antenna.
   ii. Repeat with the foil in place and
   iii. Repeat again without the foil.

Exposure times were kept to a minimum to reduce the loss of sensitivity. This test was done at 3, 7 and 11 GHz, and in all cases there was a strong response (rod angle > 40 degrees) to the microwaves, no response with the foil in place and a strong response once the foil was removed. This result confirms that the microwave detector location is in the head, consistent with the prior reports for the dowsing detector. The same test was performed while dowsing over the sewer line and similar results were obtained, ~ 50 degrees change in rod position before and after without the foil, and zero response with the foil in place. This result confirms that the dowsing sense organ is in the head and provides additional support for the theory that the dowsing signal from underground objects is due to microwave radiation and that the physiological detector for the dowsing signal is the same detector that is responding to microwaves.

One of the more remarkable aspects of the dowsing physiological response is the high degree of collimation of the detection process. The Oumefar antenna has a wide angle of radiance, as is shown in Figure 15.5. This graph shows that while the antenna radiates with a higher intensity along its primary axis, there is still significant radiation at all angles. The difference from maximum to minimum was only 5.2 dB or 3.3 times. Yet, when walking forward with the dowsing rods from about a meter away, the rods only started to move about 15 cm away from the antenna (measured from toes to antenna). If the dowsing sense organ is in the lower brain, or about 1.5 meters higher than the end of the antenna, and these two dimensions can be considered as the adjacent and hypotenuse of a right angled triangle, then the angle is ~5.7° or 0.10 radians. This angle for detecting microwaves is analogous to the angle used for dowsing, which is discussed in more detail later in the book. For now, the key point in that this angle is yet another indicator that the dowsing signal from underground objects is low GHz microwave radiation.

15. Electromagnetic Fields and Dowsing

The work described in this chapter has demonstrated that

- Humans are sensitive, at least at a subconscious level, to microwaves in the low GHz range, detected using basic L-shape dowsing rods.
- The microwave energy levels where this effect is first observed are orders of magnitude below the current microwave exposure limits, which are largely based on thermal effects; the U.S.-FCC's specific absorption rate limit for devices operating in close proximity to the body is 1.6 W/kg.[326]
- As discussed above, exposure to microwaves gives a dowsing response, but continued exposure weakens the response until it eventually reaches zero; increasing the exposure power can temporarily restore the response.
- The response to microwaves subjectively feels the same as a dowsing response.
- The response to microwaves occurs over a narrow angle, the same angle, within the margin of error calculated from dowsing responses.
- Metal foil covering the chin and neck blocks the dowsing response to microwaves and the dowsing response to an underground pipe.
- Prolonged exposure to microwaves with the antenna parallel to the direction of walking lessens/blocks the response to microwaves and the dowsing response to an underground pipe on walking forward, but not sideways.
- Prolonged exposure to microwaves with the antenna perpendicular to the direction of walking lessens/blocks the response to microwaves and the dowsing response to an underground pipe on walking sideways, but not walking forward.

In sum, these observations provide convincing evidence that the dowsing signal from underground objects is due to microwave radiation.

16

Dowsing Frequency Band

If you want to find the secrets of the universe, think in terms of energy, frequency and vibration.
—Nikola Tesla

Chapter summary: We have seen that the dowsing signal is in the microwave, and various techniques have been used to measure the frequency of the signal. These techniques show that the dowsing signal is in the 1 to 10 GHz range.

As discussed earlier in this book, many people have suggested that the dowsing is EM in nature, and further experiments have shown that the dowsing signal is in the microwave region of the spectrum. The goal of this chapter is to provide a better estimate of the frequency range of the dowsing response using a wide range of methods; some just general inferences, others more accurate calculations. Before considering the feasibility of this plan, it may be helpful to review the frequencies of the EM spectrum. Table 16.1 below shows the frequencies of the major regions of the EM spectrum.

Table 16.1. Frequency Bands of the Electromagnetic Spectrum

Description	Approximate Wavelength	Approximate Frequency	Associated Molecular Processes
Radio waves	1 mm to 100,000 km	3 Hz to 300 MHz	
Microwaves	1 mm to 10 cm	300 MHz to 300 GHz	Molecular rotation
Infrared	700 nm to 1 mm	30 GHz to 30 THz	Molecular vibration
Visible	400nm to 700 nm	4.3 PHz to 7.5 PHz	Electronic transitions
Ultraviolet	1 nm to 400 nm	7.5 PHz to 300 PHz	Electronic transitions and some ionization
X-rays	10 pm to 1 nm	300 PHz to 30 EHz	Ionization
Gamma Rays	1 pm to 10 pm	30 to 300 EHz	Nuclear processes

Note: In the SI system of units, mega (M) = 10^6 giga (G) = 10^9 Tera (T) = 10^{12} peta (P) = 10^{15} and exa (E) = 10^{18} so, for example, 300 MHz is 300,000,000 Hz.

Prior Estimates of Dowsing Frequency

Maby and Franklin performed a series of tests examining the cause of the dowsing effect and claimed it was due to radio waves with a wavelength of about 9 to 10 m, among many other potential causes; however, this measurement was based on the separation between bands near a stream and pipe, which they assumed was caused by wave superposition. As discussed earlier, this explanation does not hold up to scrutiny. Ellison reviewed their work and commented that the amount of experimental description was insufficient to support these claims, and he did not like that they showed smoothed data with the noise removed.[327] I agree with Ellison on the latter point, though I thought there was enough experimental description to understand what they were doing. One of the best measurements of the wavelength of the dowsing signal was made by Jennison, who estimated it to be on the order of centimeters, which is in the microwave region of the spectrum.[328] His experiment started with covering the floor with aluminum foil and then making a hole about 30 cm (1 ft) in diameter in the foil: this now gave a strong dowsing response. He then placed a sheet of aluminum (2.4 × 1.2 m) at about 45 degrees over the hole so that the dowsing signal would be reflected as a horizontal beam. Jennison mentioned that the experiment was obeying optical principles (probably reflection) and so he added a strip of aluminum across the hole, creating a double slit experiment, analogous to Young's double slit experiment, discussed later in this chapter. If the beam is wave, then it will be split by the aluminum strip and the two beams, one from each side, will form an interference pattern with peaks and valley. From the separation between these peaks, the wavelength can be calculated. However, Jennison commented that it "was difficult to establish precisely because of the asymmetry in the on/off responses of the dowsing stimulus."

Anne Miller,[329] whose experiment was discussed in Chapter 13, also measured the wavelength of the dowsing response, but she obtained wavelengths of 0.1 to 0.3 mm (3 THz to 1 THz), significantly shorter wavelengths than most other estimates. Several other investigators have tried to measure the dowsing frequency, for example, Anthony Hopwood suggested in 1980 that "ley lines," or lines of hidden energy on the Earth's surface, may react with frequencies in the range of 30 to 100 MHz, but he did not elaborate on how he came to those numbers.[330] Hopwood previously had conducted a series of investigations on the effect of electric fields on dowsing in which he dismissed any connection with radio frequencies,[331] but a good scientist must be ready to change his or her opinion when the evidence points a different way.

Estimate of Dowsing Frequencies Based on Penetration of the Ground

The EM spectrum is very broad, but we can narrow down the potential frequency range based on what we know about dowsing. Dowsers can detect objects one or more meters (yards) below the surface, so the dowsing signal must be able to penetrate soil and rock at least to some extent. We know from everyday experience that visible light cannot penetrate normal soil very far and certainly not a meter, so we can rule out those frequencies. Infrared, too, does not penetrate very far. In an underground car park, for example, there is very little UV light, x-rays or gamma rays (unless there is a nearby radioactive source), but dowsing works, so we can rule out those frequency bands. This simple approach has left us with radio waves and microwaves. Fortunately, this conclusion is the same as that drawn using similar arguments in the experiments with cardboard described in a previous chapter.

Estimate of Dowsing Frequencies Based on Physiology

There are probably several reasons why the dowsing response is based on microwaves. In a radio, the first level of selectivity is the antenna length. For a simple dipole antenna, a much stronger signal is received if the length of the antenna is half or some multiple of the wavelength. Wi-Fi, for example, typically operates at 2.4 and 5 GHz under the 802.11 IEEE standard. 2.4 GHz has a wavelength of 12.5 cm, so a half wavelength is about 6 cm, which is why the Wi-Fi antenna on computers, routers, etc., are typically around this length.

If there is a dowsing sense organ, then the signal needs to penetrate the human body at least enough to reach that sense organ. If the detection occurs at a nerve or some other organ, then it is likely to be best received if the dimensions of that organ are close to the wavelength of the radiation and induce a resonance. A typical person is about 1.5 to 1.7 m (five to six feet) and an EM wave with a wavelength of this magnitude corresponds to a frequency of about 200 MHz, i.e., at the high end of the radio wave spectrum. Most of our internal organs and other structures are in the order of centimeters in size and the frequency for a 3 cm (1.2 in) long structure (chosen to make the numbers easier), is about 10 GHz. This frequency is in the microwave region of the spectrum. The relationship between body size and potential resonance frequency is shown in Table 16.2 below.

Table 16.2. Predicted Resonance Frequencies of Body Parts for Half-Wave Dipole Antenna

Body Part	Length[332]	Frequency (Quarter Dipole) (GHz)	Frequency (Half Dipole) (GHz)
Whole body	1.5 to 1.8 m (5 to 6 ft)	0.18	0.35
Length of spinal column	45 cm	0.65	1.3
Shoulder to shoulder	40 cm (1.5 ft)	0.75	1.5
Head length	30 cm (12 in)	1.0	2.0
Brain length	16.7 cm	1.8	3.6
Head width	15 cm (6 in)	2.0	4.0
Brain width	14 cm (5.5 in)	2.2	4.3
Brain height	9.3 cm	3.3	6.5
Size of pons (part of brain stem)	2.5 cm	12	24
Pineal gland	5–8 mm	20	40
Thickness of cerebral cortex	1.5 to 4 mm	150	300

These frequencies should not be taken as precise numbers, more an indication of the order of magnitude to get an idea of what the resonance frequencies are—if there

16. Dowsing Frequency Band

are any, that is. As discussed earlier, the most likely location of the dowsing sense organ is near the base of the brain, perhaps the brain stem or cerebellum. The diameter of the cerebellum in a typical adult is about 2.6 cm and the length is about 4.6 cm,[333] so the resonance frequency for a half wavelength will be around 23 GHz and 13 GHz, respectively. While these frequencies are larger than some of the estimates for the dowsing frequency which are about 2–5 GHz, they are reasonably close considering the gross assumptions made. This approach may be helpful in identifying potential dowsing sense organs; however, it is not known if the antenna resonance is relevant to the detection of the dowsing signal.

In order for the microwave to be detected in the body the microwave also has to reach the sense organ. As the frequency increases the absorption by water also increases and so the penetration of microwaves into the body becomes more limited. The human body is about 68 percent water, with some organs such as the brain being very high in water content (73%), and other parts of the body, such as the bones, being lower (32%).[334] If the dowsing sense location is in the brain, then the microwaves have to pass through several centimeters of skin, skull, tissues and brain matter. Again, water with its high relative permittivity (dielectric constant) is the dominant microwave absorber, so the penetration of microwaves into the skull can be estimated based on the penetration of microwaves in water, scaled by the percent of water. The graph in Figure 16.1 shows such as estimated penetration, where again the penetration is the depth at which the microwave intensity has been reduced to 1/e (about a third). (See Chapter 20 for an explanation of the curve.)

If the dowsing sensor organ were located 5 cm (2 in) into the body and it can detect 5 percent of the signal then it would be inaccessible by microwaves with a frequency much greater than ~6 GHz, which has a wavelength of 5 cm, as shown in Figure 16.4. Higher frequencies will not be able to penetrate that far. Of course, these penetration

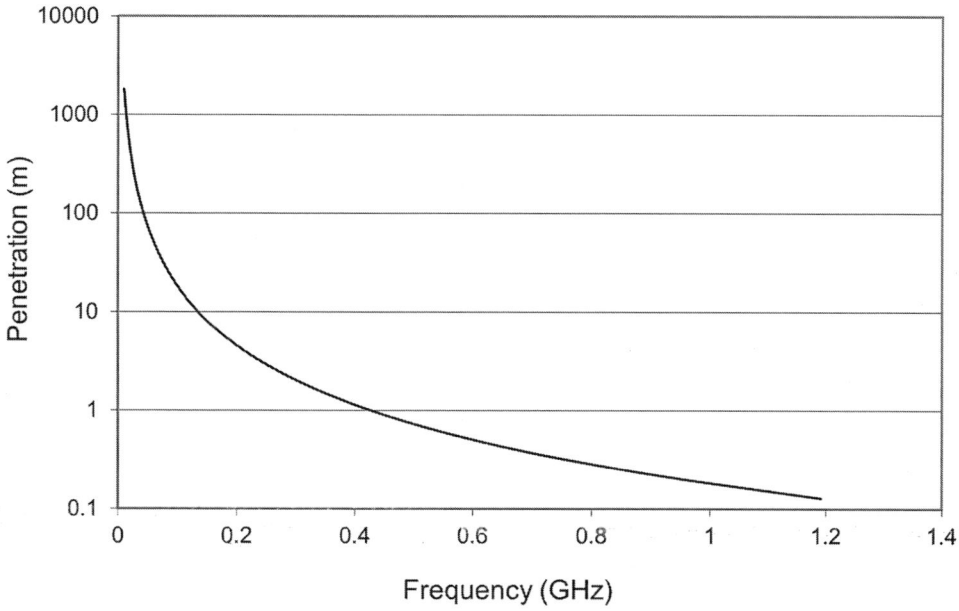

Figure 16.1. Estimated microwave penetration in human body versus frequency.

estimates are very crude, and we know from the prior chapter that the dowsing sense is very sensitive, and so it is unclear to what extent the absorption of microwaves limits the frequency range of the dowsing signal. Harvalik identified the region of the brain around the pineal gland as the center for the dowsing response. The pineal gland sits at the bottom of the brain, in front of the brain stem. The dowsing signal therefore has to pass through quite a lot of tissue before it can reach this location. It is likely, though not proven, that this absorption sets the upper limit on the dowsing frequency.

Estimate of Dowsing Frequency from Dowsing Resolution

One of the mysteries of dowsing is the high resolution described in some writings. Hume reported that it was possible to detect metal objects as small as a paper clip.[335] I am not sure that every dowser can achieve such a high resolution, but for a very simple case, such as over a PVC pipe in the ground, the resolution is around ~ 2 to 5 cm (~1–2 inches). If the dowsing signal is caused by an EM wave, then the resolution is limited by diffraction, which depends on the wavelength of the radiation. With the best optics visible microscopes can resolve objects larger than about half a wavelength or 0.2 µm and larger,[336] but they cannot resolve objects below 0.1 µm, unless special techniques such as the recently developed sub-diffraction methods, are used.[337] Electron microscopes on the other hand use electron beams with much shorter wavelengths and can resolve distances of 1 to 20 nm.[338] If we apply the same ratios for optical resolution to dowsing, then the wavelength is 4 to 10 cm (~2-4 in) and the frequency is estimated to be 3 to 7.5 GHz.

Wavelength and Optical Resolution[1]

The optical resolution of two light spots is the distance apart where the spots can be distinguished. Consider an aperture with two light beams coming through it, forming two spots, as shown in the sketch in Figure 16.2.

The angle between them θ and their wavelength λ determines whether the light spots are distinguishable or if they overlap. Rayleigh suggested that the spots are distinguishable when the first minimum of one falls on the central maximum of the other. Two peaks can be distinguished using Rayleigh's criteria, as illustrated in the sketch in Figure 16.3.

The two spots in part A of the figure overlap slightly but are well resolved; but the two spots in part B are so close that only a single combined peak can be observed. In part C the two spots overlap but can just be resolved. The resolution depends on how much the light is diffracted by the aperture and so depends on the size of the aperture in relation to the wavelength of the light. The resolution can be calculated based on the diffraction equation, and for a simple slit aperture the resolution is described by the equation

$$\theta = \lambda/a$$

The angle θ can therefore be considered as the minimum angle of resolution. Similarly, the resolution of a circular aperture is given by

$$\theta \sim \sin(\theta) = 1.22\,\lambda/a$$

---

1. P.M. Welan and M.J. Hodgsonm, *Essential Principles of Physics* (John Murray, 1978).

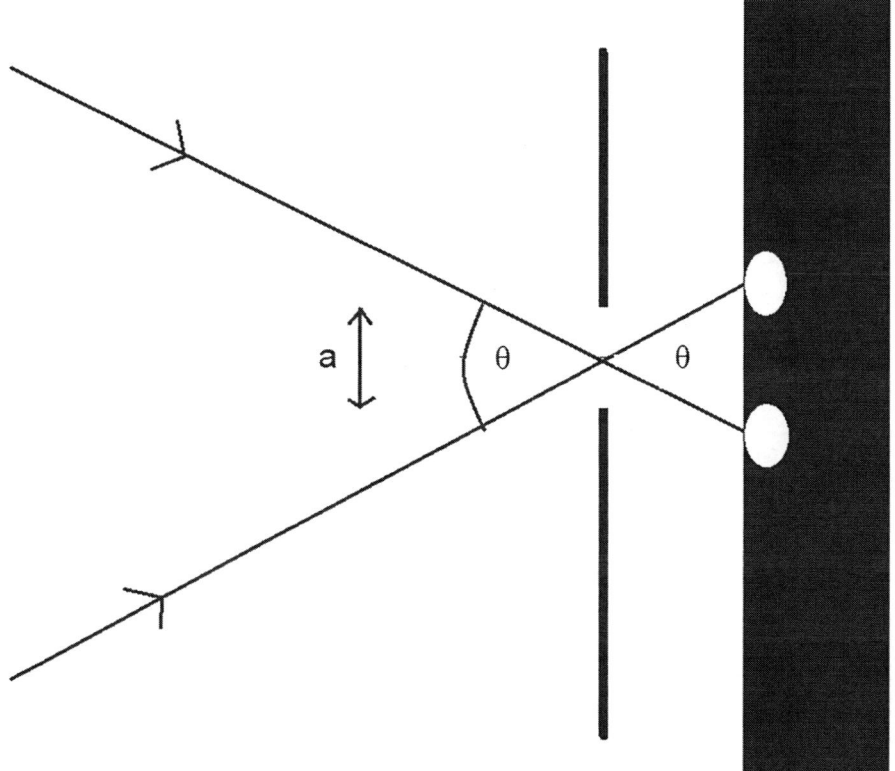

Figure 16.2. Sketch of two light beams passing through an aperture and striking a screen behind.

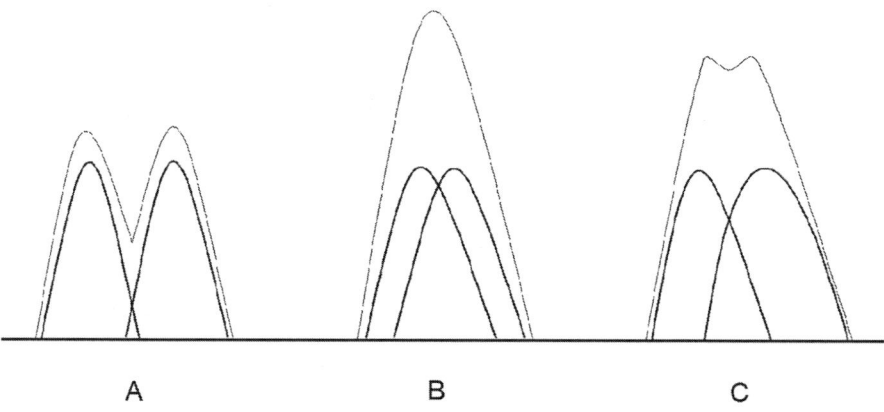

Figure 16.3. Sketch illustrating resolution as described by Rayleigh's criterion. The heavier lines represent the individual light spots and the lighter lines the combined spot.

This equation is applicable to telescopes and many other optical instruments. For the human eye, when the pupil is small, the minimum angle of resolution, θ is approximately 10^{-4} radians of arc, or about 0.006 degrees, which corresponds to a being just able to resolve two points 0.1 mm apart from 25 cm (10 inches) away (I wish).

There are several other related equations for different scenarios, but most of them are of similar form, with the wavelength over a length.

To test the dowsing resolution, at least mine, I placed two aluminum foil strips each about 9 to 10 cm wide parallel on the floor over the dowsing source and varied the distance between them. If the strips were close together, there was only one signal (rods crossed and uncrossed) when stepping over them. If the strips were far apart there were two separate signals (rods crossed, uncrossed and cross again). The point where it was hard to distinguish between one and two signals was about 18 cm. Assuming the dowsing sense organ is 1.5m above the ground, then applying a right angle triangle analysis, $\tan(\theta)$ = 18cm/1.5m = 0.12, θ = 0.12 radians, = 6.9 degrees. The wavelength $\lambda = \theta a$, using the equation above, and so λ = 0.12*18 cm = 2.2 cm (14 GHz).

Measurement of Dowsing Frequency by Interference

Interference (see Chapter 7) is an important property of waves that does not apply to classical particles. Prior to the 18th century the nature of light was a mystery and in particular, the question of whether light consists of waves or particles. Thomas Young did some elegant experiments and showed that light could be diffracted and form interference patterns, thereby showing it has wave-like properties. If dowsing depends on the thermal emission of microwaves, then it should be possible to use interference to measure its wavelength using similar methods. Jennison also used this method to measure the wavelength of the dowsing signal, as discussed earlier.[339]

Dowsing Frequency by Double Slit Experiment

An attempt was made to measure the wavelength using interference. Light will diffract from an edge as well as a slit and so the double slit experiment can be performed using a single thin barrier in a light beam. For example, a common school science project is to measure the thickness of a hair by suspending the hair in the beam of a laser pointer and measuring the distance between interference fringes on a wall and substituting the values into the equation $n\lambda = dD/x$.

Because aluminum foil blocks the dowsing signal, strips of aluminum foil placed on a concrete floor can be used to create a double slit experiment, using dowsing rods to detect the signal. I placed a strip of aluminum foil on the floor in an area with no dowsing signal and placed a wooden (transparent to microwaves) meter rule perpendicular to it (Figure 16.5), and then measured the dowsing response at different distances to the aluminum strip.

The experiment involves walking to or from a double slit at ground level and recording the distances where the dowsing-rods respond. Applying the above equation, d is the distance between the slits, X is the distance of the response to the middle of the slits, and D is the height of the dowsing sense organ, which for now will be assumed to be roughly ear height. If interference signals are detected, they will be parallel to the slits and roughly equally spaced. The one closest to the slits will be for n =1, and successively

Young's Double Slit Experiment

In 1801 Young set up two small parallel slits and saw an interference pattern, thus establishing that light was a wave. The premise of the double slit experiment is that a single slit with a width similar to the wavelength of the wave will cause any wave reaching the slit to diffract as it passes through it. If there are two slits next to each other, then the wave will diffract through both slits and the two diffraction patters will overlap, giving an interference pattern (see Appendix for discussion of diffraction and interference). If the wave is light and the interference pattern is projected onto a screen, then a series of bands is observed, corresponding to where the two diffracted waves reinforce to give bright areas or cancel each other to give dark areas. The distance between the bands depends on the wavelength, the spacing between the slits and the distance to the screen.

The sketch in Figure 16.4 shows a monochromatic light source of wavelength λ behind a barrier with two slits in it, S_1 and S_2. The light diffracts through the two slits and the resulting interference pattern (not shown) is projected onto the screen containing points P and O.

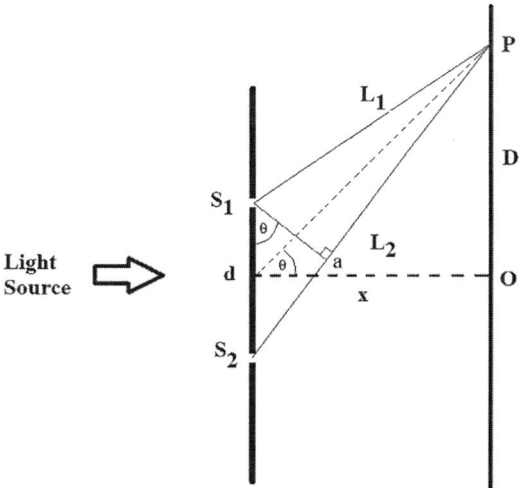

Figure 16.4. Sketch of double slit diffraction experiment showing derivation of diffraction equation.

The point P represents a lit point where the two waves superimpose. For the two waves to reinforce at P, the difference in distance from S_1 and S_2 to P (= L_2-L_1) must be a whole number of wavelengths, i.e.,

$$L_2 - L_1 = n\lambda$$

where n is an integer, and so long as d << L_1 and L_2, the increase in path length from trigonometry using the triangle S_1, S_2 and point a is

$$n\lambda = d.\sin(\theta)$$

Point O is the point on the screen corresponding to the midpoint between the slits, distance × from the slits. The distance from O to P is D, and from geometry the angle between O, the midpoint between the slits and P is also θ. Therefore $\sin(\theta) = D/x$, and hence:

$$n\lambda = dD/x$$

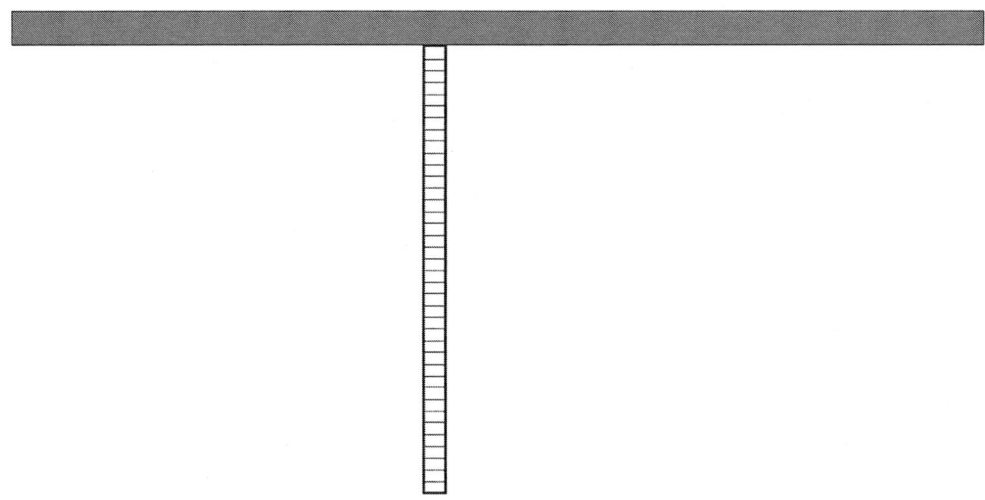

Figure 16.5. Sketch of diffusion test apparatus, a strip of aluminum foil and a perpendicular wooden meter rule.

larger n as one gets further away from the slits. The responses were very weak, and the results in Table 16.3 were obtained.

Table 16.3. Results from Double Slit Experiments

Strip Width (cm)	Distance from foil (cm)	Wavelength (cm)	Frequency (GHz)
5	11 & 27	0.31 & 0.38	97 & 79
20	12 & 70	3 & 5	10 & 6

The frequencies calculated with the 5 cm strip are far above the frequency range that is expected to be applicable for dowsing, since it will lack the ability to penetrate the ground and the human body. The frequencies calculated with the 20 cm strip are in line with the results of other frequency experiments; however, the signals were so weak with both strips that neither measurement should be considered reliable.

Wavelength Determination by Grid

I tried a simple experiment. If there is a location where there is a strong dowsing response, such as an underground pipe, then placing a large sheet of aluminum foil over that area will block the dowsing response for the pipe. However, there will be a strong response at the edge of the aluminum foil. The experiment blocking the dowsing signal was repeated but instead of aluminum foil a sheet of square wire mesh with a hole size of 1.25 × 1.25 cm (half inch square) was used, again directly over the pipe and again the dowsing signal was lost. If the mesh is able to block the EM wave, then the wavelength must be much longer than the mesh size, so greater than about 1–2 cm. A 1.5 cm wavelength corresponds to approximately 30 GHz frequency, so this simple experiment says the dowsing response is caused by EM frequencies less than 30 GHz.

A second observation was that there was now a strong dowsing response at the edge of the mesh, where before there had been no response. The same effect was observed with cardboard covered on both sides with aluminum foil. This result is consistent with the mesh and the foil blocking the EM wave because there is a steady intensity away from the foil, and close to zero intensity over the foil, and a step change in intensity as one crosses the edge of the foil.

On repeating with a larger mesh size, the dowsing response was restored. When the mesh hole was about 2.5 cm (1 inch), there was weak response, and a 5 cm (2 inch) mesh gave a moderate response, and with a 10 cm (4 inches) mesh the response was the same as if the mesh was not there. This result means that the wavelength of the EM radiation is larger than 1 to 2 cm (half inch) and is less than or equal to four inches. The wavelength is therefore estimated to be between 2 and 10 cm (15 to 3 GHz).

EM radiation has been extensively studied for hundreds of years, and while new aspects of it continue to be discovered, EM radiation is very well understood. The microwave explanation also provides an explanation for the results with the row of neodymium magnets discussed in Chapter 8. The magnets were causing a dowsing response, not because of their magnetic field, but because they were 1¼ inch (3 cm) metal disks lying in a row on the ground and they were disrupting the passage of the microwave radiation, since microwaves can't pass through metals; and the disruption to the microwaves was the basis of the dowsing response.

The experiment was repeated using a set of metal grids made from 5 mm (~ ¼ inch) adhesive copper metal tape on cardboard. Grids were made with copper tape spaced 2 cm, 5 cm, 10 cm, 20 cm and 40 cm apart, with corresponding hole sizes of 1.5, 4,5, 9.5,

---

Passage of Waves Through a Grid

If an EM wave reaches a metal grid, the wave passes through the grid or it may be reflected back, depending on the size of the openings relative to the wavelength. Assume that the openings in the grid are rectangular, then the grid can be viewed as a waveguide, with directions x and y in the plane of the grid and z passing through the grid. The wave in z direction is a travelling wave, but the components of the wave in the x and y directions form standing waves in the cavity formed by the reflective surfaces of the grid (transverse electric and magnetic modes). If we first consider wave in the x direction only, then for a standing wave between two walls, the amplitude will be zero at the walls, and so the longest wavelength (λ_{max}) will be the twice the distance between walls. or in the case of a wire grid twice the size of the opening:

$$\lambda_{max} = 2a$$

where a is the width of the opening. The same applies to the y direction, except that the maximum wavelength is twice the height of the opening in the grid. The cutoff wavelength depends only on the dimensions of the opening. Therefore, we can say that the wavelength is about twice the opening size. A more detailed analysis for EM radiation is available, though the final result is the same.[1]

---

1. David (no last name given) "What Is the Relationship Between Faraday Cage Mesh Size and Attenuation of Cell Phone Reception Signals?" *Physics Stack Exchange*, April 12, 2015, https://physics.stackexchange.com/questions/149607/what-is-the-relationship-between-faraday-cage-mesh-size-and-attenuation-of-cell?rq=1, accessed September 3, 2022.

19.5 and 39.5 cm. In addition, another sheet of cardboard covered with aluminum foil on both sides was also used (grid spacing = zero). These grids were placed on the ground where a dowsing signal had been recorded and with aluminum foil the dowsing signal was blocked. The foil was moved away, and incrementally larger grids were tested until the dowsing signal was restored. In almost every case, the dowsing signal was blocked by the 2 cm grid, was about half to three quarter strength with the 5 cm grid and was full strength with the 10 cm grid. Larger sized grids (20 cm & 40 cm) made no difference beyond the response with the 10 cm grid. This result means that the dowsing signal has a wavelength greater than 3 cm (1.5 cm grid) and less than or equal to 20 cm (10 cm grid). 3 cm corresponds to 10 GHz and 20 cm corresponds to 1.5 GHz. This experiment was repeated many times for many underground objects, at a variety of depths, and the same result was consistently obtained.

Summary of Wavelength Determination

The ability of EM radiation to penetrate the ground and cardboard suggests that the dowsing radiation is in the radio wave or microwave region of the spectrum. Within the microwave region of the spectrum, the ability of microwaves to penetrate the ground and the human body place an upper limit on the frequency to about 10 GHz. Several methods were used to estimate the frequency, and the values obtained were around 7.5 to 15 GHz or 2–4 cm. The wavelength measurements are summarized in Table 16.4.

Table 16.4. Summary of Dowsing Wavelength Measurements

Method	*Wavelength (cm)*	*Frequency (GHz)*
Dowsing resolution	2	15
Angle of Diffraction	4	7.5
Double slit	3 to 5	10 to 6
Grid	3 to 10	10 to 3

The grid results in Table 16.4 are probably the most reliable, since they were repeated many times under different conditions. The signals in the double slit experiment were very weak and so those results are less reliable. The diffraction and angle of diffraction were the same basic experiment, but with different analyses. The diffraction values and the dowsing resolution are looking at phenomena from the surface; i.e., the diffraction slit was on the surface and the resolution was similar to aluminum foil on the surface. The resolution calculation is also based on diffraction and so the wavelength obtained is not an independent value. It is possible that the wavelength of events at the surface is different from that at greater depths. However, these methods all indicate that the dowsing signal wavelength is in the low cm range. These results are in general agreement with those of Jennison described earlier.[340]

SPOILER ALERT—The most likely source of microwave radiation is blackbody radiation, as discussed in the next chapter. Blackbody radiation in the microwave region of the spectrum increases in intensity as the frequency increases into the terahertz. Therefore, dowsing signals from objects lying on the ground, such as a sheet of aluminum foil, are likely to be dominated by the higher frequencies, since thermal emissions from near the surface do not need to pass through ground and so absorption is not an issue. Therefore, it is likely that the highest frequency detected is limited by our physiological detection mechanism and the decreasing ability of the radiation to penetrate into biological materials as the frequency increases. It is likely that the absorption of the signal before reaching the dowsing detector may limit the upper frequency range of the dowsing signal.

17

Source of Electromagnetic Radiation

The first [uncontested philosophical rule] is, that there emanates or exhales generally from all bodies some subtle particles, which with good reason might be called spirits if they did not come from matter.
—Nicholas Jean (1680)[341]

Chapter summary: The last chapter showed the dowsing signal was in the low GHz microwave region, and so it is reasonable to ask where this radiation comes from. The most likely source of microwave radiation is from thermal emissions, also known as blackbody radiation. Thermal emission is the same source of microwaves as detected by some weather satellites.

The preceding chapters have shown that the dowsing signal is comprised of microwave radiation in the low gigahertz range. The next obvious question in determining the mechanism of the dowsing effect is to ask where this microwave radiation is coming from. Tromp considered radio waves and microwaves (Hertzian waves) and assumed that they came either from the sun or from a radio station.[342] Maby and Franklin also considered radio waves and believed they were generated by the impact of cosmic radiation on surface and subsurface materials.[343]

Since dowsing microwaves are blocked by a metal sheet on the ground, and the dowsing signal contains information about subsurface structures, these microwaves are clearly coming out of the ground. However, the question remains of where they originally come from, and are these microwaves natural or man-made? Man-made radio waves are unlikely to be the source, since dowsing is practiced all over the world, and it was used for centuries before radio waves and microwaves were discovered. This fact indicates that the dowsing signal comes from natural sources. There are three conceptual natural sources of microwaves:

   i. Emissions from the earth.
   ii. Emissions from the sun.
   iii. The cosmic microwave background radiation that is best known for providing experimental evidence for the Big Bang theory formation of the universe.

As discussed in Chapter 3, dowsing underground pipes works day and night and so the microwaves are not coming from the sun. Another possibility is that the microwaves are coming from the universe, for example, from the cosmic background radiation in the microwave region of the spectrum which was used to develop the Big Bang theory of the formation of the universe.[344] To test the idea that cosmic microwaves are the basis of the dowsing signal, I placed a sheet of aluminum foil folded to about 15 by 30 cm (6 in. by 1 foot) and placed it on the ground in two places along a trail that passed through an old railway tunnel. The first location was outside the tunnel and the second location was in the middle of the tunnel. The response to the foil was similar inside and outside the tunnel, and neither spot gave a dowsing response absent the foil. Thus the dowsing signal if coming from the universe was not significantly reduced by the 10 meters (35 feet) of rock above my head. I also repeated the test in the open and inside a gazebo with a metal roof (which would reflect microwaves and radio waves), with the same result. The conclusion therefore is that the dowsing signal is coming up through the ground and not from the sun or the universe. This result makes sense, since the cosmic microwave background radiation is so low intensity (peak brightness of I_{max} ~ 3.7×10^{-18} W m^{-2} Hz^{-1} sr^{-1} at frequency of ~ 160 GHz, equivalent to the radiation from a blackbody at 2.7K[345]) that it is negligible for our purposes and so is very unlikely to be the source of the dowsing microwaves. The most plausible source of microwaves therefore is thermal emission, so called blackbody radiation.

Blackbody Radiation

All objects emit EM radiation across the spectrum as a function of their temperature. The maximum output is from so-called blackbodies. The emissions from blackbodies were described by Max Planck, the great German physicist. Since blackbody radiation varies with the temperature of the object, it is also known as thermal emission.

Blackbody Radiation

Blackbody radiation was described mathematically by Max Planck, in an equation that bears his name. For non-blackbodies, the same equation applies, but it includes an emissivity term that varies from 0 to 1. The EM emission or spectral radiance (B_F) as a function of frequency (F) and temperature (T) from a blackbody is given by the Planck Equation:

$$B_F(F,T) = (2hF^3/c^2)(1/[\exp\{hF/k_BT\} - 1])$$

where h is the Planck constant ($6.62607015 \times 10^{-34}$ Js), c is the speed of light and k_B is the Boltzmann constant (1.380649×10^{-23} J K^{-1}). B_F is the emitted power per unit solid angle, per unit of area and per unit frequency at thermal equilibrium at temperature T (units are power/[area*solid angle*frequency] or W.s/steridan/m^2). Since frequency and wavelength are interconvertible, the Plank Equation can be recast in terms of wavelength.

$$B_\lambda(\lambda,T) = (2hc^2/\lambda^5)(1/[\exp\{hc/\lambda k_BT\} - 1])$$

The spectral radiance using the frequency equation is graphed in Figure 17.1.

The maximum of the curve is around 20 terahertz (4×10^{13} Hz) for ambient temperatures which is in the infrared part of the spectrum and provides the radiation that infrared (night vision) cameras detect. The microwave region of the spectrum is much lower emission and much lower frequency on the far left hand size

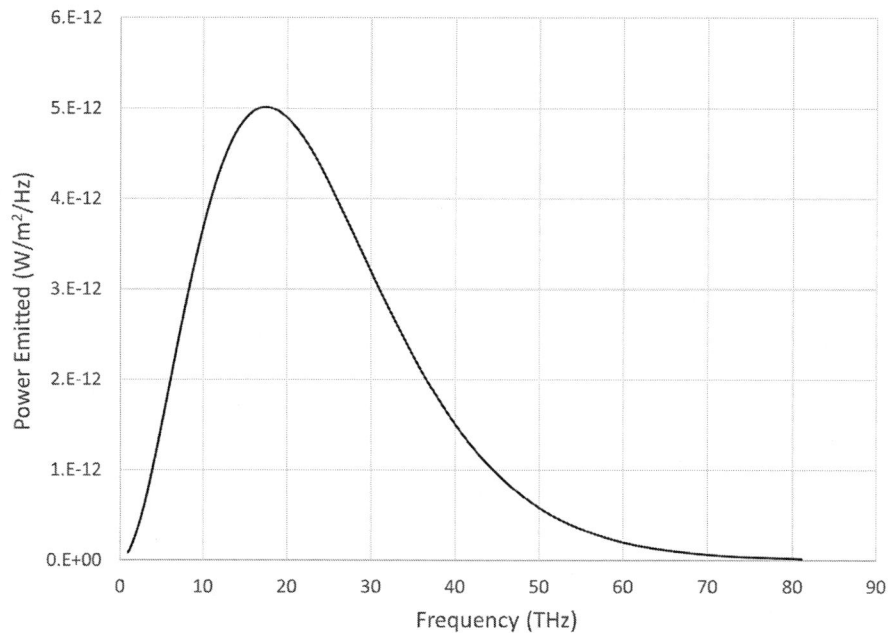

Figure 17.1. Blackbody radiation over frequency, calculated from Planck's equation for blackbody at 25°C.

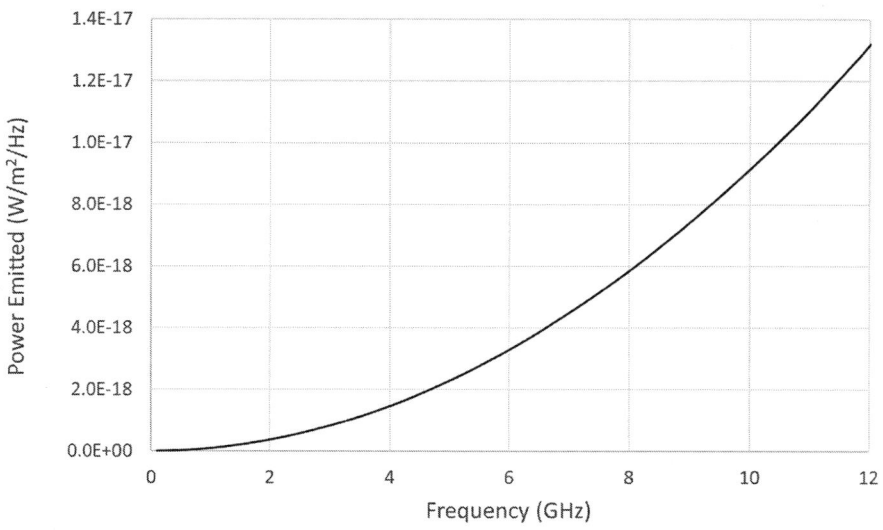

Figure 17.2. Blackbody radiation over region of microwave spectrum relevant to dowsing, calculated from Planck's equation for blackbody at 25°C.

(1 GHz = 0.001 THz). (The graph in Figure 17.1 can be rescaled to show the GHz region of the spectrum, shown in Figure 17.2).

Signal Strength of Microwave Blackbody Emissions Versus Microwave Communication Signals

The emission energy at 1 GHz (λ = 30 cm) can be estimated. For emissivity = 1, then (B_F) = 0.1 aW·sr^{-1}·m^{-2}·Hz^{-1}. A power of 0.1 attawatts (aW) is equivalent to 1 × 10^{-19} Watts per Hertz. If the emission over a broader band is considered, for example, from 500 MHz to 1,500 MHz, then the energy of emission is 0.1 × 10^{-9} W·sr^{-1}·m^{-2}, a measurable but still a low power.

This detection limit can be compared to other radio frequency receivers. For comparison, amateur signal strength is measured on the S scale, range from S9 (great signal) to S1 (poor signal). S9 is defined for the high-frequency bands to be a receiver input power of -73 dBm for frequencies below 30 MHz, and -93 dBm, for higher frequencies.[1]

S1 corresponds to –125 dBm for frequencies below 30 MHz and -145 dBm for higher frequencies. -125 dBm is equivalent to 3.2 × 10^{-16} W and -145 dBm is equivalent to 3.2 × 10^{-18} W. Comparing these numbers to the power for thermal emission, indicates that the expected signal should be readily measurable instrumentally, especially for larger bandwidths and more sensitive measuring equipment.

1. "IARU Region 1 HF Managers Handbook V8.1," http://hamwaves.com/decibel/doc/iaru.region.1.s-meter.pdf, accessed December 3, 2021; "Decibel & S-Readings, Serge Stroobandt, ON4AA," https://hamwaves.com/decibel/en/, accessed December 3, 2021.

The energy emitted depends on the frequency or wavelength. For sake of discussion in this section, and to simplify the numbers, I will assume that the dowsing effect frequency is 1 GHz (30 cm wavelength).

Fractional Band Width of an Antenna[1]

The fractional bandwidth (fbw) of an antenna is a measure of the frequency range over which the antenna can be used. If the antenna can be used between high-frequency F_1 and low-frequency F_2, then the frequency range is F_1-F_2, the center bandwidth F_c is $(F_1$-$F_2)/2$ and the fractional band width is given by fbw = $(F_1$-$F_2)/F_c$

Using a dipole antenna as an example. The bandwidth of dipole antennas is about 8 percent at 1 GHz.[2] The fbw in GHz is (1.08–0.92)/ 1 = 1.17 GHz. The energy being emitted per square meter over the frequency range can be found by multiplying it by blackbody emission per Hertz (1 × 10^{-19} W·sr^{-1}·m^{-2}·Hz^{-1} at 1 GHz) and for a solid angle at the surface of 1 steridan, the emissions are estimated to be 1 × 10^{-10} W/m.^{2} In comparison, my local radio station, has a 15 kW transmitter 14 miles away. Assuming that it broadcasts hemispherically, its signal power where I live is ~5 µW/m^2 (5 × 10^{-6} W/m^2). The background microwave radiation at 1 GHz detected by a dipole antenna is therefore 50,000 times lower power than my local radio station.

1. "Fractional Bandwidth (FBW)," http://www.antenna-theory.com/definitions/fractionalBW.php, accessed August 13, 2020.
2. "Bandwidth," http://www.antenna-theory.com/basics/bandwidth.php, accessed August 11, 2020.

128   The Science of Basic L-Rod Dowsing

Blackbody Emissivity

The emission rate (B_F or B_λ) from a non-blackbody object also depends on the emissivity, which varies from 0 (does not emit) to 1 (a perfect emitter, the same as a blackbody). Generally, if something absorbs light (or EM radiation) well, then it also emits well. A black car gets hotter in the sun because black absorbs light, but it also emits light

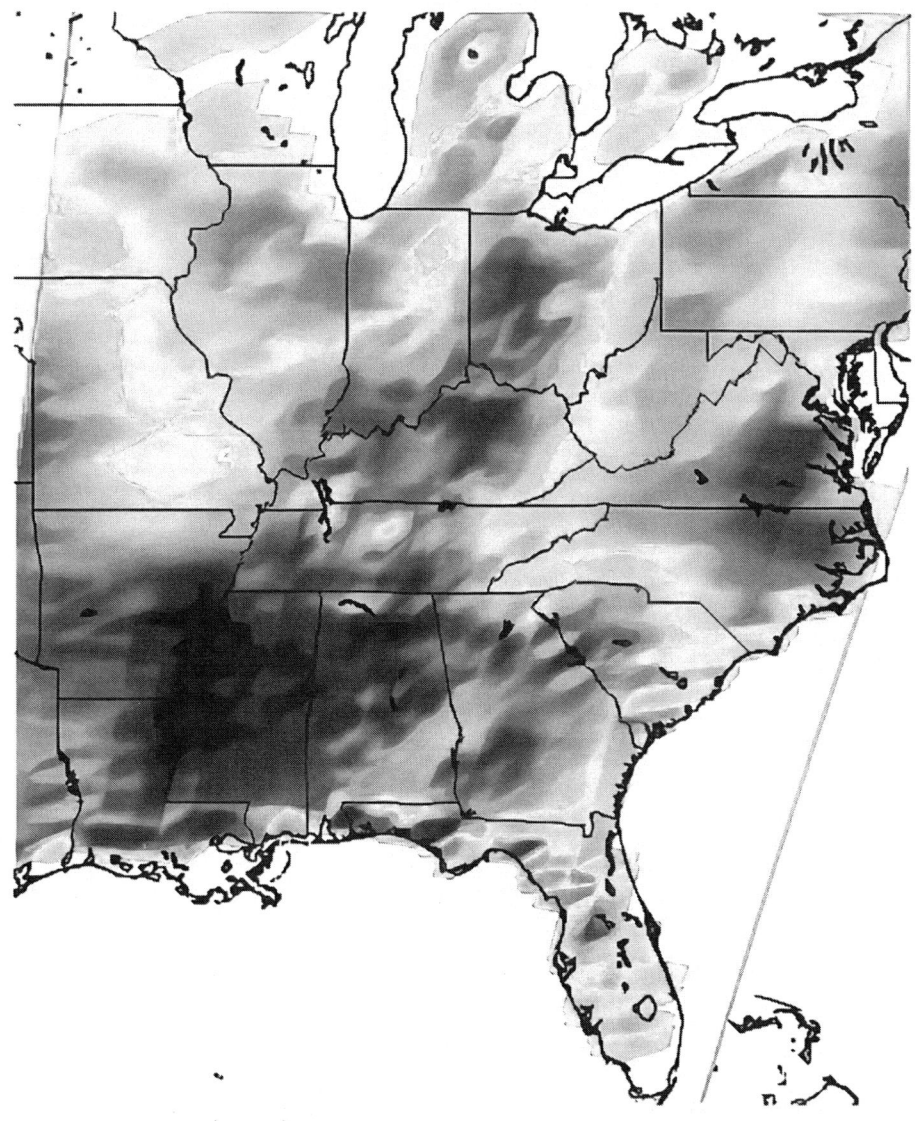

Figure 17.3. Difference in microwave image from 9/12/2002 and 9/28/2002 before and after tropical storm Isadore, taken from NASA's Aqua satellite (AIRS from Jet Propulsion laboratory, NASA, https://airs.jpl.nasa.gov/resources/144/flooding-resulting-from-hurricane-isidore-difference-image-sept-12-and-28-2002/, accessed May 15, 2023).

Satellite Studies of Microwave Emissions

All bodies emit thermal radiation, including microwave radiation, and the emission rate depends on the temperature and the emissivity or brightness of the surface emitting. Microwaves are an important part of the spectrum used for studying the Earth from orbit because radio waves longer than about 20 m and infra radiation can't penetrate the atmosphere. The microwaves are from thermal emissions, whereas most visible light coming from the Earth's surface is primarily reflected light. There are therefore narrow windows in the EM spectrum that can be used to see into space or see the ground from space, namely the visible region and microwave region of the spectrum between about 20 m and 2 few cm in wavelength, as shown in Figure 17.4.

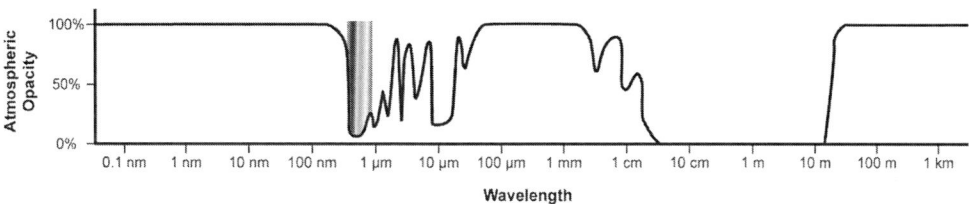

Figure 17.4. Absorption of electromagnetic radiation by the atmosphere (modified image from NASA).

If a body is a thermal equilibrium, then the rate of absorption and emission are equal. As discussed above, the penetration and emission depths depend on wavelength with the higher frequencies being absorbed and emitted closer to the surface ground. By changing the measurement frequency, it is possible to determine how the emissions vary with depth. Sequential microwave measurements from space enable measurement of the water content of soils over time, which is important for agriculture.

The water in clouds also absorbs microwave radiation, and thus satellite-based microwave observations of clouds provide a means to study the water structure of storm clouds and so better predict the weather and the consequences of storms. An example of a microwave satellite is the National Oceanic Polar Operational Environmental Satellites and Atmospheric Administration's (POES). These satellites orbit about 520 miles above the Earth's surface every 1.7 hrs.[1] One of the instruments, the Advanced Microwave Sounding Unit (AMSU) covers frequencies from 3 MHz to 6 GHz,[2] illustrating that blackbody microwaves near the frequencies relevant to dowsing are both emitted from the Earth's surface and are routinely detected.

1. "Polar Operational Environmental Satellites (POES), Office of Satellite and Product Operations," NOAA, https://www.ospo.noaa.gov/Operations/POES/, accessed February 19, 2021.
2. "NOAA POES Series—5th Generation Satellites," https://earth.esa.int/web/eoportal/satellite-missions/n/noaa-poes-series-5th-generation, accessed February 20, 2021.

and heat better, so it will also cool down faster in the winter—clearly people buy black cars for reasons other than their thermal characteristics.

One of the most important factors in determining the emissivity is the relative permittivity (dielectric constant) of the emitting surface.[346] The relative permittivities of some common materials are shown in the table below:

Table 17.1. Relative Permeability (Dielectric Constants) and Conductivities of Some Common Materials[347]

Material	Relative Permittivity	Conductivity (mS/m)	Material	Relative Permeability
Air/vacuum	1	0	Alumina	8.5
Water	88.2 (0°C)	0.1 to 30	Bitumen	2.7–3.5
Seawater	70	400	Glass (soda)	7.5
Sand (dry)	2.5	0.0001 to 1	Gypsum	5.7
Sand (water saturated)	25	0.1 to 1	Petroleum jelly	1.9–2.1
Clay (water saturated)	8 to 12	100 to 1000	Polyethylene	2.3
Ice	4	0.1 to 10	Porcelain	5.5
Granite (dry)	8	0.00001	Rubber, natural	2.4
Limestone (dry)	7 to 9	1×10^{-6}	Salt (sodium chloride)	5.9
Sandstone	10		Wood (pine)	7.3 to 8.2
Soil	3 to 10 (dry to moist)			

The most noteworthy feature of this data is that most rocks and common solids have relative permittivities in the range of 2 to 5, whereas water has a very high relative permittivity of around 80. This means that the relative permittivity of soil varies strongly with the water content, almost linearly.[348]

The greater the water content the greater the thermal microwave emissions and absorption. The satellite measurements of the surface water, forest, glaciers or desert, extent of the icecaps or the acreage felled in the Amazon are based on the variation of thermal microwave emissions from the surface of the earth. For example, the image in Figure 17.3 shows the difference in the microwave emission before and after the tropical storm Isidore taken from NASA's Aqua satellite. The difference in the two microwave images which is shown by different shading, shows the extent of flooding from the storm.

18

Resolution of Dowsing Signal

Eventually, we reach ... the utmost limits of our telescopes. There, we measure shadows, and we search among ghostly errors of measurement for landmarks that are scarcely more substantial.
—Edwin Powell Hubble (1935)[349]

Chapter summary: One of the most remarkable aspects of dowsing is the accuracy with which an underground object can be located at the surface. Dowsing rods will cross within a few centimeters directly over a pipe that is, for example, one meter down. There is not much difference in distance from the dowser's feet to the pipe where the rods cross and step back. Why does dowsing have this very high angular specificity? The answer appears to be due to a combination of the optics of microwave radiation (refraction vs internal reflection) and physiological factors.

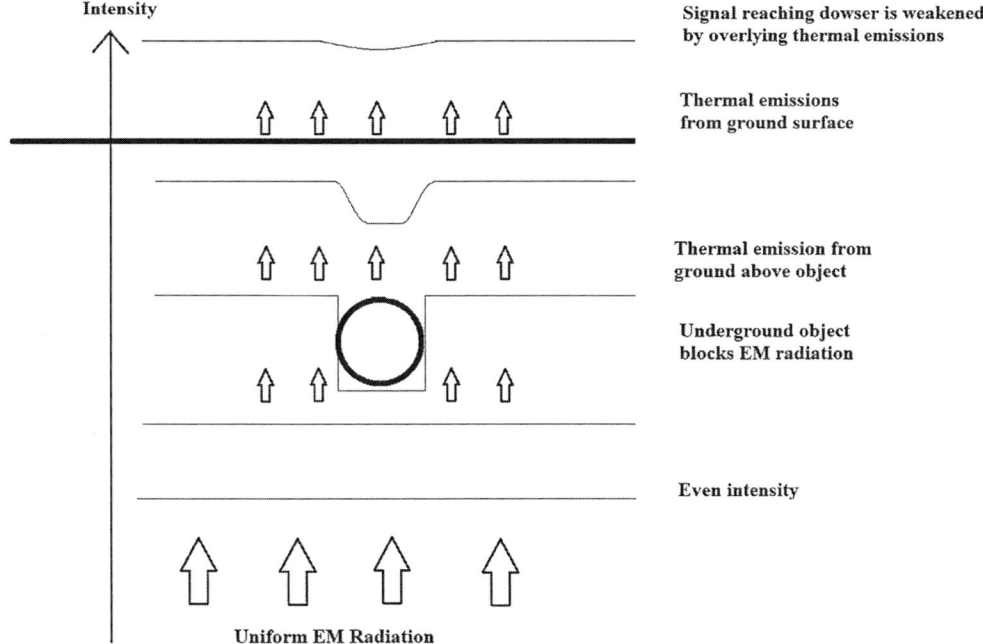

Figure 18.1. Dowsing signal from perturbations in underground thermal emissions (only showing vertical emissions).

132 **The Science of Basic L-Rod Dowsing**

One of the mysteries of dowsing is that dowsers can typically distinguish objects on the order of 2.5 to 5 cm (1 to two inches) that are several meters down. A resolution this fine is quite remarkable if the dowsing effect is caused by thermal microwave emissions, since thermal emissions occur in all directions and therefore radiation is coming towards the dowser from all directions. All objects emit EM radiation in all directions, and the dowsing signal is believed to be the perturbations in this signal caused by objects that lie in the path between the source and the dowser. As the signal rises through the rocks, some of it will be absorbed. Furthermore, since the object is below the ground, then the soil, rocks, etc., on top of the object will also emit thermal EM radiation and the final signal is a small perturbation in the combined signal as illustrated in Figure 18.1.

Since the thermal radiation is coming from all directions, how does the dowser differentiate signals coming from directly below from those from slightly in front, or to the side or from behind? If the object is a meter (~yard) down, then the distance from the object to the dowser is not very different, a step forward or a step backward, yet dowsers can pinpoint the location of an object to within a few centimeters (inches), as illustrated in Figure 18.2.

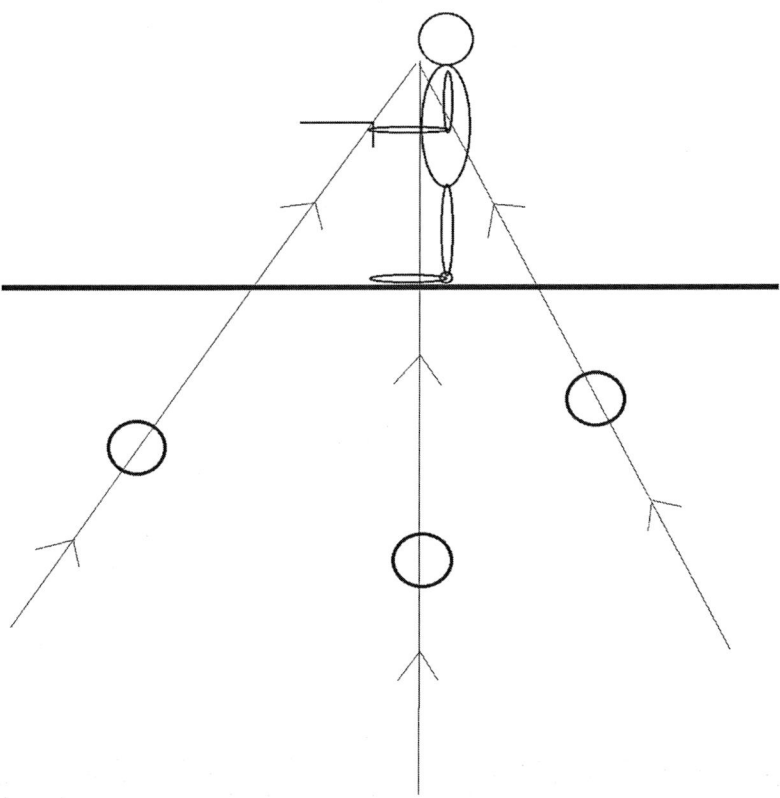

Figure 18.2. Sketch showing dowser walking along, potentially being affected by objects such as pipes below ground which are below, in front of or behind him/her, yet the dowser can selectively detect the object directly below his or her feet.

18. Resolution of Dowsing Signal

With visible light, one can narrow one's field of view to select only light coming from one direction using a collimator, such as a long tube. If one looks at the world through a long narrow tube, then one's field of view is greatly diminished, but one is only seeing light from the target. One possibility is that the microwaves are somehow collimated. There is, however, no apparent collimation of microwaves in the ground, but the laws of optics may be of help here.

Snell's Law and Internal Reflectance

A partial explanation for the collimation of the dowsing signal comes from optics. If a wave approaches an interface with another transparent medium, the wave can either pass through or be reflected at the interface if the angle is shallow enough. This effect is easy to see if one holds a sheet of clear plastic or glass towards a light. If the sheet is perpendicular to the light, then the light passes through and one can see through the sheet, but if the sheet is held almost edge on, the light is reflected (Figure 18.3) and one gets dazzled by the reflected light.

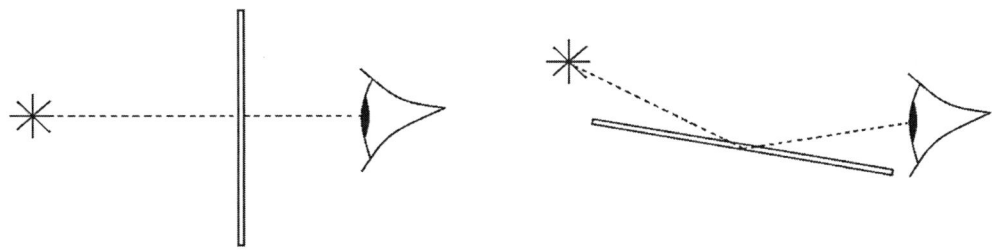

Figure 18.3. Sketch showing light transmission versus internal reflection.

Whether light passes through the glass or is internally reflected depends on the angle at which the light strikes the surface. If the angle is small, as measured to the normal (i.e., perpendicular to the surface, angle = 0), then the light passes through, but if the angle is large, then the light is reflected. The angle at which all the light is reflected is called the critical angle. Radio waves and microwaves are also EM radiation and behave similarly to light and will undergo the same process. The net effect is that only radiation reaching the surface at an angle less than the critical angle will be emitted from the surface (Figure 18.4).

For microwaves and radio waves the internal reflection (Figure 18.5) from optics occurs for an angle of 6.7 degrees. This small angle means that the dowsing signal will not leave the surface of the ground unless it is hitting within 6.7 degrees from the normal/perpendicular. This angle is small and effectively collimates the signal coming from the ground. It is noteworthy that this angle is within experimental error the same as the angle measured for first detection of microwaves with dowsing rods (5.7°) described in Chapter 15 and the angle resolution of dowsing (6.9°), and so it seems plausible that the critical angle is important to the high resolution in dowsing. Other factors must also be important, since a similar angle was measured for microwaves from an antenna which

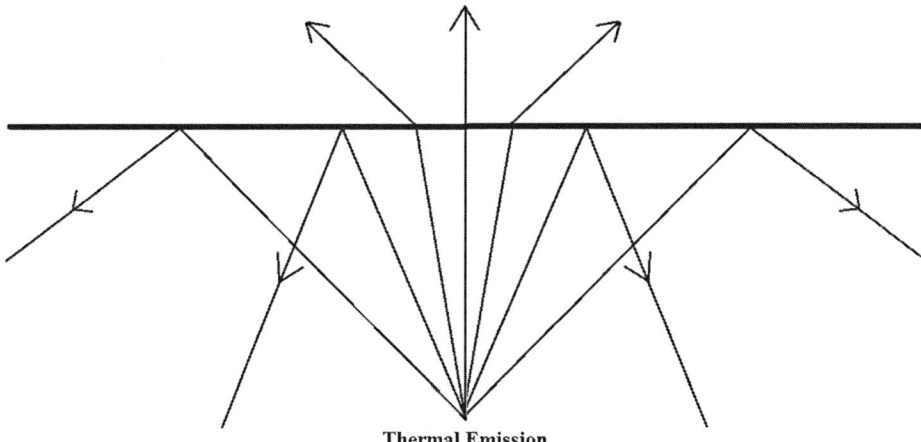

Figure 18.4. Sketch showing thermal emission radio waves and microwaves being emitted or internally reflected from the surface of the ground.

did not pass through the ground (Chapter 15) and similarly for a sheet of aluminum foil lying on the ground. This collimation may be part of the physiological detection mechanism.

Internal Reflection or Transmission

Light and other EM waves travel at different speeds (v) through different materials, and the refractive index provides a measure of the relative speed in that material compared to the speed of light in a vacuum (c). Consider a wave traveling in one medium with refractive index n_1, approaching an interface and angle θ_1 with a second transparent medium with refractive index n_2; the wave will either be transmitted by refracting at the interface, i.e., pass through but at a different angle, or it will be reflected back by the interface.

$$n = c/v$$

The fastest that light can go is in a vacuum; its speed in air is almost the same as in a vacuum, but its speed in liquids and solids is significantly lower. For example, the refractive index of visible light in water is 1.33,[1] so the speed of light in water is about 75 percent that of the speed of light in a vacuum. The angle at which the light wave will refract is given by Snell's law which says that

$$(\sin \theta_2 / \sin \theta_1) = n_1/n_2$$

As the angle of incidence θ_1 increases beyond the critical angle (θ_c), the light switches from being refracted to reflected at the interface. At the critical angle, the angle of refraction is 90°, so $\theta_2 = 90°$. Putting this value into Snell's law gives:

$$n_1 \sin\theta_c = n_2 \sin(90°) = n_2$$

and rearranging gives the result that the critical angle for $n_2 \leq n_1$ is given by

---

1. David R. Lide, ed., *CRC Handbook of Chemistry and Physics* 84th ed. (CRC Press, 2003).

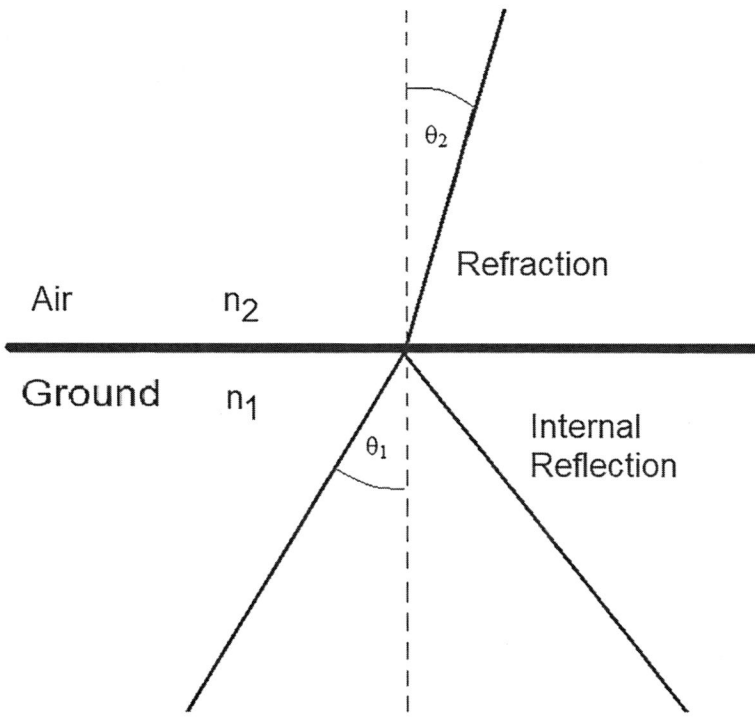

Figure 18.5. Transmission versus internal reflection.

$$\theta_c = \arcsin(n_2/n_1)$$

The refractive index of a material is a characteristic physical property of a material and is a function of the permittivity and permeability of the material.

$$n = (\varepsilon_r/\mu_r)^{1/2} = (\varepsilon\mu_o/[\mu\varepsilon_o])^{1/2}$$

where ε_r is the material's relative permittivity, and μ_r is its relative permeability, and since these parameters vary with frequency, so does the refraction index.

The refractive index of microwaves in air is close to 1.0[2] and the refractive index of microwaves in water has been found to be about 9.[3] Since there is little interaction of the magnetic field component with water ($\mu_r \approx \mu_o$), and the permittivity of water does not change much with frequency, the main variable is the permeability. The refractive index can therefore be approximated by:

$$n = \varepsilon_r^{1/2}$$

---

2. Georges Boudouris, "On the Index of Refraction of Air, the Absorption and Dispersion of Centimeter Waves by Gases," *Journal of Research of the National Bureau of Standards: D. Radio Propagation* vol. 67D, no. 6 (November-December 1963), 631, https://nvlpubs.nist.gov/nistpubs/jres/67D/jresv67Dn6p631_A1b.pdf.

3. Mark Lee Mesenbrinka, "Complex Indices of Refraction for Water and Ice from Visible to Long Wavelengths," Masters of Science thesis, Spring 1996, Florida State University College of Arts and Sciences, Department of Meteorology, https://apps.dtic.mil/dtic/tr/fulltext/u2/a312143.pdf.

The variation of permittivity with frequency has been measured[4] and so the refractive index can be calculated and plotted versus frequency as shown in Figure 18.6.

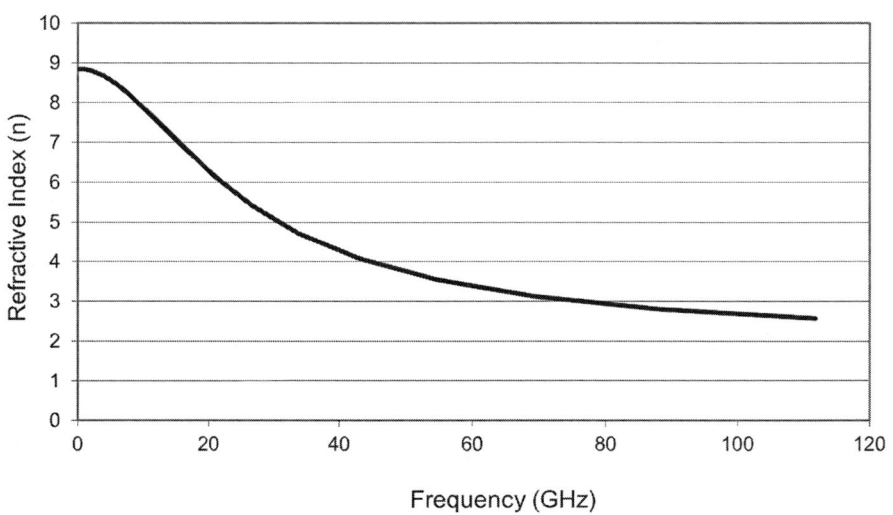

Figure 18.6. Refractive index of microwaves in water as function of frequency.

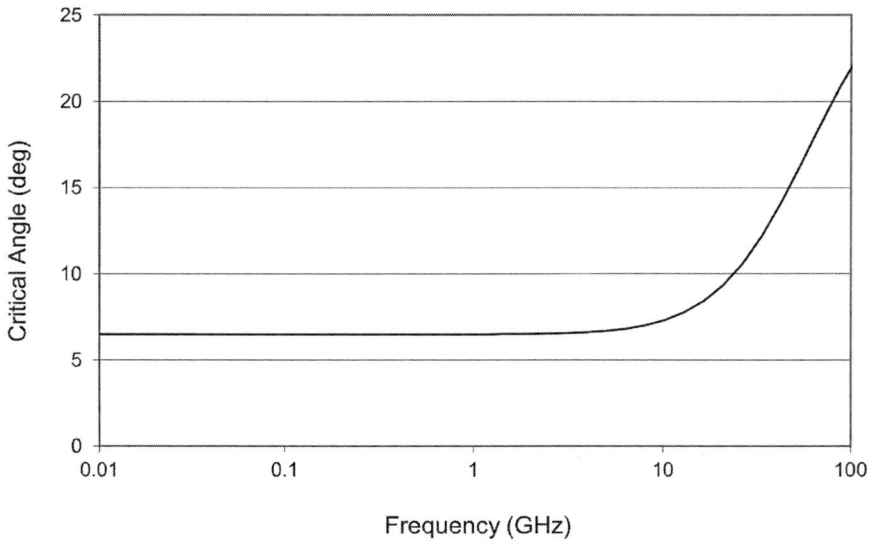

Figure 18.7. Critical angle of microwaves leaving water into air as a function of frequency.

---

4. Ravika Vijay, Ritu Jain and K.S. Sharma, "Dielectric Properties of Water at Microwave Frequencies," *International Journal of Engineering Research & Technology (IJERT)* vol. 3, issue 3 (2015), 1–3, special issue, https://www.ijert.org/research/dielectric-properties-of-water-at-microwave-frequencies-IJERTCONV3IS03027.pdf.

18. Resolution of Dowsing Signal

Using the above relationships, the critical angle can be expressed in terms of the refractive index.

$$\sin(\theta_c) = ((\varepsilon_{r\text{-air}})/(\varepsilon_{r\text{-water}}))^{1/2}$$

Since we are concerned with the water interface with air, $\varepsilon_{r\text{-air}} = 1$, so

$$\theta_c = \arcsin([1/\varepsilon_{r\text{-water}}]^{1/2})$$

Using this formula, the critical angle can be calculated as a function of frequency. A plot of critical angle versus frequency is shown in Figure 18.7.

The critical angle for water does not change much for frequencies below about 10 GHz. Any subsurface microwaves below ~ 10 GHz which reach the surface will be reflected back down again, unless they are within 6.7 degrees of vertical. This calculation shows that the only microwaves being emitted from below the surface are close to perpendicular to the surface. From the last chapter, the frequency range relevant to dowsing is most likely to be in the 1 to 10 GHz range, so a critical angle of 6.7 degrees is relevant to dowsing.

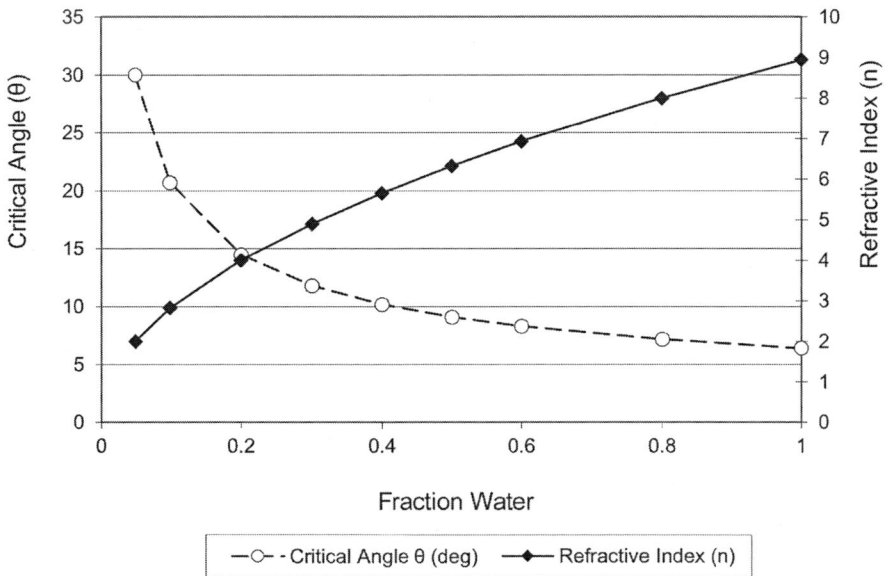

Figure 18.8. Estimate of the critical angle for rocks containing various fractions of water, assuming the relative permittivity of water is 80 and the anhydrous rock is 5.

As previously mentioned, the relative permittivity of rocks depends primarily on their water content. If a rock contains 30 percent water, then the critical angle can be estimated assuming that only the water contributes to the relative permittivity.

$$\theta_c = \arcsin([\varepsilon_{r\text{-water}}]^{1/2})$$

If $\varepsilon_{r\text{-water}} = \sim 80$ (at 1 GHz), then $\varepsilon_{r\text{-rock}}$ will be around 24 for 30 percent water, and $(\varepsilon_{r\text{-water}})^{1/2} = 3.107$, $\theta_c = \arcsin(1/3.107) \sim 0.20$ radians (12°). Figure 18.8 shows the critical angle for rocks of different water content.

> Experimentally, typical values of the refractive index are between 1.5 and 5 for the ground in many areas for 7.5 GHz.[5] Those microwaves that reach the surface at an angle of less than 11.5 degrees to the perpendicular will also pass through but will change angle due to refraction, and those which reach the surface at more than 11.5 degrees will be reflected at the surface back underground (see Figure 18.4 above).
>
> ---
>
> 5. V.L. Mironov, Pavel Bobrov, A.P. Bobrov, V.N. Mandrygina, V.D. Stasuk, "Microwave Dielectric Spectroscopy Of Moist Soils For A Forest-Tundra Region," *International Geoscience and Remote Sensing Symposium (IGARSS)*, 6 (2005), 4485–4488, https://www.researchgate.net/publication/224621911_Microwave_dielectric_spectroscopy_of_moist_soils_for_a_forest-tundra_region.

If a dowser were standing at a spot, waves would be reaching his or her feet from all directions in the ground, as though he or she were at the center of a hemisphere. The effect of the internal reflection effect is to prevent almost all of these waves, except those select few which approach the surface nearly perpendicularly, by reflecting the majority of them back down again to be absorbed in the subsurface below. If an object is a yard/meter down, then the surface horizontal distance over which the radio waves and microwaves are emitted is only eight inches (20 cm) to be within the critical angle. Similarly, if the object is two yards/meters down, then the horizontal distance is 40 cm, and so forth for other depths.

Refraction not only controls transmission vs. internal reflection but also the angle of emission from the surface. The angle at which the radiation leaving the surface refracts depends on the relative refractive index of the ground versus air, and the angle of incidence of the wave (see above). A wave approaching the surface at 10 degrees from the perpendicular will be refracted so that it leaves the ground traveling at an angle about 30 degrees to the ground's surface. Assuming the dowsing sense organ is in the brain, then this wave has to travel far enough that it can reach the height of the dowser's brain. If the dowser is average height, then their brain is probably 1.5 m (5 ft) off the ground for a man and not much less for a woman, and the radiation will have to travel a distance of 2.6 m before it has enough altitude to reach the brain.

> ## Snell's Law and Refraction of Radio Waves and Microwaves
>
> If θ_1 is 10 degrees, and assuming $n_1 = 5$, $n_2 = 1$, then from Snell's law,
>
> $$\theta_2 = \text{arcsine}(n_1/n_2) \sin \theta_1$$
>
> $\theta_2 = \text{arcsine}(5/1 * \sin[10°]) = 60$ degrees from the perpendicular or 30 degrees from the horizontal ground surface.

As the wave travels out, it spreads out and so the energy per cross-sectional area decreases, in similar manner that the beam from a flashlight spreads out with distance and becomes less intense. If the dowser is standing directly over the object, he or she will get the maximum intensity, since the beam goes straight up, and less intensity the further he or she is away.

Effect of Refraction Angle on Radiation Intensity

The relative energy over distance can be estimated from geometry. The intensity will be proportional to the cosine of the angle (θ) with respect to the perpendicular and the inverse square of the distance (r), since the power will be proportional to the area.

Relative energy $\propto \cos(\theta)/r^2$

Assuming the dowsing sense organ is in the brain, then an estimate of how the intensity of the dowsing signal will vary with distance can be made. If the dowsing sense organ is 1.5 m above the ground (~ 5 ft), then from simple trigonometry, the horizontal distance for the signal being refracted 30 degrees off the surface is about 2.6 m (~8.5 ft), see Figure 18.9. It can be seen that there is not a large difference in intensity for distances much larger than a few centimeters that dowsers can resolve. To paraphrase the old adage, what the critical angle gives in terms of resolution, refraction takes away.

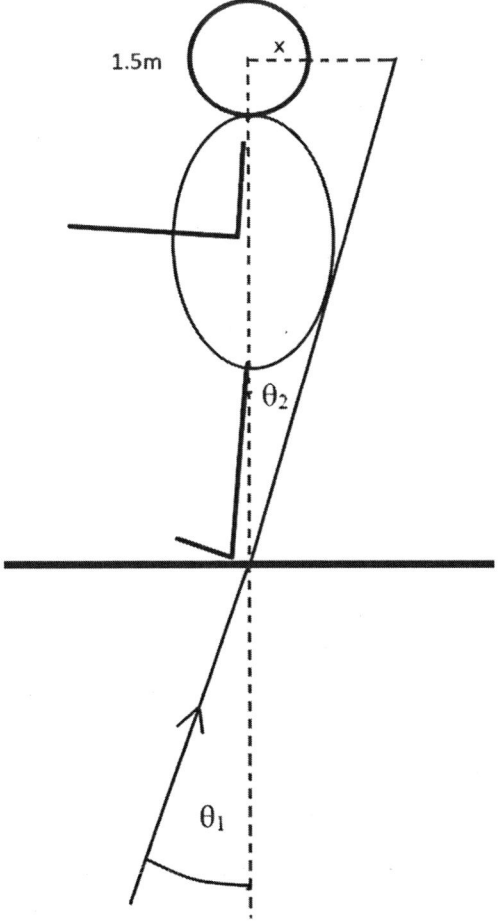

Figure 18.9. Estimate of the horizontal distance traveled by the wave before it reaches the dowser's brain.

The relative energy is shown in Figure 18.10.

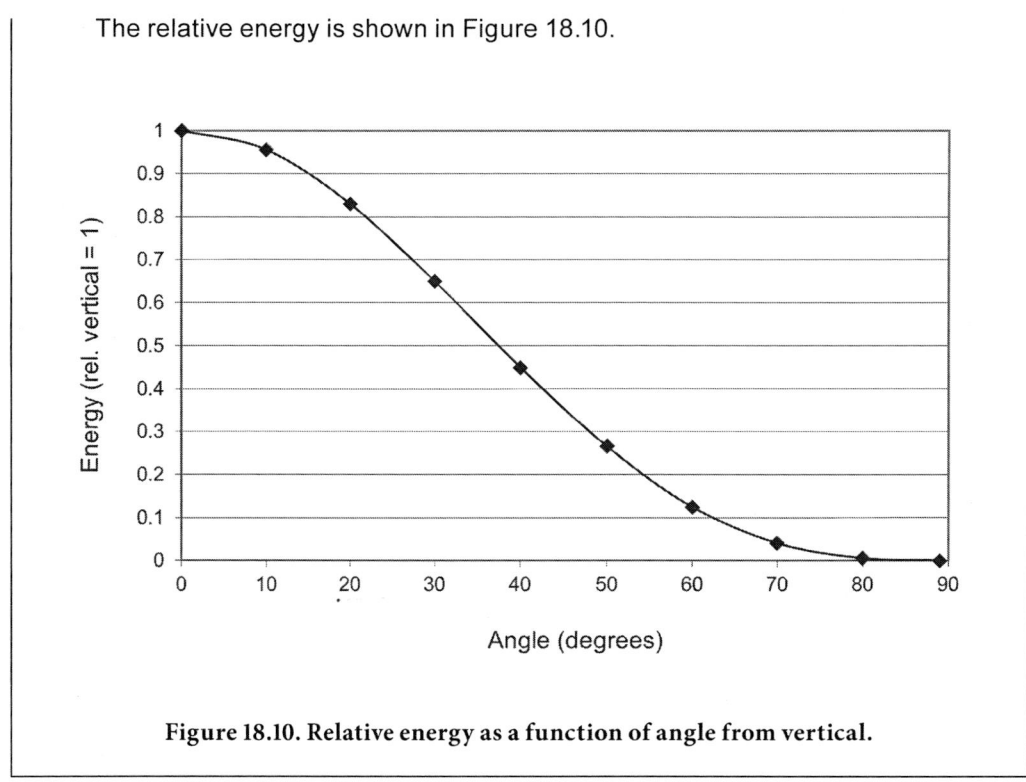

Figure 18.10. Relative energy as a function of angle from vertical.

Snell's law also shows why it is so difficult to measure the dowsing signal instrumentally. Even though only radio waves or microwave photons approaching the surface nearly vertically transmit through, these beams are then refracted to a wide range

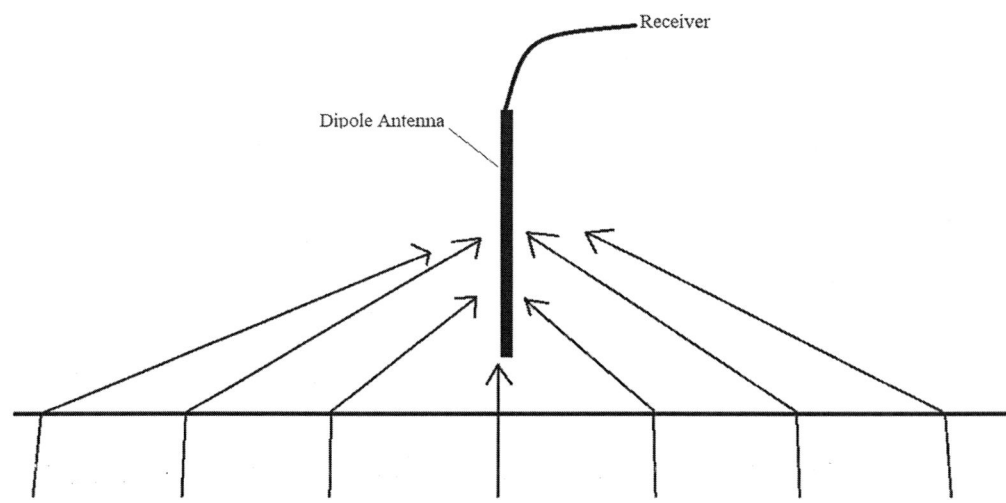

Figure 18.11. Dipole detection of dowsing signal will not detect small changes in signal with distance because of interference from neighboring sources.

Antenna Gain

The term "antenna gain" is somewhat misleading, since it suggests amplification. The gain of antenna is a measure of its directionality compared to an ideal omni-directional reference antenna, a so-called isotropic antenna. There are no completely isotropic antennas, which detect radiation equally in all directions, only a mathematical model which serves as the reference point. Even a simple dipole antenna has some directionality—it detects the electric field parallel to the dipole antenna well but detects radio waves with electric field perpendicular to the axis of the dipole poorly.

Antenna transmission and reception are reciprocal, so the same design considerations and same antenna gain applies to both. The antenna gain can therefore be expressed in terms of transmitting or receiving. The gain A_G of an amplifier is defined as the maximum radiation intensity radiated/received (I_r) by the antenna compared to that given by a lossless isotropic radiator/receiver (I_o) supplied with the same level of power.

$$A_G = (I_r/I_o)$$

If the power is transmitted or received uniformly over all directions, then $I_r = I_o$ and the gain is 1. A Yagi directional antenna may, for example, have an antenna gain of around 20 dB, and a small parabolic dish antenna such as that used for satellite TV reception may have a gain of about 30 dBi; the amplifier gain of a half-wave dipole antenna is typically around 2.2 and a quarter-wave monopole about 5.2dBi.

Equivalent Antenna Gain for Dowsing

If the dowsing signal were detected by an instrumental method, then suppose the device was monitoring the dowsing signal from a height of 1 m above the ground, with a position location accuracy of about 5 degrees. If a directional antenna is to be used, then in two dimensions, the solid angle for detection can be estimated from the area of a circle with a radius of 8.7 cm,

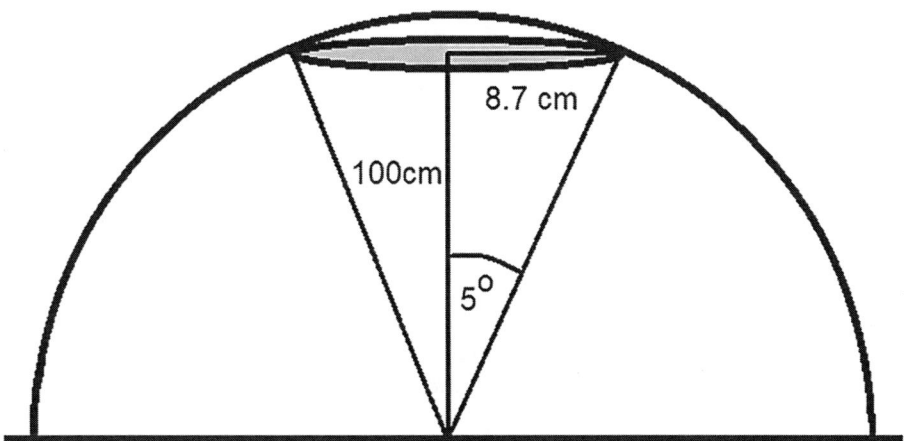

Figure 18.12. Sketch illustrating dowsing gain.

compared to the area of a semi-sphere of radius 1m, which gives a solid angle of 0.12 mSteridans (Figure 18.12). This solid angle is equivalent to an antenna gain dBi of 39.4. Such an antenna gain is difficult to achieve with a small antenna.

of angles. Thus a simple dipole antenna, for example, may detect signals coming from directly below or from two feet away and any small differences in intensity, but the dowsing signal will be swamped by the signals coming from all around, as shown in Figure 18.11.

A much more directional antenna would be needed to detect the dowsing signal. At a distance of 1 meter (~ 1 yard) off the ground, a 5 degree window corresponds to a lateral distance of +/- 8.7 cm from perpendicular (geometry: distance = tan[5°]*1m), which is a little wider than the position accuracy of a typical dowser. The antenna gain dBi needed would be around 39, which is a high value.

Dowsing for Voids

Refraction also explains why it is possible to dowse underground pipes. Consider an empty round PVC pipe buried in the ground. Microwaves will approach from all directions, but only those that reach the surface within a critical angle will be transmitted; the rest will be reflected. Microwaves coming from below the pipe will reach the PVC, which has a refractive index of 1.63 (n = $\varepsilon_r^{1/2}$, relative permittivity of 2.67 at 2.26 GHz,[350]), lower than most soils and rocks because of the latter's water content but higher than air (1.0). The microwaves will refract or reflect at the soil/PVC interface and the PVC/air interface in the pipe depending on their angle of incidence versus the critical angle. This refraction will cause most of the microwaves to be scattered in various directions. The microwaves will then pass through the PVC again and into the soil and will be transmitted at various angles. The critical angle will not apply because the radiation is passing from lower refractive index (air) into higher refractive index (PVC and ground), and so the radiation will pass through. The net effect is that the intensity of microwaves heading up perpendicular to the surface is greatly reduced, so that for a dowser standing on the surface there will be the steady background radiation and then a dip in intensity over the PVC pipe. The dowsing signal is a response to this change in microwave intensity.

Physiological Collimation?

The laws of optics have helped explain much of the position resolution of dowsing, but dowsers can often perform better than can be explained by the laws of optics applied only to the ground, and so there is probably another collimating mechanism at work. There are a couple of related mechanisms that may be at work in the dowser.

The first is that there is some collimation of the microwave signal. If one imagines the simplest type of collimator, a tube of impermeable material, then the width would have to be at least as large as the wavelength of the radiation (few cm) and the length long enough to achieve the desired collimation. Since dowsing signals can be measured walking forwards, backward or sideways, if the head had a narrow tube structure that collimated the dowsing signal, then the orientation of this passage would have to be vertical. Unfortunately for this model, there is no obvious structure in our heads that fits this description. Furthermore, the dimensions do not work out well.

Model for Physical Collimator

A simple model for a collimator is looking at an object down a long tube. The longer and narrower the tube, the smaller the area of the target that is viewed. If such a tube collimator were in our heads, it would mean that our heads were impervious to the dowsing signal except for a narrow passage leading to the dowsing sense organ. A simple model can be used to explore the feasibility of collimation by our heads. Consider a point light source at the end of a tube of diameter δ and length L_1 projecting onto a screen which is distance L_2 from the opposite end of the tube. The light will project a circle with small diameter d. The width of the diameter depends on the diameter and length of the tube, and the distance to the screen (see Figure 18.13).

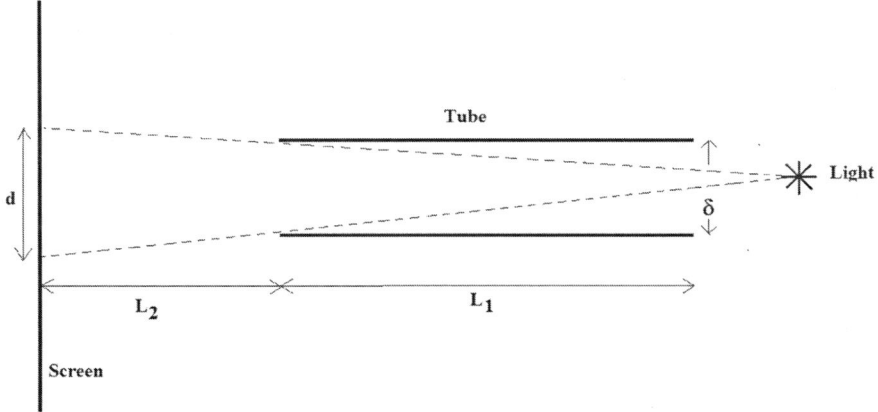

Figure 18.13. Sketch of a point light source shining through a tube onto a screen.

The triangle defined by the light source and the far end of the tube is similar (same shape and angles, though different size) to the triangle defined by the light and the light diameter on the screen. The diameter of the light spot on the screen, using the principle of similar triangles, can be determined from the following relationship:

$$L_1 = \delta L_2 / (d - \delta)$$

Applying this model to dowsing for an order of magnitude estimate of L_1. The tube diameter δ must be at least the wavelength of the radiation (~3 cm), L_2 is the height from the neck down (~1.5 m) and d is the resolution on the ground (~5 cm). Putting these values into the above equation gives L_1 = 2.3m. Clearly this number is not realistic and so the model fails.

It is interesting that the angle of detection of microwaves from an antenna was about 6 degrees (Chapter 15), which is very similar to the dowsing resolution. The microwaves came from an antenna and not from the ground and so there was no critical angle of reflection, yet the angle measured is almost exactly what was predicted for the critical angle of microwaves entering air from water (6.7 degrees, Figure 18.6). Perhaps these numbers are not coincidental, and the second mechanism is a second critical angle of reflection in our heads giving rise to the very tight angular specificity of dowsing. It is not clear exactly where that second critical angle of reflection/transmission would be. Critical angles are important in going from a material of high refractive index to one of low refractive index, and it is unclear where this may be occurring on the passage of the dowsing signal, up the front of the body, through the throat/chin and to the lower brain.

If the microwaves are collimated from the critical angle leaving the ground and in the dowser's body, then these two effects are probably cumulative. Only those microwaves that approach the ground's surface within a few degrees of the critical angle will be able to pass through; the rest will be reflected. Of those that pass through, those microwaves which are furthest from normal will be diffracted away, and only those closest to the normal (perpendicular to the surface) will make it into the dowser's head. Any microwaves which are diffracted away at more than the critical angle in the dowser's head will be rejected.

The very precise angular resolution of dowsing therefore probably results from the combination of both ground and head critical angles.

I stood in the middle of the abandoned 575 foot (~180 m) railway tunnel mentioned earlier that is now a trail and slowly turned around see if there was a difference in microwave intensity facing either the wall or towards the tunnel exits, rotating on the spot. There should be a difference in the microwave intensity facing the exits versus facing the wall (and cliff) and this difference should be over a fairly small angle. If I started facing the wall, then the rods crossed slightly when I turned towards one exit, were straight again when I faced the opposite wall, slightly crossed when I faced the second exit, and the rods were straight again as I came back facing the original wall. The effect was small, so at least in the horizontal plane, there is a slight difference facing front than side, but it is not a large effect. This result suggests that the collimation in favor of a vertical signal only is not 100 percent efficient, but close to it.

Dowsing Signal Path into the Head and Potential Collimators

An attempt was made to identify potential pathways for microwaves to the dowsing sense organ. Different anatomical structures will present different absorptions to microwaves largely depending on their water content. Soft tissues are primarily water and will strongly absorb microwaves, whereas bone has less water and will absorb less strongly, and air spaces will hardly absorb at all. To get an estimate of the relative microwave absorption, an MRI of the head was used. MRI is a form of proton nuclear magnetic resonance, discussed earlier, which looks at the spin of the hydrogen (protons). Water (H_2O) has two protons (hydrogens) and so MRI images are typically bright where there is a lot of water, fats and other hydrogen rich (soft) tissues, and are dark where there are fewer hydrogens.

Two likely locations for the dowsing sense organ in the brain are the brain stem and the cerebellum. The exact location of the dowsing sense is not known, so the intensity of the image was measured from the pituitary gland to estimate the relative microwave absorption. The pituitary gland was selected somewhat arbitrarily and is located at the base of the brain, just in front of the top of the brain stem.

The penetration of microwaves into the head will depend on the relative

> **Magnetic Resonance Imaging (MRI)**
>
> MRI is a form of NMR, as discussed earlier, except that the magnetic field is kept very uniform, and the radio wave signal is a short pulse. When the pulse is applied, the hydrogen nuclei change spin states and once the pulse is over, the protons relax back to the background state. This relaxation can be measured, and using signal analysis techniques that are well beyond this book (and the author!) an image can be generated. There are two main relaxation processes that operate on different times scales, T1 and T2. A few milliseconds after the pulse ends the proton spins will realign with the magnetic field, and this process gives rise to the T1 signal. The faster the protons realign, the greater the T1 signal. The second and slower process is a loss of resonance of dephasing of the spins, and this process gives rise to the T2 signal. The slower the dephasing, the greater the T2 signal. The rate at which these relaxation processes occur depends on the environment the protons are in and hence on the tissue type. By changing the pulse sequence, it is possible to detect the signal after different time intervals. Protons in fat realign quickly with high energy and produce high T1 signal, whereas protons in water dephase slowly. The result is that a T1 MRI shows the fat as bright areas, but the body fluids, which are largely water, as dark areas. In contrast, a T2 MRI shows both the fats and the fluids as bright areas. The resulting image therefore depends not only on the concentration of protons in that area, but also the tissue type. There are other MRI processes such as FLAIR (fluid attenuated inversion recovery) which nulls the signal from the fluids, but they are not relevant to this discussion. For the analysis of water content, the T2 MRI is the best imaging method and is used here.

permittivity of the various constituents of the head (blood, brains, bones etc.) These values are summarized in Table 18.1.

Table 18.1. Relative Permittivity (Dielectric Constant) of Head Constituents[351]

Head Constituent	Relative Permittivity at 1 GHz	Conductivity (S/m)
Air	1.0	0
Blood	61.1	1.58
Cerebellum	48.9	1.31
Bone (Vertebrae)	12.4	0.156
Brain Grey Matter	52.3	0.985
Brain White Matter	38.6	0.622
Cerebrospinal Fluid	68.4	2.46
Fat	5.45	0.0535
Nerve	32.3	0.6
Water	84.4	0.229

A T2 MRI image of a head in the axial (horizontal) plane that intersects with the pituitary is shown in Figure 18.14A.

This image was imported into Fiji[352] image processing software. The software allows one to draw a line between two points and record the integrated pixel intensity along the line. One line was placed on the pituitary gland and the other end was rotated to points around the head to measure the intensity from outside in. The results are shown in Figure 18.14B. The graph shows that the easiest path for microwaves to reach the pituitary gland via this plane is via the side of the head, near the ears. However, it should be noted that there is not much difference between the highest and lowest readings, only a factor of two, so at least on this plane through the head there is not much discrimination of microwaves based on direction.

The process was repeated with an image of a T2 MRI along the coronal (left-right vertical) plane (up/down and side to side) which intersected the pituitary gland (Figure 18.15A).

The head in this view was divided like a clock, with the viewer facing the subject and the intensities along the line were again measured. The results

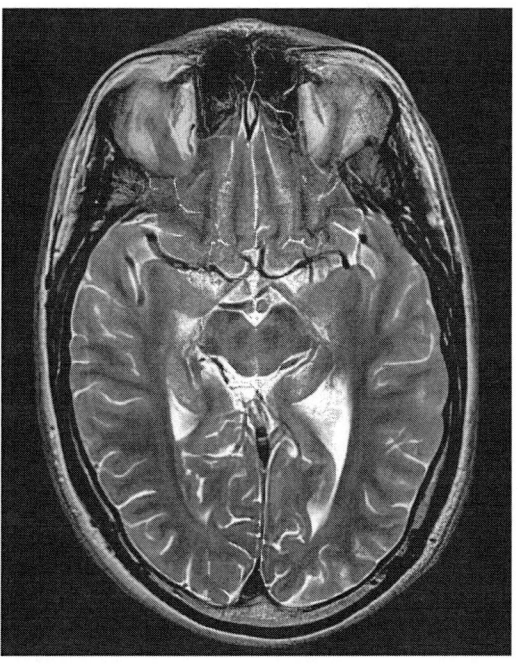

Figure 18.14A. MRI T2 image of a head in the axial plane that intersects close to the pituitary gland (author's collection).

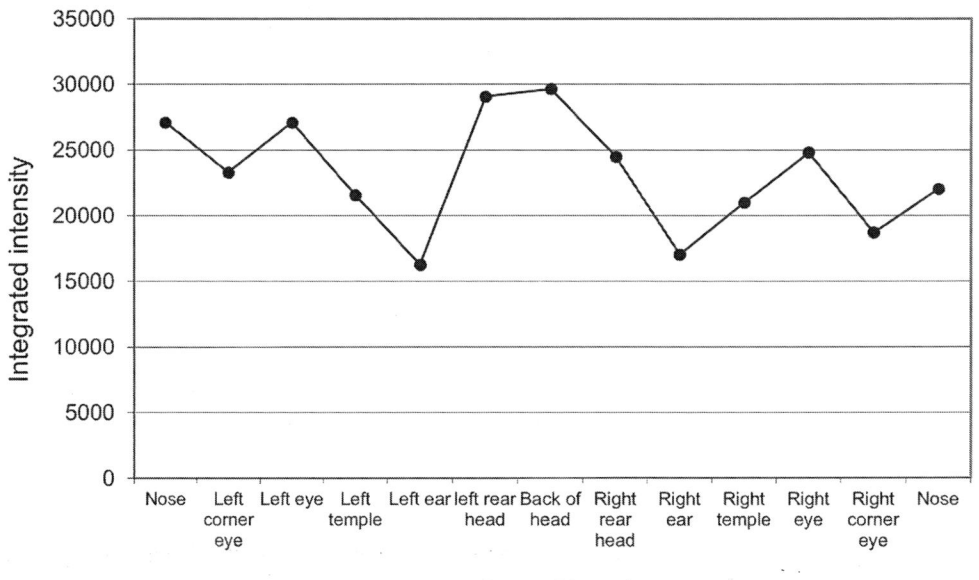

Figure 18.14B. Line graph of light intensity as a function of direction around the head in the axial plane.

are shown in Figure 18.15B. Again, there is only a factor of two between maximum and minimum, and the best path for microwaves is between 4:00 and 9:00 o'clock, so in through the bottom half of the head rather than through the top. The process was repeated with an image of a T2 MRI of a head, showing a slice along the sagittal (front-back vertical) plane, with the starting point at both the pituitary gland and close to the pituitary gland and also the center of the cerebellum (see Fig. 18.16A).

The two data sets were not correlated ($R^2 = 0.00$). Assuming that the intensity of the MRI image corresponds to higher water content, then the lower the integrated intensity the better the path for the microwaves (Figure 18.16B).

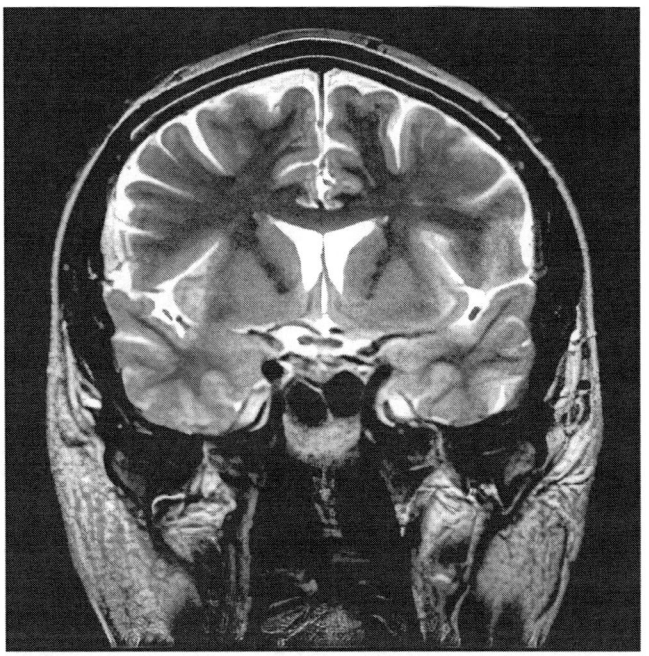

Figure 18.15A. T2 MRI image of head, corona plane, and (R.S. Swenson, *Atlas of the Brain*, 2009, available at https://rsswenson.host.dartmouth.edu/Atlas/, accessed January 1, 2023. Used with permission).

The MRI data also argues against there being a physical collimator. The

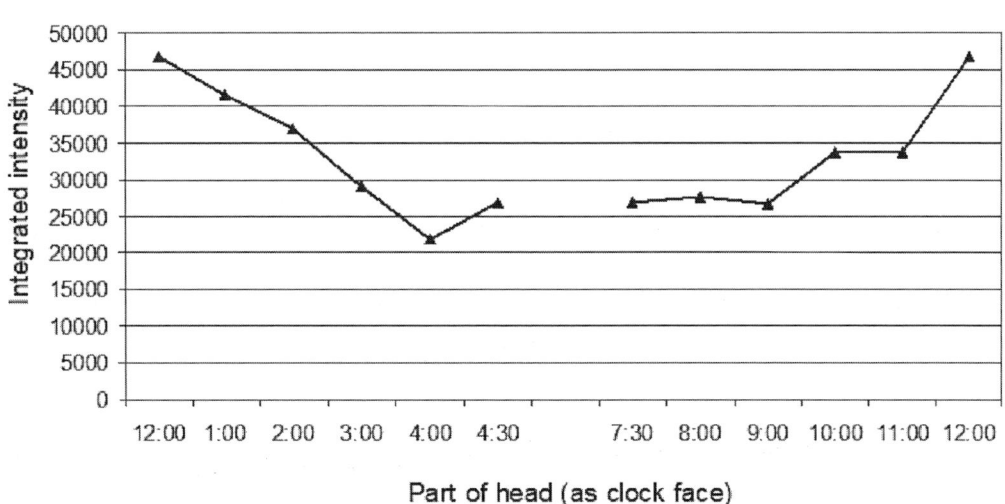

Figure 18.15B. Line graph showing relative intensities in the corona plane from pineal gland and cerebellum to outside.

difference between maximum intensity and minimum is only a factor of three, so the microwaves can come in from any direction. To be a successful collimator, the accessible path needs to be more transparent than the blocked path, by orders of magnitude. A factor of three is not going to have much of a collimation effect. The analysis done with the MRI images shown here was in three axes (three perpendicular lines around a sphere), but there are many other potential pathways that have not been tested, for example, coming out the front left or right side at 45 degrees down to the ground. It would be interesting to repeat the MRI analysis in three dimensions rather than just the three planes described above.

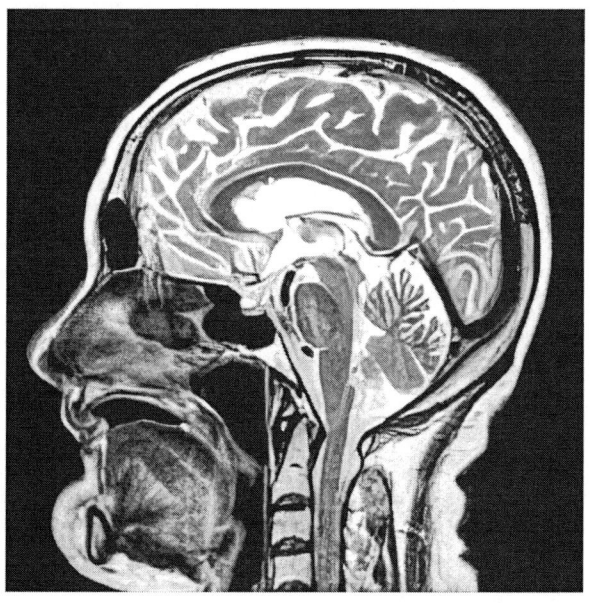

Figure 18.16A. MRI image of the head in the sagittal plane. (Ji Chan Park and Suk Young Park, "Secondary Adrenal Insufficiency Associated with Megestrol Acetate in a Patient with Lung Cancer," *Tuberculosis and Respiratory Diseases* 67, no. 1 [July 2009], https://www.researchgate.net/publication/265021872_Secondary_Adrenal_Insufficiency_Associated_with_Megestrol_Acetate_in_a_Patient_with_Lung_Cancer, accessed December 10, 2021).

If the detection center is near the pituitary, then the best path for the microwaves is through the face around the nose and mouth. Conversely if the detection center is based at the cerebellum, the best path for the microwaves is through the back of the head. Based on this data, a simple test should distinguish between these two potential sense locations. If aluminum foil is placed on the face and the dowsing response drops significantly then the sensing location is near the pituitary. Conversely if the foil is placed on the back of the head and dowsing response drops, then the sensing location is more likely to be in the cerebellum. With the foil placed behind my head, wrapping around to cover the ears, there was no difference, the dowsing response was normal. When the foil covered my face, there was no dowsing response. This result supports the idea that the dowsing sense organ is close to the pituitary gland, rather than the cerebellum. However, none of the graphs included here show a clear preferential path for microwaves that would rule out all other paths.

As seen in the image in Figure 18.16A, if the microwaves are coming in under the chin, they will pass through the tongue and then the pharynx (the hollow space that starts behind the nose and ends at the top of the trachea and esophagus), and then to the brain stem or wherever the detection center is. Perhaps it is the transition from the tongue to the air space of the pharynx that provides the second critical angle. If so, then moving the tongue may make a difference to the dowsing signal. To test this out, I tried dowsing over the sewer line in our basement again, with my

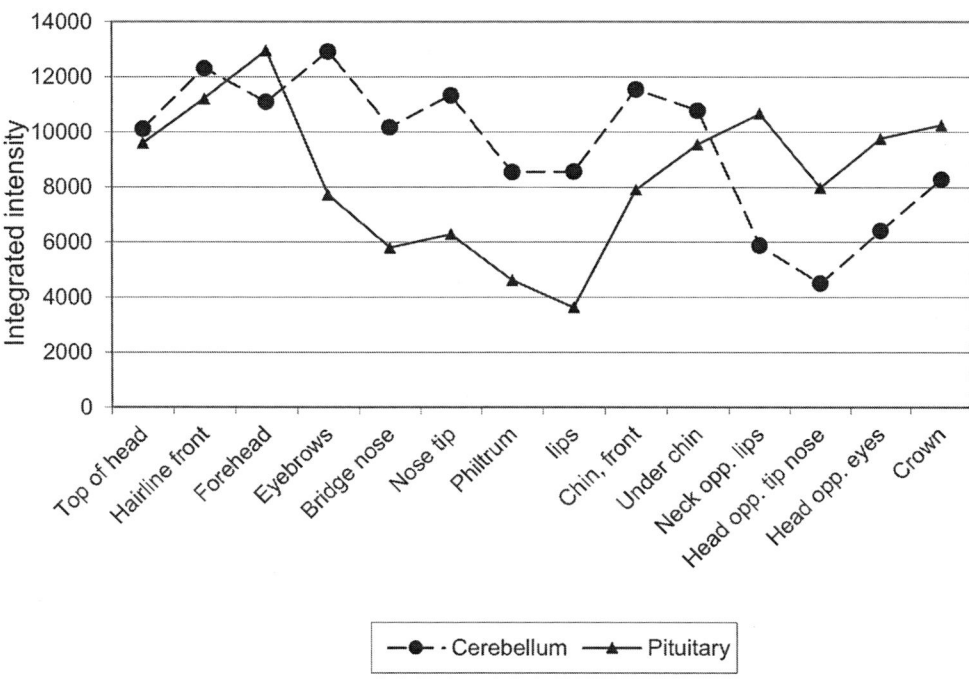

Figure 18.16B. Line graph showing relative intensities from pituitary gland and cerebellum to outside.

tongue in and tongue sticking out as far as possible (another test to only do when no one was around). The dowsing signal was gone or at least greatly reduced with my tongue out, and restored when my tongue was in its normal place. This observation would be consistent with the microwaves being reflected or reflected from the surface of the tongue, and this process being interrupted when the back of the tongue moves to a different location. While this does not prove that the tongue provides a location for the second critical angle, it supports the idea that the dowsing signal passes through the throat-chin and on to the detection center near the base of the brain via the oral cavity/pharynx. However, curiously, when stepping sideways over the same dowsing line, sticking my tongue out had little if any effect. Thus the effect of tongue position on the dowsing response depends on the polarization of the signal relative to the dowser. There are clearly more mysteries waiting to be solved in the future.

Alternative Explanations for Collimation Effect

What is the nature of the dowsing sense organ in our heads? As discussed earlier, the dowsing sense organ appears to be at the base of the brain/brain stem/cerebellum area of the brain, but no such sense organ is known. The dowsing sense operates up to the low GHz region of the spectrum and appears to be highly collimated, but most biological tissues are at least somewhat transparent to low GHz microwave. There is no apparent structure which is capable of reflecting or blocking microwaves.

One can speculate that the collimation comes from the geometry of the detector rather than from blocking unwanted signals. For example, if the detector were a string of magnetite beads strung along a neuron, each bead connected to a voltage-controlled ion gate, then if this string were parallel to the oscillating magnetic field of a microwave the response would be stronger than if the string were positioned perpendicular to the direction of magnetic field. The response of the latter would in principle be zero. However, a microwave approaching the magnetite string at 45 degrees would give half the signal (see Figure 18.17). In support of this idea is the fact that many biological systems form chains of magnetite, though the reason for them is often unclear.[353]

This model, however, has problems explaining the tight collimation observed with dowsing. In contrast the response for the system in Figure 18.17 would be much more gradual (following a cosine function). Therefore, the model needs to be improved.

Some of the most likely biological detectors of magnetic fields in mammals are magnetite particles, which are discussed in more detail in Chapters 23 and 24. The magnetite particles found in biological systems are so small that they have a single magnetic domain.[354] If they are in close proximity, for example, running along the length of a nerve, then they will tend to align with each other. The magnetic field of the assembly

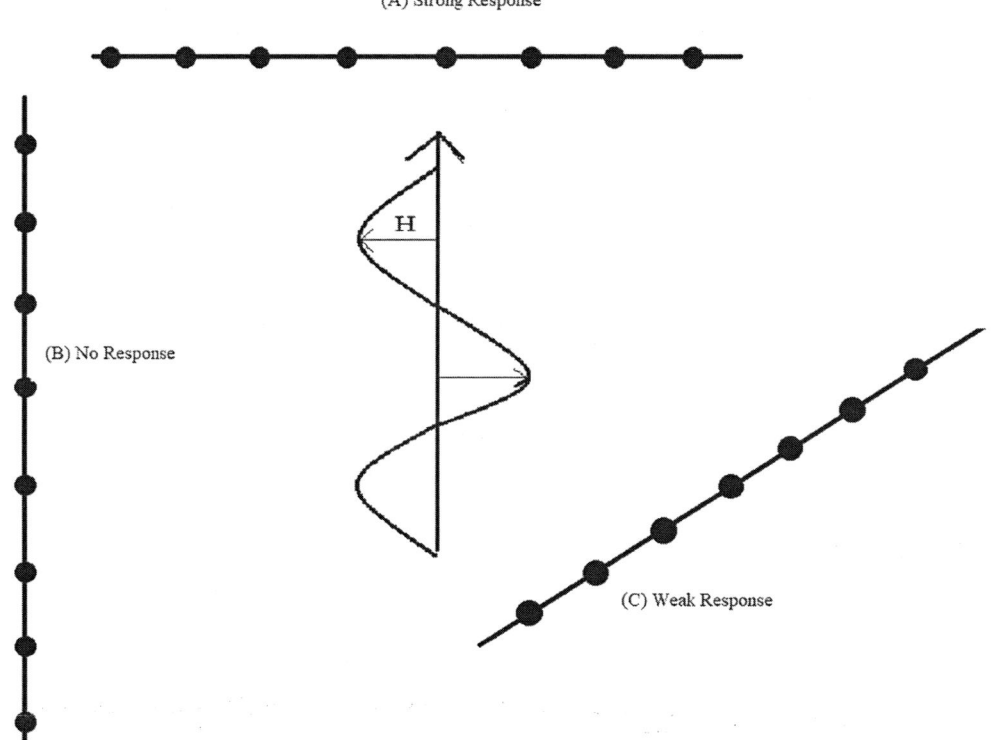

Figure 18.17. Interaction of microwave with magnetite beads on neuron. (A) Bead chain parallel to the magnetic field (H); (B) bead chain perpendicular to magnetic field and (C) bead chain at 45 degrees to magnetic field.

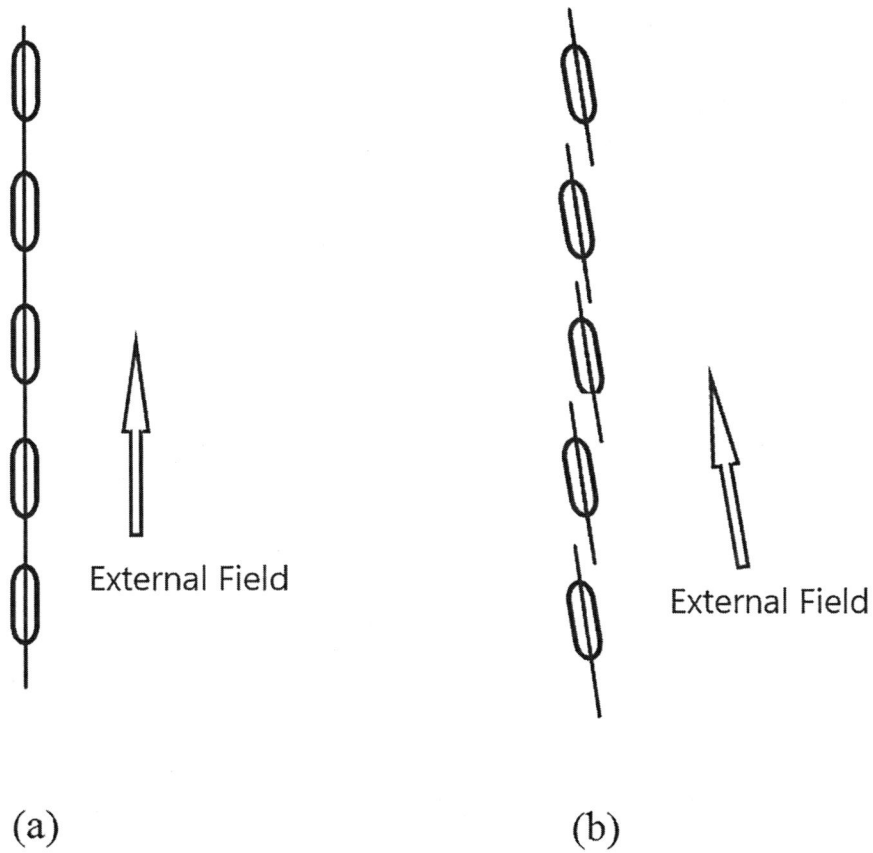

Figure 18.18. Sketch of magnetite particle orientation in external magnetic field. (A) Field is aligned with the magnetite particles; (B) Field is 10° off alignment.

may be greater than the magnetic field from the same number of particles that were not interacting in this way. The external magnetic field is likely to have a much bigger effect if it is parallel to the line of magnetite particles than if it is off-parallel (see Figure 18.18).

If the alignment of the magnetic particles is parallel to the external magnetic field, then the magnetite particles will reinforce each other. If the alignment is not parallel, e.g., only 10 degrees off, then the magnetic fields of the magnetite particles will not reinforce each other. This model gets closer to the observed acute collimation effect seen in dowsing. However, there is no evidence to suggest that this model actually describes what actually happens in either animals' magnetic direction sense or in the human dowsing sense organ. As with so many of the questions raised in this book, we will have to wait for future research to answer these questions.

19

Memory Effects

The Cosmos is all that is or was or ever will be. Our feeblest contemplations of the Cosmos stir us—there is a tingling in the spine, a catch in the voice, a faint sensation, as if a distant memory, of falling from a height. We know we are approaching the greatest of mysteries.

—Carl Sagan[355]

Chapter summary: One of the more outlandish reports of dowsing is the so-called memory effect, where if a steel object is left on the ground for a while and then moved, the ground behaves as if the object is still there for a minute or two. Outlandish they may be, but the reports of the memory effect were verified to be true.

When I first read about the memory effect, I very much doubted that it was real. But I was proven wrong (yet again). Memory, remnants or hysteresis effects have been observed in dowsing by a number of investigators and given various names. The effect describes instances where, for example, an iron pipe placed on the ground will give a dowsing response, but after the iron pipe is removed, the response remains for some time afterwards before slowly fading away.[356] For example, Dennis Wheatley wrote, "Remanence Tracking—One of the most intriguing aspects about objects is that when they are moved, they leave behind a three-dimensional etheric ghost of their past presence, and this can be readily detected with a single rod in 'search.'"[357]

Hanson similarly wrote, "Many attempts to demonstrate dowsing experimentally are probably frustrated by experimenters not recognizing that a substance seems to need time to 'imprint' a 'dowsing zone' into the ground. ... Equally confusingly, the dowsing imprint can remain when the original object that caused it is removed. For example, this imprint can be detected when a steel scaffolding pole is left in situ on the ground for some months, and then removed."[358]

An editorial in the *Journal of the British Society of Dowsers* summarized the memory effect succinctly: "A recognized phenomenon bearing some resemblance to that of scent is the existence of an immaterial residuum which can be appreciated by the dowser after the object from which it originated has been removed."[359] These descriptions are rather vague and ethereal, lacking the physical description that one would expect from a real phenomenon.

When I first read about these memory effects, I assumed that they were nonsense, since I had no reason to anticipate they existed. A steel object moved off a concrete floor would not be expected to leave any residual impact on the floor. If the ground were soft, then perhaps the weight of the steel object would compress the ground somewhat and so cause a residual distortion in the dowsing signal which would be detectable; but the same would not be possible with a concrete floor. There have been a number of reports of this memory effect, and so I tested it for the sake of completeness, fully expecting to see no results. However, a simple cast iron skillet (a type of frying pan) left a dowsing response for a short while after it was removed from the basement concrete floor. This dowsing response lasted only a minute or two, but it was there, and I readily admit I was shocked. However, I also realized that understanding this memory effect would give insight into dowsing in general. A series of tests were conducted to try to better understand what was going on. Readers who are not interested in the tests delving into uncovering the nature of the memory effect should feel free to jump to the end of the chapter, knowing that the memory effect is real.

The typical setup was to place an object on the concrete floor of our basement for a given time, remove it, start a stopwatch and repeatedly measure the dowsing response. Except where stated otherwise, the object would sit there for at least 10 hours. The extent of movement was recorded as the angle of movement of the rods. The angle was estimated by eye, and so the angle is somewhat subjective; however, this approach should be accurate to within about 10 degrees. Zero degrees indicates that the rods are straight out in front (no response), and 90 degrees indicates the rods are fully crossed in front (maximum response). A range of materials were tested to see if they would give memory effects.

A 12 mm (½ in) thick 30 × 30 cm (1 ft) square aluminum sheet was placed on the concrete floor and left for several days. After it was removed, there was no appreciable memory effect. I then replaced the aluminum sheet with a ~ 30 cm (1 ft²) diameter, 5 cm (2 in) deep cast iron skillet of about the same mass. After it was removed, there was a memory effect which lasted for about 3 minutes before it faded away. The skillet needed to be in

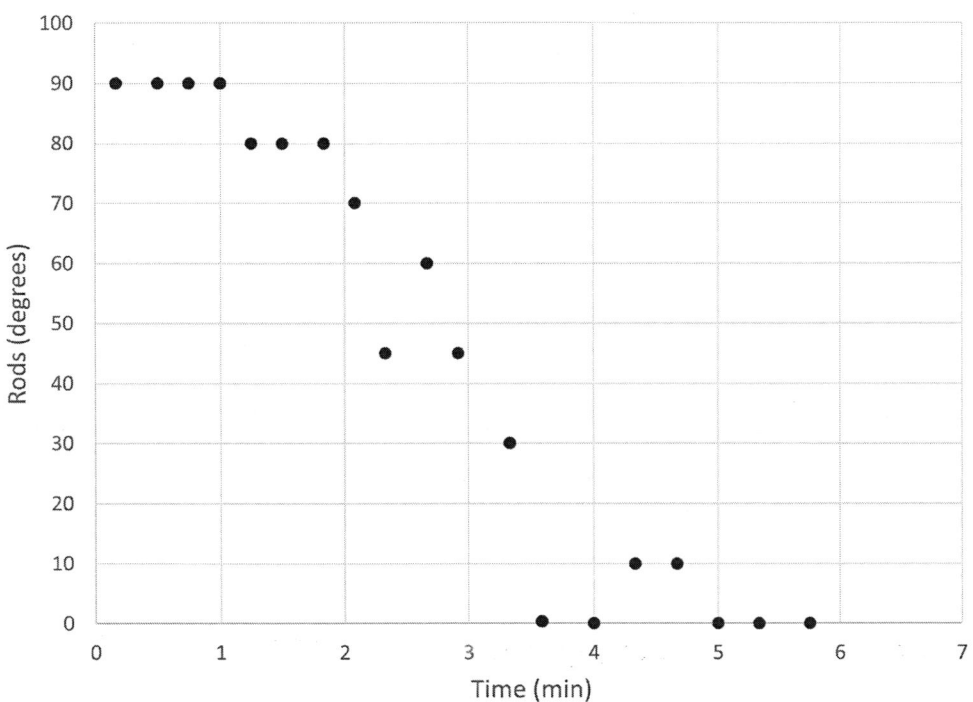

Figure 19.1. Memory response on removing the cast iron skillet after it was left on the floor overnight.

place at least an hour to see a weak memory effect which increased with residence time up to about 8 hours, after which additional time made little difference in the effect. Figure 19.1 shows a typical memory response curve after the skillet had been in place overnight.

This result confirmed that the memory effect was real, but what was going on was unclear. One thought was that the cast iron may be magnetized by the Earth's magnetic field and induced a magnetic field in any iron or iron compounds in the floor/ground (e.g., rebar in the concrete). If this occurred, then there may be a residual magnetic field after the skillet was removed, but not the aluminum, since an aluminum sheet will not have a magnetic field associated with it. However, no change in the magnetic field (x, y, z or total) was observed on removing the skillet and placing the iPhone magnetometer in its place on the floor. Therefore, the memory effect does not appear to be magnetic, or the effect is smaller than about 1 µT, the practical resolution of the magnetometer.

The next thought was temperature. Though both the skillet and the aluminum block have come to steady state temperature with the local environment, perhaps the skillet was a little cooler because it is black and so will emit more radiation across the spectrum (it will also absorb better). The skillet and aluminum block were placed next to each other on the floor and left overnight. The temperature was measured with an infrared thermometer and there was no significant difference between them (the resolution of thermometer is 0.1°C and the accuracy is 0.2°C). The skillet was removed and the temperature of the floor was measured over time. There was no significant change in temperature greater than the resolution of the thermometer. These results suggest that the memory is not caused by a temperature difference of the skillet or the ground immediately below it.

The skillet was black, and the aluminum block was silver color and very reflective (but not polished). The skillet was wrapped in aluminum foil, left overnight and the memory almost went away. Removing the foil restored the memory effect. This result suggests that the foil is blocking some kind of EM wave. The skillet is cast iron so it too will reflect radio waves and microwaves, but it is black, meaning that it is absorbing and not reflecting visible light and probably infrared too.

The experiment was repeated but with a sheet of aluminum foil under the skillet. With the skillet on the foil, there was a memory effect taking about 3 minutes to disappear. However, when the foil was placed on top of the skillet (not wrapped around it) the memory effect was barely noticeable, fading out in about 10s. This result suggests there is a two-step process. Something is coming from above and reaching the skillet, and in the second step something is leaving the skillet and going into the floor.

The experiment was repeated with three gallons of water, in one-gallon jugs in a row, and no memory effect was observed. Water has significant absorption in the microwave region, but barely any in the radio wave region (at least this quantity of water). Therefore, absorption in the microwave region does not appear to be the cause of the memory.

To get the memory effect, it appears that the object needs to be certain metals. Cast iron, and cold rolled steel worked well, but copper, silver, aluminum, and stainless steel did not. So what is the diffference? Nonmetallic objects (wood, wax, sugar, salt) do not appear to give the memory effect. Also, the color of the object appears to be important. The skillet (black) gave a strong memory effect, as did a cast iron Dutch oven (cream colored enamel on the inside, red enamel on the outside). A Dutch oven is a cast iron saucepan, much beloved by cooks everywhere. For the testing here, it was used without its lid. A steel sheet (formerly the side of a desktop computer enclosure), unpainted on one side and black on the other, was tested. Both sides gave a memory effect, but the painted side up gave a much stronger memory effect (the signal faded out after ~6 min vs. ~1.5 min for the unpainted side up). Two identical 30 cm square aluminum sheets were purchased; one sheet was painted with a blue/black automotive spray paint and the other was tested unpainted. Neither sheet gave a memory effect. This result suggests the type of metal is important. Lead shot weights in woven nylon bags for scuba diving were tested and they gave a memory effect. Various stainless steel objects were tested and none of them gave a memory effect. It is unclear if it is the metal alloy composition or the shiny color of the stainless steel, or both, that is the determining factor. Two steel panel saws with shiny blades were tested back to back so that the combined area was about the same as that of the Dutch oven. These saws gave no memory effect, suggesting that bare metal, even steel, does not give a memory effect.

Table 19.1. Materials That Give a Memory Effect on a Concrete Floor

Materials and objects that gave a memory effect	*Materials and objects that did NOT give a memory effect*
• Cast iron skillet, cast iron Dutch oven • Cold rolled steel computer panel • Lead shot diving weights in nylon net bags	• Stainless steel • Silver plated copper, coil of silicone insulated copper wire • Ferrite magnetic sheet (letter sized) • Indium tin oxide coated plastic sheet • Aluminum, foil and sheet • 1 gallon of water • Wood (pine), books, cardboard • 4.53 kg (10 lb.) package white cane sugar • 1 gallon of vegetable oil • Steel can of tomatoes (3 kg, 6 lb. 10oz)

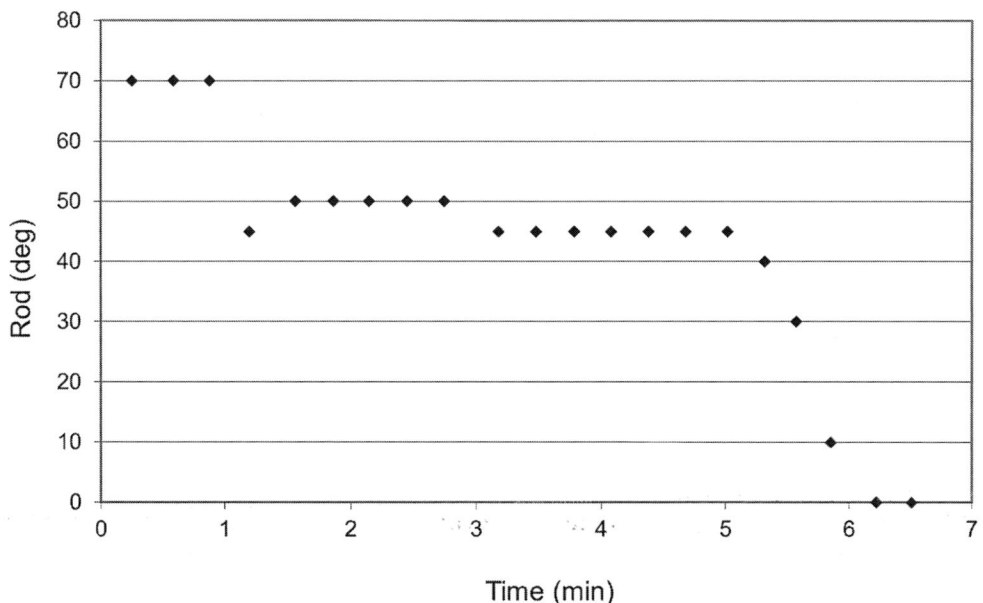

Figure 19.2. Memory effect of Dutch oven on concrete floor.

The strongest memory effect was obtained using the cast iron Dutch oven and so it was used in later testing. The results with the Dutch oven were similar to those observed with the skillet, Figure 19.2 is an example of the memory effect with the Dutch oven.

The graph is typical in form. There is a short period at high angle (~ 70 to 80 degrees), followed by a drop to about 40 to 50 degrees, which is largely flat, followed by a rapid fall to zero response. The time to completion was taken as the time needed for the rods' angles to drop to 20 degrees or below. This value was chosen because it is in the middle of the rapid fall at the end and so should be the most accurate measurement.

Memory Effect—Dwell Time

The next parameter studied was the dwell time, the time the Dutch oven was left on the concrete floor before testing was varied. The results are shown in Figure 19.3.

For short dwell times the memory duration increases with dwell time, but as the dwell time gets longer than about 4 hours the memory duration tends to plateau. This observation suggests that there is a process that saturates or comes to equilibrium after a few hours. The accuracy at which the memory duration time can be measured to 20 degrees is much better than the scatter in Figure 19.3. Therefore, it appears that there are some other environmental parameters that are not being controlled for.

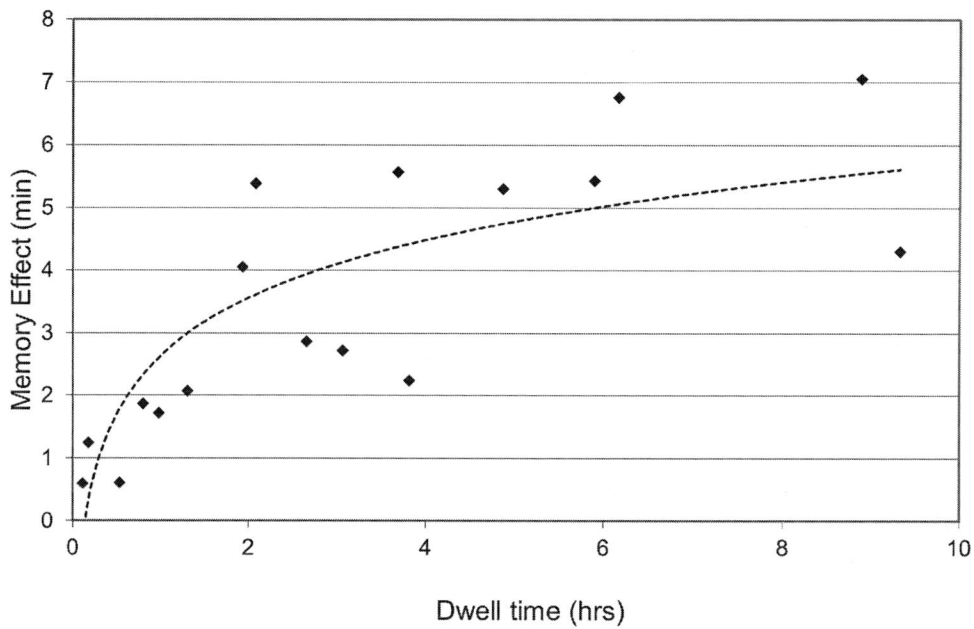

Figure 19.3. Memory duration for Dutch oven placed on concrete floor as a function of dwell time (dashed line is a logarithmic best fit).

There are three stages to the memory effect that can be explored in more detail.

1. The first is the activation stage, the process that is activating the Dutch oven to create the memory effect, and which is blocked by aluminum foil.

2. The second is the memory creation step, the process that modifies the concrete floor that constitutes the memory effect

3. The third is the detection step, measuring the memory effect by dowsing rods or other means.

Memory Effect—Activation Step

Understanding the memory activation step means exploring the radiation or whatever that the Dutch oven needs to create the memory effect. A series of quick tests were conducted, and the results are summarized in Table 19.2. In each case the Dutch oven was placed on the concrete floor and the test material was placed on top of it. After the dwell time, the effect on the memory effect was tested. The dwell time was at least 10 hours in each case, long enough as per Figure 19.3 that small changes in dwell time would not have a larger impact

Table 19.2. Memory Effect Activation by Covering for Dutch Oven

Covering	Effect
None	Strong
Aluminum foil	Blocked
Corrugated cardboard (from a cardboard box)	Blocked
Transparent plastic sheet (PPG's CR36, ~ 4 mm [3/8"] thick)	Blocked

The fact that the memory effect was blocked by aluminum foil suggests that the cause may be EM radiation. The observation that the memory effect was blocked by cardboard and the transparent plastic sheet indicates that it was not due to visible light, radio waves or microwaves (cardboard is transparent to microwaves and radio waves), and therefore the most likely part of the spectrum for the memory effect was infrared or high-frequency microwave.

To get a better idea of the wavelength, the test was repeated but with a stainless steel mesh over the Dutch oven. The memory effect responses were recorded for different mesh sizes. Memory effects were observed for mesh sizes 18, 40, 80 and 120, but no memory effect was observed for mesh sizes 150, 200 and 400. Thus the wavelength of the activating radiation must be larger than the hole size in the 150 mesh (0.11 mm) or 110 µm. EM radiation with this wavelength has a frequency of 5 THz, which is in the infrared. This result shows that to activate the Dutch oven's memory effect, the Dutch oven must be exposed to infrared radiation with a wavelength of 110 µm or less. Presumably this radiation is absorbed by the enamel of the Dutch oven or the black coating of the skillet, but is reflected from surface of shiny metals. This infrared is from ambient background thermal radiation, since there were no other intentional infrared sources nearby.

If infrared can activate the memory effect, what else can activate it? A chemical hand warmer (Megawarmer from Kobayashi Consumer Products LLC, Dalton GA) was placed in the Dutch oven, covered with the 400 mesh stainless steel to prevent ambient infrared activation, and a memory effect was observed.

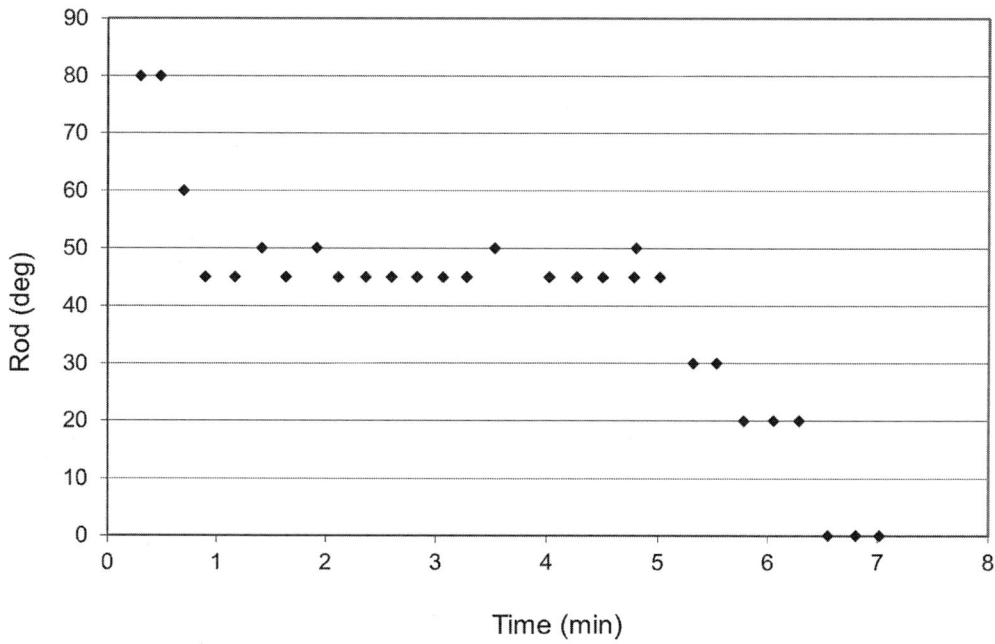

Figure 19.4. Memory effect of Dutch oven containing chemical hand warmer, under 400 mesh stainless steel, on concrete floor.

The graph in Figure 19.4 shows the same general pattern as observed with ambient infrared activation, a short period where the signal is around 80 degrees; a longer, close to flat, period in the 40 to 50 degree range; and a rapid drop-off after a few minutes. Clearly this general memory effect pattern does not depend on the type of activation.

When the Dutch oven was filled with ambient temperature water, there was no memory effect; presumably the water is absorbing the incoming infrared radiation. However, when the water is warm relative to ambient, then the memory effect is restored as shown in Figure 19.5.

The initial water temperature was 53.0°C and the final water temperature was 46.3°C, and the floor temperature when the Dutch oven was moved was 31.8°C. At the end of the run, the floor temperature had cooled to 27.2°C, at least the surface had, compared to ambient floor temperatures around 21 to 22°C. The memory curve is the same general form as other memory curves and does not look like a cooling curve, which would be continuously falling over time in an approximately exponential manner. At the end of the run, the memory effect had dropped to zero, but the temperature of the water and the floor had not returned to ambient. Hot water therefore can also activate the Dutch oven to create the memory effect, but the form of the memory effect is controlled by other factors. The extent of the memory effect also depended on the time the Dutch oven was placed on the concrete, as shown in Figure 19.6.

The memory effect was not caused by the effects of heat on the concrete. Placing the chemical hand warmers or a plastic bowl of hot water directly on the concrete floor did not create a memory effect. Figure 19.7 shows the cooling of the concrete floor.

The floor cooled slowly as may be expected, since the higher the temperature difference between the floor and the surroundings, the higher the heat flow. It should be noted that the

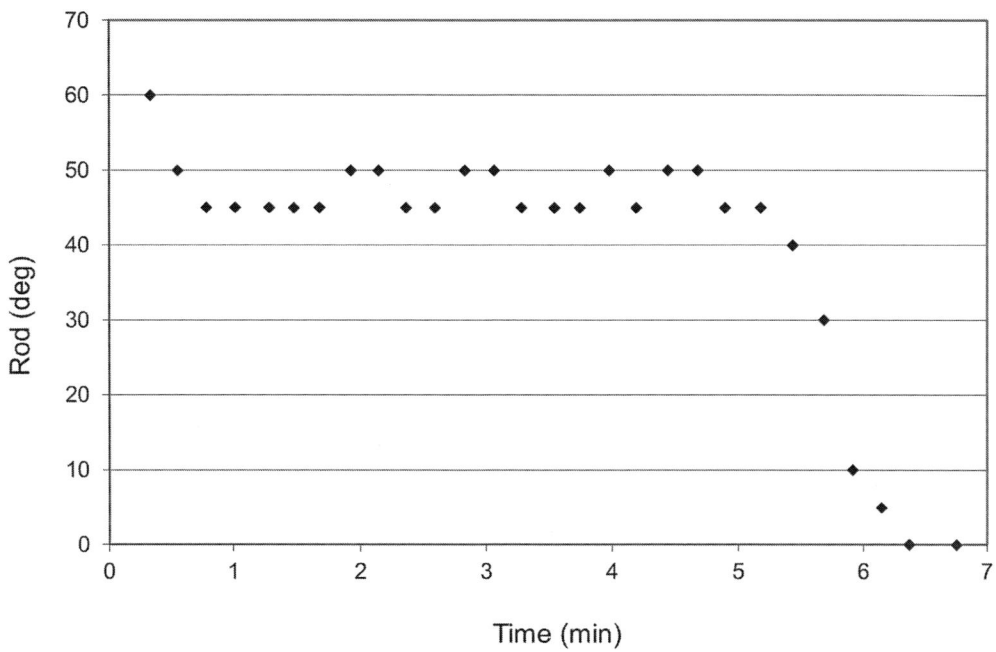

Figure 19.5. Memory effect from Dutch oven filled with hot water and covered with aluminum foil, with a dwell time of 20 minutes.

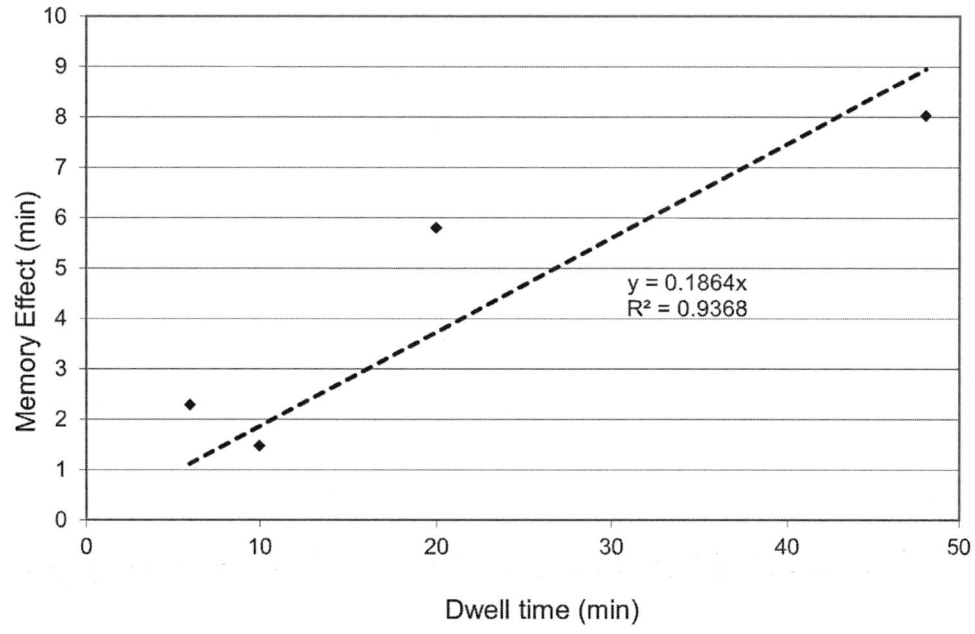

Figure 19.6. Effect of dwell time of Dutch oven half filled with hot water (~ 50°C), under 400 mesh stainless steel cloth on memory effect time.

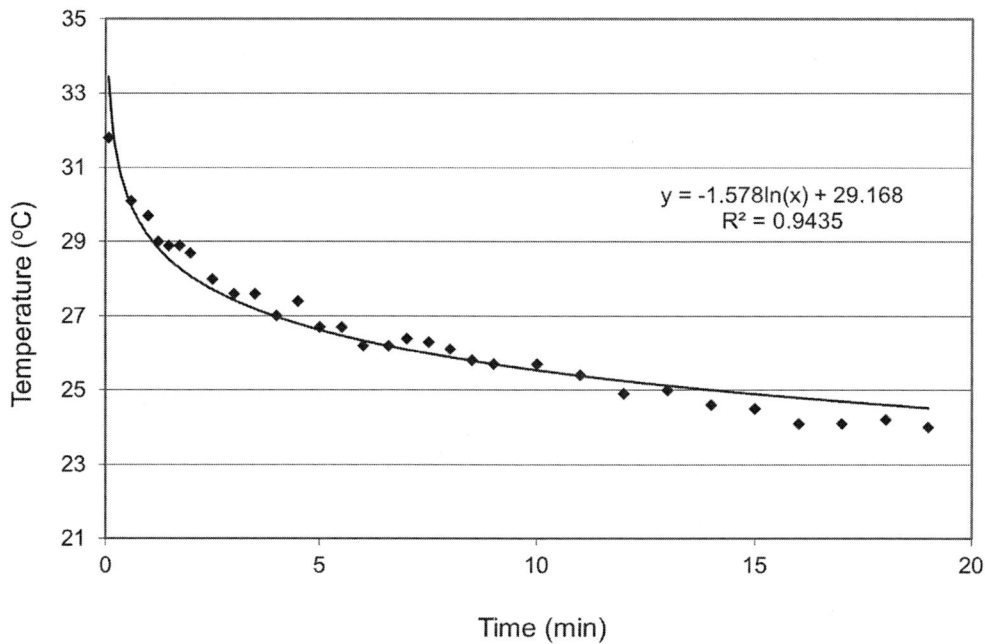

Figure 19.7. Cooling curve of concrete floor after plastic container of water initially at 51.6°C was placed on floor and removed after 15 minutes. Temperature of nearby concrete floor was 21.0°C.

shape of this curve is very different from memory effect curves such as the one shown in Figure 19.5. Unlike the curve in Figure 19.5, the floor cooling curve shows no sudden transition around 5 minutes, and so though the temperature induced the memory effect, the memory effect is not directly proportional to it or a clear function of it. This result suggests that the temperature causes something else to happen, which in turn gives rise to the memory effect.

Memory Effect Creation

Somehow the Dutch oven is changing the concrete floor to create the memory effect. Some simple observations were made.

- When the Dutch oven was placed on a cardboard box about 10 cm (4 inches) off the floor, there was almost no memory effect. The Dutch oven needs to be close to the floor to have a significant impact.
- When the Dutch oven was supported on two pine boards at its edges so that there was a ~ 2 cm air gap between the Dutch oven and the floor, there was a memory effect, but weaker than with direct contact.
- When aluminum foil covered the floor, and the Dutch oven was above the foil, not in contact with it, there was no memory effect. This result is consistent with the Dutch oven's effect on the floor being by EM radiation.
    Note: As mentioned above, when the Dutch oven was in direct contact with the foil, there was a memory effect.

- When corrugated cardboard or the CR36 transparent plastic sheet was placed between the Dutch oven and the floor, there was a memory effect. The EM signal is therefore in the microwave or radio wave region, since these materials are transparent at these frequencies.
- When a copper screen on cardboard was placed under the Dutch oven, copper screen down against the concrete, there was no memory effect for a 2 cm screen, a weak effect for the 5 cm screen and a strong effect with the 10 cm screen (same as no screen). This result is consistent with the wavelength of the radiation from the Dutch oven to the floor being longer than 2 cm, i.e., the same wavelength/frequency as the dowsing signal.

The conclusion therefore is that infrared or heat is absorbed by the Dutch oven, which in turn emits microwaves that affect the concrete floor. These microwaves have the same frequency cutoff as the dowsing signal. However, it is unclear if the emission frequency has the same cutoff or (more likely) the frequency which can effectively induce the memory effect in the concrete has the same cutoff. It is not clear what this process is, but perhaps the Dutch oven absorbs infrared at the frequency of an infrared absorption band of its enamel coating. Subsequently, the Dutch oven could emit across the lower frequency spectrum compared to the incoming infrared, similar to thermal radiation. However, if the concrete only absorbs certain bands, and only one of these bands is associated with the memory effect, then the wavelength of this band will be detected using the grid method to determine the cut off wavelength and frequency.

An equally interesting question is what is happening in the concrete floor. My initial thought was that the concrete floor was absorbing the microwaves and then emitting them later, analogous to phosphorescence. My kids used to have some phosphorescent stars or other objects that would be "charged up" by holding close to a light, and then once the lights were turned off, the object would continue to emit their greenish glow for some time later. At first glance, the concrete floor appears to be behaving as though it were a microwave phosphor. Phosphors function by absorbing the light, and then the excited states decays to a metastable state that is slow to return to ground state (spin forbidden transition). I am not aware of any microwave phosphors and a brief literature search did not find any either.

However, the story gets stranger still. If the Dutch oven is placed on a pine board (19 mm, ~ ¾ inch thick) the memory effect in the concrete floor is present, but smaller than if the Dutch oven were placed directly on the floor. However, when the Dutch oven is moved away, and the pine board is also moved to a different part of the concrete floor, now there is a memory effect from both the original location on the concrete floor and from the pine board. Whatever the "charging" mechanism is that energizes the concrete floor also energizes the pine board as illustrated in Figure 19.8.

What is remarkable is that the memory effect of the two materials was very similar, both in magnitude and in timing. The experiment was repeated with two pine boards, and on moving the Dutch oven, the memory effect of the concrete floor and both boards was recorded, as shown in Figure 19.9. When four boards were used, the four boards were tested as two pairs, top two and bottom two. The two sets of pine boards behaved similarly, but the memory effect from the concrete floor was minimal.

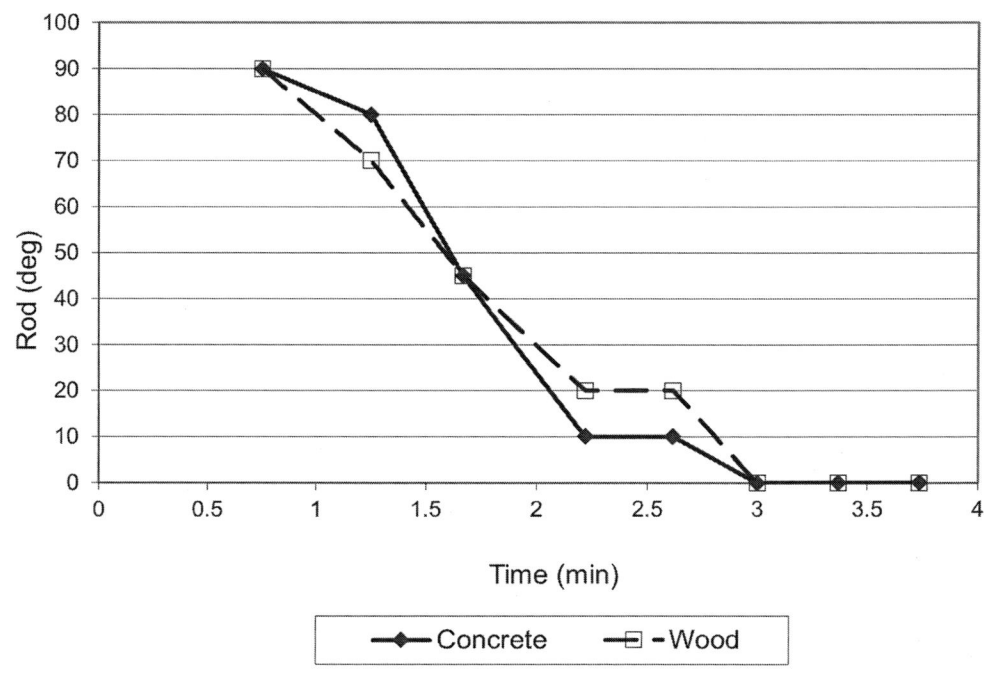

Figure 19.8. Memory effects of Dutch oven left for ~ 11 hours on pine boards on concrete floor.

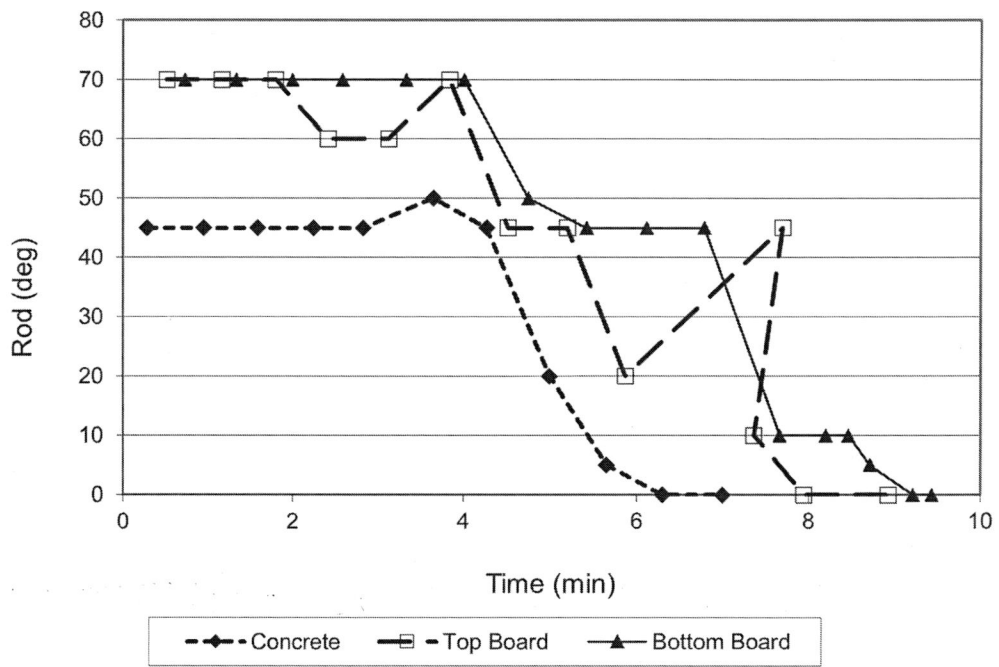

Figure 19.9. Memory effect from Dutch oven placed on two pine boards on concrete floor.

When the pine board was replaced by a sheet of expanded polystyrene (30 cm × 30 cm × 2.5 cm [1ft × 1ft × 1in]), there was a memory effect from the concrete floor but none from the polystyrene. Similarly, when paraffin blocks (8 × Gulf paraffin wax blocks each 11.4 × 5.8 × 1.8 cm [4.5 in. × 2⅜ in × ¾ in]) were laid 4 × 4 to give a rectangular sheet, there was no memory effects from the paraffin, but there was from the concrete floor. The signal had passed through the polystyrene and paraffin to affect the concrete below. When the pine board was replaced by a 3 kg pack of cane sugar, there was a weak memory effect from the sugar.

When the experiment was repeated but with the Dutch oven on a pine board and beneath the pine board was the 2 cm copper screen, then the pine board showed the memory effect, but the concrete floor did not. The radiation that induces the memory effect is blocked from reaching the floor by the copper screen, and so no memory effect.

The memory effect can be induced in concrete, wood, paper books, weakly in sugar, but not in polystyrene. One component that all of the memory active materials have in common is water in various forms (free, adsorbed, water of crystallization etc.). Perhaps the memory effect is a function of the water present in these materials. Another observation with the four pine boards is that the induction of this memory effect only goes down a few centimeters, not several meters. EM radiation in the low GHz frequencies can only penetrate a few centimeters in contrast to dowsing, which can detect signals from several meters below the surface of the ground, as is discussed in more detail in the next chapter.

Detection of Memory Effect

The dowsing signal from the memory effect was investigated. The primary measurements were made using the dowsing rods, and from the user's perspective, these tests did not appear or feel any different from other dowsing. The frequency of the signal was determined using the adhesive copper strips on cardboard grids described above, and as with other dowsing, aluminum foil blocked the signal, as did the 2 cm grid. The signal was weaker with the 5 cm grid, but full strength with the 10 cm grid. The experiment was performed by creating the memory effect with the Dutch oven and then testing bare floor with foil, bare floor with 2 cm grid, bare floor with 10 cm grid, etc. The experiment was performed several times with the same results. The characteristics of the memory signal were the same as the normal dowsing signal, with a wavelength of less than about 5 cm and so a frequency of ~ 3 GHz or higher. Whatever the memory effect is, it is repeatable, and I found nothing related to it in a search of the literature. The mechanism of the memory effect appears to be in the following steps:

1. Some metal objects emit microwaves of the right frequency when stimulated by heat or infrared.
2. These microwaves are absorbed by the concrete floor and the wood board that the metal object is lying on.
3. Afterwards a microwave dowsing signal can be detected using dowsing rods.

If this mechanism is correct, then exposing the concrete floor to microwaves of the appropriate frequency should give a subsequent dowsing response similar to that obtained using the Dutch oven.

Microwave Induction of the Memory Effect

To test this theory, a GHz signal generator (Gigatronics model 900) was attached to a horn antenna. The horn was placed face down on the floor, and the signal at the chosen frequency (no modulation, no attenuation) was applied for a minute. The horn was then moved, and the floor area was then tested with dowsing rods until the signal faded away. The dowsing responses at different frequencies after exposure for 1 minute are shown in Figure 19.10.

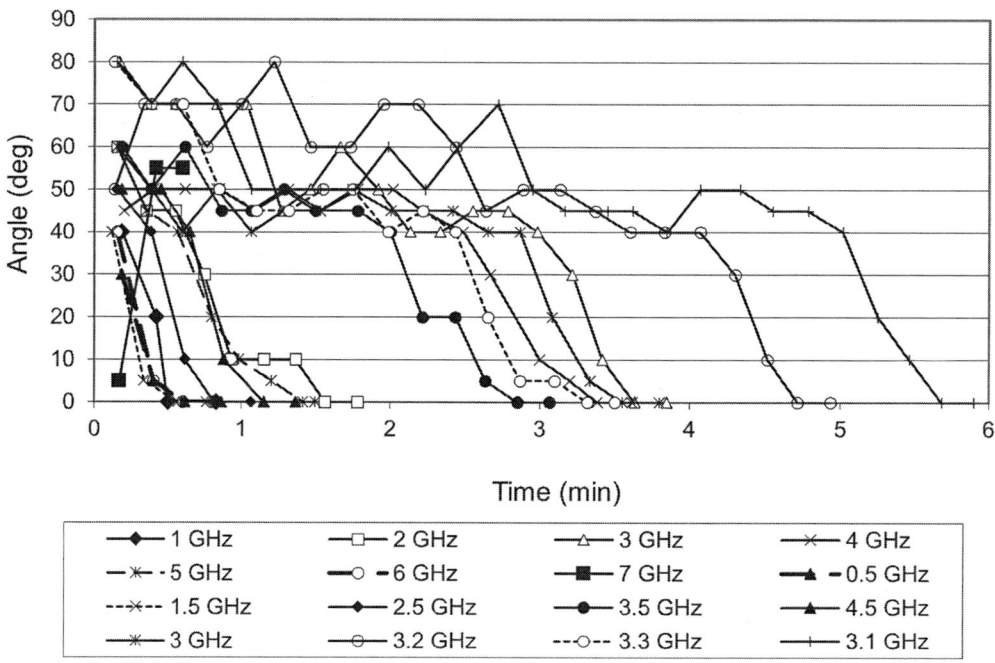

Figure 19.10. Dowsing response of concrete floor after 1 minute exposure to microwaves at various frequencies with horn antenna (power delivered to antenna ~ 1 mW).

Characterization of Horn Antenna

Two identical horn antennas were purchased from a used equipment dealer on eBay. The antennas had both an N connector and a waveguide. The antennas were described as dual frequency, the "N" connector being for 5.7–5.9 GHz and will cover the 5.65–5.925 GHz band. The waveguide is for 3.7–4.2 GHz. The antennas are linear polarized, and they had been partially dipped in some kind of conformal coating for weather resistance. A photograph of one of the antennas is shown in Figure 19.11.

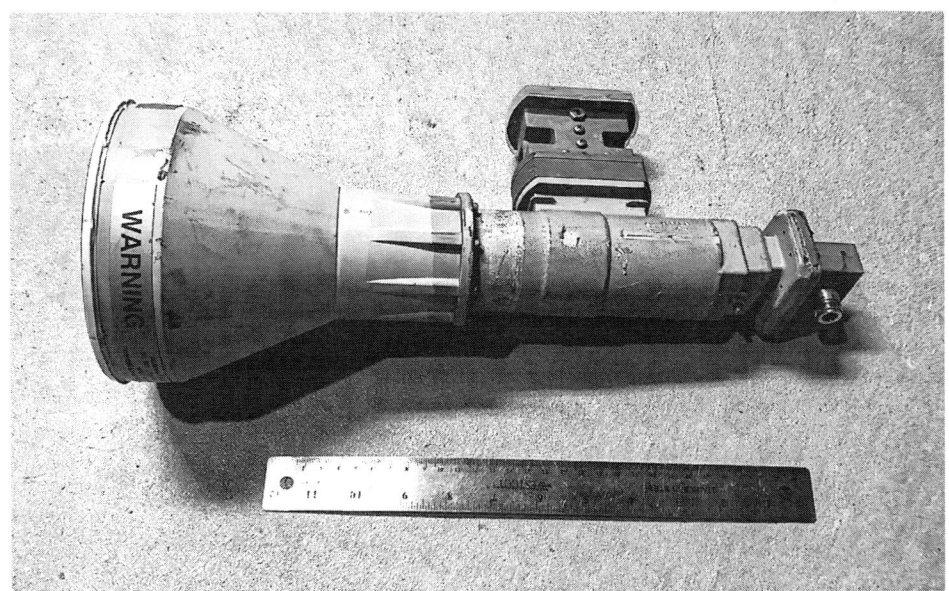

Figure 19.11. Horn antenna with 30 cm ruler for scale.

For this testing, only the N connector was used. The frequency dependence of the antenna was determined by connecting one of the horn antennas to the Gigtronics 900 signal generator and the other to an HP 437B power meter and HP 8481D power sensor, set up so that the antennas were aligned facing each other, with a separation 30 cm from horn opening to horn opening. The results are shown in Figure 19.11 and confirm that the horn antennas function best at 4 to 12 GHz and receive no significant signal below 3.5 GHz.

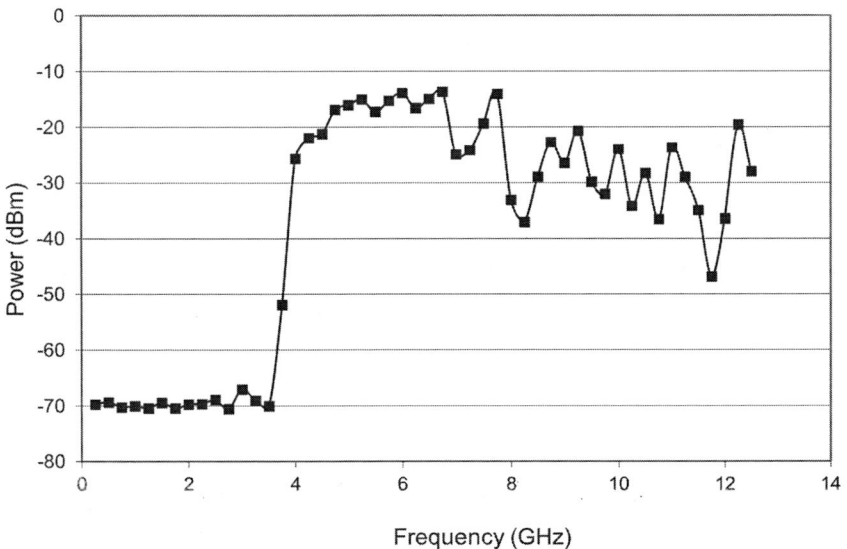

Figure 19.12. Characterization of frequency response of horn antenna.

For frequencies about 4 GHz, there was only a small and brief dowsing response, and for signals below about 2 GHz, the dowsing response faded quickly. The longest lasting dowsing signal was obtained at a frequency of 3.1 GHz. The dowsing response is shown in Figure 19.13.

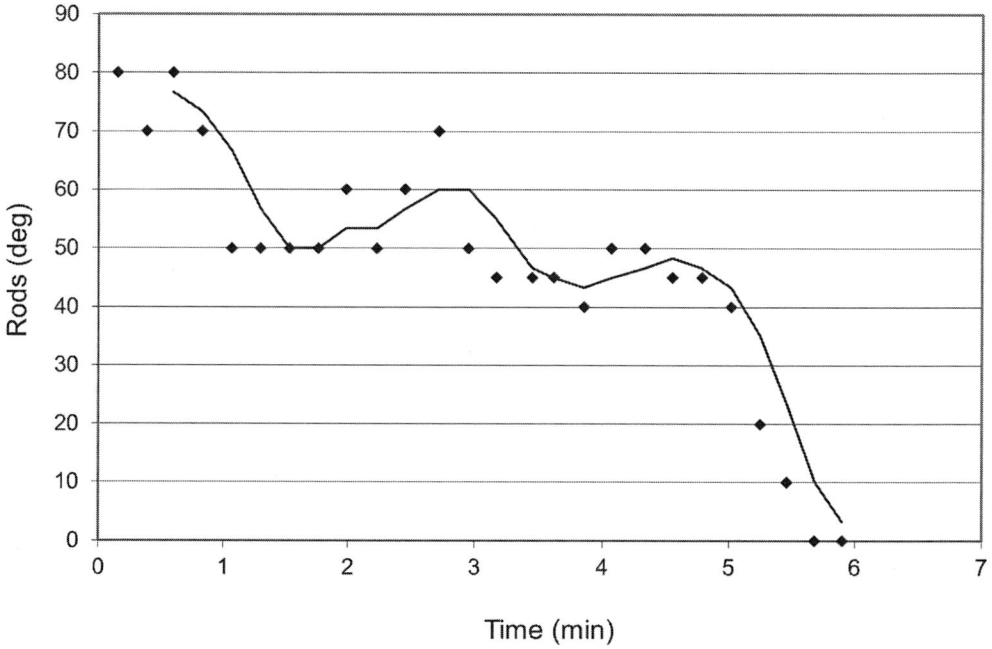

Figure 19.13. Dowsing response to concrete floor exposed to 3.1 GHz for 1 minute with horn antenna.

The graph in Figure 19.14 shows the time taken for the dowsing signal to fade way as a function of frequency.

One of the surprising features of the graph shown in Figure 19.14 is that the peak intensity is around 3 GHz, even though at 3GHz, the antenna efficiency is very low. Despite the low efficiency, there must still be enough signal strength at 3 GHz to cause this effect. It is also a testament to the very low signal strengths that the dowsing method can detect, as discussed in Chapter 15.

The response after exposure to 3.1 GHz was tested for wavelength using the copper grids. Aluminum foil and the 2 cm spaced copper grid blocked the signal, but the 5 and 10 cm grids allowed it to pass. These are the same wavelength properties as used for dowsing for underground pipes and other structures.

The memory effect was observed in pine boards using the Dutch oven, and so the pine boards were exposed to microwaves and tested for the memory effect. The result can be seen in the graph in Figure 19.15, which shows the dowsing response at 3.1 GHz. For these tests the horn antenna was placed vertically, directly on the pine board with no gap.

The frequency dependence of the dowsing rod response with frequency is shown in

19. Memory Effects

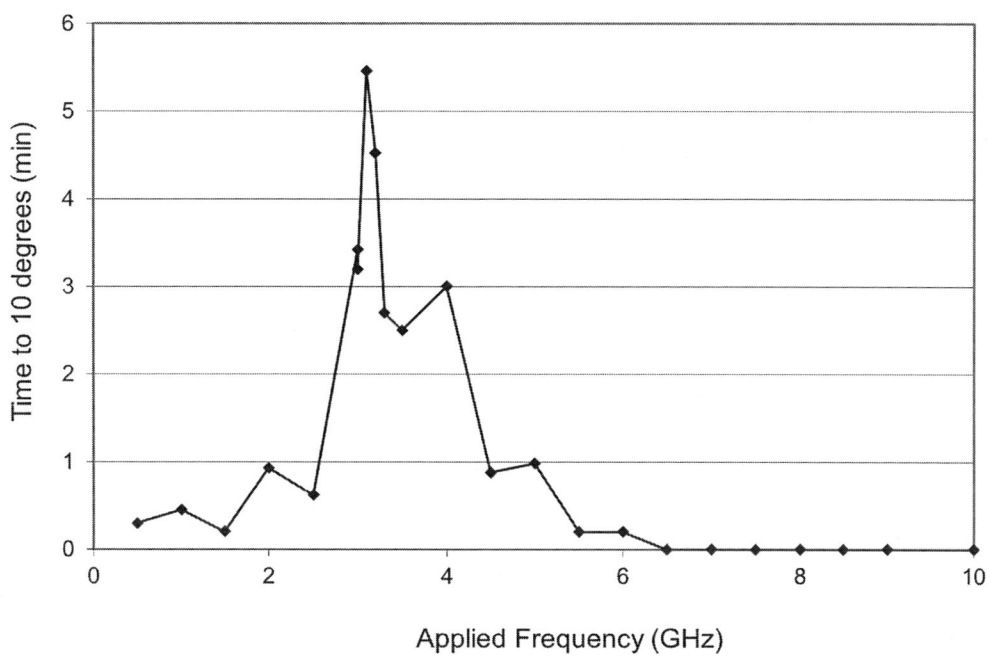

Figure 19.14. The time for the dowsing response to fall down to 10 degrees after exposure of a concrete floor to microwaves for 1 minute.

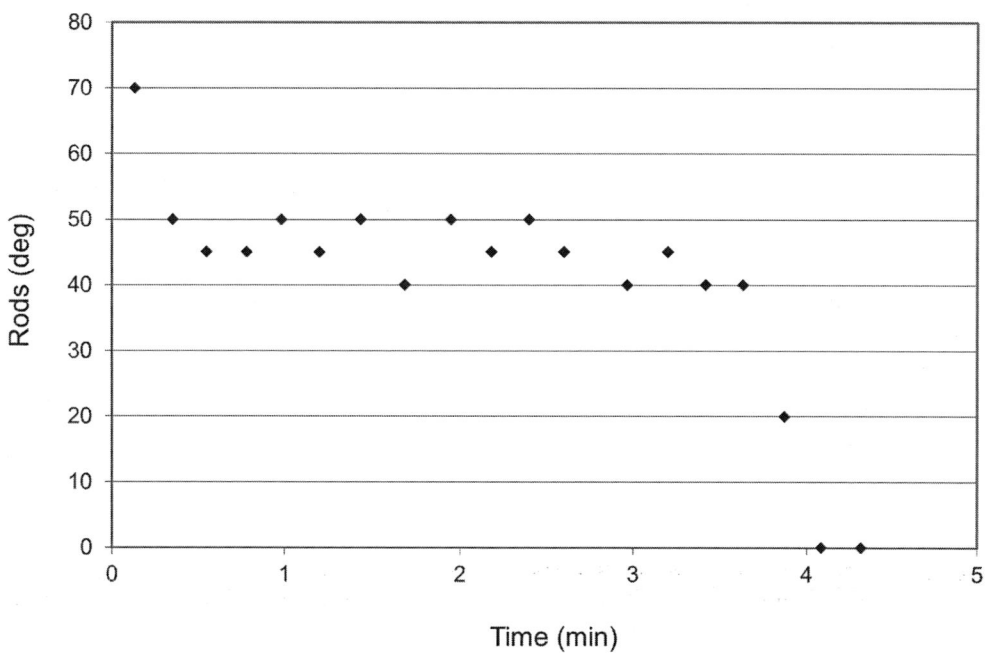

Figure 19.15. Response of dowsing rods after exposure of pine board, horn antenna, 3.1 GHz applied for 1 minute.

Figure 19.16. The general form of the response is similar to what was observed after exposure to the concrete floor, but the peak is broader with a different shape.

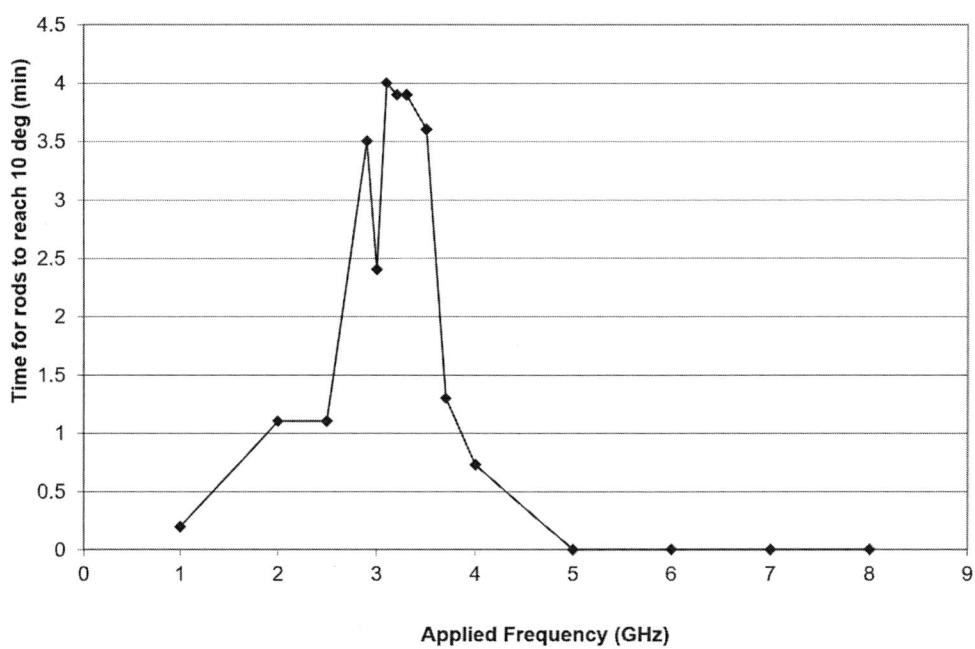

Figure 19.16. Dowsing response of pine boards exposed to microwave radiation. The time for the dowsing response to fall down to 10 degrees after exposure of a pine board to microwaves for 1 minute.

The experiment was repeated, but with the antenna directly over a plastic container of water, and no memory effect was observed in either the water or the concrete floor, suggesting the liquid water simply absorbed the microwaves. One difference was that instead of placing the horn antenna on the surface as with the concrete and the pine boards, the horn was held about 1 cm above the surface of the water. However, the water was undoubtedly exposed to the microwaves. Thus liquid water does not appear to exhibit the memory effect. The experiment was repeated but with the water frozen as a block of ice (~ 5 cm, 2 inches thick). After exposure to 3.1 GHz radiation for 1 minute, there was no memory effect from the ice but a strong memory effect from the floor, of similar magnitude to when the microwave horn antenna was placed directly on the concrete floor. These observations suggest that the ice was transparent to the microwaves and did not interact with them. The experiment was repeated at 3.1 GHz but exposing a 4 kg (10 lb.) bag of granulated white sugar or two books (each 24 × 16 × 4.5 cm, 9.5 × 6.25 × 1.8 in).[360] Both the sugar and the books exhibited the memory effect, as did the concrete floor under them, though weakly. The latter point indicates that some of the microwaves passed through the sugar or the books and excited the concrete floor.

The common component of concrete, pine, sugar and paper is water. Since liquid water does not show a memory effect, it is probably bound water or a water-related species such as hydroxyl or hydroxide. Gigahertz radiation is generally associated with molecular rotations; and rotational energy like most things on the molecular scale is quantized, i.e., only discrete values are allowed. The excitation band around 3.1 GHz may therefore correspond to the rotation of a water-related species bound to the material. In gases and liquids relaxation from energetic rotational levels is promoted by collisions with other molecules, but perhaps the collision rate of an adsorbed water-related species is much smaller, and so the stability of the excited state is much greater.

This effect appears to be a new phenomenon that has not been studied before and so that opens a whole world of opportunities. Some clear areas for further study include

- Using an antenna which is designed to operate in the 2 to 4 GHz range to induce the memory effect.
- Looking at the effect of the memory effect with different materials, to better understand how the effect varies with the material.
- Measuring the microwave emissions from the Dutch oven instrumentally. If these emissions can be measured instrumentally, then the subject becomes much easier to study quantitatively, whereas dowsing is both subjective and not very quantitative. This change is analogous to going from analyzing perfumes by smell to using gas chromatography to identify and quantify the perfume's components.
- Measuring the microwave signal from the concrete floor and other materials instrumentally, for the same reasons.

Conclusion of Memory Effect

In conclusion, the reports of the memory effect were verified. It was found that it only occurs with certain metals (steels and lead), and only when they have a coating of oxide, paint or enamel. Other metals, such as aluminum, silver, copper, stainless steel, did not appear to produce a memory effect. The memory effect lasts up to a few minutes and follows a typical pattern consisting of an initial drop in the rod angle from about 70 to 80 degrees, followed by a plateau around 40 to 50 degrees, and then a rapid drop to zero.

Three stages were identified in the memory effect. The first is the activation of the metal by ambient infrared light, or by heat. The second is the emission of microwave radiation into the substrate around 3 GHz or higher, and the third is the later emission of this radiation from the substrate, at the frequency range, which corresponds to the dowsing signal frequency. The substrate in which the memory effect could be induced included concrete, wood, sugar and paper. The common component of these materials is water. The mechanism of the memory effect is not known. The memory effect also can be stimulated by exposing the material with microwaves around 3 GHz, and later it will give a dowsing response over a time scale of several minutes. This memory effect definitely deserves closer examination by researchers better equipped than I am. A tentative explanation for this effect is offered in the next chapter. If the effect is caused by absorbed water or some other water-related species, then closer study will provide valuable information of the structure of the water in these materials; if not, then further study will reveal new hidden truths about concrete, cellulose and many other materials.

20

Depth

Mankind loves mysteries—a hole in the ground, excites more wonder than a star in the heavens.

—Josh Billings[361]

Chapter summary: Various methods employed by dowsers to estimate the depth of the object of interest are reviewed. One of the most common methods is called the Bishop's method and it was verified to be correct. How it occurs is not clear, but again, it appears to be a combination of microwave optics and physiology.

Depth Methods

Dowsing is mainly used to get information about objects under the ground, and one of the key pieces of information is depth. Several methods are used by dowsers to determine the depth of an object, be it water, a pipe, etc. A common method used to estimate depth is to count the times the dowsing stick bobs. For example, Thomas wrote, "The heavy end (of a forked willow) points toward the ground, held about a foot off the ground, and it starts bobbing up and down … and each bob represents about a foot of depth. He just counts until it stops bobbing up and down and starts moving side to side—which indicates where the water is. If it's a thick vein of water, the stick will swing side-to-side many times. But if the stick only swings side-to-side a couple times, you know there isn't as much water there."[362]

The following account describes a similar way of determining depth: "At last, at a spot not more than 30 feet from the back porch, the branch went wild. Joe said he reckoned this was where the water vein was and it was only about 30 feet deep. … Joe explained how the number of dips the branch made told him how deep the water was and the force of the downward pull told him the amount. I tried it with the same branch and it would do nothing for me. Ditto for my dad."[363]

Perhaps this method is related to Henry Gross asking his dowsing rod successive questions about depth, and the bobs down to indicate yes, until he gets to the answer.[364] A.P. Tabraham described a similar thing: "Having established the exact spot, the question is at what depth is the water, either for a well or a borehole. This is done by approaching the spot holding the dowsing rods and asking out loud or inwardly, how deep down the water is in feet, and then start counting from one. The rods will not react when counting starts, but will close when the number being counted reaches the depth in feet at which the water will be found."[365]

I am not sure what to make of these accounts. If the rods are responding to posed questions, then the process, to the extent it works, is probably not entirely physical. Another dowsing method reported for finding depth is described as follows: "After he first tested the process on various pipes buried at his house, Marshall found he can also determine how deep an object is buried by stomping his foot on the ground over it and counting off the seconds before the dowsing rods react." Each second that passes is equal to one foot of dirt over the object. "I stand right over the grave and I can tell the depth of the burial," Marshall said. "I stomp and I think it sends a reflection back."[366]

I can't explain this report. If the dowser is stomping the ground and getting a response after several seconds, he is not getting an acoustic echo either; the speed of sound in the ground is faster than it is in air (~340m/s), and in air it would only take 0.05 seconds. Likewise, it is not an EM signal coming back, since any echo would return in nanoseconds. I don't know what would give a reflected signal traveling at a speed of ~two feet per second.

Bishop's Method

One of the most common methods to determine the depth of the object of interest is the so-called Bishop's method. This method typically involves dowsing away from an underground object and determining where the first dowsing response is and using this distance as a measure of the depth. For example, in 1949 Tromp reported, "In the case of underground sources of disturbance (of equal intensity) the rule is prevalent that the deeper the source the weaker the surface reaction and the greater the diameter of the zone of disturbance."[367]

Several writers have described variations of the method. Ian Pegler described it as follows: "Having established the site of the target, the search mode is again adopted and the dowser walks away from the target until the rods again cross. This can be checked by walking away in the opposite direction. The distance from the target to where the rods cross is equal to the depth underground. Obviously there are limits to this technique depending on the nature of the terrain."[368] The following description is from the www.energydowsers.org website: "Bishop's Rule also called Depth Parallel. Walk away from the target on an imaginary line that is perpendicular to the center of flow. When the rods cross, this gives the depth. This only works if the property is very flat and the person can keep walking in a straight line without obstructions."[369] And Wheatley wrote, "An underground stream throws out to either side of the positive triad [three lines positive, negative and positive again marking the center and boundaries of the stream] a series of equally-spaced triads known as parallels. The distance from the center of the stream to the first parallel is equal to the underground depth of the stream. This is known as the 'Bishop's depthing method' (wrongly attributed to the Bishop of Grenoble!). This depthing method was actually described in the book *La Verge de Jacob*, published in the 17th century."[370]

Donald Duncan, a mining engineer, wrote, "When I asked the old fellow how he guessed at the depth he said that when he was approaching underground water he could feel a tremor in the stick, and that he counted his steps from that point until he reached the spot where the pull was the greatest. From this he could always estimate the depth quite accurately."[371] Charles Latimer also explored the effect of distance on the dowsing signal using a y-shaped stick, and explained it as follows[372]:

> Upon walking over the ground again and again, I found that the switch commenced always to turn at the same places, equally (or nearly) distant from a centre, and kept gradually turning until it pointed directly downward. To assure myself, I repeated this experiment many times, and arrived at the conclusion that the switch commenced to turn at an angle of forty-five degrees from the edge of the water, and that the distance from my hand to the water would be measured by the distance from the point where the switch commenced to turn to the point of absolute turn-down, and so it seems to be. ... Measure the distance, therefore, from the point of commencement of turning to the point of turn-down, and you have the depth from your hand to the water. I have verified this over many water-courses, upon bridges, etc., and I am satisfied it is correct, at least for the latitude in which my experiments were made. Upon this basis I made my first estimate of the depth of the water at Coloma, and gave it as from twenty-five to thirty feet. I employed an experienced well borer and had a two and one-half inch pipe driven into the ground at the exact point my switch indicated, and found water at twenty-seven feet exactly. I had the pipe driven down forty feet, and found that I had thirteen feet of water in it.

This observation sounds intuitively reasonable, but absent a clear physical basis for it, I suspected that the Bishop's method was just dowsing lore that was most likely incorrect. However, for completeness, I undertook a study to determine if depth had affected the width of the dowsing response. I looked only at pipes because pipes are well defined in that they are of a known material, at a known depth, of known dimensions, and usually of known internal composition (usually air, or sometimes water). The study involved a variety of different pipes, concrete, steel, polypropylene and PVC in different locations were tested. The test involved the following steps.

1. Find a pipe whose diameter and depth can be easily determined. Most of the pipes were therefore surface water drains.
2. Measure the depth to the top of the pipe and to the bottom of the pipe using a tape measure and calculate the diameter. Note the material of pipe construction.
3. Identify the direction of the pipe and select some relatively flat ground about 0.5 to 1 m (1.5 to 3 feet) away and dowse perpendicular to the pipe from one side and then other. Identify where the rods first start to cross and where they cross as a response to the pipe itself and put markers on the ground.
4. Using the line of the pipe (from where it is visible), determine the centerline of the pipe,
5. Measure the distance from the centerline of the pipe to the position of first movement and the position of the edge of the pipes.

The results are shown in Figure 20.1. There is a clear reasonably linear relationship between when the rods first start to move the depth of the pipe. The measured slope of this line is 0.90, so within the error of the experiment, the distance from the first response to the centerline is approximately equal to the depth of the pipe. This result provides confirmation that the Bishop's method actually works. When I started this study, I was not expecting a positive result.

The data in Figure 20.1 was collected over several months, in many different locations and for a wide range of pipe materials (PVC, steel, concrete, etc.) and pipe

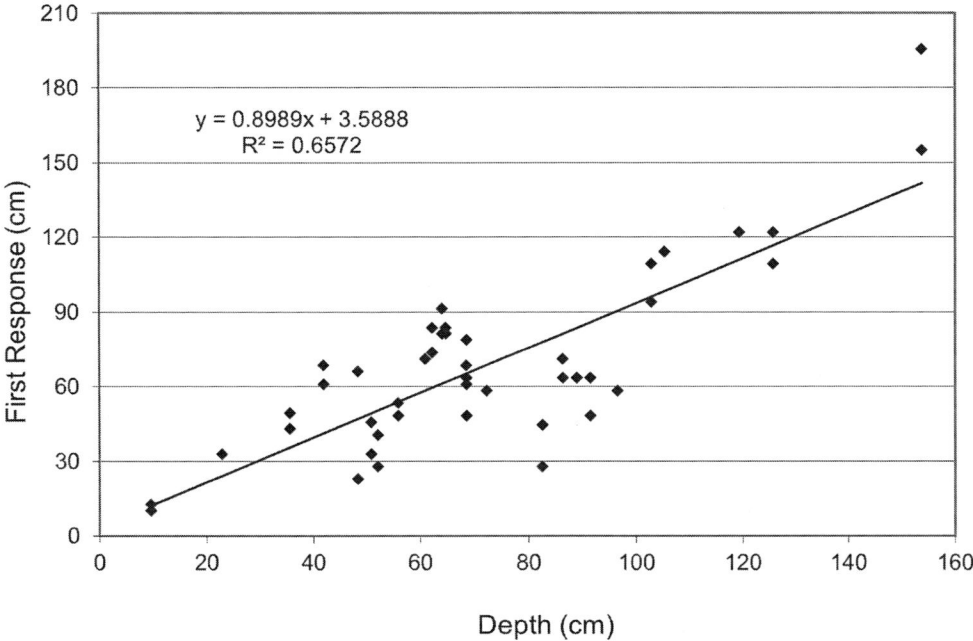

Figure 20.1. Graph of distance from when rods start to cross to the center of the pipe for various pipes at multiple locations.

diameters (from 10 cm [4 in] to 94 cm [37 in]). From our general experience with waves, one expects them to spread out as they pass an object, and the further away the object is the more they spread out.

When doing these tests, I typically found that the rods would move a little bit, perhaps 10 to 20 degrees at the Bishop's limit, and then stay fairly constant until I was directly over the object, at which point the rods would cross. If the physiological collimation discussed above is not 100 percent effective but perhaps 90 percent, then there would be two responses, a weak one (10%) when the refracted radiation as limited by the critical angle reaches the dowser's head, and the strong signal (90%) when the refracted and physiologically collimated radiation reached the dowsing sense in the dowser's head. This idea is based on refraction at the surface again and the critical angle between transmission into the air and reflection back into the ground (see Chapter 18 for more details) and is illustrated in Figure 20.2.

The black dot in Figure 20.2 represents an underground object that is perturbing the microwaves traveling towards the surface. Those microwaves which reach the surface at an angle greater than the critical angle θ_c will be reflected back into the ground. If the object is at depth D, then the maximum distance away from the vertical as defined by the critical angle is length L_1. From simple geometry, the greater the depth D, the longer is L_1 and so the longer is L_2, the first indication of the dowsing response. Those microwaves which reach the surface at less than the critical angle will be transmitted through to the air at a refracted angle of θ_r. The angle of θ_c is 12 degrees for soils and rock containing 30 percent water (see Figure 18.8) and θ_r is ~30 degrees (Chapter 18), and so the combined maximum angle is 42 degrees. The slope of the graph in Figure 20.1 is

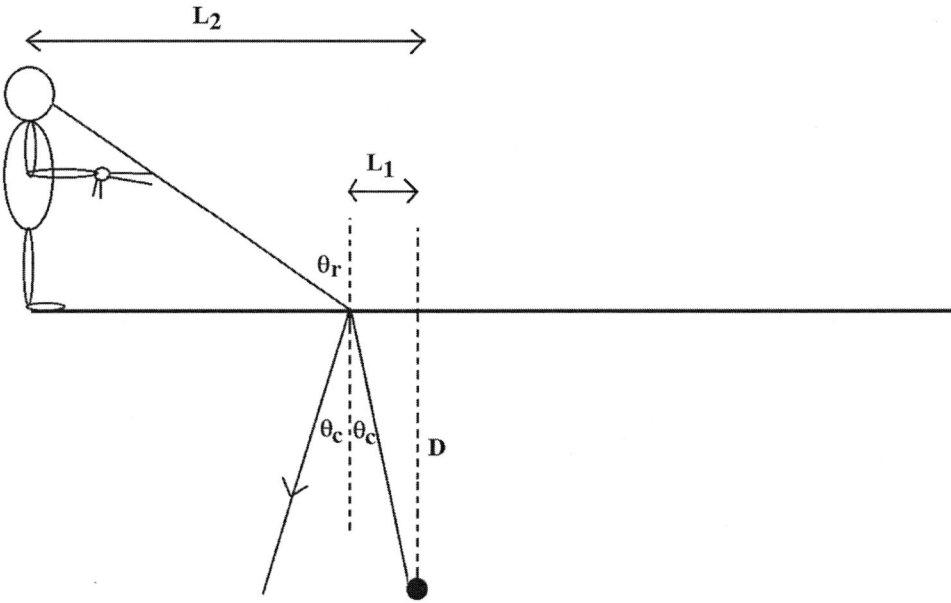

Figure 20.2. Possible basis for the Bishop's rule, based on refraction at the critical angle and inefficient physiological collimation of the signal.

about 0.9, which corresponds to an angle of 42 degrees (0.73 rad). This good agreement, however, is deceiving, since the errors in the estimate are quite large (refractive index of ground, error in the slope of Figure 20.1, height of dowser, etc.), but the agreement does suggest that this explanation is plausible.

The conclusion is that many methods are used to determine depth, often very different from each other. While the Bishop's method appears to have a physical basis, those methods involving asking questions of the rod and counting bobs in response to the question of how deep the target is sound like they are veering away from the physical and towards the psychic. Unfortunately, I cannot confirm or refute these other methods.

Signal Propagation with Depth

We know that dowsers can get information down to at least 6 m (~30 ft) depending on the soil conditions (especially water content). Some dowsers claim to be able to detect water at much greater depths (>~100 m, 300 ft)[373] and Brian Reid claimed to detect oil at 730 m (2,400 ft).[374]

The graph in Figure 20.3 shows that the penetration of microwaves into water falls with increasing frequency. The penetration is defined as the distance at which the intensity drops to 1/e (~1/3) of the original. For 1 GHz radiation, the penetration is about 10 cm, so if the intensity at the surface of the water is an arbitrary 100 percent, then as the depth in water increases, the intensity will be reduced as shown in Table 20.1.

Table 20.1. Relative Intensity of 1 GHz radiation with Depth in Water

Depth (cm)	Intensity
0	100%
10	37%
20	13.5%
30	5.0%
40	1.83%
50	0.67%
100	0.0045%

Even though the penetration of 1 GHz radiation is only 10 cm, there is some radiation at 1 meter depth, and it could be detected if sufficiently sensitive equipment were used. In the same way, if one is scuba diving in murky water, one can see quite well near the surface, but further down the visibility drops, but there is still some light penetrating the depths. There is no sharp depth above which the radiation can reach, but below which there is no radiation. The depth at which a signal can reach depends on the transmitter power, the penetration and the sensitivity of the detection equipment. For dowsing, the sensitivity appears to be very high considering how weak the thermal microwave signal is.

Most rocks contain water and water is usually a much stronger absorber of microwaves than the surrounding rocks, and so the water content of the rocks can be used to estimate the penetration into the rock. If a 1 GHz signal can penetrate water to a depth of about 10 cm, then if the ground contains, for example, 20 percent water, then the microwaves should be able to penetrate about 50 cm into the ground. To be able to detect an object at 10 m in the ground, the signal intensity will have dropped to 2×10^{-9} of its initial value or the background. If the signal from thermal radiation from an object 1 m down is getting weaker, the total signal at the surface is not necessarily dropping because the intervening rock and soil is emitting too. This signal is so weak compared to background that it is difficult to believe it can be detected. The penetration of microwaves into the ground is a challenge for the microwave theory of dowsing.

The penetration of microwaves into water is frequency dependent. In the microwave range, the higher the frequency the lower the penetration into water, as can be seen in Figure 20.3.

If the dowsing response is a response to microwaves, then the depth limitation of dowsing should be similar in magnitude to those of microwaves passing through soil. The higher the frequency the stronger the thermal (blackbody) emissions, but the stronger the absorption of the radiation as it passes through the ground. The intensity of the radiation for different frequencies can be estimated for different depths of rock, as shown in Figure 20.4.

The intensity passes through a maximum, and the maximum frequency decreases as the depth of rock increases. Thus if the source (or source of the perturbation for dowsing) is close to the surface, the higher frequencies are expected to dominate, but as the depth increases, the highest intensity may be expected to shift lower frequencies.

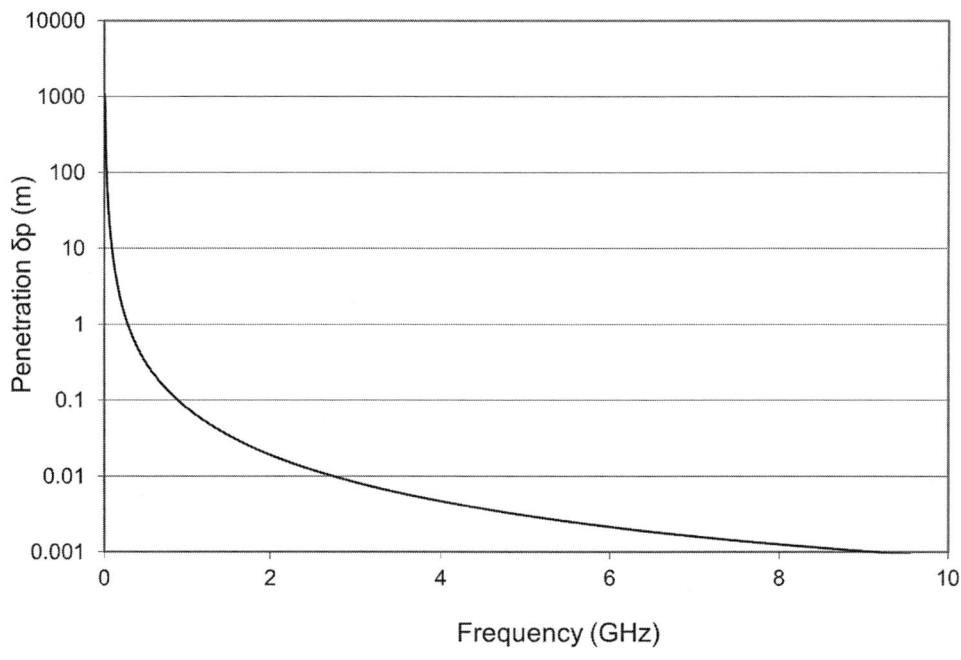

Figure 20.3. Penetration of microwave radiation into water as a function of frequency.

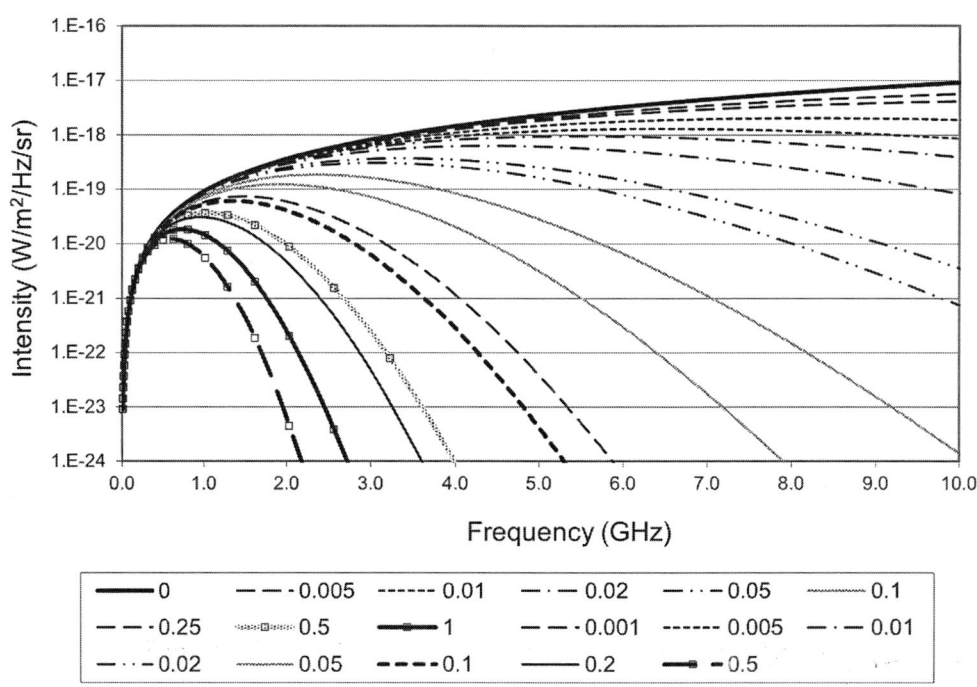

Figure 20.4. Calculated intensity of thermal radiation as a function of frequency for different thicknesses of rock. The calculation does not include thermal emissions from the rock the radiation passes through, only the absorption.

Penetration of Microwaves

The propagation of EM radiation including microwaves is described by Maxwell's equations, and from these equations the penetration depth through a material can be estimated. The propagation of EM waves through a medium depends on three parameters of the medium, namely the permittivity ε, permeability μ, and conductivity σ, however, unless the material is magnetic and electrically conductive, most of the energy absorption of microwaves by a materials will be due to the electric field component of the EM wave interacting with the material according to its permittivity, so the permeability and conductivity components will be ignored for now. The permittivity is a complex number and so it can have real and imaginary components such that

$$\varepsilon = \varepsilon' - j\,\varepsilon''$$

The real component ε' is the relative permittivity (dielectric constant) which represents the effective capacitance of a substance and serves as a measure of the ability of the substance to store electrical energy. The imaginary component ε'' is known as the dielectric loss factor, which quantifies the efficiency with which the EM energy is converted to heat. The dielectric loss factor is always positive and usually much smaller in magnitude than the relative permittivity.

The penetration of microwaves into a material is given by the following equation[1]:

$$\delta_p = \frac{\lambda o}{2\pi\sqrt{2\varepsilon'}} \left(\sqrt{1 + \left(\varepsilon''/\varepsilon'\right)^2} - 1 \right)^{-1/2}$$

1. Z. Peng, J. Hwang, J. Mouris, R. Hutcheon, and X. Huang, "Microwave Penetration Depth in Materials with Non-zero Magnetic Susceptibility," *ISIJ International* 50, no. 11 (2010), 1590–1596.

The calculated microwave penetration as a function of depth is shown in Figure 20.4, and similarly for the other penetration graphs in this book.

Permittivity and Dielectric Loss

The penetration depth δ_p is the depth at which the microwave intensity has been reduced to 1/e (~ one third) of its initial value, λ is the wavelength, ε' is the real component of the dielectric constant and ε'' is the imaginary component, the dielectric loss. The last two parameters can be calculated using the Debye equations named after Peter Debye who first developed them,

$$\varepsilon' = \varepsilon_\infty + (\varepsilon_s - \varepsilon_\infty)/(1 + \omega^2\tau^2)$$

and

$$\varepsilon'' = (\varepsilon_s - \varepsilon_\infty)\,\omega\tau/(1 + \omega^2\tau^2)$$

where ω is the frequency expressed in radians per second (= 2π times the value in Hertz), and τ is the characteristic time constant of the medium, in our case the time for the water molecule to rotate. Fortunately for us, these parameters have been determined and the variation of permittivity with frequency has been measured experimentally as a function of frequency with reasonable agreement to the theory.[1] Water absorbs in the microwave spectrum, where the energy of the microwaves corresponds to the rotation energy of water molecules. These water molecules require a certain time to rotate and if the period of the microwave wave matches the frequency of rotation, then the microwave will be absorbed.

1. Ravika Vijay, Ritu Jain and K.S. Sharma, "Dielectric Properties of Water at Microwave Frequencies," *International Journal of Engineering Research & Technology* vol. 3, issue 03, Special Issue (2015), https://www.ijert.org/research/dielectric-properties-of-water-at-microwave-frequencies-IJERTCONV3IS03027.pdf.

Comparison of Dowsing to Ground Penetrating Radar[375]

Ground penetrating radar (GPR) is a well-known method for probing underground features and structures and it has many commonalities with dowsing. GPR uses high-frequency (usually polarized) radio waves and microwaves, usually in the range 10 MHz to 2.6 GHz, which is approximately the same frequency range of interest to dowsers. A GPR transmitter and antenna emits radio wave or microwave energy into the ground. When the waves reach a buried object or a boundary between materials having different permittivities, some of the waves are reflected, refracted or scattered back to the surface. A receiving antenna records this returning signal. The depth which can be measured depends on the rock below. For dry sandy soils or massive dry materials such as granite, limestone, and concrete which have low conductivity and low water content, the depth of penetration is up to 15 meters (49 ft). However, in moist or clay-laden soils and materials which have a high electrical conductivity, the penetration may be as little as a few centimeters/inches. In certain conditions greater depths can be achieved; for example, using low frequencies, depths of several thousand meters can be achieved through ice to bedrock in Greenland. Table 20.2 shows the typical variation in accessible depth using GPR with different wavelengths and frequencies.

Table 20.2. Penetration of GPR signal with Frequency and Soil Type (data from U.S. Radar)[376]

Frequency (MHz)	Depth in wet clay (m)	Depth in dry sand (m)
100	12 (40 ft)	30 (100 ft)
250	4.5 (14 ft)	9 (30 ft)
500	1.8 (6 ft)	5 (14.5)
1000	0.6 (2 ft)	1.8 (6 ft)
2000	0.15 (0.5)	0.6, (2 ft)

The conductivities of some common rock types were shown earlier in Table 11.1. The National Bureau of Standards studied the depth of microwave penetration in clay and gravel soils for different water contents. "Assuming total reflection at the subsurface interface, as is the case with an aluminum base plate, a 0.5GHz micro-wave signal should penetrate a 150-cm layer of approximately 10% saturated clay, or a 25-cm layer of approximately 90% saturated clay. A 4.5-GHz signal should penetrate a 35-cm layer of approximately 10% saturated clay or a 1-cm layer of approximately 90% saturated clay."[377]

Dowsing and GPR share much in common. If the ground is dry, then the dowsing depth is greater, but if the ground is waterlogged, then the dowsing depth is reduced. Dowsers typically detect underground objects to depths of 10 meters (yards) or so, though sometimes people claim to be able to detect at much greater depths.[378] It is fair to say that GPR and dowsing operate over similar order of magnitude depths and with some similarities regarding dependence on the water content.

Since GPR is using radio and microwaves, lower frequency provides greater penetration but with less resolution because of the longer wavelength. The resolution at 1 GHz near the surface can be a few centimeters, whereas around 10 MHz, the resolution may be a meter at greater depths. The vertical resolution is determined by the wavelength.

For example, a 100 MHz GPR system probing an aquifer will have vertical resolution of about 15 centimeters. In contrast, the horizontal resolution is determined by the surface distance between measurements. The resolution of dowsers is comparable to GPR systems, to at least the same order of magnitude.

The GPR signal can be affected by noise from sources reflections from vehicles, buildings, fences, power lines, and even trees, and sources of EM radiation such as cellular telephones, two-way radios, television, and radio and microwave transmitters. Dowsers are not typically affected by reflections, probably because dowsers, unlike GPRs, are not emitting any EM radiation to be reflected, though there have been some reports to the contrary.[379] Dowsers, unlike GPRs, are not typically affected by cell phones, radio transmitters and two-way radios, probably in large part because of the physiological collimation discussed earlier.

One of the challenges for GPR is the detection of plastic pipes, such as PVC sewer pipes and glass fiber reinforced polymer composite pipes used for gas lines, since these materials do not strongly reflect the radar signal. One recommended practice is to use a carbon fabric and aluminum foil/tape overlay on nonmetallic pipes, which roughly doubles the amplitude of reflected radar.[380] Dowsers do not have this limitation, because they are not relying on a reflected signal.

Dowsing can be described as a passive form of GPR, responding to variations in the naturally occurring background microwaves caused by underground objects rather than transmitting a signal and recording the portion of the signal that is reflected back from those objects as with a GPR system. One major difference between GPR and dowsing is that GPR systems cost in the range of $15,000 to $50,000, depending on the complexity of the system. More advanced systems that suit more specialized needs will exceed this price considerably.[381] In contrast a dowser faces the vast expense of repurposing a steel wire coat hanger from the dry cleaner.

Variation in Dowsing Frequency with Depth

The lesson from microwave penetration and GPR is that lower frequencies penetrate the ground better than higher frequencies. Similarly, for satellite microwave imaging of soils in the deserts, where microwave radiation is estimated to come from soil layers down to depths of five wavelengths and at frequencies greater than 15 GHz, emission is proportional to surface skin temperature.[382] If one were designing a dowsing instrument, i.e., a device which measures objects underground using the dowsing signal, but without the human interface, then the dowsing signal would be a perturbation against the background radio and microwave radiation. Depth could be established by analyzing the frequency response of this perturbation, with the perturbation being shifted to lower frequencies for deeper objects, as it is with GPR and weather satellites. This idea has been explored mathematically, and a model developed for the change in microwave emissions expected.[383]

Since lower frequency signals can penetrate the soil better than high-frequency signals, one may suppose that the dowsing frequency from buried objects close to the surface may be higher frequency or lower wavelength than objects which are deeper. To test this idea, the wavelength of the dowsing signal was determined for pipes of different depths, using a series of metal grids made of 6 mm (1/4 inch) copper tape on a sheet of corrugated cardboard (as described earlier). The grid will prevent wavelengths much larger than the grid opening from passing through, and so the grids act as a frequency high pass filter. The grids made had a repeating distance of 2 cm, 5 cm, 10 cm, 20 cm or 40 cm.

The protocol was as follows:

- Measure the signal over a pipe or other sub-surface object using the rods without anything present
- Place a sheet of aluminum foil, also on cardboard down, and measure the signal.
- Place the 2 cm grid down and measure the dowsing signal.
- Repeat with larger grids until the dowsing response was comparable to the original signal without anything on the ground.

Despite my expectation to the contrary, in all cases, the aluminum foil sheet and the 2 cm grid blocked the signal, the 5 cm grid gave a normal or slightly reduced signal, and the 10 cm grid gave the same response as without the grid. This result was repeated many times, and it poses a significant problem of interpretation. From the graph in Figure 20.5, it can be seen that the penetration of microwave radiation between 3 and 10 GHz is between a centimeter and millimeter into the ground, and yet using the dowsing rods, it was possible to detect pipes and other simple objects at least 10 m (30 feet) down. Even for objects well below the penetration depth of the microwaves, the same wavelength was determined by the grids. If the dowsing naysayers are correct that dowsing is merely the ideomotor effect (Chapter 4),[384] then I would have hoped to have been wrong less often.

Dowsing Signal Propagation from the Depths

The discussion so far has shown that the dowsing signal is reflected from conductors such as aluminum foil, and additionally it has been shown to be a wave, since it can be diffracted, and so we are looking at EM radiation of some kind. Furthermore, we know that this wave is a transverse wave, as indicated by the observation that the dowsing signal can be polarized, consistent with it being EM radiation. Experiments so far have shown that the wavelength of the wave is a few centimeters, which would put the dowsing signal in the microwave region of the spectrum. The likely source of the radiation has been identified—i.e., blackbody or thermal radiation.

All in all, the data forms a neat and tidy story, but there is a major discrepancy that needs to be reconciled. The problem is that dowsers can routinely detect structures such as pipes to depths exceeding 10 m (30 ft), and many dowsers can go much deeper. I used pipes in these studies because they are widely available, and of defined size, composition and depth. However, water absorbs in the microwave region of the spectrum and the penetration of low GHz radiation through water is perhaps a centimeter (½ inch) or so. Most soils contain a significant amount of water and so even allowing for the soil to only contain 20 percent water, the penetration is only 5 cm (2.5 in) maximum. So how can dowsers detect to greater than 10 m (30 ft) and why is there is no difference in the wavelength dependence of the dowsing signal with depth?

Currently there is no good theory explaining how dowsers can detect objects at great depths. One theory that has been proposed for how microwaves emitted during earthquakes can travel through rock and provide information from below is that cracks

20. Depth

and faults in the rock act as waveguides, thus enabling the microwaves to travel much further through rock than would otherwise be expected.[385] This effect may occur in some rocks, but most rocks do not have channels through them of the magnitude of microwaves (centimeters for dowsing) to serve as waveguides.

Another explanation is that dowsers are really sensitive to detecting the dowsing signal and that even though the signal is greatly attenuated, the dowser can still detect it. The problem of course is that the microwave signal passing through the ground is so strongly absorbed that it is rapidly attenuated well below plausible detection limits (sensitivity and signal to noise) and so could not be detected. Dowsers are remarkably sensitive to microwaves (see Chapter 15), the biological collimation helps with the signal to noise, and an order of magnitude calculation indicates that dowsers may be able to detect the change in the thermal emissions from 10 m down. However, to go down another 10 m to 20 m deep would require the detector to be another billion times more sensitive, which is stretching credulity too far.

Attenuation of Microwaves Through the Ground

A quick order of magnitude calculation can be done to check the feasibility of detecting microwave emissions from the ground. The blackbody emissions at 20°C are 2.425×10^{-17} W/m²/nm at 3 GHz (λ = 10 cm) as a typical value. If the frequency is twice as high or low, it will not make a huge difference to this calculation. Assuming the detection band width is 20 percent or 2 cm (= 2×10^7 nm), then the blackbody emission energy is ~5×10^{-10} W/m.² If the dowsing resolution is 10 cm, the area of emission of interest is 10×10 cm² = 0.01 m,² so the blackbody emission energy is ~5×10^{-12} W. At 3 GHz the penetration into water is about 10 cm (Figure 20.3), and if the soil is 20 percent water, then the penetration is about 0.5 m. The penetration describes the depth at which the signal is attenuated to 1/e or 0.368. For 3 GHz, the attenuation is about 0.135 per meter.

Table 20.3. Attenuation of 3 GHz Microwaves with Depth

Depth (m)	Depth (ft)	Depth/Penetration	Power (W)
0	0	0	5×10^{-12}
0.5	1.6	1	2×10^{-12}
1	3.3	2	7×10^{-13}
2	6.6	4	9×10^{-14}
3	9.8	6	1×10^{-14}
5	16	10	2×10^{-16}
7	23	14	4×10^{-18}
10	33	20	1×10^{-20}
15	49	30	5×10^{-25}
20	66	40	2×10^{-29}
30	98	60	4×10^{-38}
50	164	100	2×10^{-55}
75	246	150	4×10^{-77}
100	328	200	7×10^{-99}

These results are summarized in Figure 20.5, which shows the logarithm of the power reaching the surface as a function of depth and the same number expressed as a percentage of the initial power.

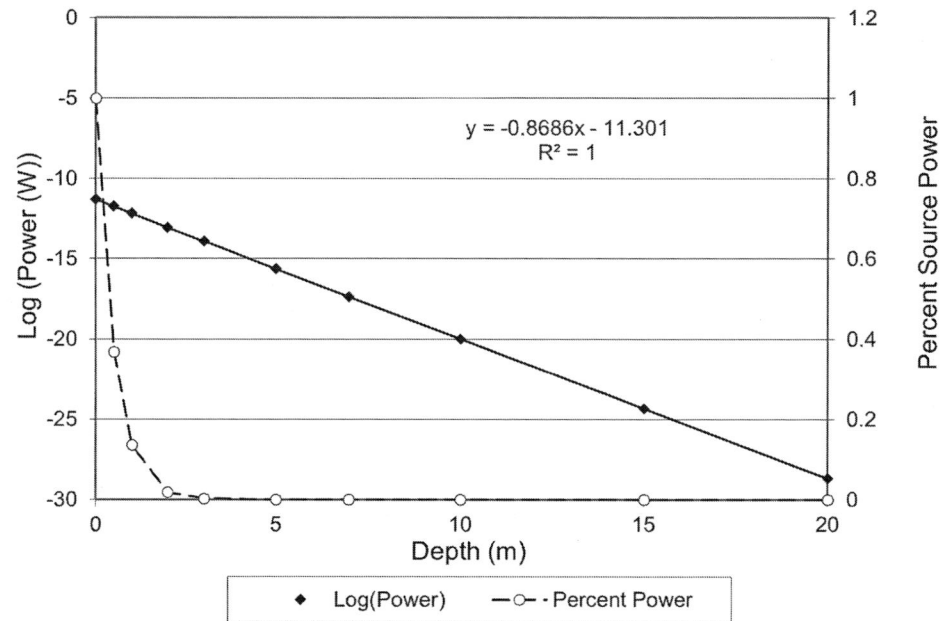

Figure 20.5. Graph showing the power reaching the surface versus depth.

The results in Table 20.3 and Figure 20.6 show that for 10m depth, the signal has decreased to 2×10^{-9} compared to that of the thermal power emitted at the surface over this frequency range, or about 1×10^{-20} W.

However, this power is not taking into account the dispersion of the microwaves' waves. The microwaves are not traveling to the surface in a parallel beam, but in all directions. Imagine a sphere (because it makes the math easier), 10 m (30 ft) down, with diameter of 1 m. The area of the sphere ($4/3\pi r^2$) is 1.05 m². If this sphere is radiating in all directions, then by the time the signal reaches the surface, the power will have dropped due to dispersion by a factor of 441 (radius at 10 m/ radius of sphere)². The power from a 10 cm × 10 cm area 10m down will therefore be reduced by several hundred times.

Dowsers are very sensitive to microwaves, for example, I was able to detect powers of ~ 10^{-16} W power delivered to the antenna (1mW signal from signal generator attenuated by ~ 130 dB, see Chapter 15). The antenna undoubtably has some inefficiencies and at any time, only a small amount of power being broadcast would be detected because of the narrow angle of the physiological collimator. While there are large uncertainties in the actual minimum power that can be detected, the power is below the estimated signal from a depth of 10m. Thus the high sensitivity of the dowser remains for now a plausible explanation. However, to detect the emissions from 20 m (60 ft) down, the detection mechanism would need to be 10^9 times more sensitive. That level of sensitivity may be asking too much even of the most sensitive dowser.

Proposal: Dowsing via Stimulated Emission

In addition to the question of sensitivity, the memory effect in concrete and other materials that contain water remains to be explained. A tentative explanation for both the sensitivity to depth and the memory effect is that the signal is transmitted to the surface by stimulated emission. While the rest of this book is based on well-known science, this section requires stretching the known science to an uncomfortable extent, and so I offer this suggestion largely as a place holder until a better explanation comes along. Readers who are not interested in such questionable practice are welcome to skip to the end of the chapter.

Stimulated emission is the physical basis behind lasers, and it has the unique feature that it amplifies the signal. Under the right conditions for stimulated emission from a molecule, one photon in gives two photons out. These exiting photons travel in the same direction, with the same wavelength, and same phase as the incoming photon. The "right conditions" for stimulated emission are the challenging part, which is why stimulated emission is not observed naturally nearly as often as the spontaneous emission. Stimulated emission does occur naturally in the microwave region of the spectrum sometimes, for example, water vapor can form a maser under astronomical conditions and emit light by stimulated emission around 22 GHz and several higher frequencies.[386]

Spontaneous and Stimulated Emission of Radiation

A photon also is a quantum entity, and it has a discrete energy $E = hF$, where h is the Planck constant and F is the frequency. The energy levels in atoms and molecules are also quantized and if the photon energy equals the energy difference between two energy levels in a molecule, then the photon may be absorbed and the molecule will be in an excited state. The excited state has several potential outcomes (see Figure 20.6).

1. The molecule may relax back to the ground state through collisions with other molecules and the energy of the photon ends up as heat. This mechanism is why black roads get hot in the summer sun.
2. The photon could be emitted from the excited state and the emitted photon would be the same energy as the incoming photon, but in a random direction, so called spontaneous emission.
3. If the excited molecule is hit by another photon of the same frequency, then the molecule may emit two photons with same frequency, with the same direction and phase as the second incoming photon, so called stimulated emission.[1] Stimulated emission was first predicted by Albert Einstein in 1916 and since then has become well understood.

If there are a lot of molecules in the excited state and a photon of the right energy interacts with one of them, then the molecule will emit a second photon with the same wavelength, phase and same direction as the first photon. These photons can go on to interact with more excited state molecules in a cascade, with the result that a low-intensity beam going in results in an intense beam coming out. The result is a laser or maser. Most of us

---

1. "Absorption, Spontaneous Emission, Stimulated Emission," Libre Texts 7.1, last updated May 22, 2022, https://eng.libretexts.org/Bookshelves/Electrical_Engineering/Electro-Optics/Direct_Energy_(Mitofsky)/07%3A_Lamps%2C_LEDs%2C_and_Lasers/7.01%3A_Absorption%2C_Spontaneous_Emission%2C_Stimulated_Emission.

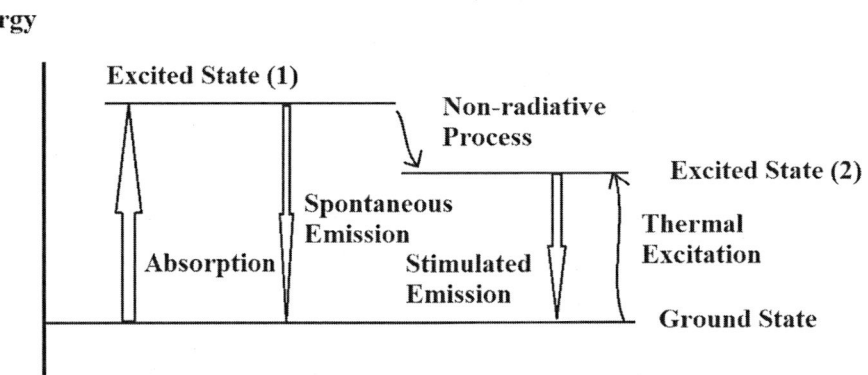

Figure 20.6. Sketch showing emission and stimulated emission from excited state.

have heard of a laser but fewer have heard about the lesser known older sibling the maser. Masers (microwave amplification by the stimulated emission of radiation) and lasers (light amplification by the stimulated emission of radiation) are essentially the same thing though operating at different wavelengths.

Recapping a few pertinent dowsing observations:

- It can be shown using an aluminum foil sheet, polarizer and grids that the dowsing signal is an EM transverse wave with a frequency in the low GHz range.
- This frequency does not change with the depth of the object and applies to depths in excess of 10 m (30 ft).
- Exposing concrete, cellulose and sugar to ~ 3 GHz radiation results in a microwave memory effect that can be detected using dowsing rods and that lasts several minutes.

Typically for optical lasers, $k_B T$ is less than the excited states and so the number of excited states is small compared to the ground state and an incoming photon is more likely to be absorbed than to stimulate emission. Lasers only function by having a means to pump molecules up to the excited states by applying energy in a variety of ways including chemical (chemical lasers), gas discharge (e.g., excimer lasers), a lower frequency radiation (e.g., solid state lasers), and electricity (e.g., laser diodes).[387]

For masers, the difference in energy between the excited state and ground state is much lower than $k_B T$, and so the excited state is well populated at ambient temperatures through thermal excitation. At thermal equilibrium there will be less excited states than the lower energy ground states and so the rate of absorption will be greater than the rate of stimulated emission. If the system is at thermal equilibrium, then the rate of absorption will equal the rate of emission, both spontaneous and a minor amount of stimulated, and no net change in energy will occur.

Rate absorption = rate of spontaneous emission + rate of stimulated emission

> **Masers**
>
> Masers (microwave amplification by stimulated emission of radiation) were proposed independently by Weber[1] and by Basov and Prokhorov[2] in the early 1950s, and the first maser was built in 1955 based on ammonia gas[3] and with hydrogen in 1960.[4] The optical equivalent of the maser, the laser, was invented in 1960,[5] and lasers have since become widely used, leaving masers in anonymity. Solid state masers were developed[6] but they required cryogenic temperatures, since for a maser to function there must be a sufficiently high population in the excited state and the energy gap between the excited state and ground state must be much greater than the system temperature k_BT (see section on Molecular Energy in Chapter 14 for explanation of k_BT), and the decay back to ground (spin-lattice relaxation rate) must be slow enough that a significant population can form in the excited state. Microwave photons are very low energy and so very low temperatures are required.
>
> In astronomy water masers have been detected at 22 GHZ along with absorbances from hydroxyl radicals (OH) at 6 GHz and hydroxyl masers are 1.6 GHz.[7] Atomic hydrogen masers have also been observed astronomically and in the lab, and are used as frequency standard at 1.420405751 GHz.[8] The water masers, however, correspond to interstellar water vapor, not liquid water. For a maser to exist in nature indicates that water vapor can form meta-stable states that can relax to baseline by stimulated emission. In a rock there is some, but not much water vapor and there is no obvious means for exciting the molecules to the excited states. At ambient temperature, the energy of a microwave photon is less than k_BT and so masers are unlikely to form in terrestrial rock and soil.
>
> 1. J. Weber, "Amplification of Microwave Radiation by Substances Not In Thermal Equilibrium," *Trans. IRE Prof. Group Electron Devices*, PGED-3 (1953), 1–4, https://doi.org/10.1109/IREPGED.1953.6811068.
> 2. N. Basov and A. Prokhorov, "About Possible Methods for Obtaining Active Molecules for a Molecular Oscillator," *J. Exp. Theor. Phys.* 1 (1955), 185.
> 3. J.P. Gordon, H.J. Zeiger, and C.H. Townes, "Molecular Microwave Oscillator and New Hyperfine Structure In The Microwave Spectrum Of NH3," *Phys. Rev.* 95 (1954), 282, https://doi.org/10.1103/PhysRev.95.282.
> 4. H.M. Goldenberg, D. Kleppner, and N.F. Ramsey, "Atomic Hydrogen Maser," *Phys. Rev. Lett.* 5 (1960), 361–362, https://doi.org/10.1103/PhysRevLett.5.361; D. Kleppner, H.M. Goldenberg, and N.F. Ramsey, "Theory of the Hydrogen Maser," *Phys. Rev.* 126 (*1962*), 603–615, https://doi.org/10.1103.
> 5. T.H. Maiman, "Stimulated Optical Radiation in Ruby," *Nature*, 187 (1960), 493–494, https://doi.org/10.1038/187493a0.
> 6. H.E.D. Scovil, G. Feher, and H. Seidel, "Operation of a Solid State Maser," *Phys. Rev.* 105 (1957), 762–763, https://doi.org/10.1103/PhysRev.105.762.
> 7. J. Wagner, "22 GHz Water Maser Search In 37 Nearby Galaxies, Four New Water Megamasers In Seyfert 2 And OH Maser/Absorber Galaxies," *Astronomy & Astrophysics* 560 (2013), A12, https://doi.org/10.1051/0004-6361/201322655.
> 8. Irv Diegel, "Hydrogen Maser Frequency Standard," Honeywell Technology Solutions Inc., https://ivscc.gsfc.nasa.gov/meetings/tow2013/Diegel.MW.pdf, accessed July 22, 2022.

Typically, the rate of absorption from the ground state to an excited state is fast, and the rate of spontaneous emission is also fast, but for some molecules the excited state can transfer from one excited state to another from which spontaneous emission is slow.

As mentioned above, if the energy difference between the ground state and the excited states is small compared to k_BT, then a large proportion of the molecules will be in the excited states. If these molecules were blasted with microwaves there will be a lot of absorption from the ground state to the excited state (1), and near simultaneous spontaneous emission from the excited state (1) back to the ground state and relaxation of the excited state (1) back to ground level by the release of heat (cf. microwave oven)—see Figure 20.6. In addition, there would be a lot of stimulated emission from the excited state (2) back to the ground state resulting in a population deficit in the excited state (2). Once the microwave source is turned off, the excited state (2) will repopulate either by thermal excitation from the ground state or by non-radiative processes from the excited state (1). IF (big IF) this process is slow then there will be a deficit in stimulated emission over time until the excited state (2) repopulates.

This model predicts several things:

1. At steady state signals from the depths will be amplified by stimulated emission. This effect will only occur at low microwave intensities, because at high microwave intensities the population of molecules with excited (2) level will be depleted and the effects of stimulated emission will no longer be observed.

2. An experiment measuring the absorbance of microwaves by a soil sample with a transmitter on one side and receiver on the other side would just observe absorption and not see the effects of stimulated emission unless the energy throughput were very low.

3. After exposing the ground to microwaves, there will be a decrease in the signals from below for a short time until the excited state (2) has time to repopulate.

The next question is what kind of system could potentially behave this way.

Water, Water, Every Where, Nor Any Drop to Drink (Samuel Taylor Coleridge)

There are many types of rock found in the ground and many different minerals present, but dowsing works on them all. So, is there a common ingredient to them all? The answer is probably water, since water is found in almost all rock to some extent. Some rocks, however, contain more water, especially sedimentary rocks (e.g., limestone, shales, sandstones) and man-made rocks such as concrete also contain some water. Concrete is a mixture of sand, aggregate and cement as a binding agent. Portland cement contains anhydrous calcium sulfate with reacts with water to form hydrated calcium sulfate which binds everything together. In addition, there may also be adsorbed water and unbound water that has diffused into the concrete.

Microwave absorptions usually correspond to molecular rotations, and water is extensively hydrogen bonded. Hydrogen bonds are weak bonds that connect one water molecule to other water molecules or to polar molecules. The oxygen (O) in a water molecule (H_2O) can be viewed as having four binding sites, two of which are occupied by its hydrogens and two of which are available. These vacant binding sites each have a pair of electrons (negatively charged) associated with them and so they are looking to bind to something positively charged. A hydrogen atom typically has one bond to another atom, but under some circumstances can form bonds to two other atoms. However, hydrogens tend to be positively charged, since the oxygen is more electronegative and pulls some of the charge density away from the hydrogen. The hydrogens can therefore form weak bonds with something negative, like an electron pair on another oxygen (molecular infidelity). The result is that in solid water (ice), each oxygen has four bonds, roughly tetragonally spaced, two to its own hydrogens and two shared hydrogens from other water molecules. Conversely, every hydrogen atom forms two bonds, one to its oxygen and one to the oxygen in another molecule.

The bonds between oxygen and its own hydrogen are normal chemical bonds, whereas the bonds between an oxygen and another water's hydrogen is a weaker and longer bond called a hydrogen bond. The bond strength of the normal O—H bond is about 464 kJ/mole, whereas the bond strength for a hydrogen bond is about 5 percent of the normal bond or 21 kJ/mol. The hydrogen bond may not sound much, but it is the reason that water is a liquid at room temperature, and not a gas.

In liquid water the molecules are always moving, making and breaking hydrogen bonds, but the average number of hydrogen bonds at any instant is about 3.5.[388] Small molecules in the vapor phase can rotate about their center of mass, and like all energetic processes on the atomic scale, rotation is quantized. It is as though there are only certain rotational speeds are allowed, and there are discrete energy differences between these rotational energy levels. The energy differences for small molecule rotations correspond to the microwave region of the spectrum.

This separation of charge in a molecule is called a dipole, and this dipole oscillates with the electric field of the incoming radiation. If the frequencies match, then the

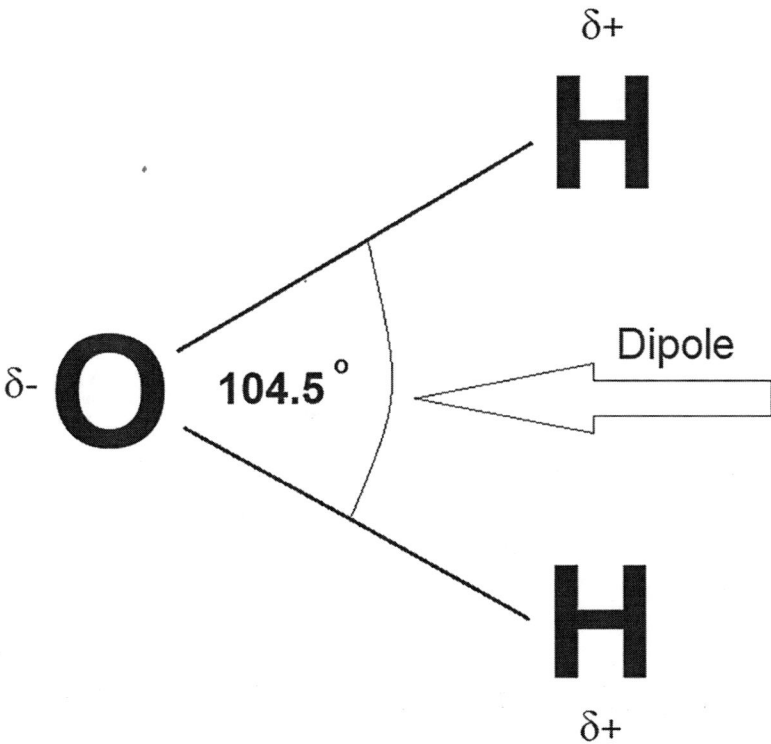

Figure 20.7. Sketch of water molecule showing partial charges δ+ and δ- and the net dipole moment.

radiation may be absorbed. In ice, the water molecules are locked in place and so cannot rotate and so ice absorbs microwaves much weaker than does liquid water. In liquid water the molecules and hence their dipoles can move somewhat and so can absorb the microwaves, but they are prevented from rotating by the hydrogen bonds and so the absorbed energy is converted to heat. Liquid water therefore has no rotational spectrum just a broad absorbance peak.[389] Water vapor can rotate freely and so it has a strong microwave absorbance.

A water molecule adjacent to a hydrophobic surface forms fewer hydrogen bonds than a bulk molecule because other water molecules cannot approach from the surface side.[390] The hydrogen bonding of coordinated water therefore depends on what the water is bound to. For certain materials such as silver iodide, water forms ice like hydrogen bonding.[391] In porous hydrophilic materials, hydrogen bonding also occurs between water molecules and between the water and the substrate.[392] Hydrogen bonding is very important in organic materials such as wood.[393] Many crystals have water of crystallization, for example, hydrated copper sulfate ($CuSO_4 \cdot xH_2O$, $x = 1,3,5$) has up to five waters, all of which take part in hydrogen bonding,[394] and so cannot rotate.[395] The limited ability of adsorbed water to rotate and move means that adsorbed water has been found to absorb microwave radiation only 53 percent as strong as liquid water in some rock core samples.[396]

It is proposed that while most of the adsorbed water is locked into place by hydrogen bonding either to other water or to the substrate, a small fraction of the water is not hydrogen bonded, and therefore is free to rotate, but only about the bond binding the water the surface, as illustrated in Figure 20.8.

It is difficult to estimate what proportion of the adsorbed water will not be hydrogen bonded, but the fraction is likely to be very small. If the only factor was energy, then we could estimate the number assuming a Boltzmann distribution and a bond energy for hydrogen bonding around 2.1×10^4 J/mol or 3.5×10^{-20} J per hydrogen bond and twice that for two hydrogen bonds per water. The fraction having no hydrogen bonds is 4×10^{-8}. However, many other factors control hydrogen bonding including nature of the substrate, local environment, water content, etc., and so this fraction is fairly meaningless except to say the number is very small.

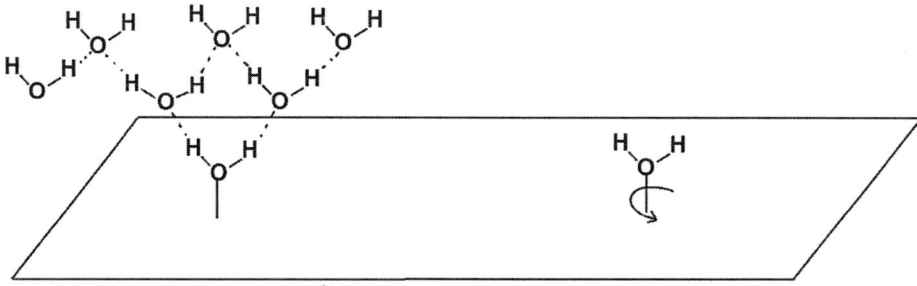

Figure 20.8. Sketch showing (A) adsorbed water hydrogen bonded to other waters and so unable to rotate and (B) non-hydrogen bonded water which is able to rotate.

The proposal is that the rotation of non-hydrogen bonded water is responsible for the propagation of the dowsing signal. The rotation is quantized and many of the water molecules will be in the energetic state (1), since the difference in energy between the ground state and excited state (1) is less than $k_B T$. Microwaves of the correct frequency can be absorbed to increase the rotation from the ground state to the excited state (1) and conversely cause the excited state (1) to relax to the ground state by spontaneous emission of a microwave. If there is a second energetic state (2), that is populated by non-radiative decay from the first energetic (1) state or by thermal excitation, then this energetic state can emit a photon by stimulated emission. Since there is water in most rocks, this stimulated emission provides amplification of the low-intensity microwave signals from all around including from below. This amplification is only for low-intensity signals and so it increases the depth to which dowsers are sensitive. Experiments with higher-intensity microwaves would saturate the system, after which the behavior would be dominated by absorption and spontaneous emission.

Microwave photons emitted by thermal emission will travel in all directions. Some will head straight for the surface. On the way, some will be absorbed, and some will interact with the excited adsorbed water (2) through stimulated emission, thus creating two photons with the same frequency and direction (and same phase). If the rate of stimulated emission is close to the rate of absorption, then the signal will propagate further than without the stimulated emission. As the signal rises to the surface, it may pass through or be obstructed by various materials, objects, etc., and change in intensity. This intensity pattern will then also be carried towards the surface to give the dowsing signal. The same is true for other directions, but dowsers are only interested in the signals heading to the surface.

The rate of spontaneous emission and stimulated emission at steady state will be determined by the thermal properties of the material. If an external microwave source is applied at the correct frequency, these photons will cause stimulated emission, and the population of excited rotational states will decrease. If the microwave source is removed, there will be a difference in microwave thermal emissions from the material for a short time until the excited state populations return to thermal equilibrium. While this explanation does explain the observations, much more data will be needed before the explanation can become an accepted theory.

There are several potential applications of this memory effect in concrete, beyond the fact that it is an interesting phenomenon. If this drop in thermal microwave emission can be measured instrumentally, then this method could potentially provide a new form of spectroscopy that would allow examination of the internal structure of the concrete from a new perspective. It is likely that the absorbed water will vary with the local environment, and so this technique has the potential to reveal information about the internal structure of concrete and similar hydrated materials in a non-destructive manner. Similarly, it may offer some quality control applications. For example, for a material whose memory effect varies with the composition, product on a production line could be irradiated at one location and tested downstream after a known time and the measured values compared to statistical norms for that product.

In summary, this idea explains how the dowsing signal can reach the surface and why dowsers are able to detect what is happening below the surface. This idea also partially explains the memory effects described in the previous chapter and is explored in more detail there. However, this idea has a number of weaknesses.

- There is no evidence that absorbed water forms metastable rotational states (water vapor does, so it is not beyond the realm of possibility). The absorption and emission of GHz radiation from water has been extensively studied in the past,[397] and if this mechanism occurred to a significant extent, it would probably have been reported, but nothing showed up in a literature search. Perhaps the intensity of this effect in prior studies was too small to see this effect.
- Typically, thermal processes are quite fast, much faster than the timescale of the memory effect.

Much more work is needed before these questions can be answered. Hopefully, in the future with more research, this idea will either be validated by experimental evidence or replaced with a better theory.

21

Measuring the Dowsing Response Instrumentally

The heart of science is measurement.
—Erik Brynjolfsson[398]

Chapter summary: One of the drawbacks of studying dowsing is the subjectivity of the response. The goal of this chapter was to detect the dowsing signal using a microwave detector. The detector was shown to respond to thermal microwave radiation, and responses to water and to metal foil were obtained that are similar to dowsing responses.

If the dowsing effect is indeed a physiological response to a physical effect, then that physical effect should be amenable to measurement using physical instruments. Several people have claimed to have developed dowsing instruments, often with little detail and with uncertainty as to what they are actually measuring.

Maby claimed to be able detect the dowsing response using a couple of devices. The first was the coherer, an early type of radio detector. It seems unlikely to be very reliable for detecting a dowsing response both from a sensitivity perspective and due to its

---

Coherer[1]

The coherer was used as a form of radio detector during the start of the 20th century until about 1907 and preceded semiconductor rectifiers such as a wire touching a galena crystal (lead sulfide), the so called cat's whisker detector. Radio transmissions at the time were radio pulses, such as from a spark generator, and the coherer provided a means to measure these very transient signals. A coherer consisted of a sealed tube containing two electrodes spaced a small distance apart with loose metal filings in the space between. When a radio pulse is applied to the device, the metal particles would stick together or "cohere," providing a conductive path allowing a much greater direct current to flow through it that would activate a bell, or a Morse paper tape recorder to record the received signal. Once the pulse had passed the metal filings remained stuck together so that the coherer had to be "decohered" by tapping it with a clapper actuated by an electromagnet each time a signal was received.

1. "Coherer," Wikipedia, https://en.wikipedia.org/wiki/Coherer, accessed December 4, 2021.

limited ability to measure small changes in the background thermal radiation intensity. However, I am not sure how one would use a coherer to detect a dowsing signal, so that may be the issue rather than any reflection on Maby.

Neon Lamp/Tube

Maby's other device was a neon filled voltage regulator tube operated close to the potential at which the neon discharge lit.[399] Glow discharge detectors are well known as a cheap rugged detector for high-intensity microwaves.[400] The principle of detection is that if a high potential is applied to two electrodes placed in a low pressure gas, the gas will ionize, a current will flow and a glow will form (cf. fluorescent lights). Once the discharge starts, the resistance across the gas drops sharply and a much larger current flows. If the potential is reduced to just below the bare minimum needed for the discharge, then the potentials induced by high energy microwaves can be enough to cause the gas tube to discharge. The circuit shown in Figure 21.1 is an example of such a circuit which allows the detection of low-intensity microwaves, since their presence will make it easier for the lamp to light and so it changes the frequency of the lamp flashes. In my first attempt I used a neon indictor lamp instead of the neon voltage regulator that Maby and Franklin and their contemporary Louis Rota used,[401] but otherwise the circuit shown in Figure 21.1 is similar. Unfortunately, I was not able to detect any dowsing signals. Gas discharge tubes can be used to detect high-intensity microwaves. Their application to the very low-intensity thermal microwaves remains unverified.

Glow Discharge Detector Circuit

The DC voltage was provided by eight 9V batteries in a series which produced over 70V. This circuit is a Pearson-Anson oscillator, which was invented in 1922.[1] When an increasing voltage is applied to the neon bulb by varying the potential divider R_1, there is initially no current flowing until the voltage is large enough to cause a discharge in the bulb. Once the current starts flowing the resistance drops sharply, the current increases very rapidly and without a load resistor (R_3) in series with the bulb, the latter is likely to burn out. The voltage needed to light the neon bulb is about 45 to 65 V. In the Pearson-Anson oscillator, the voltage charges the capacitor C through resistors R_1 and R_2 until the voltage across C is sufficient for the lamp to light. When the lamp lights, the capacitor can now discharge through the lamp and resistor R_3 until the voltage across the capacitor drops so low that the lamp turns off, and the process repeats. This circuit thus gives flashing output, with a frequency which depends on the values of R_1, R_2, R_3, C and the input voltage. By varying R_1 and R_2 in the above circuit the lamp frequency can be set to about one flash a second. Microwaves are detected by a change in the flash rate.

---

1. S.O. Pearson, H. St. G. Anson, "Demonstration of Some Electrical Properties of Neon-filled Lamps," *Proceedings of the Physical Society of London* 34, no. 1 (December 1921), 175–176, doi:10.1088/1478-7814/34/1/435.

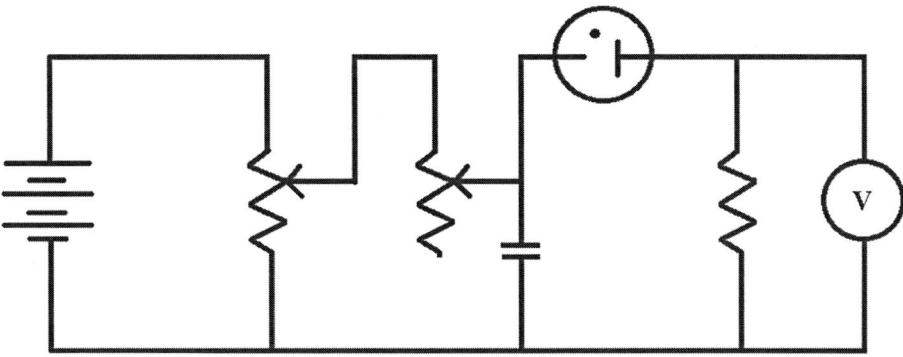

Figure 21.1. Neon indicator bulb detector.

Microwave Detection

The next approach was to try something more modern to detect the high-frequency radio waves/microwaves of dowsing. There are two aspects to this investigation. The first is to find a suitable detector and the second is to find a suitable antenna.

The primary detector I used was an HP 473B power meter, with HP 8481D power sensor. This instrument can record the power received above a ~-70 dBm noise floor across its frequency range (10 MHz to 18 GHz). I also used a software defined radio (SDR) and looked at the baseline between radio sources over the MHz to ~1 GHz range, the maximum frequency that the system would respond to. SDR systems are remarkable in that for less than $30 one can set the frequency or scan over whatever frequency one wants from KHz to a GHz. To accomplish the same a few years ago would have required purchasing a spectrum analyzer which would have cost significantly more. The SDR I used as the Nesdr Smartee using HDSDR free software version 2.80 from http://www.hdsdr.de/. The software was installed on a Windows 10 tablet with a full-size USB port allowing the unit to be fully portable. I was able to see the human-made radio sources but the baseline was about –50 dBm and did not appear to change over the dowsing line corresponding to the sewer line beneath the concrete floor of our basement.

Software Defined Radio (SDR)[1]

Most radio systems are comprised of a receiver, transmitter, mixers, filters, amplifiers, demodulators, etc., which are built with dedicated hardware. Software-defined radio (SDR) performs the same functions but using software on a personal computer or embedded system, thus allowing very simple hardware. A simple SDR system may consist of a radio frequency front end, connected to personal computer equipped with a sound card, usually via a USB port. The SDR concept produces a radio which can receive and transmit widely different radio protocols based solely on the software used and can be updated or changed to a different system merely by changing the software.

1. "Software Defined Radio," https://en.wikipedia.org/wiki/Software-defined_radio, accessed December 6, 2021.

My next attempt was using a Tiny spectrum analyzer, which has two inputs, one a high quality MF/HF/VHF input for 0.1 MHZ to 350 MHz, and the second lesser quality UHF input for 240 MHz to 960 MHz. This device, which was only released March 2020, is another incredible piece of technology for the price. Costing about the same as an SDR unit, the Tiny SA has a graphic display which shows the spectrum, which can be configured for start/stop frequency, etc. Again, my plan was to look for deviations in the baseline on and off locations that give a dowsing response (like the sewer pipe). However, even though the Tiny SA has been optimized to be very quiet and has an impressive noise floor of less than −104 dBm for its high-frequency range (240 MHz to 960 MHz) and −85 to −90 dBm over the low-frequency range (0 to 350 MHz), with both the SDR and the Tiny SA I saw no difference in the baseline in my basement where there was no dowsing response and where there was a dowsing response over the sewer line. I also went to a local park which has a stream running through it that is often stocked with trout (so good water flow). Again, I saw no difference in the baseline between dry land about ~15 meters from the water's edge and standing on a stone holding the devices over the water. For these tests, I tried a simple monopole antenna,

Power in Decibels

The decibel is a convenient way to compare the power of a signal against a reference, whether radio frequency or audible. The decibel scale is a logarithmic scale, so if the power of a signal is 0 dB, then it is the same power as the reference. If the power increased by 10 dB, then the power is ten times that of the reference and so forth. For radio waves signals it is convenient to use a reference value of 1 mW, indicated by the units of dBm, and so the dBm value is an absolute measure of the power.

Table 21.1. Correlation between Power and dBm

Decibel	Power Relative to Reference	Power Relative to 1 mW (dBm)
30	1000	1W
20	100	0.1 W
10	10	10 mW
0	1	1 mW
−10	0.1	0.1 mW
−20	0.01	10 μW
−30	0.001	1 μW
−40	1×10^{-4}	0.1 μW
−50	1×10^{-5}	10 nW
−60	1×10^{-6}	1 nW
−70	1×10^{-7}	0.1 nW
−80	1×10^{-8}	10 pW
−90	1×10^{-9}	1 pW
−100	1×10^{-10}	0.1 pW

inside a cardboard box that had been lined with aluminum foil on all surfaces except the bottom to reduce outside interference. A monopole antenna has almost no directionality in the plane perpendicular to the antenna. A monopole antenna is like half a dipole, with the other half mirrored in a (virtual) ground plane. I also tried a Yagi antenna, and a combined Yagi/parabolic antenna, which have much better directionality. Various experiments were run with combinations of these antenna and the receivers without much success.

Ku-Band Low Noise Block

Experiments described earlier support the idea that that the dowsing signal is EM radiation in the low GHz range. Low GHz radiation is often used for satellite communications, such as satellite TV, and so perhaps this equipment can be used to measure the dowsing response. To test this idea a low noise block (LNB) detector from a satellite television dish was used.

The goal was to detect similar phenomena with the LNB as can be detected using dowsing rods. Two such responses are to aluminum foil on the ground and the presence of water at the surface. For the initial test, the output of the LNB was tested with the bare LNB facing down about 16 cm (6 inches) off the concrete floor, with and without a sheet of aluminum foil on the floor. The results were very disappointing with no response seen; i.e., there was no difference in the power reading with and without the foil present. The LNB is designed to detect across a wide angle, at least the wide angle of a parabolic dish, and so with signal coming in from all around, there may not have been much difference with and without the foil. The LNB was therefore mounted at the end of a PVC tube, wrapped in aluminum foil, to collimate the signal beam, as shown in Figure 21.2. This configuration was used in all the later room temperature tests with this LNB.

Ku-Band LNB

Most satellites used for video streaming are in the Ku band (12 to 18 GHz), but this frequency does not pass through coax cable very well. Therefore, the LNB detects the signal, amplifies it and reduces the concentration down to the high MHz or low GHz range. Signals at this lower frequency range can be much more easily transmitted through the coaxial cable that takes the signal from the LNB detector to the satellite receiver. The LNB reduces the frequency using the heterodyne principle by mixing the input signal and an internally produced oscillation at 9.75 GHz, and then subtracting the two. Therefore a 1 GHz signal corresponds to a source frequency of 10.75 GHz and a 2 GHz signal corresponds to a source frequency of 11.75 GHz. The LNB detector was connected to a power inserter to provide power to the LNB via the coaxial cable, and the signal was then passed to a microwave power meter. The output was measured with an HP 8481D power sensor connected to an HP 437B power meter, which in turn was connected to a PC for data logging.

The baseline level for the LNB was around −33 dBm, and there was no change on passing the LNB on and off a sheet of aluminum foil. Either the baseline was swamping the response to the aluminum foil, or there was no response. To improve the signal/baseline ratio, the LNB was placed at the end of a PVC pipe (5 cm [2 in] ID, × 64 cm [25 in] long), and the pipe and LNB were covered with foil so that the LNB was isolated from the outside world except through the open end of the pipe.

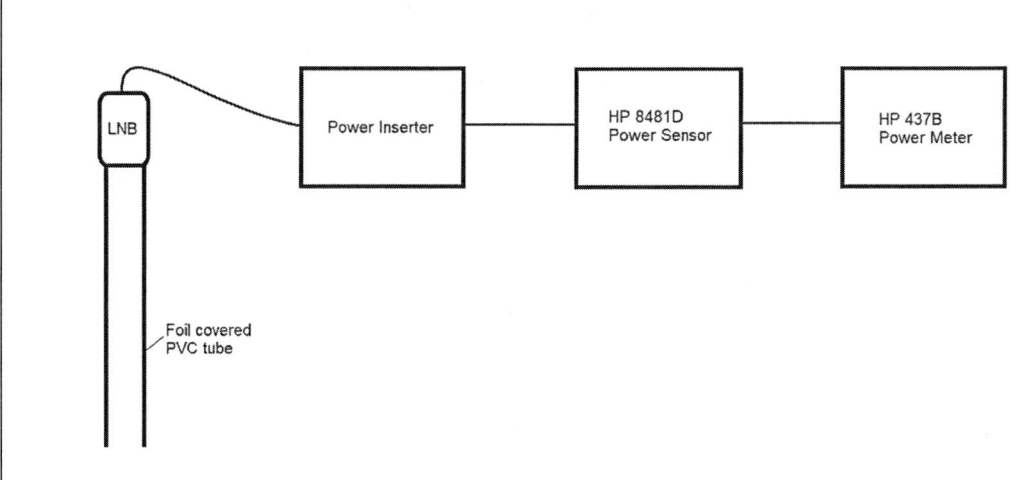

Figure 21.2. Ku-band LNB test setup.

Note: The power level increased on closing the end of the pipe with foil by about 2.0 dB. Perhaps some emission from the LNB was reflected back by the foil closed pipe end. This observation was not investigated further.

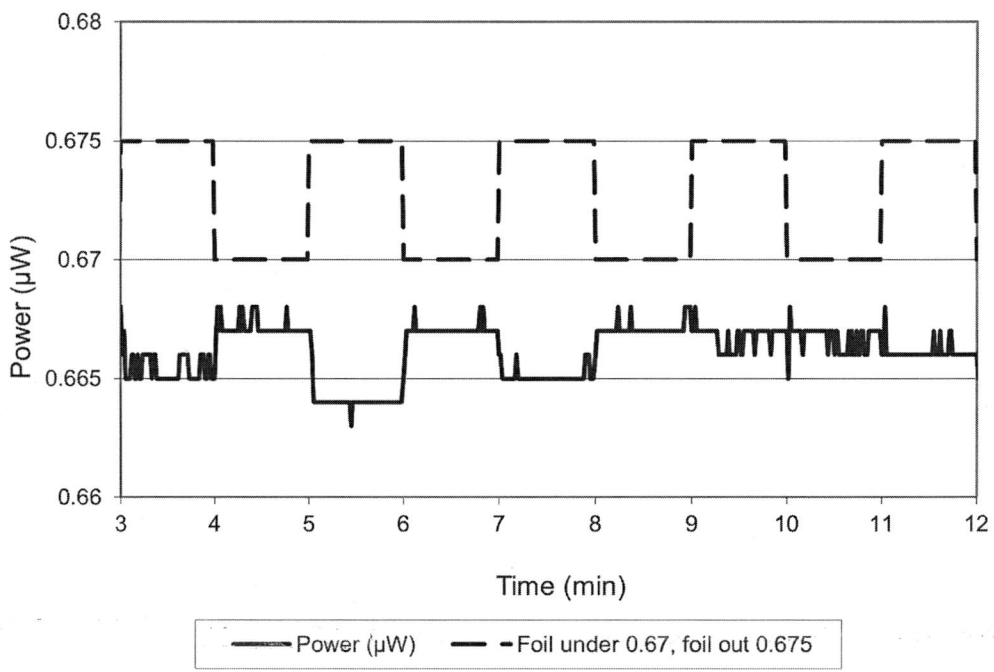

Figure 21.3. Output from room temperature Ku-band LNB with and without aluminum foil, with the foil 20 cm from the end of the collimating tube.

21. Measuring the Dowsing Response Instrumentally

The LNB in its pipe was mounted vertically, with the open end about 5 cm (two inches) from the concrete floor and a piece of aluminum foil was placed under the LNB and removed repeatedly. A small but repeatable difference in signal with and without the aluminum foil on the floor directly below the detector was observed. Bare concrete gave a signal of -31.58 dB (0.695 µW) and the foil covered concrete floor gave a signal of -31.66 dBm (0.682 µW), This power difference is very small, and corresponds to a power difference of 12.7 nW or 1.83 percent of the total baseline signal.

Decreasing the distance from the end of the collimating tube to the aluminum foil increased the difference in signal between foil and no foil (Figures 21.3 and 21.4).

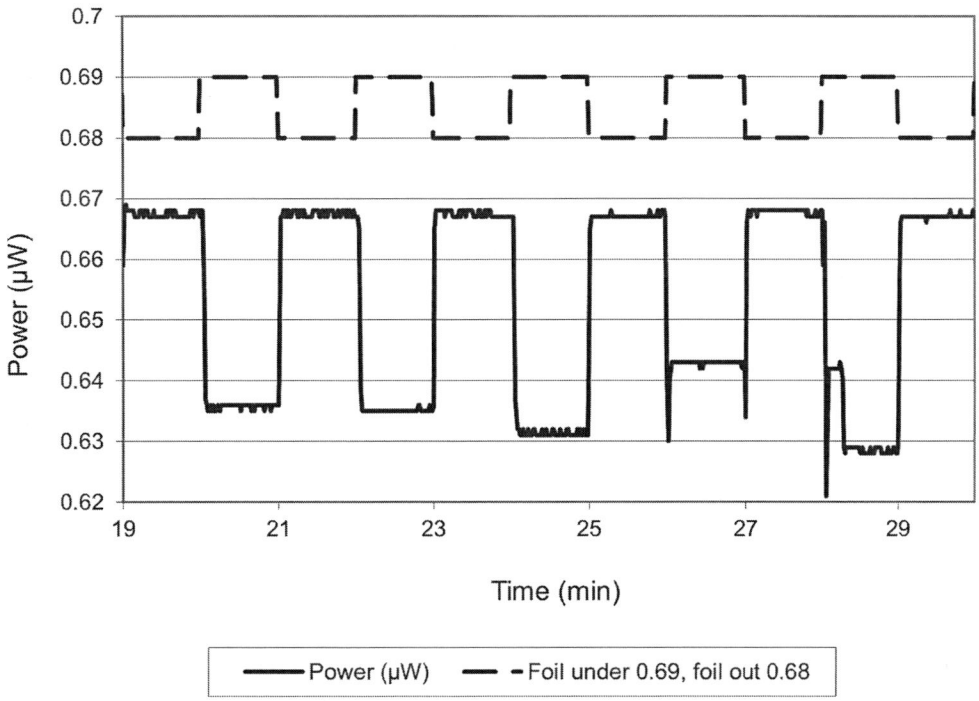

Figure 21.4. Output from room temperature Ku-band LNB with and without aluminum foil, with the foil 1 cm from the end of the collimating tube.

This percentage is not a change in the thermal radiation caused by the foil, but rather the change in the total signal. The vast majority of that signal arises from noise within the LNB detector itself, as was demonstrated by disconnecting the coax cable at the LNB, after which the power meter read ~-70 dBi, the noise limit of the power meter. Since most of the baseline is coming from the LNB, the percent change in the external thermal emissions by adding water or aluminum foil was much greater than 1.83 percent calculated above.

The foil could be functioning by blocking radiation coming up from/through the floor reducing the power reaching the detector, or it could be reflecting radiation coming down from above and the sides and so increase the power reaching the detector. The decrease in power on placing the foil under the LNB detector pipe suggests that the foil is blocking the signal coming from/through the concrete floor. This mechanism is believed to be the same as how an aluminum sheet on the concrete floor will give a dowsing response. The alternative suggestion is not without merit, for if the foil is first placed horizontally on the floor and then held at an angle (~ 30° by eye), then the LNB power increased from ~0.695 to 0.700 µW, a small but significant change. The decrease in power measured with the foil is consistent with the majority of the signal coming from the floor below, but some coming from the sides as well, as may be expected from thermal radiation which is coming off all objects above zero Kelvin in all directions, as illustrated in Figure 21.5.

Replacing the foil with a 2 cm thick sheet of pine wood held at different angles made no difference to LNB reading. This result is consistent with the pine wood being essentially transparent to low GHz radiation, whereas aluminum foil will reflect the radiation.

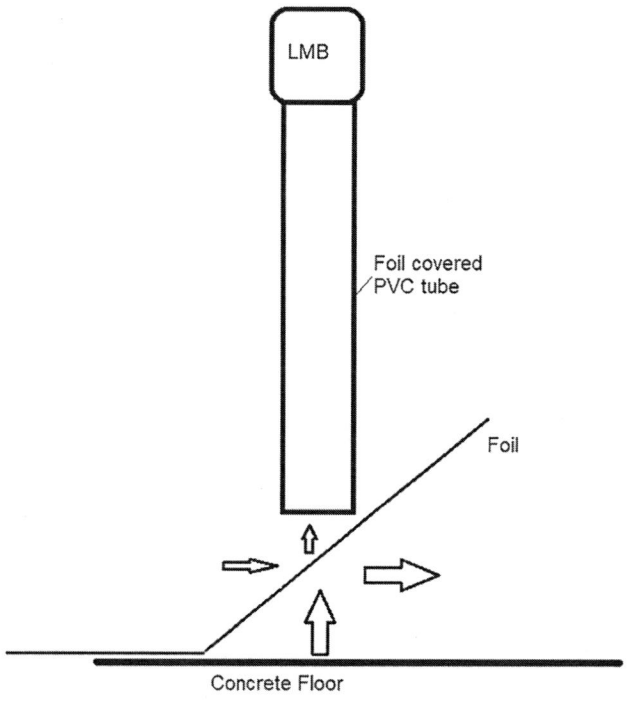

Figure 21.5. Sketch showing foil reflecting thermal radiation coming from the concrete floor away from the Ku-band LNB but reflecting thermal radiation from the side into the LNB.

The next experiment was to place a small plastic container of water under the LNB detector tube instead of the foil. Adding and removing the empty plastic container had no significant effect on the power reading. The power reading did vary repeatably with and without water, with lower power being observed with the water (Figure 21.6), and thus the LNB detector was able to replicate the second dowsing response.

The baseline tended to drift, but the power was found to vary with the depth of the water, and the results are shown in Figure 21.7, which show a reasonably linear behavior. Note the baseline was corrected each time before the water was placed under the LNB.

The greater the water depth the smaller the signal, so the water is clearly having an effect. The signal with no water was 0.695 µW, and so the reduction in power per cm of water based on the line of best fit is 7.4 nW, or 1.06 percent. This result is consistent with the water absorbing the signal coming up through it from the concrete floor below. Again, this percentage is not a change in the thermal radiation caused by the water, but rather the change in the total signal. Much of that signal arises from noise within the detector.

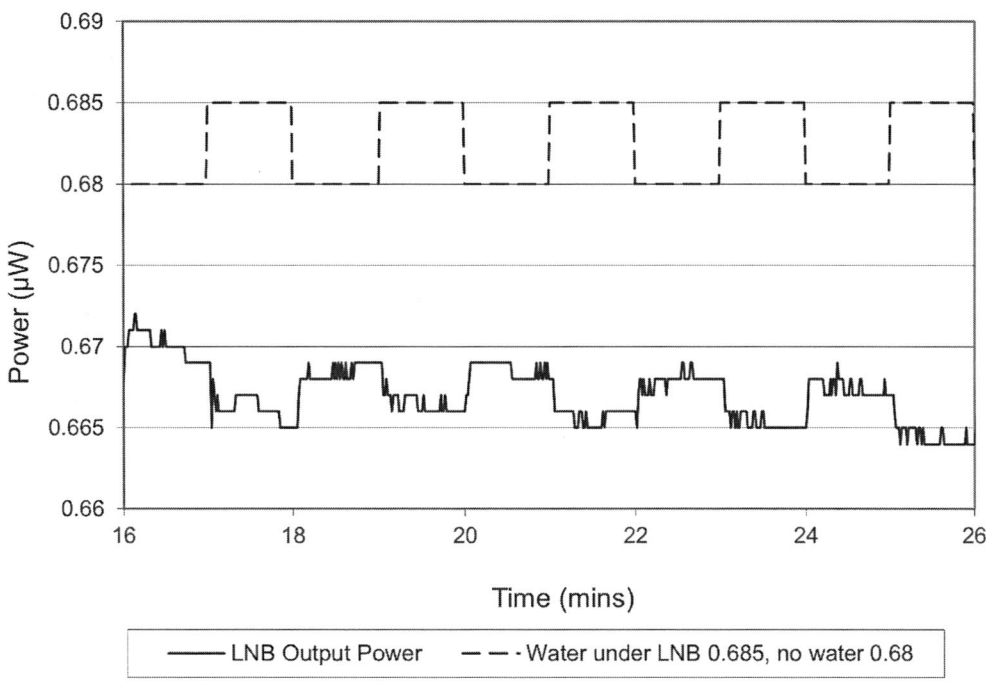

Figure 21.6. Output from room temperature Ku-band LNB with and without 4 cm of water. Water bowl sitting on a 5 cm thick book.

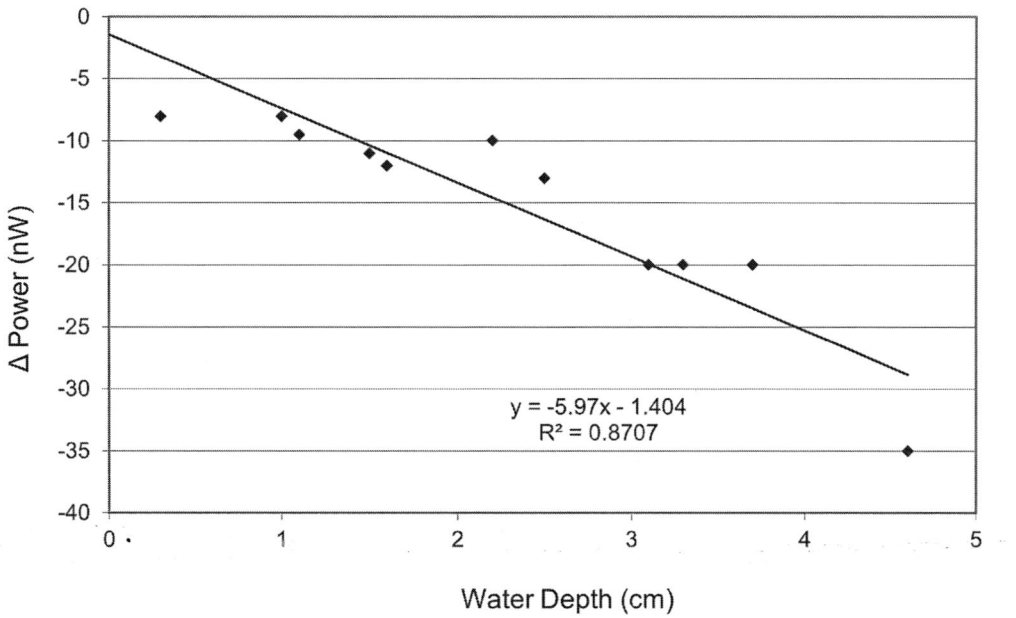

Figure 21.7. Graph of the change in Ku-band LNB power with the depth of the water compared to bare concrete floor.

When the plastic container with water was placed under the LNB the signal would jump and decay over several seconds until the water stopped sloshing in the container. If the container was bumped to slosh the water again, the reading would again jump up before decaying back down again as illustrated in Figure 21.8. This behavior might be because when the water is sloshing, there is less water in the middle of the container and so more radiation can pass through. As the sloshing quiets, the depth of the water in the middle below the LNB increases and the signal drops to a steady state. If the sloshing rate is less than the time averaging of the data, then a simple decay will be observed.

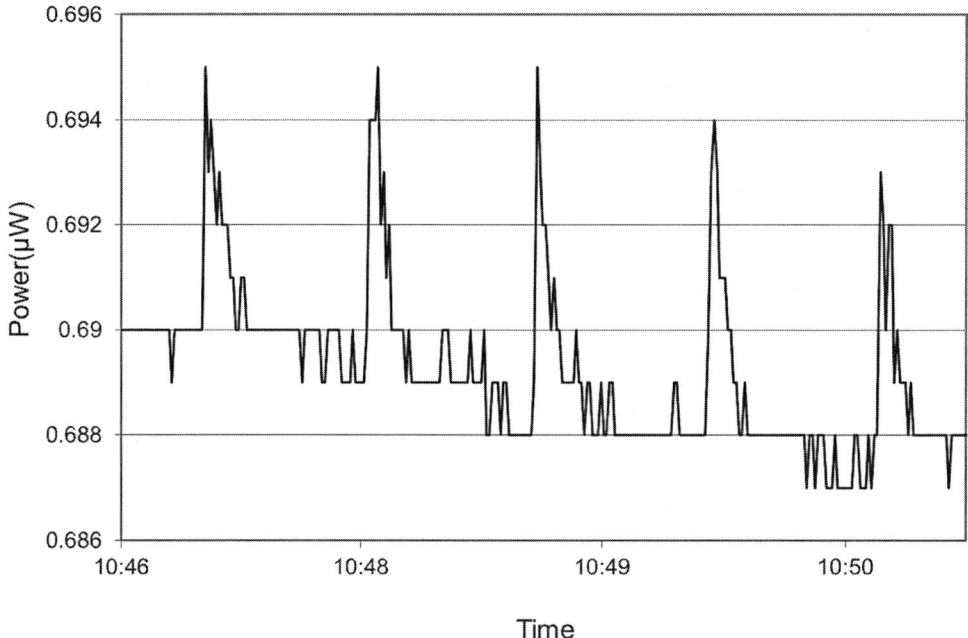

Figure 21.8. Output from Ku-band LNB to HP Power meter, over a container of water that was repeatedly sloshed.

These two experiments show that the Ku-band LNB detector can reproduce two of the dowsing detection feats, water and aluminum foil, though the signals are very weak.

The next question was to identify the source of the radiation that the LNB was detecting. The same setup was taken to the kitchen and the LNB in its foil-covered PVC pipe was pointed at the inside of the freezer, heated oven and electric stove top heating surfaces and the power measured, and nearly simultaneously the temperature of these surfaces was measured using an infrared thermometer. The output from the LNB varied with the temperature; see Figure 21.9. Incidentally, the infrared thermometer uses the same principle; it is measuring the infrared radiation from thermal emissions, and calculating the temperature assuming the surface has blackbody behavior, but in the infrared region of the spectrum rather than in the microwave region.

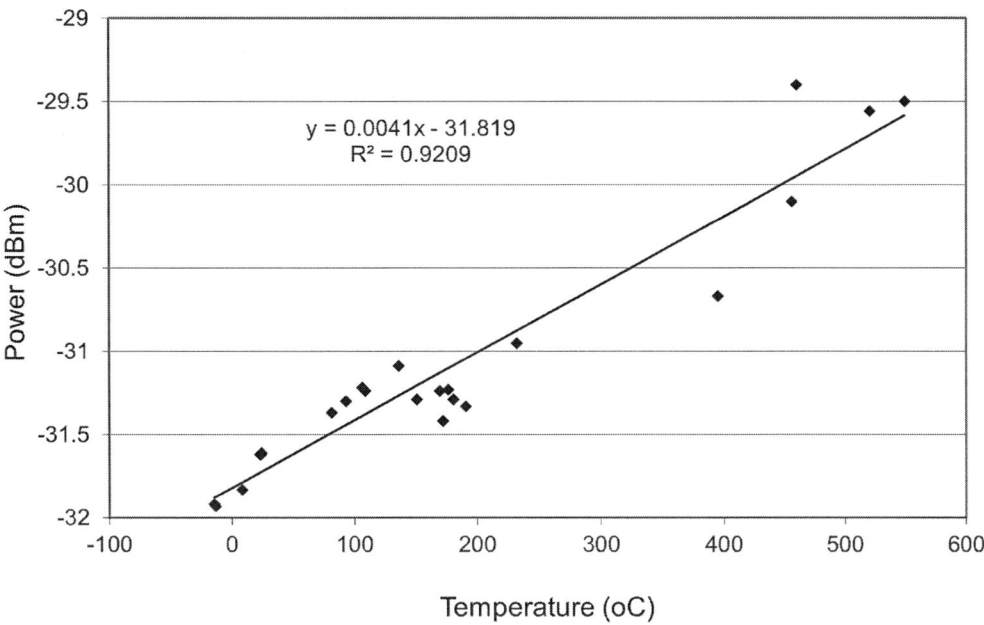

Figure 21.9. Response of room temperature Ku-band LNB detector to various surfaces vs. temperature recorded with an infrared thermometer.

The power measurements recorded with the water and foil fall in this range, which is consistent with the LNB responding to the thermal radiation from these surfaces. The LNB experiments have shown that thermal microwaves can be detected using instrumentation and using these methods it is possible to replicate some of the responses seen with dowsing. Aluminum foil on the floor gives a dowsing response by blocking thermal emissions and the LNB shows a drop in the intensity of thermal emissions. Water also absorbs microwaves and gives a dowsing response and the LNB also shows a decrease in intensity which varies with the depth of water consistent with the dowsing response. This result provides strong support for the idea that the dowsing signal comes from changes in the background thermal radiation.

Most of the background signal from the Ku-band LNB detector is probably thermal noise and so the next step was to try to improve the response of LNB by lowering the temperature. An outer surround (15 cm, 6" diameter PVC pipe) was placed around the LNB detector and packed with dry ice (sublimation temperature −78.5 °C [−109.2 °F]). Using dry ice lowered the background signal from about 0.7 μW to 0.55 μW. The LNB was set up vertically over the concrete floor and a bowl of water or a sheet of aluminum foil was placed below the LNB. Figure 21.10 shows the response to water. The water bowl was placed under the LNB for one minute, removed for one minute and the process repeated. It can be seen that the signal drops when the water is present and increases again when the water is removed. Repeating the experiment with the empty plastic water bowl had no effect on the signal. The water was at the same temperature as the room. This result is consistent with the water absorbing some of the thermal radiation coming from the concrete floor before it can reach the LNB.

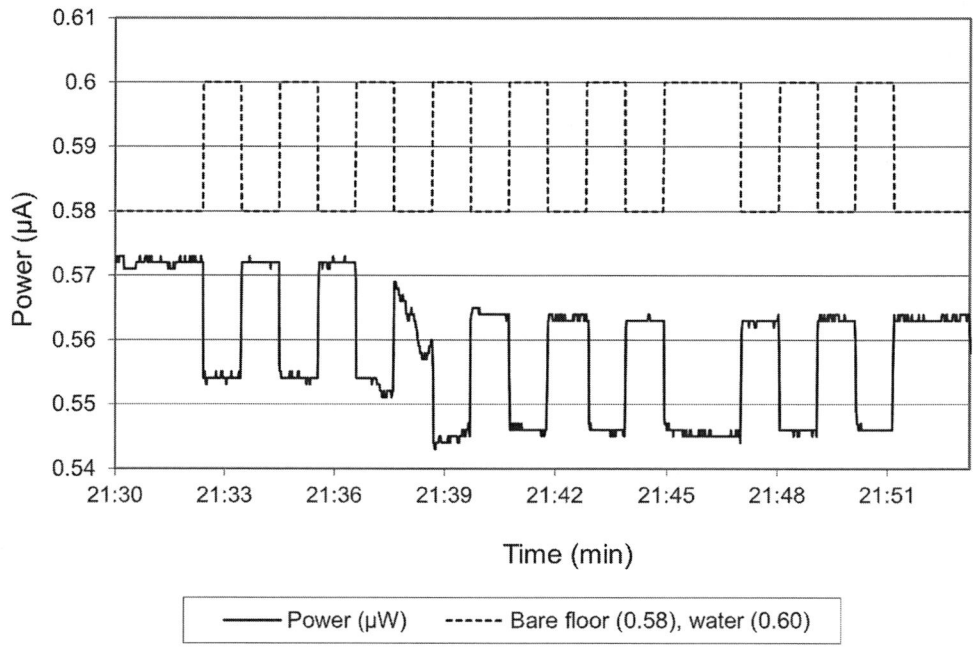

Figure 21.10. Graph showing the response of the dry-ice cooled Ku-band LNB to water.

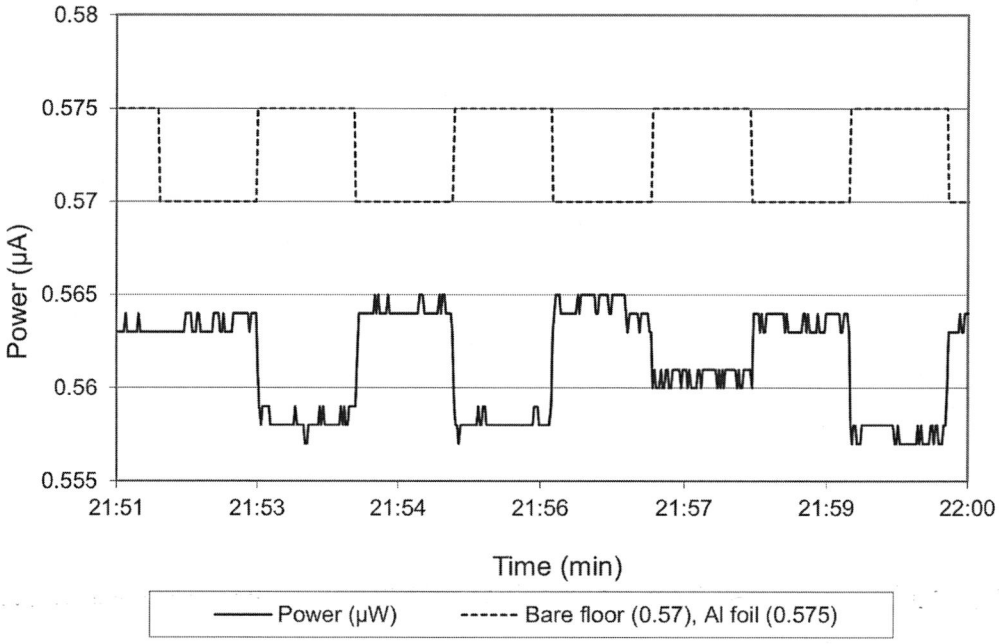

Figure 21.11. Graph showing the response of the dry-ice cooled Ku-band LNB to aluminum foil.

A similar experiment was performed using aluminum foil, as shown in Figure 21.11. This result is consistent with the foil blocking some of the thermal radiation from the concrete floor and so preventing it from reaching the LNB.

C-Band Low Noise Block

The test was repeated with a C-band LNB that uses a 5.15 GHz local oscillator. Figure 21.12 shows the effect of placing a bowl of water under the LNB. The C-band LNB was used without the collimating tube needed for the Ku band LNB.

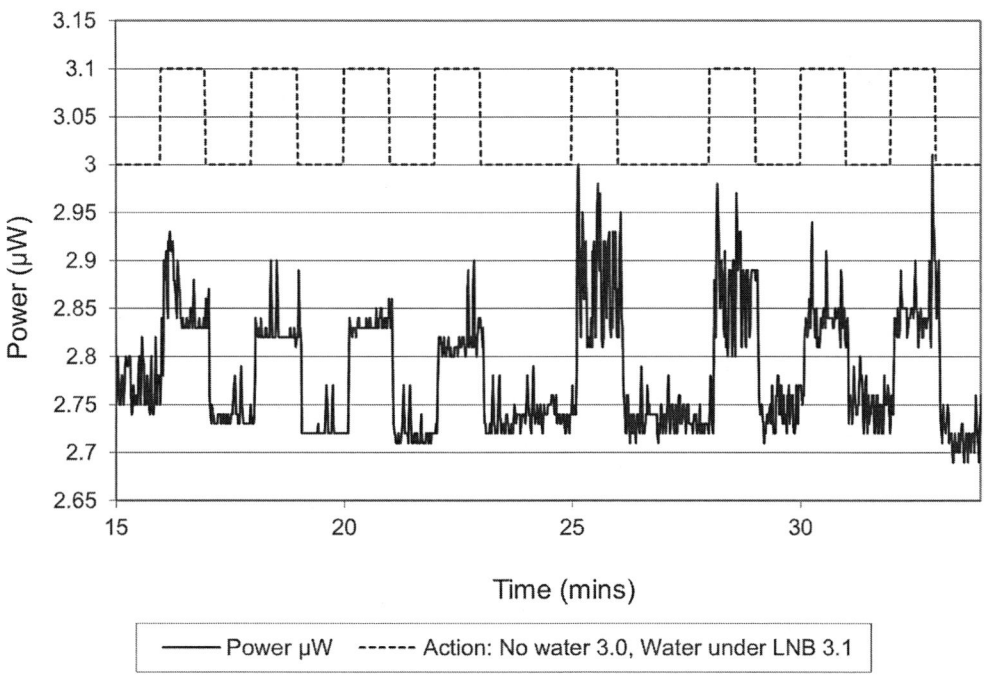

Figure 21.12. Graph of power vs. time for a C-band LNB mounted vertically over a concrete floor. A bowl of water was repeatedly placed under the LNB and removed.

The results with the C-band LNB are consistent with those obtained with the Ku band LNB, though the former was used without the collimating tube needed for the latter. The C-band LNB without the collimating tube appears to have a higher power output than the KU-band LNB with the collimating tube, but the signal to noise does not look any better. While these tests do not show the LNB is picking up the dowsing signal, the results are consistent with that explanation.

LNB and SDR

The power meter measures the signal power across the spectrum and so tests were run connecting the LNBs to an SDR receiver to see if there was any frequency dependent dowsing-related response. Again, the dowsing response was assessed using a sheet of aluminum foil and a plastic bowl of water.

The Ku-Band LNB was mounted vertically over a bare concrete floor and was connected to the SDR to see if the dowsing effect could be observed. If present, it should show up as a decrease in the baseline when microwave absorbent or blocking materials are placed beneath the LNB. The results are shown in Figure 21.13. There is no apparent effect on the baseline when aluminum foil or a bowl of water was placed under the LNB.

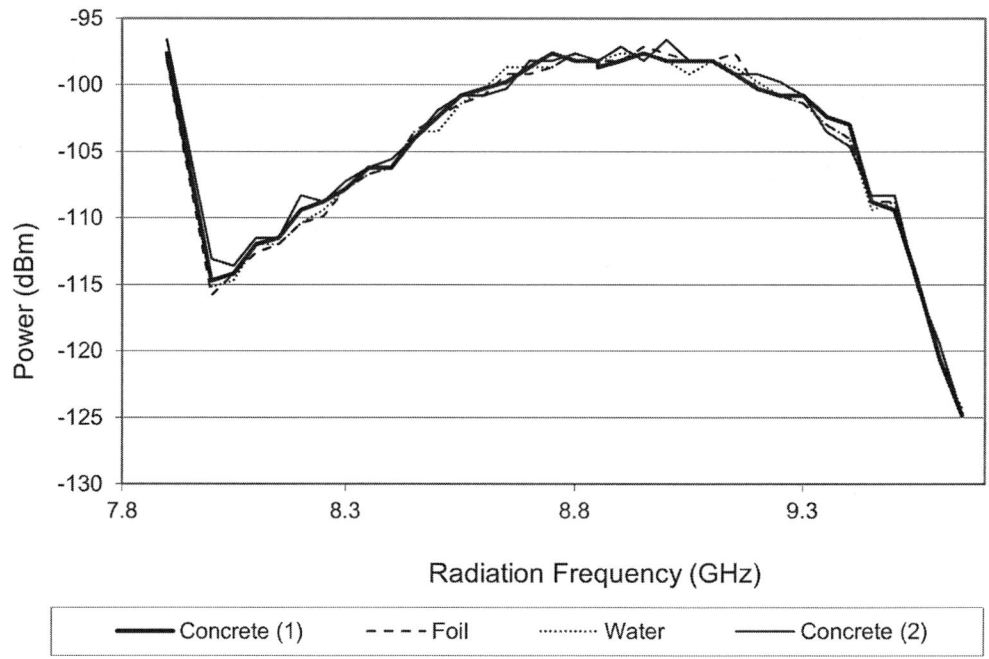

Figure 21.13. Graph of KU-Band LNB output to SDR when exposed to a concrete floor, a sheet of aluminum foil, a bowl of water and a bare concrete floor again.

The experiment was repeated with a C-band LNB mounted vertically 12.5 cm (5 inches) above a concrete floor. Readings were taken at different frequencies for bare concrete, aluminum foil sheet, a plastic bowl of water and bare concrete again. The results are shown in Figure 21.14, and again there was no significant difference between the bare concrete and the water—the small differences observed with water were not greater than between the first and last run with bare concrete. There was an unexpected oscillation with the aluminum foil. The cause of this oscillation is not known, but it corresponds to a frequency of about 100 MHz and may be a resonance between the cavity formed by the LNB and the foil and an internal oscillator, perhaps an internal clock. Whatever the cause of the resonance, it does not appear to be related to dowsing.

These results make sense on comparing the LNB/SDR data with the results from the LNB and HP 437B power meter. The changes in the power meter reading were only about 3 percent of the signal and if the baseline curves above decreased by this

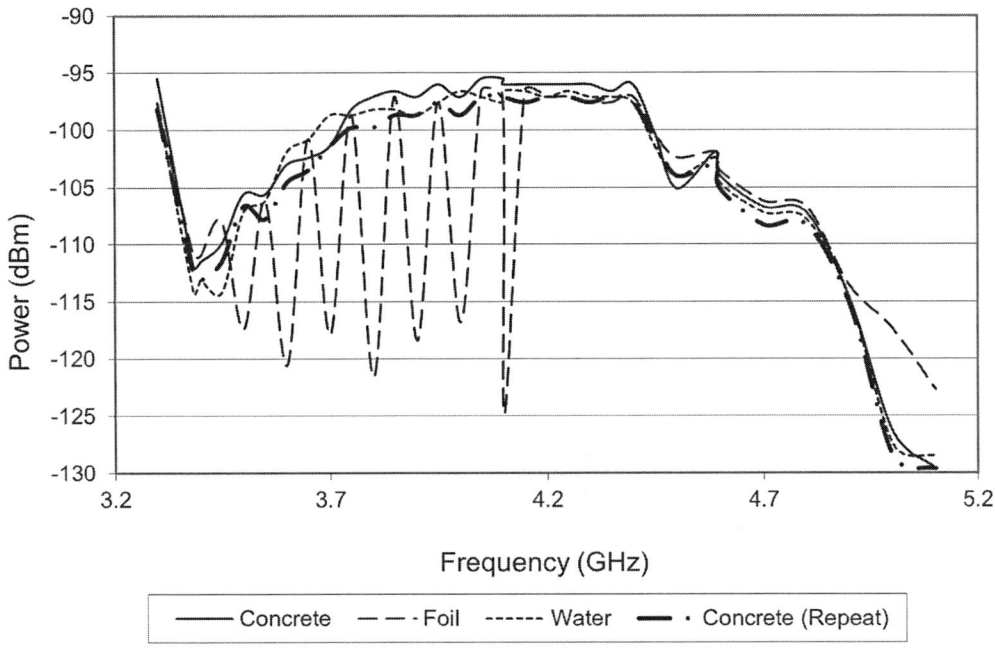

Figure 21.14. Graph showing the response from the C-band LNB with SDR, for bare concrete, aluminum foil, water and concrete.

percentage, the decrease would only be about 0.14 dBm. However, the resolution is about 2 dBm on a baseline of 100 dBm.

Estimate of Change in Power in LNB/SDR Baseline from Water and Foil

From the tests with the power meter, the size of the signal from the dry-ice cooled LNB without water was 0.572 µW, and with water 0.554 µW, a decrease of 0.018 µW or 3.16 percent.

The power for the LNB/SDR baseline was about -100 dBm, which is equivalent to 1×10^{-13} W. Assuming the power decrease with water is uniform across the spectrum, a decrease of 3.16 percent gives a remaining 9.68×10^{-14} W. Converting back to dBm gives -100.14 dBm. The SDR and spectrum analyzer do not have the signal/noise resolution to distinguish such a small change.

The results presented in this chapter have shown that dowsing-like behavior can be detected instrumentally, but the dowsing signal is weak, and the detection is at the limits of the equipment used. The LNBs used were readily available detectors for satellite TV, and so if more sensitive detectors were used, and a lower noise receiver than the SDR employed above, perhaps the dowsing response would be stronger. It is recommended that future attempts to measure the dowsing signal instrumentally detect the signal at ~3 GHz with a very sensitive, highly colimated detector.

22

Dowsing in Three Dimensions

A mind that is stretched by a new experience can never go back to its old dimensions.
—Oliver Wendell Holmes, Jr.

Chapter summary: Dowsing is normally thought of in terms of detecting objects or material beneath one's feet, but objects overhead can also cause a dowsing response, as can shadows from outdoor sunlight, again consistent with microwaves being the basis of the dowsing effect.

Dowsing Overhead

We normally think of field dowsing as someone walking across the land looking for things hidden below the surface. However, that is a limited view, since dowsing works in three dimensions. I first observed it in my basement, noticing several parallel dowsing lines across the floor. It took an embarrassingly long time for me to look up and see that these lines coincided with the steel I-beams supporting the house, and the sheet metal hot air ducts directly above my head. Since then, I have made many other observations that confirmed that, yes, dowsing does occur from above as well as below.

To confirm this idea, I tried a simple experiment in which I wore a 30 cm (12 in) diameter fedora covered in aluminum foil. I expected the downwards signal to go away, but it did not. There was no apparent difference with and without the foil covered hat. Of course, this type of experiment is best done in the privacy of one's own basement, since running around with a foil hat on one's head looking for unknown radiations from above is not something to share with the neighbors, or one's close family either for that matter.

The fedora was a little small and so rode high on my head, about 4 cm (1.5 in) above the top of the ears. Perhaps the microwaves were coming from the side? I repeated the test with a foil covered sombrero, about 71 cm (28 in) diameter, and with this cultural improvement the signals from the overhead I-beams and heating ducts disappeared but the signals from the sewer line beneath the basement floor remained the same as before. It may be that dowsing signals from overhead come in from the side to reach the bottom of the brain, since penetrating that 10 cm or 4 inches of brain tissue from above may be too much to ask for. The longer path in air and the more oblique angle may be more than compensated for by the shorter distance through high water content brain tissues. Clearly there was more work to be done studying the path taken by the dowsing signal from above.

To test this further I walked into the entrance of the same abandoned railway tunnel discussed earlier. The rods partially crossed on entering the tunnel and fully crossed about two yards/meters into the tunnel. Looking from the outside, the partial cross corresponded to the concrete surround to the tunnel which jutted out from the hillside a couple of meters/yards by eye. The rods did the same at the other end of the tunnel. While this result is not definitive, it supports the idea that dowsing is a three-dimensional phenomenon, and the universe, atmosphere and rocks above a tunnel will also contribute to the dowsing signal through the emission of thermal radiation.

Other people have also reported that dowsing can be detected from above; for example, William Highcock wrote, "Three bamboo canes will be required, two about seven feet long … and one four foot long.… The canes are made up to form a bridge with sufficient height and width to allow the dowser to pass beneath without touching them. A length of copper wire is then hung along the cross piece, so that the ends of the wire can hang down almost to the ground on each side. … If the dowser now walks beneath the bridge with the rods in the search position, there should be a dowsing reaction on passing under the cross piece."[402] Similarly Hume wrote that "Unfortunately, the extreme sensitivity of the dowsing coat hangers [L-rods] proves their principal drawback, for they not only pick up buried metals but will also react when one passes beneath pole-strung telephone wires or moves about ten yards of a parked car, and like mine detectors, they react splendidly to modern nails, bottle caps, and bits of bicycles."[403]

Maby and Franklin[404] also reported the three-dimensional aspect of dowsing, but not in so many words. They found that metal posts in the ground gave a dowsing response which varied with the time of day. I was able to confirm their observation by testing steel high-voltage pylons and lights in an outdoor car park. The lights were off at the time of the test and so there was no current and an overhead light is essentially a metal pole set in concrete or mounted to a concrete base. Around each of these structures were various dowsing signals which were fixed, corresponding to the power supply for the light ground wires, cracks in the asphalt in one case, and other unidentified sources. However, there was a strong dowsing signal from the shadow of the pole in the light cast by the sun. Walking across the shadow, the rods would cross as my head crossed the edge of the shadow and uncrossed as it extended outside the shadow on the other side. This shadow moved with the sun's position in the sky as reported by Maby and Franklin, though their interpretation was different.

This result makes sense. The surface of the sun is about 6,000°C (10,000°F)[405] and so it radiates EM radiation across the spectrum, and the sun is by far the largest blackbody radiator in the solar system, including in the radio wave and microwave regions. Radio waves and microwaves are reflected by metal surfaces and so there is a sharp drop in intensity in the shadow cast by a metal pole in the sunlight. On days with heavy rain clouds, this dowsing signal was found to be greatly diminished. Presumably the radio wave and microwave radiations were absorbed or scattered by the water in the clouds in similar manner to the visible light.

Dowsing Near Large Steel Objects

I tested large steel boxes (a Pod storage container and a steel shipping container) and found that the rods crossed about 50 to 64 cm (20 to 24 inches) away from the steel surface regardless of the direction from which I approached it. Walking up to the middle of a large shipping container (2.5 m [100 in] tall, 12m [40 ft] long, and made of 0.64 cm [1/4 in] steel) with dowsing rods caused the rods to start to move about 1.2 m (4 ft) away and finally cross at about 0.5m (~20 in). In contrast, walking up to large aluminum structures, such as road signs, did not cause the rods to cross, suggesting the response with the shipping container may be magnetic.

There are several possible explanations, though none of them seem completely satisfying. A possible explanation is that the steel surface reflects incoming radio wave and microwave radiation from all directions and so emits it in all directions, along with a small amount of its own thermal emission. However, as the dowser walks towards the surface his or her body will block incoming radiation, and so when about a body's width away there will be a drop in the intensity of the reflected radiation and this drop will be observed by the rods crossing. The same effect can be seen with visible light. Under conditions of diffuse lighting, if one faces a wall painted white, there is no shadow, but as one approaches the wall a shadow forms and becomes darker as one gets closer. However, this explanation does not seem viable, since walking up to large aluminum metal sheets (road signs) gave almost no response.

Another possible explanation is that a large steel object will have or will create a magnetic field around it. The neodymium permanent magnets discussed in Chapter 14, though very strong magnets, were very small, and so their magnetic fields were indistinguishable from the Earth's magnetic field using the iPhone magnetometer beyond about 20 to 30 cm (8 to 12 inches). In contrast a steel shipping container is very large, and even if it is only weakly magnetized, the resulting magnetic field is detectable

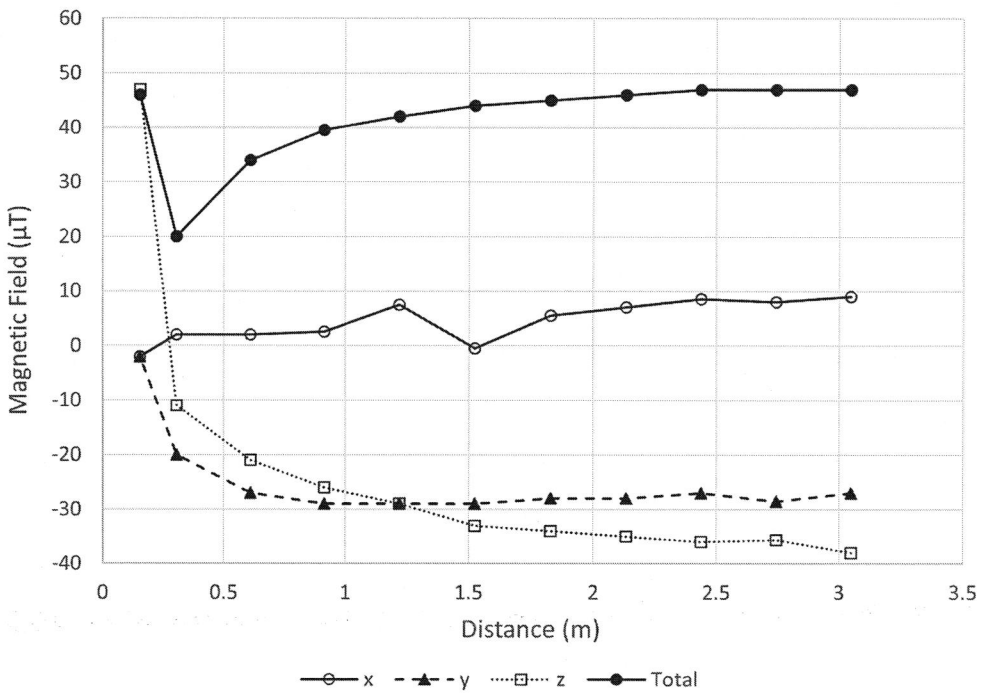

Figure 22.1. Magnetic field as a function of distance approaching a steel shipping container.

from much larger distances away than were observed with the neodymium magnets. Using the iPhone magnetometer, the magnetic field was measured a distance away from a shipping container. There are two effects, a changing magnetic field on the distance of meters (feet) and then a short-range effect on the range of centimeters (inches). The former is probably the magnetic field, and the latter may be an inductive effect of the metal, since similar behavior is seen with an aluminum block, which is not magnetic. It has been reported that with a little coding the output from the iPhone's magnetic sensor can even be used to convert the iPhone into a metal detector,[406] which supports the idea that inductive effects are important close to large conductors. The iPhone magnetometer application provides x, y and z components as well as the total magnetic field. The results are shown in Figure 22.1.

The iPhone was held horizontally, screen up, with the home button away from the shipping container. It can be seen in Figure 22.1 that the magnetic field in the x-axis (parallel to the wall of the shipping container) did not change much with distance, but both the y-axis (towards the shipping container) and the z-axis (vertical) increased on approaching the shipping container. The total field at 1.2 m is about 5 µT below ambient, or ~ 10 percent of the Earth's magnetic field. However, this result contradicts earlier tests that indicate no effect from magnetic fields generated by coils of wire carrying electric current (Chapter 14), though as discussed in that chapter, some other investigators have observed a response to magnetic fields.

Another possible explanation relates to the observations made of the memory effect, discussed in Chapter 19. In these experiments it was found that cast iron and steel emitted microwaves that could trigger the memory effect in the concrete floor, but aluminum objects of comparable size had no such effect. It is not entirely clear what, but something is going on. For example, if the side of a shipping container is emitting microwaves of the appropriate wavelength, are they generating a dowsing response directly or by inducing a response from the ground below? Clearly, the dowsing response from large steel objects is another area that needs further study.

23

Mechanisms for Detection of Magnetic Fields in Animals

Something is as little explained by means of a distinctive vital force as the attraction between iron and magnet is explained by means of the name magnetism. We must therefore firmly insist that in the organic natural sciences, and thus also in botany, absolutely nothing has yet been explained and the entire field is still open to investigation as long as we have not succeeded in reducing the phenomena to physical and chemical laws.
—Jacob Mathias Schlelden[407]

Chapter summary: The dowsing response may be related to the magnetic field sense in animals, including humans. The mechanisms of the magnetic sense are reviewed and considered for applicability to the dowsing response.

The question of whether dowsing is a sense or an artifact of our physiology has been posed several times in this book. One idea that seems promising is that there is not a specific dowsing sense organ, but rather the dowsing response piggybacks on the magnetic field sense organ. Even though most people can't consciously sense magnetic fields, many animals can, and it is possible that this ancient mechanism lies dormant within us all. To explore this idea more, this chapter explores the detection of magnetic fields by animals.

Detection of Static Magnetic Fields in Animals and People

The ability of animals to detect static magnetic fields is an active area of current research but remains poorly understood. The ability to sense the Earth's magnetic field is very important for many types of animal that migrate over large distances. It has been found that many creatures can detect the earth's magnetic field and use it for orientation and navigation. Bacteria and phytoplankton generate biological magnetite crystals that allow them to sense Earth's magnetic field, as do bees.[408] Sharks are known to navigate using the Earth's magnetic field,[409] as are salmon,[410] and experiments with loggerhead turtles which migrate thousands of miles have shown that they can detect not only the orientation/intensity of the Earth's magnetic field, but also its inclination.[411]

There is evidence that dogs too are sensitive to the Earth's magnetic field. Dogs use it to find shortcuts,[412] hunting dogs use it to navigate,[413] and wolves have been observed to align in a north-south orientation when resting.[414] Vlastimil Hart et al.

studied 70 dogs of 37 breeds during defecation (1,893 observations) and urination (5,582 observations) over a two-year period and found that dogs align themselves with the Earth's magnetic field when they relieve themselves.[415] I did a much more limited study with only one dog, for over 300 pooping events. Our male dog was either off the lead or on an 8 m (26 ft) retractable lead, so he had freedom to choose his direction. There appears to be a weak correlation with northwest-southeast orientation (see Figure 23.1), but whatever the cause of this orientation preference, he does not appear to be aligning with the Earth's magnetic field.

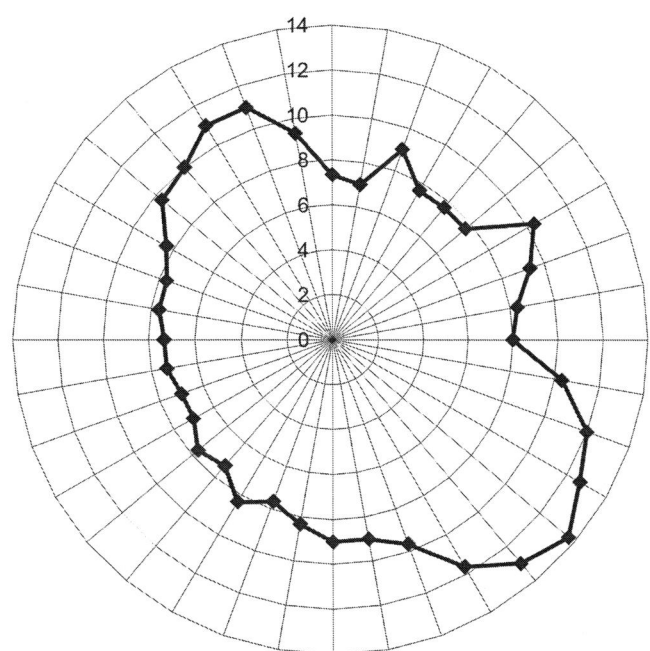

Figure 23.1. Orientations for one dog for over 300 pooping events, measured to nearest 10° using an iPhone 7 compass, with 30 degree running average.

There is more evidence that dogs can sense magnetic fields; for example, dogs have been trained to find a bar magnet by selecting one of three possible containers and were found to do better finding bar magnets than food treats.[416] Even cows have been observed to align with the magnetic field,[417] though these results have been questioned.[418] The key point is that many animals, including mammals, have the ability to detect the orientation of the Earth's magnetic field, and some also have the ability to detect the inclination as well as the magnetic field orientation.

There are two main theories to explain how many animals can detect magnetic fields. The first theory is that the magnetic sense is achieved by means of a pair of radicals in the eyes' cells that modulate the animal's vision as a function of the magnetic field.[419] The second proposal is that small granules of magnetite found in many animals are used to measure the magnetic field. Both of these theories are discussed in more detail below.

Cryptochromes[420]

The first potential magnetic receptor in mammalian and other animals are a group of flavoproteins called the cryptochromes, found in plants,[421] insects,[422] reptiles, birds and mammals that are sensitive to blue light. In birds and mammals crytochromes are found in high concentrations in the retina. Foley et al. showed that fruit flies use a cryptochrome protein in their eyes to detect magnetic fields, and flies without the gene for this protein were unable to detect magnetic fields. When fruit flies were bred with the human version of the gene, they could sense a magnetic field.[423] In humans these cryptochromes are associated with controlling circadian rhythms,[424] and thus our crytochromes have the ability to be used for sensing the Earth's magnetic field, even if these proteins have been repurposed.

Proposed Mechanism of Magnetic Field

Cryptochromes are found in the retinas of many birds and mammals, and it is proposed that blue light is absorbed and two radicals (unpaired electrons) are formed, then the electron spins will align with the magnetic field and doing so may direct the reaction products of the radical.

Detection by Crytochromes

While there is data to support this theory (e.g., birds can only sense the magnetic field if certain wavelengths of light are available), the exact mechanism remains elusive.[1] This radical pair has a resonance frequency at 1.315 MHz (Larmor frequency), and birds exposed to radio waves were disoriented at this frequency down to radio frequency amplitudes of 15 nT, while 150 nT administered at non–Larmor frequencies had no effect.[2] Ilia Solov'yov and Klaus Schulten have written a nice summary of the current theory of how birds might use the crytochrome protein for sensing the Earth's magnetic field.[3]

1. Ilia Solov'yov and Klaus Schulten, "Cryptochrome and Magnetic Sensing," http://www.ks.uiuc.edu/Research/cryptochrome/, accessed August 18, 2020.
2. C. Nießner and M. Winklhofer, "Radical-Pair-Based Magnetoreception in Birds: Radio-Frequency Experiments and the Role of Cryptochrome," *J Comp Physiol A* 203 (2017), 499–507, https://link.springer.com/article/10.1007/s00359-017-1189-1; Michael Le Page, "Radio Waves From Electric Devices May Affect the Body Clock Of Insects," *New Scientist*, September 18, 2019, https://www.newscientist.com/article/2216690-radio-waves-from-electric-devices-may-affect-the-body-clock-of-insects/.
3. Ilia Solov'yov and Klaus Schulten, "Cryptochrome and Magnetic Sensing," Theoretical and Computational Biophysics Group, University of Illinois at Urbana Champaign, http://www.ks.uiuc.edu/Research/cryptochrome/, accessed January 25, 2021.

In a recent survey of the major mammalian families, many members of the Carnivora canidae family (dogs, foxes, racoons, ferrets and others) and some primates (Bornean orangutans, rhesus macaques and crab eating macaques) had the cryptochrome 1 protein in the retinal cone photoreceptors in their eyes, suggesting that they may see the inclination of the Earth's magnetic field.[425]

Some mice have the crytochrome 1 protein in their retinal nuclear cells,[426] and mice are magneto sensitive. Wood mice have been observed to build their nests north-south, and when a magnetic field was applied east-west, the mice built their nests east-west. Based on tests exposing the mice to radio frequency radiation, the authors concluded that their results provided the first evidence for a radical-pair mechanism for magnetic field detection in a mammal, i.e., that mice use a cryptochrome to detect magnetic fields.[427]

Interestingly, Sherrard et al. showed that repetitive magnetic field exposure in human cells stimulates the production of reactive oxygen species such as superoxides, peroxide radical, etc., via interaction of the magnetic field with crytochrome proteins.[428] A similar mechanism has been proposed to explain the response of plants to sub microTesla magnetic fields in the presence of light,[429] suggesting that these magnetic sense mechanisms are both very widespread and arose early on the evolutionary timescale. There is some evidence to suggest that men but not women so far (for reasons that are not clear) are sensitive to magnetic fields using crytochrome proteins and blue light.[430] These results help explain the observation of free radical species in mammals after exposure to radio waves and microwaves (see next chapter).

Magnetite

Pigeons and some other birds have been found to have a magnetite particle–based magnetic sensing organs in their beaks.[431] Other animals also use magnetite to orient themselves to the magnetic field, including bees, some mammals, and some bacteria.[432] Magnetite (Fe_3O_4) is a naturally occurring magnetic material that will align with an external magnetic field. Magnetite particles have been observed in humans too.

Evidence for Magnetite in Humans

Baker et al. reported that the phenoid/ethmoid sinus complex bones contain deposits of ferric iron and are magnetic,[1] and Schultheiss-Grassi et al. found magnetite particles in the hippocampus.[2] Kirschvink et al. found magnetic crystals in human postmortem brain tissue with similar morphology to those formed in magneto-bacteria and fish. Magnetic and high-resolution transmission electron microscopy measurements of brain samples imply the presence of a minimum of 5 million single-domain crystals per gram for most tissues in the brain and greater than 100 million crystals per gram for pia and dura (two of the three layers of the meninges, the membrane that surrounds and protects the brain). Magnetic property data indicate the crystals are in clumps of between 50 and 100 particles[3] and resemble magnetosomes, the magnetic organ in some bacteria. A typical human brain contains about 170 billion cells, half of which are neurons, and weighs about 1,350g,[4] so each gram contains about 125 million cells, and so on average about 4 percent of cells have these magnetite particles. However, since the magnetite crystals are clumped, these numbers suggest that some cells (~0.05%) have clumps of magnetite particles but most cells have none.

The authors also showed by simple calculation that the response of these "magnetosomes" to earth-strength extremely low-frequency fields are capable of opening trans-membrane ion channels[5] and thus have the potential to cause nerves to fire. This last observation suggests a possible mechanism for the magnetic sense and perhaps even the dowsing sense.

---

1. R. Baker, J. Mather, and J. Kennaugh, "Magnetic Bones in Human Sinuses," *Nature* 301 (1983), 78–80, https://doi.org/10.1038/301078a0.
2. P.P. Schultheiss-Grassi, R. Wessiken, and J. Dobson, "TEM Investigations of Biogenic Magnetite Extracted From the Human Hippocampus," *Biochem Biophys Acta.* 1426, 1 (January 4, 1999), 212–6, doi: 10.1016/s0304-4165(98)00160-3.
3. J.L. Kirschvink, A. Kobayashi-Kirschvink, and B.J. Woodford, "Magnetite Biomineralization in the Human Brain," *Proceedings of the National Academy of Sciences* 89, 16 (August 1992), 7683–7687, doi: 10.1073/pnas.89.16.7683.
4. Eric H. Chudler, "Brain Facts and Figures," https://faculty.washington.edu/chudler/facts.html, accessed February 16, 2021.
5. Joseph L. Kirschvink, Atsuko Kobayashi-Kirschvink, Juan C. Diaz-Ricci, and Steven J. Kirschvink, "Magnetite in Human Tissues: A Mechanism for the Biological Effects Of Weak ELF Magnetic Fields," *BioEM S Supplement*, vol. 13, issue S1 (1992), https://doi.org/10.1002/bem.22501307101992.

Role of Magnetite in the Human Brain

Gilder et al. recently also found that there is magnetite in the human brain and that it is most concentrated in the brain stem and secondly in the cerebellum. While the magnetite particles respond strongly enough to trigger a nerve cell, no magnetic sensory cells that use magnetite have been found.[433] Kirschvink et al. used electroencephalography (EEG), and found changes in human brain activity in response to changes in highly controlled magnetic fields equal in strength to Earth's.[434] This observation suggests that there is still some magnetic sense functionality in the brain, even if only at the subconscious level, a mere vestige of its former glory; and also that even though the magnetic sensory cells have not been found yet, they are probably out there. Wang et al. did similar EEG testing and found that the alpha waves in their human subjects responded to static magnetic fields of similar intensity to the Earth's magnetic field and also that the response was triggered only by horizontal rotations when the static vertical magnetic field was directed downwards, as it is in the northern hemisphere; but not by the same horizontal rotations when the static vertical component was directed upwards. This result indicated that the response varied with location of the subject, at least northern versus southern hemisphere.[435] This observation is interesting, since it suggests an up/down orientation that could possibly be related to the acute angle sensitivity of dowsing.

Magnetite Particle Sizes

Kirschvink and Gould estimated the sensitivity with which animals with magnetite sensor organs could theoretically detect magnetic fields in a very good paper from 1981.[1] The magnetic properties of magnetite (Fe_3O_4) depend strongly on the size of the particle and its width to length ratio. If the particles are very small (< ~ 0.03 to 0.05 μm) and long, then they are superparamagnetic, which means that their microscopic magnetism changes with ambient magnetic field, so whichever way the magnetic field is pointing the internal microscopic magnetism will align with it. The next size up is 11 μm and up, depending on shape, and this size particle is the single domain magnetite. For these grains, all the magnetite is aligned the same way, but the grain will not change its internal microscopic magnetic orientation in the presence of an external field (unless very large). There will however be a force on the whole grain to align it with the external field. For larger particles larger than 11 μm the magnetite particle is so large that there will be more than one magnetic domain in the particle, which may or may not be pointing in different directions. The maximum magnetic response is therefore obtained using the single domain particles, and these particles are very stable at ambient temperature and keep their magnetism for many years[2]

1. J.L. Kirschvink, J.L. Gould, "Biogenic Magnetite as a Basis for Magnetic Field Detection in Animals," *Biosystems* 13 (1981), 181–201.
2. Robert F. Butler, Subir K. Banerjee, "Theoretical Single Domain Grain Size Range in Magnetite and Titanomagnetite," *Journal of Geophysical Research, Solid Earth and Planets* vol. 80, issue 29 (October 10, 1975), 4049–4058, https://agupubs.onlinelibrary.wiley.com/doi/abs/10.1029/JB080i029p04049.

Induced Currents

There is another theory for how birds detect the magnetic field which has received very little attention. Nimpf et al. proposed that animals detect magnetic fields by EM induction within the semicircular canals of the inner ear.[436] They showed experimentally that magnetic stimulation can induce electric fields in the pigeon semicircular canals that are within the physiological range of known electroreceptive systems and have identified a voltage-gated calcium channel (CaV1.3) in the pigeon's inner ear that is similar to the channels which mediate electroreception in skates and sharks. Wu et al. traced the neurons involved and found that they activate those parts of the brain involved in orientation, spatial memory, and navigation.[437] Malkempter et al. searched for magnetite in the pigeon's inner ear but found none, thus ruling out the magnetite theory.[438] This line of research is fairly recent and the details are still being worked out, but it appears that birds, and perhaps other animals, have at least three different types of magnetic field sensors.

In conclusion it appears that animals have three magnetic senses, one based on magnetite particles, one using radical pair processes in the retina using a cryptochrome and one involving induced currents in the inner ear. The cryptochrome appears to provide more information such as magnetic inclination than is possible with the magnetite or the induced currents but also requires light, but the magnetite and induced current both work in light and dark conditions. Which magnetic sense animals use depends on the species, and some such as many migrating birds appear to employ more than one sense for navigation.[439] More details about avian magnetic sensing can be found in a 2010 review.[440]

Possible Origin of the Dowsing Sense

Life on earth developed in the presence of the terrestrial magnetic field and background EM radiation. A possible explanation relies on the proposal earlier that the dowsing response is a vestige of our ancestors' magnetic field sense. For a four-legged animal to navigate by a magnetic field, it needs to do more than just detect the presence of the Earth's magnetic field; it needs to be able to detect very small differences in the magnetic field with orientation such that it can sense which way is north (or south) and so get its bearing. Not only must the magnetic field be detected, but the animal must detect the component which is parallel to its main axis, i.e., parallel to its head or spine. Being able to detect the orientation of the magnetic field as well as its magnitude is a sensory challenge, but one that nature has remarkably achieved given how many animals use the Earth's magnetic field to navigate. If the Earth's magnetic field is around 50 μT, then roughly each degree rotation corresponds to (50 μT/90° =) 0.56 μT per degree (field goes from 50 μT facing north to zero facing east-west).

To navigate using the Earth's magnetic field, an animal needs to be able to determine the direction of the magnetic field (the so-called magnetic lines of force), so that it knows what direction it is traveling with respect to the magnetic field. A dog, for example, running along will typically have its head out in front. The dog's brain has the same major structural components as humans, but the orientation is different, especially the older parts of the brain, around the brain stem, through which the spinal cord connects to the brain. In a dog, the brain stem and spine are roughly horizontal, and a similar configuration is found with most quadrupeds. Whereas, in a human, standing on two legs, the head is positioned on top of the shoulders, the brain stem and spine are roughly vertical.

If the magnetic sense in mammals is in the brain stem (location unclear at this time), then the magnetic sense organ used by quadrupeds living near the equator and in most temperate climates would work much less well for upright humans near the equator and better as one heads north or south towards the poles. Even if the magnetic sense organ is not in the brain stem, it is presumably oriented with the animal's horizontal axis. The magnetic sense must be able to detect the direction of the Earth's magnetic field accurately if it is to be useful. For example, if the deviation from magnetic north were a mere three degrees, then after traveling 100 km (62 miles), the error would be over 5 km (3.1 miles) from where the animal wanted to go as illustrated in Figure 23.2.

Ancestral humans evolved hands to do other things such as make tools and skim stones across lakes, but at a cost of moving much slower and perhaps a significant weakening of the magnetic orientation sense. While the magnetic sense organ may not work so well for orientation in upright humans, this organ is positioned well for sensing changes in the EM radiation coming up from the ground, the dowsing sense. If the magnetic sense is based on magnetite, then particle size will be very small (< ~ 0.03 to 0.05 μm) and superparamagnetic to get the sensitivity. If these tiny particles are appended to a gate protein, then the response time probably depends on the mass of the particle and the force of its tether, by analogy to Hooke's law for a spring. The smaller the particle and stronger the tether, the higher the frequency. If the frequency of the particle vibrations is greater than the frequency of incoming EM radiation, then the magnetite

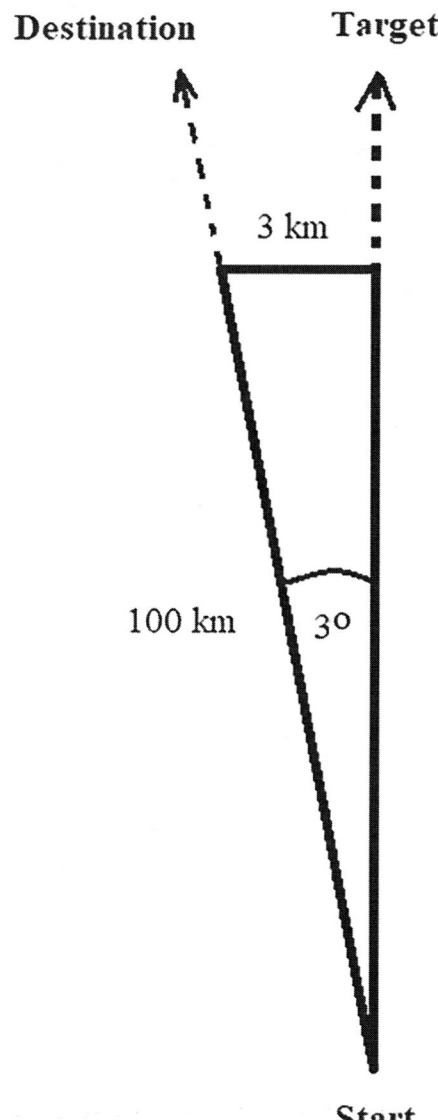

Figure 23.2. Direction deviation with angle when navigating.

particle should be able to respond. If the frequency of the radiation is higher than the magnetite particle's frequency, then it will not be able to respond. Unfortunately, this idea is just conjecture, with very little evidence to support it. We are still in the early days in the exploration of receptors for many types of stimuli; for example, the first detailed description of a human olfactory receptor was only published in 2023,[441] so the next few years should rapidly expand our knowledge.

This chapter started with the question of whether the dowsing response is using the dormant magnetic sense. While there is evidence that the cryptochrome found in the human eye can be used for magnetic field detection,[442] it is unlikely to be the mechanism of the dowsing effect, because dowsing works in the dark. The induced current is also unlikely to be behind the dowsing response, since any currents would have to be at GHz frequencies. The human brain has been found to have magnetite particles in it, especially in the brain stem and cerebellum, close to the same region that the dowsing sense location is believed to be found in. Magnetite could potentially interact with the magnetic fields of microwave radiation if the particle size was small enough that it could oscillate with the magnetic field of the microwave radiation, and of the three magnetic sense mechanisms it appears to be most likely to be relevant to dowsing. One possibility is that the dowsing sense is an artifact of the disused magnetic field sense. It is, however, odd that our sensitivity to static magnetic fields is now below conscious perception, but the dowsing response is highly sensitive.

24

Interaction of Electromagnetic Fields with Biological Systems

My body was a buzzing antenna into which radio waves flooded from the entire cosmos. I was the living switchboard of the universe. My skull was a magnetized globe.

—Simon Critchley[443]

Chapter summary: Prior chapters that shown that the dowsing response relies on low-intensity thermal microwave radiation. If this statement is true, then the human body must be able to detect these microwaves. This chapter reviews the interaction of very low-intensity microwaves with humans and other animals and possible mechanisms for the dowsing sense.

The earlier chapters of this book demonstrated that the dowsing signal comprises EM radiation in the low GHz range. For the dowsing signal to be detected there must be some interaction between very low-intensity microwaves and us. This chapter reviews the literature on the effects of EM radiation on biological systems, especially microwave

Table 24.1. Typical Microwave Applications and Frequencies

Application	Frequency range (MHz)
FM radio and TV broadcasting antennas	80–800
Mobile phones	453.5–1980.0
Mobile phone base station	463.5–2170.0
Microwave links	1000
Cordless phones	1880–1900
Terrestrial trunked radio	380–470
Wi-Fi, cell phones and Bluetooth devices[1]	2450
Baby monitors	40, 446, 864, 1900 and 2450
Wireless local area networks	2400 and 5000
Microwave ovens	915–2450
Radar	30–300,000

1. Bluetooth is a registered trademark of the Bluetooth Special Interest Group.

radiation. Table 24.1 shows some of the common microwave frequencies and their applications.

The microwave region of the spectrum is associated with low energy molecular rotations, and there is not enough energy in a microwave photon to ionize a molecule, or break chemical bonds, including forming free radicals. Ionization is the process where an atom or molecule receives enough energy to lose one of its electrons. Chemical bond breaking and ionization typically only happen in the ultraviolet and x-ray regions of the spectrum because photons at these wavelengths carry much more energy than microwaves (a 300 nm UV photon carries one millions times as much energy as a 1 GHz microwave photon). Since microwaves cannot ionize molecules, they are assumed to pose no significant risks to the users of microwave communications equipment, so long as the intensity of the microwaves is too small to cause heating effects.

Heating Effects of Microwaves

High-intensity radio and microwave frequencies below 3 GHz are harmful, since they can penetrate the outer layers of the skin, be absorbed in the underlying tissues, and result in heating, including burns, cataracts, and possibly death. This heating effect is the same action as heating food in a microwave oven. For example, the U.S. military developed an active denial system that was briefly deployed in Afghanistan before being withdrawn. This non-lethal weapon fires a burst for a few seconds of 95 GHz microwaves at the target which is absorbed by the outer layer of the skin causing severe pain, but minimal physical damage.[444] The thermal effects of radio waves and microwaves are reasonably well understood and government regulators around the world set microwave exposure limits so as to ensure that the amount of tissue heating due to the absorption of energy will not cause injury.[445]

Effect of EM Radiation on Biological Systems

There is increasing evidence that radio waves and microwaves can have effects on biological systems at intensities well below those associated with thermal effects; for example, microwave exposure of mammals, including rodents, can cause high blood pressure, oxidative stress, and other adverse symptoms.[446] The biochemistry of rodents is fairly similar to humans, so there is a risk of similar adverse effects occurring in humans too. In recent years there have been reports that microwaves can cause cancer[447] and other problems, which is interesting because, as mentioned earlier, microwaves were previously believed to be incapable of ionizing molecules and/or creating highly reactive species such as radicals. However, in the last chapter we discussed the formation of radical species being formed by interaction of changing magnetic fields with crytochrome proteins. Such radicals and highly oxidizing species may be capable of damaging DNA. Perhaps, the microwaves are triggering a reaction with the cryptochrome proteins, rather than directly causing the breaking of DNA and formation of free radicals. The International Agency for Research on Cancer (IARC), which is part of the WHO, classified microwave emissions at the frequency used in cell phones as possibly carcinogenic to humans (Group 2B), based on an increased risk for glioma, a malignant type of brain cancer, associated with wireless phone use.[448] These results do suggest that influence of microwaves on biological systems has been greatly underestimated because of the prior assumptions based on the low photon energy.

Effect of Sub-Thermal Microwaves on Mammalian Brains

Microwave radiation has also been found to have an effect on behavior in rats and college students, with less movement,[449] cognitive decline,[450] reaction times,[451] deficits in spatial learning and memory,[452] anxiety, greater depression and for the male mice decreased learning and memory (females were apparently unaffected).[453] Most of these studies are statistical rather than mechanistic, though a recent review concluded that most changes in behavior on exposure to microwaves can be ascribed to thermal effects.[454] Behavioral changes indicate that the microwaves are having an effect on the brain. In addition to changes in subjects' behavior microwave exposure can cause changes in their brain activity as measured by electroencephalogram (EEG). At very low frequencies, these effects result in physiological changes but at higher frequencies the effects are not apparent to the subject and are only seen in techniques such as the EEG, as summarized below.

Very Low Frequencies

- Repetitive transcranial magnetic stimulation (rTMS) at 1 Hz caused changes to the EEG.[455]
- Nineteen volunteers exposed to two-second bursts of 1.5 and 10 Hz EM fields, 0.2–0.4 gauss (20–40 µT), exhibited altered brain electrical activity at the frequency of the EMF during the time of stimulation, as determined by EEG.[456]
- Human subjects exposed to 7 and 1000 Hz modulation frequencies exhibited significant changes in their EEG and various neurological parameters.[457]

Kilohertz Frequencies

- Exposing volunteers to a 10-minute, previously recorded 10 kHz-sferics impulse, presented with a pulse repetition frequency statistically varying between 1 and 3 Hz, resulted in changes to the volunteers' EEG patterns.[458]
  Note: An sferic is a broadband electromagnetic impulse that occurs as a result of natural atmospheric lightning discharges.
- Volunteers exposed to the 10-minute of 10kHz-sferics impulses without modulation resulted in increases in absolute alpha and beta frequency in their EEG.[459]
- Exposure of volunteers to EM fields ranging from DC to at least 40 kHz resulted in decrease in the alpha frequency band in the EEG.[460]

Megahertz Frequencies

- The EEGs of cats changed after exposure to low-intensity (1 mW/sq.cm or less) microwaves, at 147 MHz electrical fields, amplitude-modulated at biological frequencies (1–25 Hz).[461]

- Exposing volunteers for 30 min to a 920 MHz GSM-like signal resulted in changes to their EEGs.[462]
- Subjects were exposed to low level (0.16 mW/cm^2) 450 MHz microwave radiation modulated with 7 Hz, 14 Hz, 21 Hz, 40 Hz, 70 Hz, 217 or 1000 Hz frequencies. Between 12 percent and 30 percent of subjects exhibited statistically significant changes in EEG rhythms energy and dynamics.[463]

Gigahertz Frequencies

- Animals exposed (2 h daily for 21 days) to 1 kHz square wave-modulated 2450 MHz microwave radiation showed changes in their EEGs.[464]
- Exposure of volunteers to 2.45 GHz Wi-Fi resulted in changes to their EEGs, but no changes to their sleep patterns.[465]
- Radar microwave radiation leads to a decreased reaction time and lower short-term memory performance. Among radar workers exposed to 14–18 GHz microwaves, somatic symposium anxiety and insomnia, social dysfunction and severe depression were observed.[466]
- For rats treated with long-term exposure to microwave radiation, their neurons exhibited edema and irregular hippocampal neurons, compared to controls.[467]
- Applying UHF radiation (field strength field of 1,000 V/m to a neuronally isolated strip of cerebral cortex in a non-anesthetized rabbit increased the amplitude of the EEG potentials coming from it).[468] The UHF band ranges from 300 MHz to 3 GHz.
- Young albino rats of both sexes exposed for 60 days to 7.5-GHz microwaves (1.0-kHz square wave modulation, [average power 0.6 mW/cm^2] for 3 h daily tended to eat and drink less with smaller gain in body weight).[469]
- Rats exposed to pulsed 2.45 GHz microwaves (pulse width 2ms, 500 Hz, 2 mW/cm^2, for 1 hr in a circular waveguide system immediately before each training session in a maze caused a deficit in spatial "reference" memory compared to unexposed rats).[470]
- Exposure of rats to 1.5 GHz microwaves at 5, 30 & 50 mW/cm^2 resulted in spatial memory dysfunction, hippocampal structure changes, and changes in protein levels in rats, with a defined dose-dependent effect.[471]

EEG has the advantage that it is a passive measurement that does not require the conscious involvement of the subject. Effects in the EEG are seen from very low frequencies all the way up to GHz. It is interesting that Harvalik reported that some dowsers were responsive to EM radiation from 1 Hz to 1 MHz,[472] and if not coincident, then these observations may suggest a common mechanism.

These reports show that nonthermal microwave frequency radiation can interact with the brain and affect the EEG and potentially have a wider impact on the brain. The dowsing signal is a response to sub-thermal microwaves and the first part of understanding the detection mechanism is showing that sub-thermal microwaves can have an effect on the brain or nervous system.

Possible Mechanisms for the Effect of EM Radiation on Biological Systems

Radio and Microwave Hearing

Radio frequency (RF) hearing is a well-known effect, where subjects hear clicks or buzzing in the presence of pulsed radio frequencies, usually at fairly high intensity. Elder and Chou studied these effects and concluded[473]:

- Effective radio frequencies for this RF hearing ranges from 2.4 MHz to 10 GHz, but an individual's ability to hear RF induced sounds depends upon his or her being able to hear sounds in the kHz range above ~ 5 kHz. [The microwaves are absorbed creating vibrations with frequencies between 5 kHz and 20 kHz, the latter being the upper limit of human hearing.]
- The RF hearing sounds are caused by audible sounds produced by rapid thermal expansion resulting from an estimated temperature rise of only 5×10^{-6}°C in tissue at the threshold level due to absorption of the energy in the RF pulse in or close to the cochlea. [Microwaves are absorbed, the materials heat up causing local temperature changes, and expansion, which in turn create vibrations.]
- The site of conversion of RF energy to acoustic energy is within or close to the cochlea. [The same effect may occur away from the Cochlea, but it goes undetected since the sound vibrations never reach the cochlea.]
- The fundamental frequency of RF induced sounds is independent of the frequency of the radio waves but dependent upon head dimensions. [This result suggests that there may be a resonance effect, either acoustic or from the microwaves.]
- Once the sound reaches the cochlea, it is detected the same way as an acoustic sound. [Sound is vibration. Using the speed of sound in sea water (1500 m/s) as an approximation for sound through biological tissues, the wavelength at 5 kHz to 20 kHz is 7.5 to 30 cm. These dimensions are similar to the dimensions of the head and the structures within it.]
- The auditory response has been shown to be dependent upon the energy in a single pulse and not on average power density. [This result suggests it is specific structures which are absorbing and heating rather than an overall thermal effect.]

Subsequent research has confirmed Elder and Chou's conclusions.[474] The energy absorption needed per pulse of around 16 µJ/kg needed to produce the microwave hearing effect is 36,000 times lower that the maximum microwave exposure limit of 576 J/kg of the IEEE C95.1 radiation safety standard.[475] This energy corresponds to a temperature pulse of temperature of only about 10^{-6}°C, but on the microsecond timescale.[476] Microwave hearing is a well-documented and generally accepted phenomenon that demonstrates that microwaves at sub-thermal exposures can have physiological effects.

There is some evidence that radio waves can interact with humans in a way more directly related to dowsing. Huttunen reported that radio waves could cause movements of the hands of car passengers. The passengers were repeatedly driven along a 2 km stretch of road with motion detectors in their hands that logged the output to a computer which also logged the amplitude of the local FM radio tower located 30 km way, operating at a frequency of about 100 MHz. The results showed that involuntary hand movements of the test subjects correlated with EM field. The involuntary hand movements also correlated with the location of a geomagnetic anomaly along the road, confirmed by the geological maps of the area.[477] Interesting result, but there may be other explanations, such as any peaks and dips along the way may have affected both hand-movement and radio intensity, making the association a correlation rather than causal.

Huttunen also reported that humans respond weakly to radio waves, and that this response is similar to a dowsing response. Huttunen had seven test subjects walk one at a time along a line between two rural houses, while their hand movements were recorded. The houses were located about 5 km (2 miles) from a TV broadcast transmitter (~190 MHz frequency). The experiment assumed that waves reflected from the wall of the second house, forming a set of standing waves between the houses. Huttunen stated that "clear reproducible reflexive hand movements took place when the person crossed the maximums of the standing waves generated by video and voice transmitting signals of analog TV (p=0.001)."[478]

Huttunen et al. further tested subjects holding dowsing rods for how they responded to radio frequency standing waves, using a movable reflective wall. "When the reflector was moved, the position of the maximums of the standing waves changed.... The computer with an AD-converter registered the signals of the hand movement transducer and the RF-meter with 100MHz dipole antennas. A total of 29 adults of different ages were tested. There were 9 persons whose hand movement graphs included features like the RF-meter. Six showed responses that did not correlate with the RF-meter. There were also 14 persons who did not react at all. Sensitive persons seem to react to crossing standing waves of the FM-radio or TV broadcasting signals."[479]

As mentioned above, Harvalik showed that a very sensitive dowser (Mr. De Boer) was able to respond to EM radiation from 1 Hz to 1 MHz,[480] and results described above extend this sensitivity to GHz. These results indicate that the human body can respond to EM radiation over a wide range of frequencies and that this exposure can lead to muscle movements and a dowsing response. It also suggests that the dowsing response is not relying on a specific resonance for detection, such as the resonant circuit in an AM or FM radio. Instead, the response is apparently broad spectrum. These results are consistent with the dowsing response being a response to changes in the EM field. This conclusion is somewhat contradictory to the results discussed earlier that the dowsing response frequency is in the low GHz range.

Penetration of Microwaves into the Body

The penetration of microwaves and radio waves into the body is primarily determined by the high permittivity of water. Our soft tissues are largely water and even bones are about 30 percent water.[481] The typical penetration of EM radiation is approximately 1.5–0.5 cm for muscle tissue for 0.5–2.5 GHz and above 10 GHz, it is only about 0.2 mm and less.[482] The calculated values of radiation intensity at a depth of 10 cm are shown in Figure 24.1. The calculation is based on the absorption of EM radiation by water and assumes that a human body contains 60 percent water (see Chapter 20).

The depth of penetration depends on the frequency of the microwaves and the tissue type. Lower frequencies penetrate deeper; for example for 5.8 GHz (3.2 mm) most of the energy is dissipated in the first millimeter of the skin; 2.45 GHz frequency

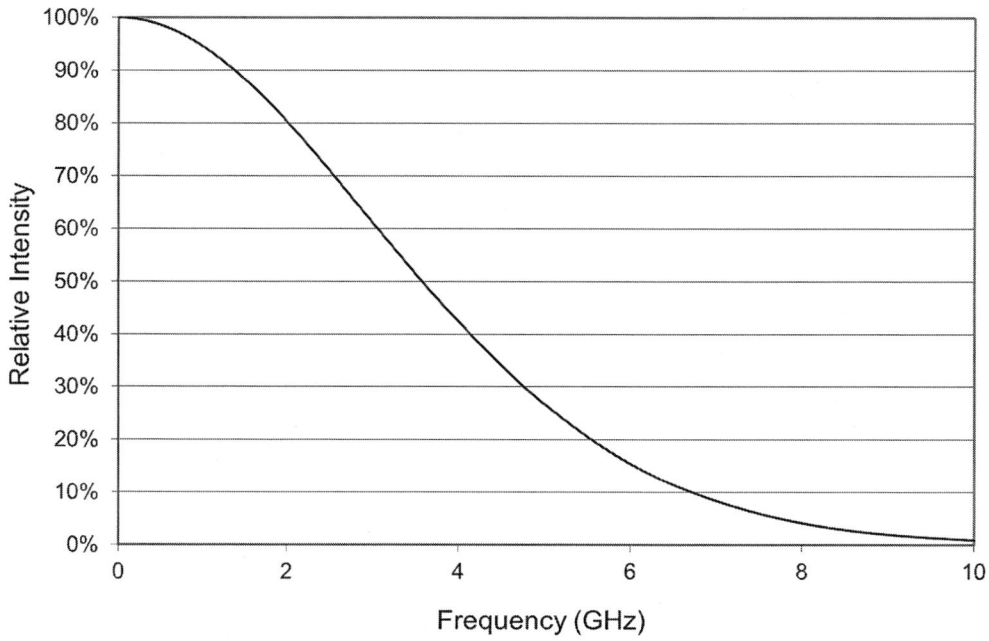

Figure 24.1. Calculated relative intensity of microwave radiation at a depth of 10 cm into human body, assuming 60% water, compared to incoming radiation.

microwaves commonly used in microwave ovens can deliver energy deeper into the tissue; the generally accepted value is 17 mm for muscle tissue.[483] If the penetration is 17 mm, then it is plausible that a significant amount of microwaves can reach near the base of the brain or the brain stem.

Over the years there have been many suggestions for how the dowsing sense works, some more plausible than others. Some of these mechanisms are described below, though the selection is not intended to be comprehensive.

Interaction of the Dowsing Signal with Nerves

Dowsing results in muscle movement and so the dowsing signal must interact with the human body and most likely the nervous system. Several possible theories for how EM radiation interacts with nerves are discussed.

Maby and Franklin believed with certainty that the dowsing response is not controlled by the brain, but rather that it is a local reflex and furthermore, based on the slow response time, they concluded that the dowsing response was in the muscles, not the nerves. Not everyone shares their viewpoint. As Professor Charles Richet, winner of the Nobel Prize for Medicine and Physiology in 1913, said[484]:

> This emanative force which acts through the muscles certainly does not act on the muscles themselves, but on the nervous system which gives movement to the muscles; the muscles are never anything but the passive slaves of the mystery of the nervous system. And here we are thus led to a conclusion whose importance will escape no one; a force emanates from metals, from veins of water, from metallic salts, and acts on the nervous system.

The observation that there is discrete dowsing sense location argues in favor of Richet's opinion.

Action on Nerves

In 1933 Dudley Wright proposed that nerve cells can act as parts of a resonant circuit to detect the dowsing signal,[485] with the insulated nerve cells providing capacitance and the coiled DNA in the chromosomes providing inductance. It is true that nerve cells (and other cells) comprise electrically conducting fluids on both sides of an insulating lipid bilayer membrane (discussed later in this chapter) and so have capacitance which can be measured (0.9 $\mu F/cm^2$).[486] However, since 1933 the study of genetics has advanced and we have learned that chromosomes have functions in the cell other than to provide inductance and so the idea of nerves and chromosomes forming LC oscillators to detect EM radiation can be discounted.

If the length of the neuron is comparable to the wavelength of the radiation, it is conceivable that the neuron will act as an antenna and have an oscillating electric field formed in it. It is known that electric fields applied to brain tissue can affect cellular properties by hyperpolarizing the ends of cells closest to the positive part of the field, and depolarizing ends closest to the negative; and hyperpolarization/depolarization of neurons can affect excitability.[487] If the neuron is electrically compact, the change in transmembrane potential becomes an almost linear function of distance in the direction of the field. Neurons from the mammalian hippocampus, maintained in tissue slices in vitro, are significantly affected by fields of around 1–5 V/m.[488] However, these electric fields are many orders of magnitude greater than the anticipated fields from dowsing, and so this mechanism does not satisfactorily explain the dowsing response. Radicheva et al. took muscle fibers from frog legs and found that microwaves (2.45 GHz, 20 mW/cm²) can cause them to twitch.[489] Other physical stimuli can also cause frogs legs to twitch, such as application of voltages as discovered by Luigi Galvani in the 18th century, or just applying salt.[490] However, the microwave power in these experiments is many orders of magnitude larger than in dowsing, and so if and how these modes of action are related to the dowsing response is unclear.

Nerve Triggering

The nerves are crudely analogous to wires connecting a microprocessor to peripheral actuators and sensors, where the signal to or from is typically a voltage, or perhaps a current. Whereas voltage changes in a wire are created by the movement of charge along the wire, the signal voltage in a nerve is created by the movement of ions across the cell membrane by a truly remarkable process, described in very simplified form below to provide some background when discussing later the importance of ion gates in cell membranes.

Cells in humans and other animals are awash in electrolyte fluids. On the inside of the cell is the cytoplasm and on the outside is the intercellular fluid, both of which contain proteins and ions. The outside of the cell is defined by a cell wall, which in animals consists of a lipid bilayer.

Lipid Bilayer

Lipids are long chain fatty molecules which are hydrophilic (water loving) at one end and hydrophobic in the middle and the far end. Just as oil does not want to mix with water, so the hydrophobic ends stick to each other and avoid contact with the water, and the hydrophilic ends immerse themselves in the water. Lipids accomplish this compromise by forming sheets with two layers of lipid arranged with hydrophobic ends together in the middle of the sheet with the hydrophilic ends sticking out both sides in contact with the solution inside and outside of the cell (Figure 24.2) forming the cell wall.

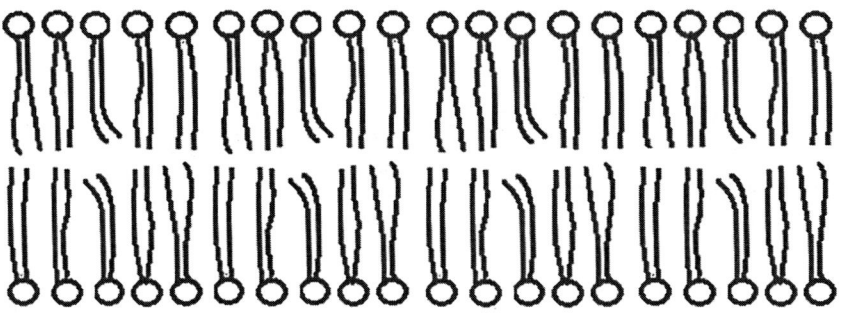

Figure 24.2. Sketch of lipid bilayer.

This lipid bilayer is only about 10 nm thick and is electrically insulating and also provides a physical barrier to ions such as sodium ion (Na^+), potassium ion (K^+) or chloride ion (Cl^-). Small neutral molecules such as oxygen and carbon monoxide can diffuse through the cell wall. Cells need to have supplies enter and waste products leave, so there are gates in the cell wall which allow certain things to pass through.

There are many different types of gate in the cell wall, but they can be broadly grouped into two types. One type allows things to pass through by diffusion and the other by active transport. Diffusion is the result of random motion of the molecules and ions making up gases and liquids. If there are two regions next to each other and one has a high concentration and one has a low concentration, then random movement is going to even out the concentrations; i.e., there will be a net movement from the area of high concentration to the area of low concentration.

Diffusion is analogous to walking downhill, so called passive transport. Sometimes it is necessary to walk uphill, for ions and molecules to be moved against the concentration gradient. Such changes are thermodynamically unfavorable, decreasing entropy, and so energy is needed to make the ions and molecules move in this way. This type of movement is called active transport.

Cell membranes have gates that use both passive and active transport. One of the most important classes of gates are the voltage-controlled ion gates. The voltage-controlled gates in the cell wall open or close depending on the potential

Diffusion

Diffusion is the net movement of ions or molecules due to a concentration gradient, so whenever there is a concentration difference between two adjacent areas, there is the potential for diffusion. However, the rate of diffusion also depends on what is between the areas. If for example, there were two areas separated by an impermeable plastic sheet with a small hole in it, there would be diffusion through the hole. If the hole were made larger the rate of diffusion would increase in proportion to the area of the hole (Figure 24.3).

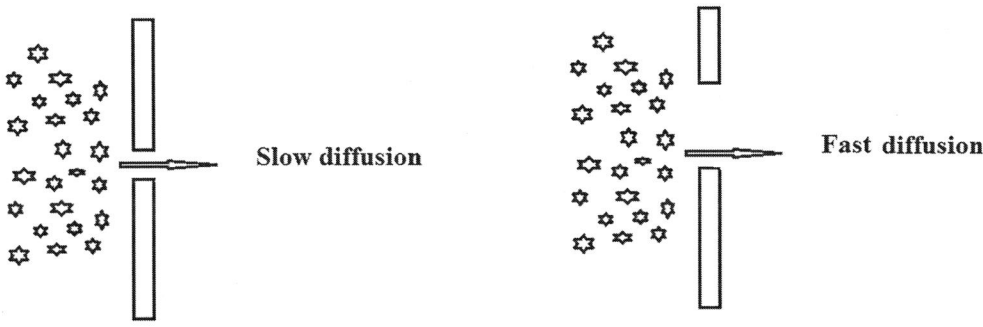

Figure 24.3. Sketch showing slow and fast diffusion.

The rate of diffusion is described by Fick's first (steady state) and second (time dependent) laws of diffusion. Diffusion occurs by the random movement of ions and molecules in gases and liquids and is thermodynamically favorable, since the final mix has higher entropy than the starting conditions with different concentrations.

Sodium Potassium Pump

One of the most remarkable active transportation gates is the so-called sodium potassium pump. This gate has a transport cycle that creates the electrode potential of the cell. The gate starts out open to the interior of the cell, exposing three binding sites for potassium ion. Once loaded up with potassium, it binds an adenosine triphosphate (ATP) molecule which hydrolyzes to adenosine diphosphate (ADP) providing energy to the gate to reconfigure so that it is now closed to the interior and open to the exterior. This new configuration makes the potassium ions bind less strongly and they leave, but it presents two empty sodium binding sites. Once these are occupied with sodium ions, the gate closes on the outside and reopens on the inside releasing the sodium ions and the cycle is ready to start again. The net effect of a complete cycle is that the inside of the cell lost three potassium ions and gained two sodium ions, so it is down a positive charge. The counterbalancing negative ions are unable to cross the membrane, and so an electrical potential develops across the membrane. The sodium potassium pump establishes the rest potential of the cell, ~-70 mV difference between the inside and outside (inside negative).

The cell membrane is about 10 nm thick and so the electric field across the membrane is very high (electric field = potential difference/distance = 700 kV/m). As the pump moves more potassium out of the cell, it has to work against this electric field and so energy is needed (ATP to ADP). This electrical potential provides a driving force to move positive ions into the cell. The sodium potassium pump also reduces the concentration of the potassium ion inside the cell and increases it outside the cell. Therefore, there is a concentration gradient which drives potassium ions into the cell and sodium ions out of the cell whenever an appropriate gate opens and there is a diffusion path for the ions.

across the cell membrane. These gates have a protein which changes conformation (shape) based on the voltage. If the potential is low, then the gate is closed and ion diffusion cannot occur. If the voltage rises, then the protein switches to open and now the ions can pass through the gate. Most of these ion gates are specific to the type of ion they allow through, so there are voltage-controlled sodium gates which pass sodium ions and voltage-controlled calcium gates which allow calcium ions to pass through.

Nerve Firing

For a neuron, the voltage-controlled gates are normally closed in the resting state, but if there is a stimulus voltage greater than the trigger voltage, then the gates will open and the selected positive ions can move by diffusion and/or be driven by the electric field. This triggering voltage can be provided by a connecting neuron or other electrical stimulus. Once the triggering voltage is reached, the gates open and the potassium and sodium ions flood in drawn by the electrical potential and by diffusion, causing the voltage to spike positive and the cell to depolarize at the the so-called action potential. Once the cell depolarizes, the gates close and the sodium potassium pump starts work again to reestablish the resting potential. The time for the cell to depolarize and repolarize is only one to two milliseconds.[1] While it is doing so, the cell is unresponsive to stimulation. The sudden change in the potential in one region of the nerve cell provides the trigger for the adjacent region, whose

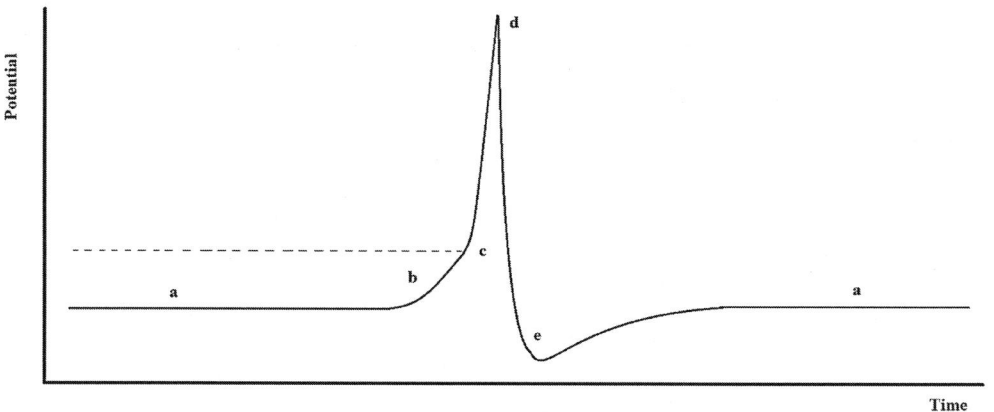

Figure 24.4. Sketch of a typical action potential shows its various phases as the action potential passes a point on a cell membrane.

---

1. "Action Potential," Wikipedia, https://en.wikipedia.org/wiki/Action_potential, accessed January 2, 2023.

> voltage-controlled gates now open. The signal thus passes along the length of the neuron as fast as these voltage-controlled gates can open, change the local potential and trigger the adjacent gates. The speed varies with the type and size of nerve, but it is typically in the range of 4 to 120 m/s. The sodium potassium pump restores the potential, overshooting a little because of diffusion before it returns to the resting potential. Figure 24.4 shows the action potential of a section of cell wall when triggering potential is received.
>
> The membrane potential starts out the rest potential (a) in Figure 25.4, which is approximately −70 mV. If a stimulus is applied which is able to reach the threshold limit (dashed line ~ −55 mV) (b), then the voltage activated gates will open and the potential swings positive (~+40 mV) (c), the gates close, the sodium potassium pump restores the steady state again (a), sometimes overshooting a little (d) before returning to the rest potential (a).
>
> If an interaction between microwaves and a neuron is large enough to generate a potential needed to open the gates, then the nerve may fire. This explanation provides a possible mechanism for sensing the dowsing signal.

The interaction of low-frequency EM fields with the brain has recently been reviewed,[491] including observations that[492]

- Extremely low-frequency magnetic fields (ELF-MF) with frequencies from 1–3 Hz provoke action potentials in large-diameter myelinated nerve axons.
- EM fields of 50 Hz have empirically increased the frequency of action potentials in isolated nerves.
- Exposure to 50 Hz ELF-MF resulted in an increase in the peak amplitude of action potentials, and after hyperpolarization potential and magnetic fields decreased in a time-dependent manner as well as the firing frequency and the duration of the action potential.

Both low-frequency and microwave frequency EM radiation can cause changes to the EEG, as discussed above, and if microwaves can be shown to affect action potentials, we are closer to understanding the sensing mechanism of dowsing.

Many animals show signs that they are affected by EM radiation, though to date there is no clear evidence that animals can sense radio waves or microwaves. Maby and Franklin noted that pigeons appear to lose their sense of direction near high-power radio transmitters and fly in circles, apparently unable to find their bearings in the usual way.[493] Henrik Mouritson similarly found that robins respond to specific radio frequencies between 5 KHz and 2 MHz, which corresponds to AM broadcasting.[494] The disturbance was not at specific frequencies but across the range tested (low-level AM EM noise between 20 kz and 20 MHz).[495] The birds are presumably navigating using their magnetic field sense, and these observations suggest that their magnetic field sensor mechanism can respond fast enough to the radio frequency signal to block the effect of the Earth's static magnetic field. Hutchison et al. found that anthropogenic EM fields from undersea power cables affected several types of bottom-dwelling creatures.[496] It is likely that other animals that use the Earth's magnetic field for navigation may be affected too. Tromp found that some people can tell whether a microwave transmitter is operating, others experience psychological disturbances after a few days, and the head seems to be the most sensitive part. He reported that wavelengths greater than 10 m are harmless, but below 10 m (30 MHz) the influence increases with decreasing wavelength[497]; it is possible the subjects were experiencing RF hearing.

Interaction of EM radiation with Ion Channels

There is evidence that nonthermal EM radiation from 50 Hz to microwave can activate the voltage-controlled calcium gates. In addition, effects can be observed from static electric fields, static magnetic fields and nanosecond pulses. The evidence for this finding includes the observation that calcium channel blockers block EM field effects.[498] Voltage-controlled calcium gates are found in very high densities throughout the nervous system and are essential to the release of neurotransmitters and neuroendocrine hormones. It has been proposed that radio waves and microwaves may activate the voltage-controlled calcium gates, releasing excessive neurotransmitter / neuroendocrine as well as causing oxidative/nitrosative stress and other responses. D'Agosti et al. also found that that exposure to the extremely high-frequency electromagnetic fields (EHF-EMF 40 GHz to 120 GHz) induces a potassium efflux from lipid vesicles and that exposure to the EHF-EMF enhances the action of valinomycin, a potassium ion carrier, thus increasing the extent of potassium ion transport across the lipid membrane.[499] These results show that it is not just calcium ion gates which are affected, but other cation gates too.

Pall identified the primary mechanism of interaction of microwaves with cells as being activation of the voltage-gated calcium channel by the microwaves with only minor contribution from activation of other voltage-gated ion channels.[500] He also reported that pulsed EM radiation is usually more active than are non-pulsed radiation; polarized (artificial) radiation was more active than unpolarized (bad news for all of us with cell phones). He also found that the dose-response curves are non-linear and non-monotone, so lower intensities have a greater effect than expected from simple proportion. The effects are often cumulative and appear to impact young people more than adults.[501] If the dowsing signal is caused by changes in the background radiation in the radio wave and microwave spectrum, then interaction with voltage-controlled metal ion gates is a promising mechanism. However, a 2021 review article by Wood and Karipidis found that there was no effect of radio wave and microwave frequencies on voltage-controlled calcium gates,[502] which casts doubt on this mechanism as the basis for the dowsing response.

Magnetite Crystals and Ion Channels

If EM radiation can affect ion channels, then the question is how. A possible mechanism involves calcium ion gates with magnetite particles attached.[503] Kirschvink proposed that low-frequency magnetic fields affect biological systems by interacting with magnetite crystals in cells oscillating in a 60-Hz, earth-strength field exerting enough force on a mechanically sensitive ion channel to cause it to open or close. Kirschvink estimated that the minimum magnetic field needed to open an ion channel was 0.5 mT, and the response time of the channel was about 25 mS. These results provide an explanation of the effects brought on by 60 Hz mains power. Kirschvink went on to say that depending upon where such a channel is located, and whether it is coupled to secondary messenger systems, this could influence the cell membrane, DNA synthesis, RNA transcription, calcium release, and virtually any ionically mediated cellular processes.[504] Goychuk has modeled ion channels controlled by magnetic nanoparticles and found that such structures are plausible.[505]

As discussed earlier in the chapter on the magnetic sense, magnetite has been found in many cells in the brain. If magnetite is used as part of the magnetic sense, then the response of the magnetite to the magnetic field must be connected to nerves. Many of our senses (e.g., taste) operate by attaching a responsive molecule to the calcium ion channels so that when the target is present, the gates open and a response is triggered. Perhaps the same mechanism operates for the detection of magnetic fields or EM radiation. In support of this theory, some calcium ion channels have been found to have magnetite particles attached to the gates. For example, Dutta et al. and Goychuk et al. studied such channels and found that in a culture the magnetite opens the channel, releasing calcium ions into the cell, and so changes the membrane potential.[506] If the cell is a nerve cell and the potential changes enough, then it may trigger the nerve cell. If the response time of the magnetite crystal was shorter than the period of a radio wave/microwave, then it too could open the gate. Kletetschka et al. examined brains of people with Alzheimer's disease and found they had an increased number of magnetite particles in their brain.[507] These particles, which are about 40 nm across, have magnetic moments which fluctuate in a broad spectrum of frequencies, ranging over nine orders of magnitude, from Hz to GHz. This top frequency is in the range expected for dowsing, and as discussed above, dowsers are reported to be sensitive to EM radiation from Hertz to GHz.[508]

Nerve as Rectifier

Another potential mechanism for microwave interaction with the ion channels was proposed by Panagopoulos et al., who wrote that "an oscillating external electric field will exert an oscillating force to each of the free ions that exist on both sides of all plasma membranes and that can move across the membranes through trans-membrane proteins. This external oscillating force will cause a forced vibration of each free ion. When the amplitude of the ions' forced vibration transcends some critical value, the oscillating ions can give a false signal for opening or closing channels that are voltage gated (or even mechanically gated)."[509]

Since the EM radiation is an oscillation, it is unclear whether even if this mechanism were operative there would be any net movement of ions under the influence of the oscillation electric field, since the ions would be moved one way and then back again. However, if there were some mechanism by which they moved one way and were prevented from moving back, i.e., the signal was rectified, then the EM radiation would have a significant effect.

One potential model for the nerve rectifier is the electrolytic rectifier, which was a type of detector (demodulator) used in early radio receivers from 1903 to about 1913, before it was superseded by crystal detectors and vacuum tube detectors. The electrolytic rectifier was even able to detect AM radio.[510] Electrolytic rectifiers most commonly had an aluminum anode and a lead or steel cathode in a solution of triammonium orthophosphate. These devices operate on the principle that an aluminum electrode in an electrolyte will only conduct when it is negatively charged and hydrogen gas will form on the surface, but when it is positively charged, the surface quickly becomes covered with an insulating layer of aluminum oxide, which prevents further current flow. For this model to be applicable to a nerve there must be a process which only allows the current to flow one way. Selective ion flow through some of the gates is one possibility.

Ion gates operate by allowing selective ions to pass one-way through the gate. If an alternating electric field were imposed on the nerve at steady state, then those ions moving through the gate in the direction of the electric field would get a boost, but when the electric field were reversed, the gate would prevent ions moving the other way. The ion channel would therefore be acting as a rectifier. Wust et al. found that nonthermal radio frequency EM fields have an influence on human colon cancer cells and found that the cells reduce proliferation and clonogenicity when exposed to 13.56 MHz compared to controls. They believed the RF electric field component was rectified and smoothed in the ion channel, resulting in a DC voltage of ~ 1 μV. They suggested that this voltage change may induce ion fluxes and disturb the cell's equilibrium.[511] The difficulty with this idea is that the voltages induced are very small, compared to the action potential of a cell ~−55 mV, or 15 mV above the resting state, so a 1 μV change is not going to make much difference. However, Matthie et al. commented that while such changes in membrane potential seem orders of magnitude too small to significantly influence neuronal signaling, there are a number of mechanisms in the central nervous system which amplify signals. This may allow such small changes in membrane potential to induce significant physiological effects.[512] Overall, the message that comes across is that some researchers have seen some interesting effects, but the science is still being developed and so many questions remain.

Dowsing appears to operate up to GHz frequencies and so the next question is whether this rectifying process would work at GHz frequencies. It will depend on whether an ion can move through the channel in the cycle time of the electric field; if not, then the ion will just oscillate in the channel.

Estimate of Maximum Frequency of Neural Rectifier

Ion movement results in the net movement of charge which is an electric current. By measuring the conductivity of an ion channel, a rough estimate of the time needed for the ions to pass through the channel can be made. The conductivity of a single sodium channel in giant squid has been measured, and its conductance is 14 pS.[1] A giant squid was used because its neurons are large and so easier to measure.

- If the conductance is 14 pS, then the current (i) at the 70 mV rest potential will be 1 pA per channel.
- The sodium flux can be calculated from Faraday's law, flux = I/nF_c, where F_c is the Faraday constant (9.648×10^4 C/mol) and n is the charge per ion (n =1 for sodium). Sodium flux = $1 \times 10^{-12}/9.648 \times 10^4$ ~1×10^{-17} moles/s.
- Sodium ion flux is molar flux times Avogadro's number = $1 \times 10^{-17} \times 6 \times 10^{23}$ = 6×10^6 sodium ions per second.
- Assuming that the sodium ions pass through one at a time, the average travel time is $1/(6 \times 10^{-6})$ ~ 0.2 μs.

The maximum frequency which this sodium voltage activated gate is expected to be rectifying is therefore (1/0.2 μs =) ~ 5 MHz.

1. Francisco Bezanilla, "Single Sodium Channels From The Squid Giant Axon," *Biophys. J*, vol. 52 (December 1987), 1087–1090, https://www.cell.com/biophysj/pdf/S0006-3495(87)83304-0.pdf

A rough estimate for a squid neuron is 5 MHz, which is several orders of magnitude below the upper frequency for dowsing. There are, however, many different types of ion channel, and the gates in a human are likely to be very different from those of a giant squid. For example, at least nine distinct types of sodium channel have been detected in the nervous system.[513] The single-channel conductance of ion channels ranges from 0.1 to 100 pS.[514] Putting the higher limit of 100 pS into the calculation above gives a maximum frequency of 500 MHz, which is within an order of magnitude of the frequencies observed from dowsing. This calculation is very crude and there is still much to be learned about ion channels, but this calculation suggests that this rectification mechanism remains, for now at least, plausible.

The Mechanism of Voltage-Controlled Gates

The mechanism of how the voltage-controlled gates function is still being worked out, but a likely mechanism is that the protein gate has an internal electric dipole which interacts with the electric field across the gate, inducing a torque on the protein that aligns the dipole and protein along the direction of the applied field, causing motion that closes the gate.[515] On activation the conductance of the gate can change 150 times for only a 10 mV change in membrane potential.[516] If EM radiation with an electric field strength of this order of magnitude is present and it has a frequency whose period (=1/frequency) is less than the time needed for the dipole to respond, then this EM radiation may affect the opening and closing of the gate.

Saunders and Jeffries proposed that the mechanism of interaction between low-frequency magnetic fields and voltage-controlled calcium gates is achieved by direct effects on the electric dipole voltage sensor within the ion channel.[517] A stationary electric dipole will not experience any force in a static magnetic field. If either the dipole or the magnetic field is moving relative to the other, then there will be a force on the dipole, as the magnetic field interacts with the positive and negative charges of the dipole. An EM wave has an oscillating magnetic field component, and potentially this field could interact with the dipole of the gate and cause it to be more likely to open or more likely to close, or perhaps just be less responsive to the membrane potential. However, it is likely that the effect of the magnetic field will be small compared to the electric field component of the EM wave, which will have a much stronger effect on the dipole. It is unclear if the effects of the electric and magnetic fields of the EM radiation that constitute the dowsing signal will cause a significant effect on the gate, but it is a tantalizing theory. Researchers at MIT found that the movement of synthetic 100 nm magnetite disks along the outside of a neuron was enough to trigger it.[518] It seems unlikely that this is the mechanism behind dowsing, since they needed a large number of magnetite disks to get a response, but it does indicate the sensitivity of neurons to small movements.

There are some other ideas for how microwaves could interact with ion channels. In the discussion on the transmission of the dowsing signal from depths (Chapter 20), it was postulated that the EM radiation of the dowsing signal propagates through the soil by means of stimulated emission of some kind of water species, perhaps adsorbed water. If correct, then this idea means that the dowsing frequency is set by a resonant frequency of this water. This interaction was observed in a concrete floor, a pine board, a book and in sugar, a wide range of water-containing materials, each of which contained absorbed water. One can envision water bound to a protein that controls an ion channel in a neuron. A change in the intensity of the radiation at the resonance frequency would cause adsorbed water to change rotations, affecting the ion channel and thus a signal. Currently this idea is mere speculation, and there is no data available to support it.

Along a similar line, Hinkius et al. proposed[519] that the effect of microwaves (and dowsing too) on the brain was the result of brain neural oscillations caused by microwave excitation of water affecting hydrogen bonding forces between water molecules, causing enhanced diffusion and so affecting the neurotransmitters' transit time and neuron resting potential.[520] Theirs is an interesting theory for how sub-thermal microwaves can have an effect on the brain, but again there is little or no data to support this idea.

All of the ideas for the detection of the dowsing signal have major gaps; however, at this time, the theory that appears to be the most plausible mechanism for detection of the dowsing signal is the magnetite particle controlling an ion channel. Such a detection mechanism is clearly not accidental and may be related to the detection of the Earth's magnetic field. The interaction of electric and magnetic fields with the ion channels is an area of active research and while much has already been learned, there remains much more to be discovered.

25

Remaining Mysteries and Interesting Reports

Every answer given arouses new questions. The progress of science is matched by an increase in the hidden and mysterious.
—Leo Baeck (1949)[521]

Chapter summary: This book has explained many of the characteristics of dowsing, in a systematic way, largely relying on existing science. However, dowsing still has many other mysteries and some of these are briefly discussed in the chapter.

While most of the data presented in this book can be explained, there are many mysteries in the world of dowsing that remain. Some of these are described below.

Defects in Steel and Plastic

As described earlier, Weschcke and Slate[522] reported that dowsers identified hidden cracks and air bubbles in steel and plastic samples respectively in double-blind testing. A metal surface such as a steel object will reflect radio waves and microwaves, and so if the dowsing signal is in the low GHz frequency range, then it should be impossible to detect internal defects in a steel object using microwaves. Internal defects in a plastic object are also likely to be difficult to detect unless they were very large, just because the wavelengths of radiation employed in dowsing measure several centimeters and so a minor defect in a microwave transparent medium is not expected to have much effect. Assuming these results can be repeated, it is difficult to explain them with the current theory of dowsing and so perhaps some other mechanism is at work.

Ley Lines and Geopathic Stress

Ley lines are reported to be dowsing lines between important Neolithic and later landmarks that exist and apparently extend around the world.[523] Guy Underwood spent many years investigating such geodetic phenomena around Stonehenge and other Neolithic structures in the United Kingdom and Ireland. His book makes for fascinating reading, though the physical mechanism behind his observations remains unclear.[524] There is quite a lot of mythology about what ley lines are and how they work. I have no personal experience of them, and so am not in a position to comment on their credibility. It is possible that ley lines do exist, and they correspond to geologic fault lines and that the Neolithic builders chose their monuments based on these ley lines. If so, then perhaps ley lines are part of the natural order of things with a few embellishments to the story added over time to make them more interesting. If not, then they must remain unexplained.

Geopathic stress lines are reported to form a grid across the planet's surface and these rays have adverse effects on people if the lines cross where they sleep. It has been suggested that these energies are EM, with little if any supporting evidence, and that their harmful effects can be blocked by quartz and other crystals,[525] none of which are likely to block EM radiation (aluminum foil would work much better).

Animals are reported to be sensitive to geopathic stress and most, including dogs, try to avoid it. Some animals, such as cats, seem to enjoy it and ants choose to build their mounds on ley lines.[526] Geopathic lines so far have only been detected by dowsing. For example, the Guild of Energists described a person whose prior dogs had all contracted and died of bone cancer, and whose current dog had been diagnosed with the same problem: "This seemed to me almost certainly a case of geopathic stress, so I did some dowsing and then rang and told her that her kennels and all but one room of her house were affected by geopathic stress. She called in a dowser who confirmed my findings; the kennels were both built over crossed lines, which gives rise to the strongest effects, and the house was affected by a grid with only one room clear apart from the area close to one wall."[527]

Sufferers of geopathic stress or so-called Earth rays have found significant relief after placing a copper net under their beds (same idea but more expensive than aluminum foil), though a Norwegian study found that four independent dowsers gave four completely different maps of the lines in a gymnasium during testing, casting doubt on the physical basis of the remedy.[528] A statistical study of the health of 44 children and the location of the beds in their homes relative to the Earth rays as determined by dowsers found no significant difference between those whose beds were exposed and those who were not exposed.[529] With the limited data available, the question of the significance or occurrence of geopathic stress remains open. The problem with disbelieving researchers is that the placebo effect no longer works on them and this limitation may explain why they observed no effect.

Ley lines and geopathic stress both relate to a broader field of Earth energies. Many dowsers have investigated various forces that may be collectively called Earth energies and described them with a high degree of detail. Jeffrey Keen gave the following brief description of the subject: "As most readers will know, at the largest extreme are two global dowsable grids—the Hartmann and Curry grids that cover the surface of the earth; the former having cosmic connections, whilst the latter probably has terrestrial origins. Then there are earth energy currents that flow river-like across continents, such as one from Israel to Ireland. At the next level down are numerous dowsable energy lines that meander across countries, such as the well-documented Michael & Mary Line from Lands End to Norfolk, or the less well-known Belinus Line which runs from the Isle of Wight to Scotland."[530]

Keen went on to discuss how these lines have masculine and feminine, positive and negative energies, though I am not sure what he meant. He also said that these lines vary with the weather, the position of the sun and the moon as well as geological effects. Unfortunately, I have no idea what this author was observing and can offer no physical explanation.

Circular Objects

Wheeler reported, "So, walking over a linear object causes a rod rotation and so does walking between two trees. Associating the trees with circular bases, I placed dinner plates on the floor of my living room and obtained the same rod rotations. Diagrammatically, the rods turned from to [sic]. It then transpired that any object with a circular base (e.g., a wine bottle or saucepan) would initiate the crossing of the dowsing rods."[531]

To test this theory I placed two 28 cm (11 inches) diameter ceramic dinner plates on the concrete floor of my basement, 80 cm (31.5 inches) apart as measured from the center of the plates, and I did not get a dowsing response walking between the plates. I am not sure what Wheeler was observing.

Water Vapor

In 2000, Highcock issued a short article describing his experiments with dowsing[532]: He poured 20 to 30 ml of cold water onto a rubber-backed carpet placed in an area with no dowsing lines and still found no reaction. He then heated the carpet with a hair dryer and saw a dowsing response. Highcock wrote, "The carpet is now exposed to the radiation from an infra-red lamp or hot air from an electric hairdryer for about 5 seconds. On dowsing again it should be possible to detect a strong reaction over the centre line of the carpet. There should also be an equally strong reaction in the first floor room immediately above the spot where the carpet is sited. If the carpet is now covered with a piece of aluminium cooking foil and the first floor room dowsed again, it will be found that the dowsing reaction will have disappeared."

I tried to repeat Highcock's experiment. Using a 100 ml measuring cylinder I poured 25 ml of water onto a polyester carpet over a concrete floor over about two feet (~60 cm) that previously had not shown any dowsing response. The water initially coalesced into drops on the carpet and there was little if any dowsing response. As the water seeped into the carpet the dowsing response got stronger (rods half crossed). Blowing a hot air gun at the water for about 10s made little difference. I suspect that Highcock's hair dryer either helped to disperse the water into the carpet directly, or the time needed to use the hair dryer allowed the water to spread out enough until the surface area was larger enough to give a dowsing response. Five seconds of heating with a hair dryer is not going to evaporate much of the 20 to 30 ml of water. I was using a hot air gun, which is more powerful than a hair dryer, and the carpet was still very wet after 10s.

Boat Dowsing

Michael Fercik reported that it was possible to dowse the minerals under a lake from an aluminum boat down to 200 feet.[533] If these results are confirmed, the mechanism is clearly not by the detection of thermal radiation, since any such emissions from the lake bottom would be absorbed by that depth of water, and any that did make it to the surface, would not make it through the aluminum hull. The same conclusion can be drawn about people who claim to have dowsed successfully from aircraft and cars.

Tabraham's Observations

A. P. Tabraham discussed a very diverse set of experiments on dowsing along with other observations in a charmingly written booklet.[534] Most of his dowsing observations are summarized below, though in much less poetic form than the original:

- Tabraham believed that the basis of dowsing was microwaves, since he got a response whenever he held his dowsing rods over the magnetron in the microwaves, whether powered on or off.
- ○ I found that the rods did cross when I was standing over a microwave oven (not plugged in), but it made no difference whether one walked from the magnetron end or the other end. I saw the same effect with an old desktop computer, and even just the metal side-panel from the computer. A microwave oven is a large metal box, and the dowsing signal is likely to be reflected by the metal case of the microwave and give a dowsing response, whether there is a magnetron in there or not.
- He also found that a dowsing line formed between a cooking ring or hot plate and a microwave oven, and that heat was transferred along this line whenever the hot plate was turned on. Whenever the line was activated, the dowsing rods would respond whenever they crossed the line.
- ○ The hot plate on our range is approximately 2.5 meters from the microwave oven. I saw no difference in response walking between them with the burner on or off. The microwave oven was plugged in but turned off for this test.

This result was confirmed by placing two thermometers on the top of the microwave, one near the magnetron end and the other at the far end. When the hot plate or other heat source was turned on, Tabraham found the magnetron thermometer gave a temperature rise of up to 6°C higher than the one at the other end.

- ○ I measured the temperature of the top left and top right of our microwave oven. The microwave oven was plugged in but not turned on, and the magnetron is located on the right hand side. The initial temperatures were both 20.6°C (69°F). I turned on the hot plate on the range approximately 2.5 m in front of the microwave and let it run a few minutes. The temperature of the microwave oven was unchanged.
- Tabraham found that placing a sheet of lead between the hot plate and microwave killed the "force field."
- ○ Since lead is a metal, a sheet of lead is expected to block the dowsing signal, but I have been unable to find any trace of this force field between a burner and a nearby microwave oven magnetron.
- Tabraham determined the frequency of the dowsing signal, writing, "That the dowsing effect has a radio wave length was found quite by accident, … it was noticed that the dowsing rods closed when held over a radio receiver tuned to Radio Cornwall but would not close at any other wavelength. It was possible to follow the radio signal out from the radio receiver in the direction of the mast on the island. This indicates that the wavelength of the dowsing effect is 97.3 MHz which can be checked by anyone with a radio receiver and a pair of dowsing rods."
- ○ I attempted to repeat this experiment using an analog radio. There was a small dowsing response (rods moved slightly), but it did not change whether the radio

25. Remaining Mysteries and Interesting Reports

was plugged in or not, nor whether the radio was tuned to 97.3 MHz or across the FM band or the AM band.
- Tabraham also claimed that a viable beehive with an active queen gave a strong dowsing response because of the "'life force' inherent in the fertile queen," whereas a hive with a weak queen or no queen would not give a dowsing response.
  ○ I have not repeated this test. However, a strong bee colony usually has many more bees than a weak colony, and better honey reserves, and so the total water content of a strong colony will be higher than that of a weak colony and perhaps the difference was water content rather than life-force.
- Similarly, Tabraham claimed that viable seeds of every sort will give a strong dowsing response if the rods are held over them, but seeds that are too old will not give a dowsing response.
  ○ I have not tried to repeat this experiment, but one possible explanation is that old nonviable seeds have dried out and the lower water content causes the rods to cross less compared to the viable seeds. I doubt very much is due to the life-force of either the seeds or the bees.
- He also stated that arable land which had been burnt gave a positive dowsing response and was a few degrees warmer compared to unburned areas, months later, and up to two years later. He ascribed the warming effect to the dowsing signal which protected the plants in the winter.
  ○ One possible explanation is that if burning straw turns the ground black, then the amount of graphitic carbon in the surface is increased. Graphite is conductive and so is likely to partially absorb and partially reflect the dowsing signal differently from the unburned ground. I suspect the black soil from carbon increased the absorption of sunlight, which raised the surface temperature a few degrees above that of the non-burned areas. However, I did not attempt to repeat this test.
- Rocard suggested that magnetic iron oxides, presumably magnetite, can form from nonmagnetic iron compounds in organic material when burned in fires resulting in a dowsing signal.[535] Magnetite nanoparticles have been synthesized by thermal decomposition of hematite (Fe_2O_3) powder in the presence of high boiling point solvent,[536] so Rocard's suggestion appears plausible.
- Lastly Tabraham claimed that rainwater would not give a dowsing signal until after it has passed through the ground and if rainwater is collected in a container it will not give a dowsing response.
  ○ I have not tried to confirm this result; however, it is unclear what constitutes passing through the ground. Would surface runoff after a rainstorm or passing through a few centimeters of soil count, or does the water have to pass through several meters of soil and rock before it becomes dowsing active. I suspect that Tabraham also decided against running systematic studies on this and some of the other conclusions above.

Psychic Effects

There are aspects of dowsing which are hard to explain based on physical principles, and while these are outside the scope of this book, they need to be acknowledged.

For example, Roberts wrote that "inexperienced dowsers' rods respond to many different things, but experienced dowsers only work for water or whatever their target is."[537]

Clearly, to be able to only respond to water, the dowser must be able to distinguish what lies below his or her feet. It is easy to ascribe anything unknown to psychic effects, but just because the mechanism is unknown does not mean that it is caused by psychic effects. There will be differences in the signal coming from water versus a metal or an empty void, since water absorbs some frequencies, metals reflect them and voids will refract them. Perhaps experienced dowsers are able to distinguish between the signals from different materials, or perhaps more sensitive people can distinguish differences in the frequency spectrum that are impossible for the rest of us to identify.

According to Roberts, Henry Gross could touch the tip of his rod to a target and search for that item. For example, if he touched his rod to a bottle of rye whiskey, then he would only detect rye and not bourbon, scotch or any other liquor; if he touched his rod to copper, then his rods would seek copper. The rod will continue to search for this item until the tip is washed or wiped on grass. There is no obvious mechanism why touching the tip of a rod should make it specific for that target, or why wiping it on grass should clear the effect. Michael Fercik described how to make dowsing rods specific to a particular metal (gold, silver, etc.) by attaching 3.1 g (0.1 troy oz) of the metal to rods.[538] Interesting enough, Nicholas Jean used a very similar method, but in his case contacting the rod with a material to make the rod insensitive to that material and thus identifying the composition of underground objects through a process of elimination.[539]

Renowned dowser Evelyn Penrose described how she could sense water in the ground up to a mile away, and so once on-site she did not need to scan the ground for water but could instead just walk to the strongest water source on the property.[540] Michael Fercik also reported that he could detect dowsing targets (minerals) up to two miles away walking or 10 miles if in a car and down to a depth of half a mile.[541] Unfortunately, a physical explanation is not readily forthcoming for these remote dowsing abilities.

Gross could also ask his rod questions, such as distances to a spring, or depth of a water vein, or depth of a pond or shipping channel, the direction of flow and flow rate. He could also ask how many people were in a house and use the rod to find them, and lost items, individuals in a lineup given only their name.[542] To the extent that these events happened (and Gross's biographer Kenneth Roberts clearly believed them to be true), the mechanism remains a complete mystery.

In later life, Evelyn Penrose did a lot of map dowsing, so she was not even on-site, and she was reported to be very successful.[543] Henry Gross was also successful at map dowsing, successfully locating the sites for three wells in Bermuda, while he was in Maine. Bermuda at that time got almost all of its water from rain collection and was not believed to have any freshwater underground resources. When I lived there in the early 1970s, most houses, including ours, had a tank under the house to collect rainwater. Following Gross's predictions, three wells were drilled and found to be productive. According to Roberts, Penrose on being sent a map found water in Bermuda that roughly corresponded to Gross's locations. Gross later visited Bermuda and while there located a well in Vermont, which was also drilled, and found to be productive.[544]

Journalist Dan Schwartz described Steve Herbert's method of dowsing a field for water: "He draws a single L rod from his hip and, gripping it like a revolver in his right hand, pans it slowly across the job site. He is scanning, which seems like a sensible thing to do. ... Herbert's arm continues panning, but the L rod rotates in his hand, as if the tip has locked onto an invisible magnet. He wiggles his hand back and forth for emphasis: Stuck, see? It is uncanny. I look for some sleight of hand but can't detect any movement in his wrist."[545]

Herbert used this method to locate a water source that could be drilled. At present there is no apparent physical explanation for what Herbert was doing. Another very curious account discussed how the ability to dowse can be shared between people. "Joe Loman, a local dowser and well driller, ... cut a forked green willow tree branch. ... At last, at a spot not more than 30 feet from the back porch, the branch went wild. ... I tried it with the same branch and it would do nothing for me. Ditto for my dad. Then Joe showed us that by simply touching our wrist with his hand, it would work for us also. It sure did! When he placed his hand on my wrist, I could not control the branch. Same for my dad and mom."[546]

Vogt and Golde reported a similar case where a dowser who had a brother could not dowse, but when the dowser walked behind the brother and held on to his ears, the divining rod worked like normal in his brother's hands.[547] Others have reported similar effects.[548] If dowsing is the response to EM radiation in the radio wave or microwave region of the spectrum detected by our nerves or magnetite nano-crystals in our brains or some other physiological structure, then it is hard to reconcile this explanation with the story of Loman and the other unnamed dowser. How Loman and this other dowser were able to share their dowsing ability with several people by touching their hands/ears remains a mystery. Clearly, dowsing has many more secrets that hopefully will be revealed in the future.

There is also an account of a dowser called Edith Greene from Montgomery, Vermont, who was well known for finding water wells, typically locating about 50 a year using her trusty L-rods. Some people found radon in their water, and Greene claimed that she could solve that problem by getting the radon to move to another location. She identified a water source for the town, but analysis showed that it contained high levels of uranium. Greene did her thing and brought the level down to 6 ppb and repeated her process and brought it down to a very respectable 2.5 ppb, well below the state maximum of 30 ppb. The report described her process: "When she encounters radon (which appears, she says, in either an endless band or a floor-to-ceiling vortex) her rods swing apart as though they've bumped against an invisible wall. After protecting herself by envisioning a healing blue light, she sternly commands the radon to move. Occasionally she plants the tip of one rod on the ground and strikes its shaft with the other for emphasis: Move that radon over to the lawn.... Nearly always they reveal that the radon has moved precisely where Edith intended."[549]

I have no explanation for this story except that it sounds impossible from what I know of dowsing and radon for that matter too. A possible explanation is that the uranium contamination was introduced into the water by the drilling process from elsewhere in the borehole, and as the water flowed, it flushed the contamination out such that the reading fell with time. Another possible explanation that was suggested in the article was laboratory error (analysis was done twice with the same result). I am not sure how to explain Greene's success with radon, but asking the radon to move over seems improbable.

Psychics also claim that dowsing rods can be used to reveal the presence and location of spirits and to find lost articles, and as Henry Gross also reported, answer yes/no questions for a wide range of subjects.[550] Again, whatever is going on here, whether they are actually talking to spirits, tapping mystical information or the ideomotor response is kicking in, the answer has nothing to do with the physical detection mechanisms described in this book.

Dowsing is also used to measure the auras that are said to surround people. The following description was given by Penelope Quest as part of her Reiki training: "Holding the rods ... at mid-chest height ... tune in to the person's unique energy vibrations by saying aloud or silently 'I am looking for this person's aura' (insert the name of the person). Providing you are far enough away from the person, as you walk very slowly and evenly towards them, when the rods react by crossing or opening out ... you will have found the outer edge of their aura. ... Slowly walk forward again until you reach the next area where the rods change their reaction. ... But do stop before the dowsing rods crash into the person!"[551]

Marcel Vogel demonstrates detecting the aura of a young woman and how it changes size with her thoughts in a video.[552] Some dowsers claim to be able to identify which people and animals have particular diseases, which may be related to their aura, since auras reportedly change color depending on a person's health.[553] I say reportedly because, unfortunately, I have never seen anyone's aura. Similarly, D. Abel Martin is reported to have used a pendulum to diagnose which cattle, sheep and horses had tuberculosis as part of his thesis for his doctorate in veterinary medicine from the University of Paris.[554] To the extent that these dowsing practices actually work, it does not appear to be related to physical principles outlined in this book.

Jeffrey Keen has proposed that dowsing is the product of the mind and a cosmic informational field, writing, "The mind is a conceptual entity existing between the brain and the structure of the cosmos. The latter is believed to comprise at least a 5-dimension, holographic, quantum universe that is based on information, geometry and fractals, ratios including harmonics, irrational numbers such as phi (φ), chaos theory, and yin-yang properties (e.g., male/female, positive/negative, dipoles, abstract/physical, matter/anti-matter, etc. Are these different manifestations of the same basic structure?). This mix, together with free-will and intent creates consciousness and dowsing."[555]

Whether Keen's explanation is correct for the basis of psychic effects and dowsing, or whether it is just a collection of cool sounding words used completely out of context, I can't say, since I know very little about psychic experiences. Whatever the answer, he is relying on a number of assumptions which are clearly outside of currently understood science.

There are many more examples of strange and unexplained reports from the world of dowsing, and over time, some of the questions will be answered with careful study.

26

Conclusions

> The strongest arguments prove nothing so long as the conclusions are not verified by experience. Experimental science is the queen of sciences and the goal of all speculation.
> —Roger Bacon[556]

Chapter summary: This chapter summarizes the findings of this book from source of the dowsing signal to physiological detection. The dowsing signal comprises microwave thermal emissions in the 1 to 10 GHz range. These microwave emissions are perturbed by objects in the ground, and the very small changes in the intensity are detected in the brain in basic L-rod dowsing, resulting in a small movement of the arms, causing the dowsing rods to move in the hand. While this theory appears to be reasonable, there are still large gaps, especially regarding the physiological aspects of detection.

Dowsing has been used for at least 500 years, and for at least 500 years people have wondered how it worked, and to this day many questions remain unanswered. Five hundred years is too long for a testable physical phenomenon to remain a mystery, and so the goal of this book is to provide some explanation of basic L-rod dowsing. Those readers who have read through from the start already know the answer, but for those people who prefer to go straight to the last chapter of mystery novels to find out who did it, this chapter is for you.

Observations of Basic L-Rod Dowsing That Any Theory Needs to Explain

There have been many theories proposed for L-rod dowsing, and again I am limiting this only to basic L-rod dowsing in the field, looking for things below the surface. L-rod dowsing appears to be a physical effect and a technique that most people can do after simple training and will be treated as such. Below is a list of observations that any theory of dowsing needs to take into account. This list is not comprehensive, and other people can certainly add their own thoughts to this list. However, it provides a good basis to challenge any proposed theory.

- The rods themselves do not respond; they simply provide a visual indicator or mechanical amplification of subtle muscle movements. More specifically, the dowsing response appears to be due to slight involuntary movement of the

muscles that lift the elbows, primarily the deltoid muscle. The rods are held at a balance point and so small movements cause them to move away from the balance point.
- The response is a relative response, i.e., the rods respond to changes in the signal, rather than absolute values, and in most cases the response is relative to where the dowser balanced his or her rods. The rods, however, do not respond to the rate of change of the signal.
- The material of the rods is unimportant from a detection point of view.
  ○ Steel wire (e.g., from a coat hanger) or copper wire work well because they are dense, and because the rods move when gravity exceeds friction. Therefore, the smooth dense steel wire may work better than a rougher, less dense material such as wood; but wood, plastic or aluminum rods will still work.
- The rods detect a wide range of objects in the ground, PVC pipes, voids, metal objects, cables, water, etc.
  ○ Therefore, the mechanism is not substance specific, nor does it appear to be strongly dependent on the type of material.
- Dowsing works similarly at night when it is dark as during daylight.
  ○ The dowsing signal is not coming exclusively from the sun, unlike, for example, visible light, and works underground and under a metal roof, so it is not coming from the sky. The dowsing signal appears to come from the ground.
- No dowsing signal was observed from an artificial magnetic field stronger than the Earth's magnetic field, though some other researchers have drawn the opposite conclusion.
- Placing a metal foil sheet on the ground blocks the signal, but the edges of the metal sheet now create a new signal.
  ○ EM waves and electric fields are commonly blocked by electrical conductors. This result suggests that the dowsing signal may be an EM wave.
  ○ This observation also rules out sound waves, gravity abnormalities, static magnetic fields and other waves and fields which can pass through metal foils.
- Placing a cardboard sheet on the ground does not affect the signal, so cardboard is transparent to the dowsing signal.
  ○ If the wave is EM, then the transparency of cardboard limits it to radio waves, microwaves, x-rays and gamma rays. The last two can be excluded, since they are high energy and are not commonly found in everyday life.
- The dowsing signal from an underground pipe is polarized to be parallel to the pipe.
  ○ This observation says that the dowsing signal comes from a transverse wave.
  ○ This observation also rules out static electric fields, static magnetic fields and sound waves.
- Placing a steel or copper mesh with a 2 cm (~0.8 inch) hole size on the ground blocks the signal, but a mesh with a 10 cm (4 inch) mesh does not block the signal. Larger size meshes do not increase the sensitivity.
  ○ The wavelength of the dowsing response is larger than 2 cm but less than or equal to about 10 cm.
  ○ This wavelength range is in the low GHz microwave region of the EM spectrum.
- The human body can resolve dowsing signals with an angular precision of about 6 degrees, which is about a few cm on the ground.

- ○ This narrow angular resolution is remarkable.
- Microwave sources in the 1 to 12 GHz range can trigger a dowsing response, as can a cell phone broadcasting at 2.4 GHz.
- Dowsing typically detects changes beneath the surface of the ground, but dowsing responses can also be obtained from objects overhead such as metal heating ducts.
- ○ The dowsing signal is not just coming from the ground.
- The shadow from a metal object illuminated by direct sunlight (not through heavy clouds) will give a dowsing response.
- ○ Sunlight includes the radiation that gives the dowsing response.
- ○ This supports the idea that the dowsing signal is EM in the microwave region, since most of the sun's radiation is absorbed by the atmosphere except for narrow windows, including the microwave and visible.
- There is a specific location in the body where the dowsing signal is detected.
- ○ There is an organ that detects the dowsing signal as opposed to a general systemic response such as from the entire nervous system.
- The dowsing sense organ appears to be located in or near the base of the brain, with possible locations including the brain stem, but the exact location is unclear.

Probable Mechanism for L-Rod Dowsing

The dowsing signal is EM radiation, with a wavelength of a few centimeters, which corresponds to a frequency in the low GHz range, which is in the microwave region of the spectrum. The source of this microwave radiation is thermal emissions, which occur from all objects across the spectrum as a function of temperature. The ideal form of this thermal radiation is known as blackbody radiation and is described by Planck's law of blackbody radiation.

As this radiation travels through the ground it is perturbed by metals which will reflect it, water which will absorb it, voids which will refract it, and changes of density of material which may refract or reflect it. Thus the intensity of radiation traveling in any direction will depend on what the radiation has already passed through as it carries that information with it. Dowsers detect these perturbations in the background radiation.

The detection of the dowsing signal appears to occur near the base of the brain (perhaps the brain stem, or cerebellum), which causes a slight subconscious lifting of the elbows and rotating of the wrists. These muscle movements can be seen by electromyography. The rods provide a simple visual amplification of this movement, and thus the material of rods is of little consequence except that they should be fairly dense and fairly smooth to increase the force of gravity and decrease the opposing frictional forces. Copper and steel rods work well. Aluminum is less dense, and wood is less dense still, so they still work, but not as well. Since the movement of the rods is under subconscious control, the rods can appear to be moving on their own, and this is why dowsing rods are also used by people seeking to speak with ghosts, detect auras, etc., and to the extent that these activities are real or believed to be real, they reflect the ability of the subconscious mind to control the rods. Subconscious control also explains the ideomotor effects which also limit the accuracy of dowsing. I suspect that one day psychologists will use dowsing rods as a means to communicate with the subconscious mind.

The exact identity and mechanism of the detection system is unclear. Many research groups have shown that nonthermal microwaves can have significant effects on physiology, so the biological detection of microwaves is not unreasonable. One possibility is that the dowsing sense organ is the now dormant magnetic sense shared with many branches of the animal kingdom. There are several proposed mechanisms, including the use of cryptochromes (used by some birds to detect magnetic fields and inclination) and magnetite particles (used may many animals to detect magnetic fields). Cryptochromes are found in birds' eyes and human eyes and require light to detect magnetic fields. The most likely detection mechanism is magnetite particles, especially since these particles have been found in the brain stem and cerebellum. Based on the current evidence, the most likely sensors are neurons with magnetite particles linked to ion channels in neurons. However, these magnetic receptors have not been found (yet). There are thousands of different types of ion channels that provide sensing to chemicals, temperature, voltage, and parameters and their study is an active area of current research. However, there is not enough information available yet to definitively identify the dowsing detection mechanism. Hopefully more answers will be forthcoming in years to come.

One of the roles of the cerebellum is motor control. The brain stem also conveys motor and sensory signals between the rest of the brain and the body. If the dowsing sense organ is in the cerebellum or brain stem, then it does not seem too large a leap of logic to connect activation of these parts of the brain with movements of the shoulders, elbows, resulting in rotation of the wrists and the rods crossing.

One of the remarkable aspects of dowsing is the angle specificity or collimation, a mere ~6 degrees. One possible explanation for the angle selectivity is that the dowsing sense organ is the former magnetic field sense, but flipped to vertical when our ancestors decided that hands were more useful for holding stuff, and two feet was all that was needed for walking. The magnetic sense organ must be able to detect the Earth's magnetic field direction very accurately; otherwise, it would not be much use for navigation. While an appealing idea, the mixed results reported for the detection of static magnetic fields by dowsers means that the overlap between dowsing and the static magnetic field sense remains an open question.

This book has also looked at methods of determining the depth of an object. Many methods have been employed, including some methods that seem not to be entirely physical. The most common method is called the Bishop's method, where the depth of an object is determined by the distance of the first dowsing response from the object. This method was investigated and surprisingly found to work, and a theory based on refraction and internal reflection of microwaves was proposed.

The memory or hysteresis effect was also tested and, even more surprisingly, it was found to work too. The memory works with some metals (cast iron, cold-rolled steel, lead) which appear to emit microwaves but not others (aluminum, copper, silver, stainless steel). These microwaves then cause a microwave memory effect in concrete, wood, etc., that the metal object is on. Using a cast iron pot on a concrete floor as an example, once the pot is removed, the concrete floor continues to give a dowsing response for several minutes before it fades away. This effect can also be induced using a microwave signal generator and antenna at certain frequencies, ~ 3GHz. Exactly what is going on is unclear, but there is clearly a lot of new science to be developed in this area.

Final Words

The book is an exploration of dowsing to investigate the mechanism involved, but it is not a proof of dowsing; there are no double-blind tests or large statistical surveys that may contribute strong evidence of dowsing. One of the challenges for investigators is that the dowsing response is subjective and there is wide variation in dowsing ability between people. Such variance may be expected from a process where the human is the sensor, and the signal must be analyzed through human perception. Any of us can press a piano key, many people can play the piano to some extent, but only a few people can hear the piano well enough to tune it by ear. Dowsing, like most human abilities, has its Olympian athletes, people who can play the game, while the rest of us who may have tried sports in school now only watch it on TV.

The conclusion, therefore, is that dowsing is a broad subject, and it's a study that draws from a range of areas from physics to psychology to psi effects. This book has focused exclusively on the science of basic L-rod field dowsing and does not address the subject of map dowsing and the more intuitive side of dowsing, which for now must remain a mystery. This book has reviewed the current theories of basic L-rod dowsing and it describes a theory of dowsing detection which explains many of the observations. However, even this theory has some large gaps as outlined above, and much of the science upon which the actual physiological detection mechanism occurs is still being investigated. Despite the limitations of this theory, I hope this book provides a step forward towards a more comprehensive understanding of how basic dowsing works. A full exploration of the mechanism will require additional work and it is likely that many of the ideas suggested here will be superseded by others armed with more accurate data from their testing, a prospect the author welcomes. Ideas in science become accepted facts only when others can reproduce the work, and so this book is intended to be an invitation to other researchers to repeat the experiments in this book. To that end I have included detailed descriptions of the experiments, the equipment used and the results obtained. One of the goals of this book is to provide evidence that basic dowsing has a physical basis and therefore dowsing is worthy of more serious study by scientists.

To the extent that this book has helped place dowsing on a firmer scientific footing and made utility workers everywhere a little less embarrassed when they pull out the rods to find a lost pipe, this book will have been a success.

Appendix

Properties of Waves

An ocean traveller has even more vividly the impression that the ocean is made of waves than that it is made of water.
—Sir Arthur Stanley Eddington)[557]

Dowsing is frequently attributed to some kind of wave, and so this appendix reviews the properties of waves and can be used as a reference for the chapters in this book where wave properties related to dowsing are discussed in more detail. More specifically, this appendix discusses frequency, wavelength, phase angle, reflection, interference, diffraction, refraction and polarization.

Waves vs. Particles

We are all familiar with waves, and our common experiences of wave include waves on the ocean, sound, earthquakes and light. Typically a wave is a form of energy traveling in a medium or through the interface between media. For a water wave, the wave moves across the surface of the water contacting the air. For a sound wave, the sound moves through the air, and an earthquake is the movement of a wave through rocks or along the surface. A wave can be brief or long, a single frequency such as a beep corresponding to a sustained middle C note, or a complex waveform with many overlapping frequencies, such as when someone is singing.

In contrast to waves, particles are usually thought of as solid things, and typically for physical models as small solid, incompressible spheres, i.e., tiny hard balls. Waves and particles share many similar properties, and at the macroscopic level, the main difference is that particles include the net movement of a solid object along the direction of travel, whereas wave results in the net movement of energy, but not a solid object along the direction of travel. For example, a water wave rolling in towards a beach may have traveled for hundreds of miles, but the water, apart from moving up and down with the wave as it passes, does not travel with the wave. Sound waves traveling through the air allow a person on one hilltop to shout at their friend (or foe) on the next hilltop, but the air is not moving between hills at the speed of sound. The sound travels through the air, but the air molecules just juggle back and forth and do not travel with the wave. Of course, if one of the people shoots at the other with a high-powered rifle, then both a particle and wave traverses the valley. There are certain behaviors which are characteristic of waves which are not seen in particles, including diffraction, interference, refraction and polarization.

250 Appendix: Properties of Waves

The discussion here is focused on these macroscopic effects. At the microscopic level of subatomic and atomic particles, the rules of quantum mechanics prevail. Under this regime, particles have wave-like properties and waves are quantized and so have particle-like properties, and so the distinction between waves and particles is often lost.

Transverse and Longitudinal Waves

The first distinction of waves is whether they are longitudinal or transverse, and these terms refer to whether the motion of the wave in the medium is in the same direction that the wave is traveling or at right angles to the direction the wave is traveling. Going back to our example of a water wave traveling across the surface of the ocean; if a seagull is swimming as the wave passes, the bird will be lifted up and then drop down again before coming back to its original position. The movement of the seagull is at right angles to the direction of the wave, so surface water waves are transverse. Most waves in nature are transverse, including EM radiation, in which the electric and magnetic fields are at right angles to the direction of propagation. The most common form of longitudinal wave is sound. Sound waves move though air as a pressure pulse or compression wave where there are regions of high compression and low compression, as illustrated in Figure A.1.

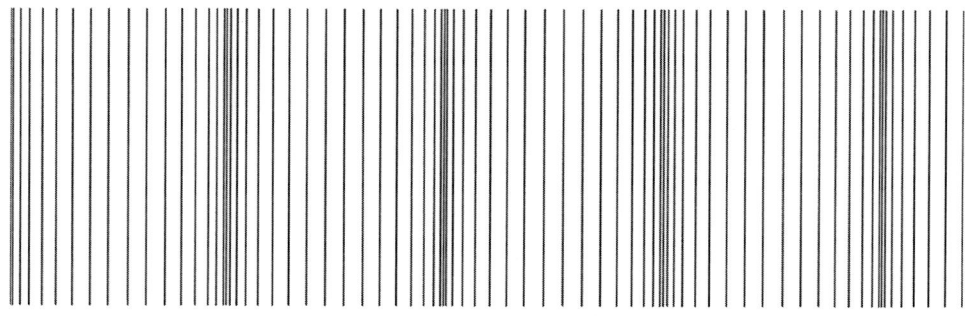

Direction of Travel of Wave ⇨

Figure A.1. Sound waves move through air, compressing and expanding the air as they go.

Both longitudinal and transverse waves have frequency, wavelength and speed, and both types of waves undergo refraction, interference and diffraction, but only transverse waves can be polarized.

Frequency, Speed and Wavelength of Waves

Waves have several characteristics. The most important are wavelength (λ), frequency (f) and speed (v), which are interrelated by the equation

$$v = \lambda F$$

For EM radiation, which is also a wave, the speed is given the symbol c (c is the speed of an EM wave in a vacuum), the speed of light, so the above equation becomes **c = λF**. Many waves, including EM waves, can be described by sine waves and any periodic wave form can be described as the sum of sine waves.

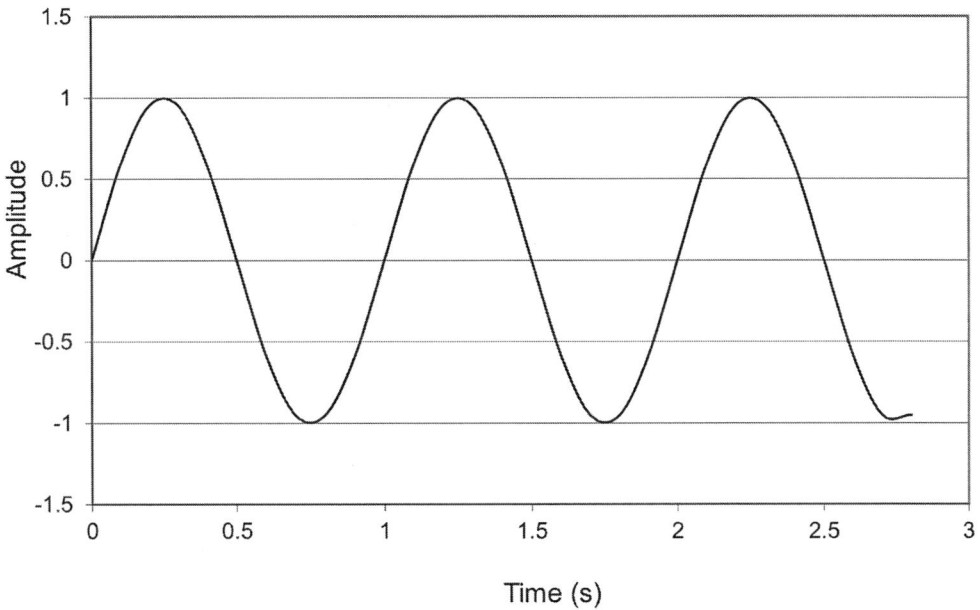

Figure A.2. Sine wave.

Figure A.2 shows a sine wave. Suppose the wave is passing a point over time. At this location, the amplitude (intensity of the wave) rises and falls as the wave passes by. The number of times the wave rises and falls per second is the frequency. In Figure A.2 the wave goes through one complete cycle (the period of the wave) in 1 second, so the frequency is 1 Hz. If we wait for 1 second, the time for one cycle, the distance the wave has traveled is the wavelength. If, for example, the wave is moving at 2 meters per second (v = 2 m/s), then the wavelength is 2 meters.

Phase Angle

The phase of a wave is an indicator of the relative timing of the peaks and valleys of two or more waves moving in parallel at the same frequency. Figure A.3 shows four waves with different phases, zero (solid line and our reference) and the other curves are 90, 180 and 270 degrees phase shifted from the first.

Degrees and Radians

Degrees and radians are two different methods for measuring angles. Degrees are fairly simple, if one goes around in a complete circle, one has gone 360 degrees. If one goes only halfway round, then the angle is 180 degrees, a quarter turn is 90 degrees and so forth. Why 360 degrees rather than some other number? Apparently the ancient Babylonians knew that the Earth's orbit was 365 days a year, and rounded down to make 360, since the math is easier...[1] in other words a fairly arbitrary number. A more systematic measure for angle is the radian. From geometry, the circumference of a circle is $2\pi r$, where r is the radius. For a unit circle where r = 1, the circumference is 2π and the unit is the radian. Therefore, angles in degrees or radians can easily be converted to the other.

360 degrees = 2π radians,
180 degrees = π radians
90 degrees = $\pi/2$ radians

The frequency can be viewed as how often a point in space on the unit circle travels the circumference in a second, and so the angular frequency $\omega = 2\pi f$. Using radians to express angles is commonly used because it also makes the math easier.

A sine wave can be viewed as a point going around the circumference of a circle at constant speed. If one plotted the height of the point with respect to the center of the circle over time, the resulting graph would be a sine wave as shown in Figure A.3. A complete wavelength can be represented by a circle, and so a 90 degrees shift means the two waves are a quarter wavelength apart ($\pi/2$ radians).

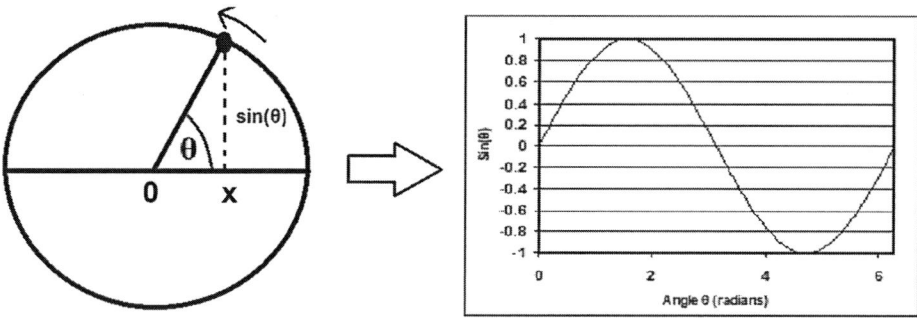

Figure A.3. A point moving around a circle maps out a sine wave.

The position of the point on the circumference can be described by a right angle triangle, and so trigonometric functions can be used. Compared to the starting point, the position around the circle is described by the equation

$$y = \sin(\theta)$$

where θ is the angle. This equation is also the reason that these waves are called sine waves. If there are two sine waves with a different phase, then the second wave can be described by the equation

$$y = \sin(\omega t + \phi)$$

where ω is angular frequency = $2\pi F$, t is time and ϕ is the phase angle between the two waves.

---

1. "Why Has Geometry Not Been 'Metricked'? Why 360 Degrees instead of 1, 10, 100 or even 1000?" *The Guardian*, 2011, https://www.theguardian.com/notesandqueries/query/0,,-185569,00.html, accessed January 6, 2023.

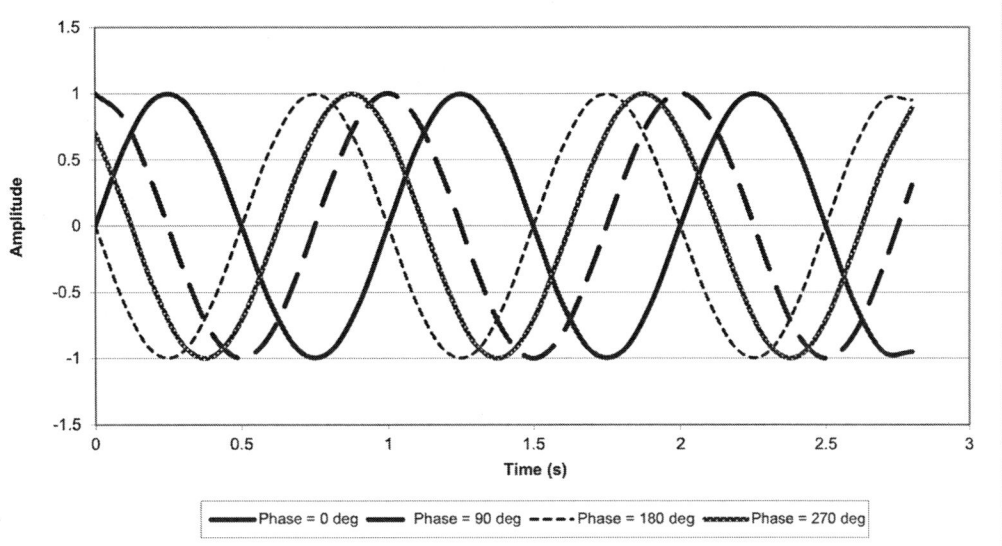

Figure A.4. Four sine waves with different phases.

Superposition and Reflection

If two solid particles collide, they will bounce off each other, whereas if two waves meet, they will pass through each other, but as they do the waves will superimpose (add

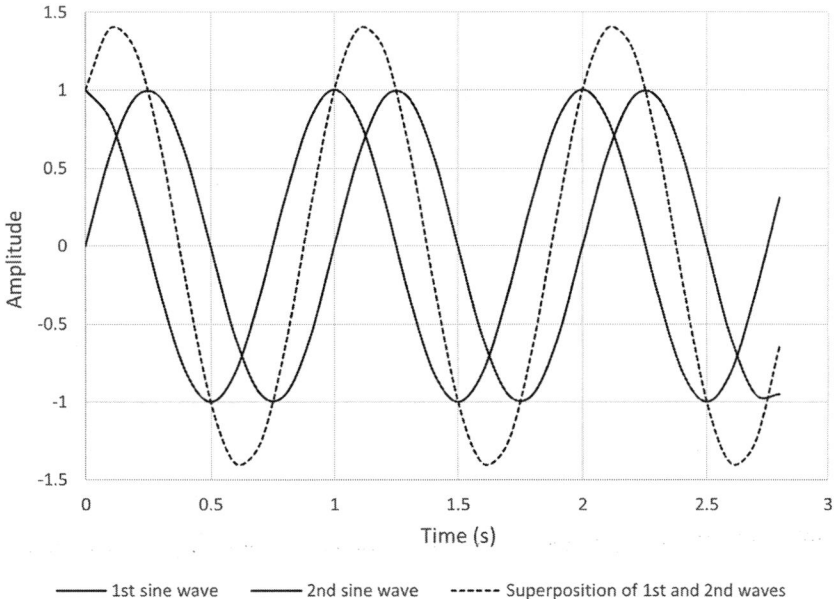

Figure A.5. Image showing superposition of two sine waves and the resulting sum of the two waves.

together); the net signal becomes the sum of the two waves. If both waves are positive of the baseline, then the result will be greater (see Figure A.5).

If one wave is greater and one is less than baseline, then the net result will be reduced. If the two waves are the same frequency and opposite phase (one positive, one negative) the waves can cancel each other out completely (think noise canceling headphones), see Figure A.6.

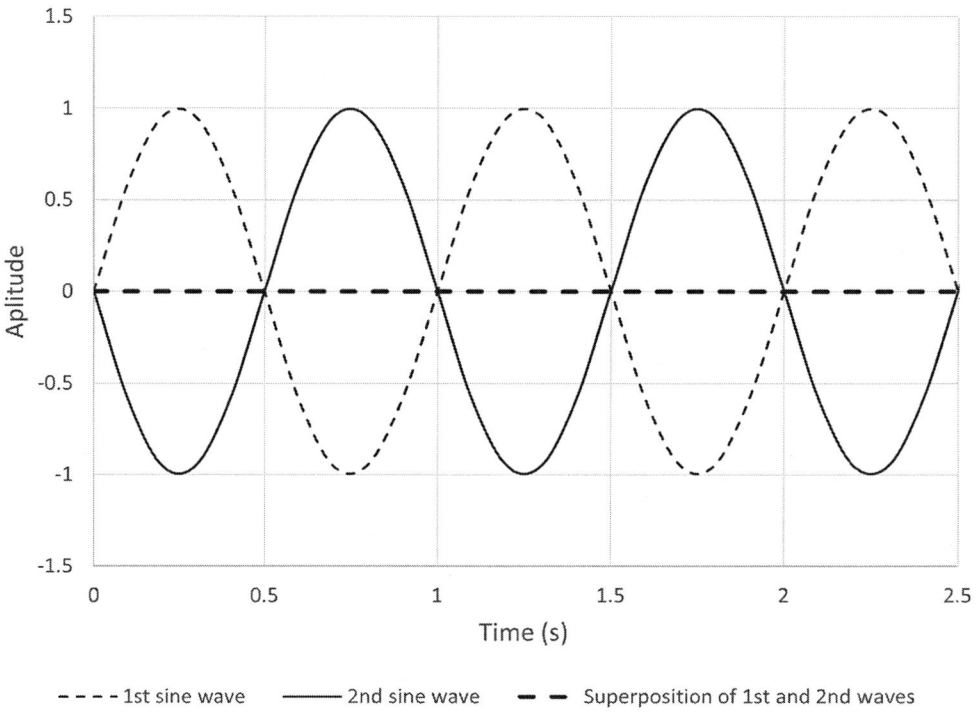

Figure A.6. Image showing superposition of two sine waves and the resulting sum of the two waves showing a net wave of zero.

Superposition occurs whether the waves are the same frequency or not.

Reflection

If a tennis ball is thrown against a hard wall, the ball will bounce off the wall at roughly the same angle as it approaches the wall. Waves do the same thing, but we call it reflection. Reflection occurs when the wave bounces off a surface at the same angle θ that is approached it, as illustrated in Figure A.7.

By convention, the angle is always measured against the normal (perpendicular to the surface). The rules of reflection are similar to a particle or a rubber ball bouncing of a wall (ignoring gravity), so $\theta_{in} = \theta_{out}$.

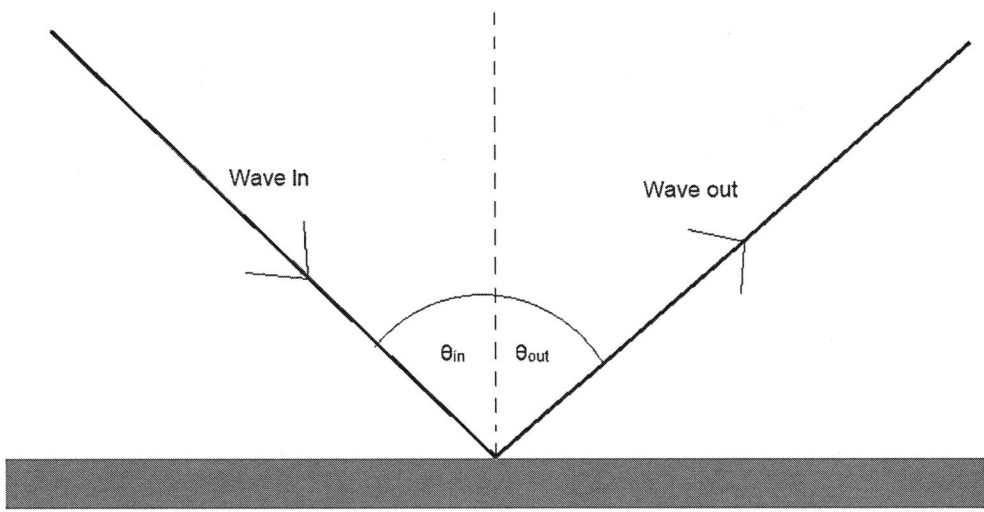

Figure A.7. Sketch of reflection of a wave at a smooth surface.

Refraction

Refraction occurs when waves pass from one medium to another. Often the speed of the wave changes if the medium changes. So, for example, the speed of sound in air is about 340 m/s, but in water it is about 1480 m/s and in steel is about 6,000 m/s,[558] and so while the frequency will be the same, the wavelength will change, since wavelength is the speed divided by the frequency.

$$(\lambda = F/v).$$

The angle of refraction is described by Snell's law, which is summarized by the equation below and illustrated in Figure A.8.

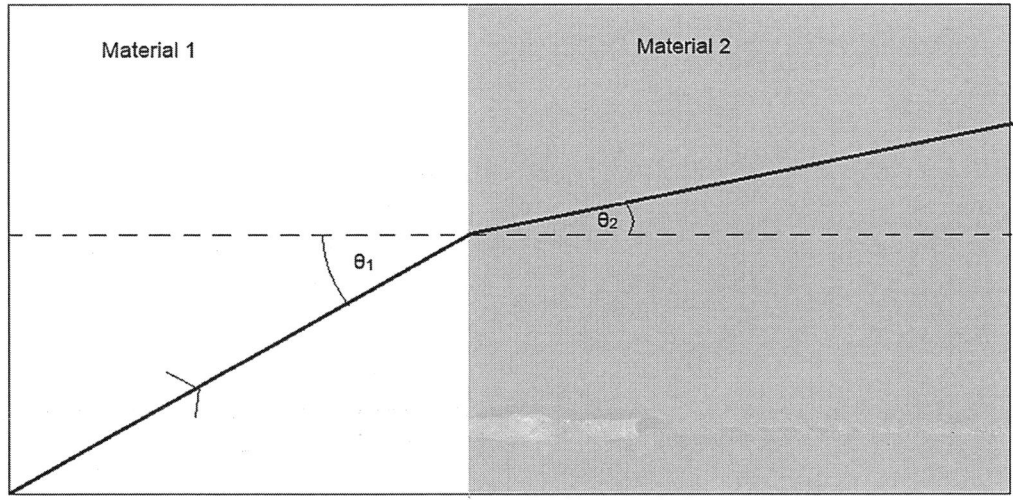

Figure A.8. Light passing from one medium to a second may change its angle relative to the perpendicular (normal), depending on the relative refractive index of the two materials.

$$n_1 \sin(\theta_1) = n_2 \cdot \sin(\theta_2)$$

The speed of light also varies with the medium, and the refractive index is a measure of the speed of the wave in that medium compared to the speed of light in a vacuum (denoted by the letter "c"). Therefore, the refractive index for light in a vacuum is 1, and the refractive index is very close to 1 in air too. The refractive index in water is 1.333 and in glass it is about 1.5 and in diamond it is 2.42.[559] The speed of light is therefore 2.4 times faster in air than it is in diamond, and this is one of the reasons why cut diamonds sparkle the way they do. The difference in refraction is also the reason why a straw in a glass of water looks bent at the top where the water contacts the air, and this effect is discussed in more detail later. The refractive index varies with frequency, and so if white light is passed through a glass prism, the extent the light bends depends on the wavelength and so we see a rainbow pattern.

Diffraction

Diffraction is a property of all waves and occurs when waves meet edges or gaps. Consider water waves at a beach approaching a short barrier. If the wavelength of the waves is much shorter than the dimensions of the barrier, then wave will continue straight on where it can and will be blocked/reflected where it can't.

If the gap is too small, the wave will not pass through. If the gap is similar in size to the wavelength, then the wave will pass through, but it will be significantly bent at the gap as the wave diffracts, see Figure A.9.

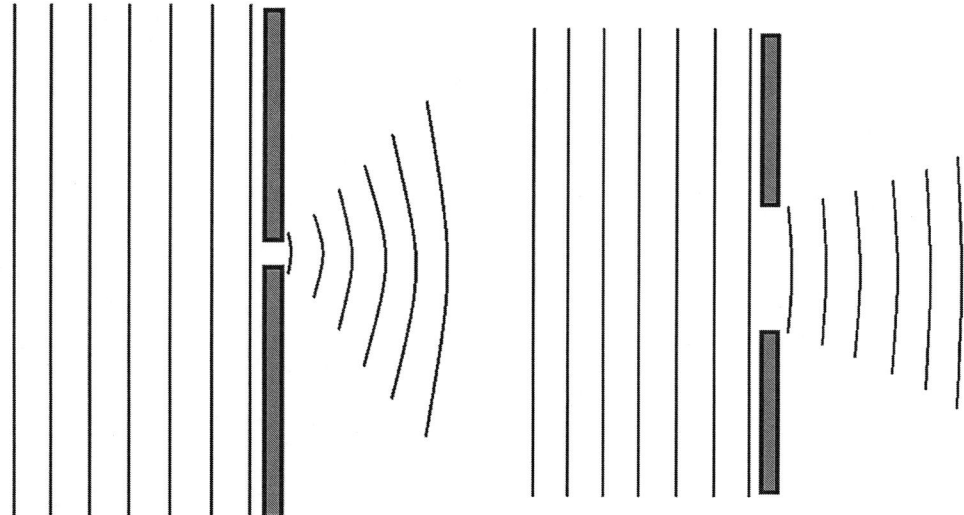

Figure A.9. Wave diffracting through a narrow gap (A, left) and wider gap (B, right).

If the gap is fairly large relative to the wavelength, then the wave bends less, but diffraction will also occur at edges, see Figure A.10.

If the wavelength is much longer than the dimensions of the barrier, then the wave will pass by and the wave fronts will rejoin on the other side of the barrier. If the wavelength is comparable in size to the barrier, then the wave will diffract around the barrier.

Interference

If a wave passes through two slits, then the resulting diffraction patterns will superimpose to create an interference pattern (see Figure A.11).

Using a laser pointer, for example, one can get interference patterns by passing the laser light through a slit and allowing the light to then land on a screen, as shown in Figure A.12. Laser light is different from normal light in that it is monochromatic, all the photons are in phase and the laser beam is usually highly collimated.

The diffraction pattern from light from a red laser pointer passing through a 1 mm slit is not really the diffraction of light through a slit, but rather the interference pattern from the diffraction of light from both edges, since the wavelength of the red laser pointer (640 to 670 nm) is over a thousand times shorter than the slit.

Polarization

If one thinks of a typical transverse wave such as a water wave, the motion of the water is up and down, perpendicular to the motion of the wave, as illustrated in Figure A.13.

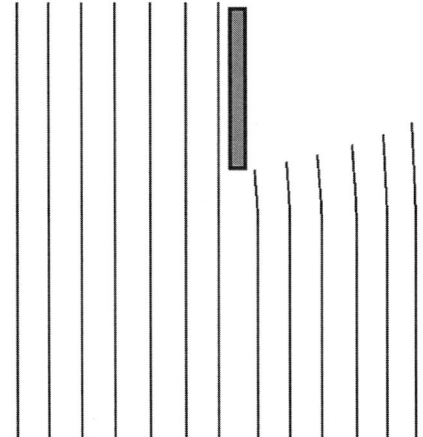

Figure A.10. Diffraction around an edge.

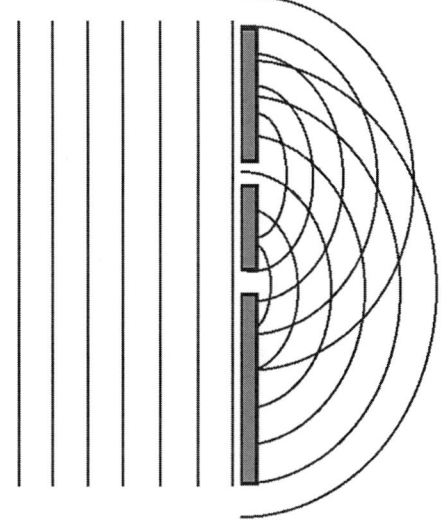

Figure A.11. Interference pattern from a wave passing through two slits.

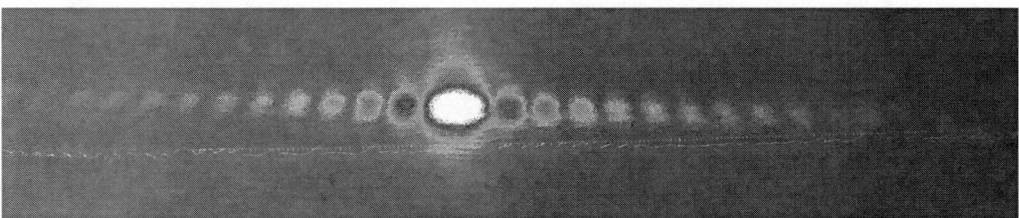

Figure A.12. Diffraction pattern produced by red laser diode (640–670 nm) passing through a narrow slit, showing diffraction pattern.

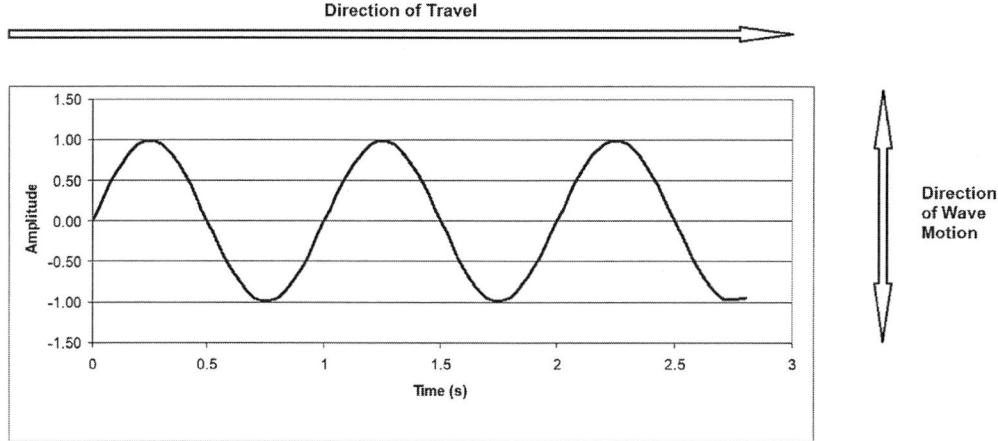

Figure A.13. Sketch showing polarization of a transverse wave.

If one "looked" down the wave, one would see a vertical line corresponding to the water going up and down. In contrast most light beams have the vibration in random orientations relative to the direction of travel. Such light is unpolarized. If an unpolarized light bead passes through a narrow slit (a polarizing filter) so that only those waves whose orientations match the slit can pass through, as shown in Figure A.14, then the light becomes polarized.

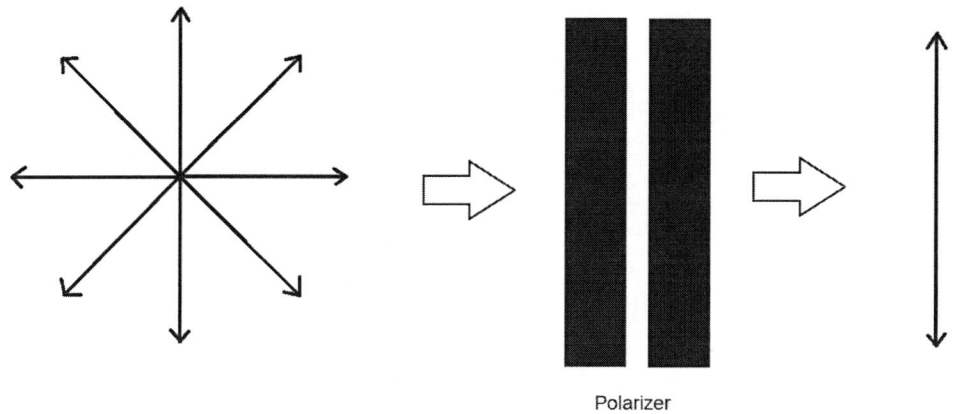

Figure A.14. Unpolarized light is polarized on passing through a polarizing filter.

This polarizing filter is how polarizing sunglasses work. Reflection can also cause linear polarization, since electric field oscillations perpendicular to the surface do not reflect. Maximum polarization occurs when the incoming and exiting light is 45° to the perpendicular, the so-called Brewster angle; see Figure A.15.

If this reflected light with horizontal polarization passes through a pair of sunglasses with vertical polarization, the reflected light will be absorbed and only the other ambient light with vertical polarization will pass through—polarized sunglasses are

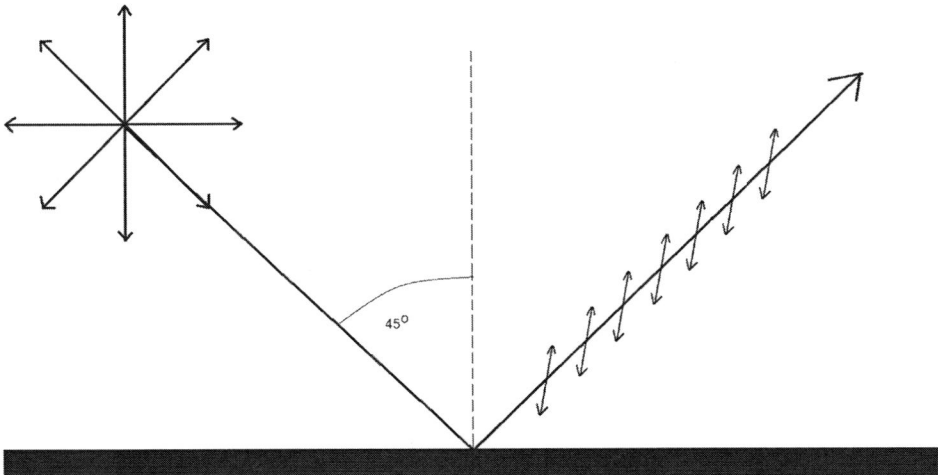

Figure A.15. Polarization on reflection. Light is partially linearly polarized on reflection with the surviving polarization parallel to the surface and perpendicular to wave direction.

great for removing the glare from reflective surfaces. More complex forms of polarization also occur, such as elliptical polarization, but these forms of polarization are beyond the scope of the discussion here.

Annex

Instrumentation Used

It matters little how much equipment we use; it matters much that we be masters of all we do use.

—Sam Abell[560]

Antenna

- MLA-30 Loop antenna Active receiving antenna 100kHz–30MHz for shortwave radio
- Griddy: The Grid Parabolic 4G LTE, 5G NR, and Wi-Fi Antenna Kit by Waveform, 26 dB, 600–6500 MHz Dish. Griddy has 12–17 dBi of gain on the 600–960 MHz frequency bands; 20–23 dBi of gain on the 1700–2700 MHz frequency bands; and 23–26 dBi of gain on 3000–6500 MHz frequency bands
- Horn antenna, 5.65–5.925 GHz band
- 15W 5–6dB 1.35–9.5GHz UWB ultra wideband logarithmic period antenna
- 3GHz dual polarized beehive feed horn
- Various monopole antennas

Cell phone

- Apple iPhone plus, model MQ962LL/A

Compass

- Apple iPhone 8 built-in compass application, set to read magnetic north (default value)

Conductivity meter

- Yellow springs Instrument Co. (YSI) Model 32

Datalogger

- Arduino Uno output to tablet running Windows 10 Home, running Cooltern Software ver. 1.8.0 (Roger Meier).
- Radioshack Multimeter, model 22–168A, serial output to Windows 7 PC, running Radioshack Scopeview software ver. 1.02

ECG

- Emay, model EMG-10, with 3M red dot electrodes

EMG

- MyoWare Muscle Sensor (AT-04-001) with 3M red dot electrodes. The sensor was connected to an Arduino Mega and the output went to a Windows 10 tablet for data logging

Low Noise Block (LNB)

- LNBs
  - SatMaximum Universal Single LNB, KU Band LNB LNBF 0.1dB FTA HD Linear Satellite Dish 1 Port
- 10.7–12.75 GHz
- LO: 9.75 & 10.6 GHz
- Noise 0.1dB
  - Direct TV LNB model DTV-SWM3-Plain
  - Titanium Satellite C-band LNBF phase lock loop
- Model C1W-PLL lite
- Input 3.4–4.2 GHz
- Output 950- 1750 MHz
- LO 5150 MHz
- NF 15 K, Gain 65 dB
  - Gardiner Communications S-band LNB
- Input 2.5–2.7 GHz
- Out 950–1150 MHz
- Local oscillator 3.65 GHz
- Gain 65 dB (typical), Noise 50 K (typical)
- LNB Power Inserter, DirectTV model P121R3–16</BULOL>

Magnetometer

- Apple iPhone 8 with Magnetomer App, ver. 1.0, Physics toolbox by Vieyra Software (available from the Apple Store) July 2020

Multimeter

- HP 3456A Digital Voltmeter
- Micronta digital multimeter
- Radioshack digital multimeter (with digital output for data logging)

RF Power Meter

- HP 473B power meter, with HP 8481D power sensor

RF/Microwave Signal Generator

- Gigatronics model 900 (0.05–12 GHz)

SDR

- NooElec NESDR Smartee
- RTL-SDR w/Integrated Bias Tee, Aluminum Enclosure, 0.5PPM TCXO, SMA Input
- Range 25MHz-1700MHz.

Spectrum Analyzer

- SA6 6 GHz Spectrum0 Analyzer & Signal Generator
- Tiny Spectrum Analyzer TinySA 2.8in Display 100KHz-960MHz

Thermometer, Infrared

- Helect Infrared Thermometer, model H1020, temperature range—50°C to ~550°C, accuracy +/1 1.5°C 0 to 550°C, and +/- 3°C -50 to 0°C
- K-type thermocouple, Professional Instruments

Chapter Notes

Preface

1. "Today in Science History," https://todayinsci.com/QuotationsCategories/S_Cat/-Superconductivity-Quotations.htm, accessed August 2, 2021.

2. Thomas Saunders, *The Boiled Frog Syndrome: Your Health and the Built Environment* (Wiley, 2003), 55.

3. Arthur J. Ellis, *The Divining Rod: A History of Water Witching, with a Bibliography* (U.S. Government Printing Office, 1917), https://archive.org/details/diviningrodahis00elligoog/page/n5/mode/2up.

4. Ken Miller, *Dowsing How Does It Work* (Sermon on the Mount Publishing, 1992).

Chapter 1

5. Charles Fort, *The Book of the Damned, the Collected Works of Charles Fort*, originally published 1919 (republished by Jeremy P. Tarcher/Penguin, 2008).

6. Henri Mager, *Water Diviners and Their Methods*, translated by A.H. Bell (G. Bell & Sons, 1931).

7. Elizabeth Brown, *Dowsing: The Ultimate Guide for the 21st Century* (Hay House, 2010).

8. Dennis Wheatley, *The Essential Dowsing Guide* 3rd ed. (Ozark Mountain, 2012).

9. Richard Webster, *Dowsing for Beginners, the Art of Discovering: Water, Treasure, Gold, Oil, Artifacts* (Castle Books, 2001).

10. "Divining Rod," Encyclopedia.com, https://www.encyclopedia.com/earth-and-environment/-minerals-mining-and-metallurgy/metallurgy-and-mining-terms-and-concepts/divining-rod, accessed August 22, 2020.

11. Dennis Wheatley, *The Essential Dowsing Guide* 3rd ed. (Ozark Mountain, 2012).

12. Babasaheb Manik More, "An Experimental Study on Water Dowsing," *International Journal of Research and Innovations in Earth Science* 2014, vol. 1, 17–19.

13. James Caviness, "How to Find Underground Plastic Pipes," https://www.metaldetector.com/learn/buying-guide-articles/industrial-use/-how-to-find-underground-plastic-pipes, accessed March 12, 2023.

14. "An Insight Into Ground Penetrating Radar and Other Methods Used for Underground Utility Detection," Scan Plus Tech, accessed July 4, 2021, https://scanplustech.ca/en/insight-ground-penetrating-radar-other-methods-used-underground-utility-detection/; Matthew Sparkes, "Two of the UK's Water Companies Are Still Using Dowsing to Find Leaks," *New Scientist,* January 27, 2023, https://www.newscientist.com/article/-2356376-two-of-the-uks-water-companies-are-still-using-dowsing-to-find-leaks/.

15. Jon Sharman, "UK Water Companies Still Use 'Magic' Dowsing Rods to Find Leaks, Despite No Supporting Scientific Evidence," *Independent*, November 22, 2017, https://www.independent.co.uk/news/uk/home-news/uk-water-companies-magic-dowsing-rods-use-engineers-leaks-no-scientific-evidence-sally-le-page-a8069616.html, accessed July 11, 2020.

16. Thomas Saunders, *The Boiled Frog Syndrome: Your Health and the Built Environment* (Wiley, 2003), 55.

17. Lloyd Youngblood, "Dowsing: Ancient History," American Society of Dowsers, https://dowsers.org/dowsing-history/, accessed July 17, 2021.

18. Michael Fercik, *The Art of Dowsing: Separating Science from Superstition* (Page Publishing, 2020).

19. William Barrett, "The History and Mystery of the So-Called Divining Rod," *Light* vol. 27, January 26, 1907, 43, https://www.google.com/books/edition/Light/LahUR0vpQzMC?hl=en&gbpv=1.

20. Roger Jennison, "A Physicist Goes Dowsing Down Under," *Physics World* vol. 8, no. 6 (1995), https://iopscience.iop.org/article/10.1088/2058-7058/8/6/15.

21. Charles Richet, Chapter 2 in *Henry Gross and His Dowsing Rod* ed. Kenneth Roberts (Doubleday, 1951); Sir William Barrett, F.R.S. and Theodore Besterman, *The Divining-Rod, an Experimental and Psychological Investigation* (University Books, 1968).

22. Sir William Barrett, F.R.S. and Theodore Besterman, *The Divining-Rod, an Experimental and Psychological Investigation* (University Books, 1968).

23. Albert Einstein, letter to Herman E. Peisach of South Norwalk, Connecticut, February 16, 1946,

cited in Richard Heggen, *Underground Rivers: From the River Styx to the Rio San Buenaventura with Occasional Diversions* (Red Hen, 2018), 716.

24. Sir William Barrett, F.R.S. and Theodore Besterman, *The Divining-Rod, an Experimental and Psychological Investigation* (University Books, 1968).

25. J.C. Maby and T.B. Franklin, *The Physics of the Divining Rod* (G. Bell and Sons, 1939).

26. Solco Walle Tromp, *Psychical Physics: A Scientific Analysis of Dowsing, Radiesthesia and Kindred Divining Phenomena* (Elsevier, 1949), 325.

27. John Wilcox, "The Use of Dowsing for the Location of Caves, with Some Results from the First Royal Forest of Dean Caving Symposium," June 1994, http://www-sop.inria.fr/agos-sophia/sis/dowsing/dowsdean.html, accessed October 3, 2020.

28. George P. Hansen, "Dowsing: A Review of Experimental Research," *Journal of the Society for Psychical Research* vol. 51, no. 792 (October 1982), 343–367.

29. Anne Miller, "Dowsing: A Review," *The Scientific and Medical Network*, https://explore.scimednet.org/index.php/dowsing-a-review/, accessed October 4, 2020.

30. Nandkumar Dharmadhikari, D. Meshram, Satish Kulkarni, Avinash Kharat, Raviraj Sorate, Sunil Pimplikar, Narang Rajkumar, Deshmukh Sunil, and Charudatta Bangal, "Use of Dowsing and Geo-Resistivity Meter for Detection of Geopathic Stress Zone," *International Journal of Modern Engineering Research (IJMER)* vol.1. (2012), 609–614.

31. Duane G. Chadwick and Larry Jensen, "The Detection Of Magnetic Fields Caused By Groundwater," *Reports* (1971), Paper 568, https://digitalcommons.usu.edu/water_rep/568, https://digitalcommons.usu.edu/cgi/viewcontent.cgi?article=1567&context=water_rep, accessed July 12, 2020.

32. John Dickinson, Richard Ellam, Manda Scott, Ann Newell, Jill Moss, Rev. Martin J. Smith, Roland Hill, and Miriam Farrell Shtaierman, "In Defence of Dowsing to Detect Water, Guardian Readers Share Their Stories on the Success of Dowsing," Letters, *Guardian*, November 27, 2017, https://www.theguardian.com/environment/2017/nov/27/in-defence-of-dowsing-to-detect-water, accessed June 10, 2020.

33. Richard Webster, *Dowsing for Beginners, the Art of Discovering: Water, Treasure, Gold, Oil, Artifacts* (Castle Books, 2001).

34. Z.V. Harvalik, "A Biophysical Magnetometer–Gradiometer," *The Virginia Journal of Science*, vol. 21, no. 2 (Spring 1970), 59–60, http://dowsing-research.net/dowsing/articles/Harvalik%20-%202%20articles%20-%20Anatomical%20localization%20of%20human%20detection%20of%20weak%20em%20radiation%20-%20and%20-%20A%20biophysical%20magnetometer-gradiometer.PDF.

35. Dennis Wheatley, *The Essential Dowsing Guide* 3rd ed. (Ozark Mountain, 2012).

36. Ivor Noël Hume, *Historical Archaeology: A Comprehensive Guide for Both Amateur and Professions to the Techniques and Methods of Excavating Historical Sites* (Alfred A. Knopf, 1974).

37. Thomas Fiddick, *Dowsing with an Account of Some Original Experiments*, ed. Chris Bond (Cornovia Press 2011), first published by the Cambourne Printing and Stationery Company, 1913.

38. Jason Koebler, "A Professional 'Water Witch' Explains How to Find Water in a Drought," *Motherboard*, March 3, 2014, https://www.vice.com/en/article/vvbeab/how-californias-water-witches-divine-water-in-a-drought, accessed Sept 4, 2022.

39. Linda Searing, "The Big Numbers: Lefties Make Up Ten Percent Of The World," *Washington Post*, August 12, 2019, https://www.washingtonpost.com/health/the-big-number-lefties-make-up-about-10-percent-of-the-world/2019/08/09/69978100-b9e2-11e9-bad6-609f75bfd97f_story.html, accessed July 12, 2020.

40. John Wilcox, "The Use Of Dowsing For The Location Of Caves, With Some Results From The First Royal Forest Of Dean Caving Symposium," June 1994, http://www-sop.inria.fr/agos-sophia/sis/dowsing/dowsdean.html, accessed October 3, 2020.

Chapter 2

41. "Charles Richet, Professor of Physiology at the University of Paris and Nobel Prize winner for Medicine and Physiology in 1913," *Nobel Prize*, https://www.nobelprize.org/prizes/medicine/1913/richet/facts/, accessed May 14, 2023; Kenneth Roberts, *Henry Gross and His Dowsing Rod* (Doubleday, 1951).

42. W. Pinchbeck, "Divining Rod at Gallipoli, A True Story of Sulva Bay," *Shapparton Advertizer* (June 5, 1916), 1, https://trove.nla.gov.au/newspaper/article/91189723.

43. *The Utility of Dowsing as a Means of Detecting Viet Cong Tunnels*, HRB Singer Inc, Project Poorboy Annual Progress Report (Provisional Report) Report Number 4139.11, April 1968, R-Annex D, citing Gordon Rattray Taylor, *Science Journal* (LLIFFE Industrial Publications, November 1, 1967), http://dowsing-research.net/dowsing/reports/Bossart%20-%20the%20utility%20of%20dowsing%20as%20a%20means%20of%20detecting%20Vietcong%20tunnels.pdf, accessed August 27, 2020.

44. "December 11, 1865: Birth of Abbé Bouly, The Most Famous Dowser In France," *Les Archives Pas De Calais*, December 11, 2020, https://archivespasdecalais.fr/Decouvrir/Anniversaires/-11-decembre-1865-naissance-de-l-abbe-Bouly-radiesthesiste-le-plus-celebre-de-France. Original in French, translated by Google.

45. "Divining Rod," *Encyclopedia.com*, citing Leslie Shepard (editor), *Encyclopedia of Occultism and Parapsychology* (Gale / Cengage Learning,

year and edition not available) https://www.encyclopedia.com/earth-and-environment/minerals-mining-and-metallurgy/metallurgy-and-mining-terms-and-concepts/divining-rod, accessed August 22, 2020.

46. Kenneth Roberts, *Henry Gross and His Dowsing Rod* (Doubleday, 1951).

47. Charles Latimer, *The Divining Rod: Virgula Divina—Baculus Divinatorius (Water-Witching.)*, 1876, Project Gutenberg EBook #45020, February 26, 2014, https://www.gutenberg.org/files/45020/45020-h/45020-h.htm.

48. "Driving," *Sunday Times* (Published 28 June 2020), https://www.driving.co.uk/news/jeremy-clarkson-takes-stab-water-divining/, accessed August 14, 2020.

49. Col. (ret.) Russell J. Gardinier and Jerome K. Clauser, "HRB Singer Inc, Project Poorboy Annual Progress Report (Provisional Report) Report Number 4139.11," Office of Naval Research, April 1968, http://dowsing-research.net/dowsing/reports/Bossart%20-%20the%20utility%20of%20dowsing%20as%20a%20means%20of%20detecting%20Vietcong%20tunnels.pdf, accessed August 27, 2020.

50. John Wilcox, "The Use Of Dowsing For The Location Of Caves, With Some Results From The First Royal Forest Of Dean Caving Symposium," June 1994, http://www-sop.inria.fr/agos-sophia/sis/dowsing/dowsdean.html, accessed October 3, 2020.

51. "Annual Report 1998," University of Calgary, Human Performance Laboratory, 1998, https://prism.ucalgary.ca/bitstream/handle/1880/110390/1998_w.pdf?sequence=1&isAllowed=y.

52. Tom Williamson, "Dowsing for Opals," *Scientist* vol. 81, 1979, 371–373.

53. Hans-Dieter Betz, "Unconventional Water Detection: Field Test of the Dowsing Technique in Dry Zones: Part l," *Journal of Scientific Exploration* vol. 9, no. I (1995), 1–43, http://citeseerx.ist.psu.edu/viewdoc/download?doi=10.1.1.458.6149&rep=rep1&type=pdf, accessed July 19, 2020; Hans-Dieter Betz, "Unconventional Water Detection: Field Test of the Dowsing Technique in Dry Zones: Part 2," *Journal of Scientific Exploration* vol. 9, no. 2 (1995), 159–189, http://citeseerx.ist.psu.edu/viewdoc/download?doi=10.1.1.558.6201&rep=rep1&type=pdf, accessed July 28, 2020.

54. J. T. Enright, "Testing Dowsing: The Failure of the Munich Experiments," *The Skeptical Inquirer* 1, vol. 23, no.1 (January / February 1999), 39, https://skepticalinquirer.org/1999/01/testing-dowsing-the-failure-of-the-munich-experiments/.

55. John Greenwood, "Locating Underground Features by Dowsing," *New Civil Engineer* (January 1, 2001), https://www.newcivilengineer.com/archive/locating-underground-features-by-dowsing-01-01-2001/, accessed October 3, 2020.

56. N.P. Dharmadhikari, V.V. Muthekar, C.S. Mahajan, N. Basavaiah, A.G. Kharat, S.I. Barde, A.K. Sharma, M.S. Patil, and M. Laxminarayana, "Vein Width Measurement of Groundwater on Earth's Surface Using Semiconductor Laser Light And Proton Precession Magnetometer," *Journal of Applied Geophysics* vol. 171 (December 2019), 103864, https://www.sciencedirect.com/science/article/abs/pii/S0926985118306682.

57. Carl Llewellyn Weschcke and Joe H. Slate, *The New Science of the Paranormal, from the Research Lab to Real Life* (Llewellyn Publications, 2016), 123.

58. Michael Martin, "A New Controlled Dowsing Experiment Putting the President of the American Society of Dowsers to the Test," *The Skeptical Inquirer* vol. 8 (winter 1983–84), 138, https://skepticalinquirer.org/wp-content/uploads/sites/29/1984/01/Issue-02-44.pdf.

59. John John Yeosock, "Physiological Studies of Persons Using Divining Rods as Detection Device," Master of Science thesis, October 1969, Dudley Knox Library Naval Postgraduate School, 93943–5101, https://core.ac.uk/download/pdf/36706173.pdf.

60. R. Foulkes, "Dowsing Experiments," *Nature* vol. 229 (1971), 163–168, https://doi.org/10.1038/229163a0.

61. "Parliament, On the Floor of the House," *The Lancet* (April 11, 1942), 457, https://www.sciencedirect.com/science/article/abs/pii/S0140673600796267; "Exchange between Mr Stokes and Mr. Sandys, Maby Dowsing Experiments," *Hansard*, Volume 378 (March 17, 1942), https://hansard.parliament.uk/commons/1942-03-17/debates/99c924a6-a0f4-4d56-8dae-0c3f1d2d5944/MabyDowsingExperiments.

62. J.T. Enright, "Testing Dowsing: The Failure of the Munich Experiments," *Skeptical Enquirer* vol. 23, no. 1 (January / February 1999), https://skepticalinquirer.org/1999/01/testing-dowsing-the-failure-of-the-munich-experiments/.

63. James Randi, "Australian Skeptics Divining Test," https://www.skeptics.com.au/resources/articles/australian-skeptics-divining-test/, accessed August 22, 2020.

64. Philip B. Stark, "Chapter 28: Does Treatment Have an Effect?" University of California Berkeley, last modified September 2, 2019, https://www.stat.berkeley.edu/~stark/SticiGui/Text/experiments.htm, accessed August 6, 2020, citing R. König, J. Moll, and A. Sarma, "Wünschelruten-Test in Kassel," *Skeptiker* (GWUP January 1991), Skeptiker, 4–10.

65. Michael A. Easter and Angi M. Christensen, "Forensic Spotlight, Dowsing for Human Remains—Considerations for Investigators," *FBI Law Enforcement Bulletin*, January 11, 2022, https://leb.fbi.gov/spotlights/forensic-spotlight-dowsing-for-human-remains-considerations-for-investigators, accessed June 4, 2023.

Chapter 3

66. "Interview with Carol Gader, The Master Dowser," *New Hampshire Magazine*, October 1,

2010, https://www.nhmagazine.com/the-master-dowser/, accessed July 17, 2021.

67. Thomas Welton, trans., *Jacob's Rod*, Translation from the French of *A Rare and Curious Work, A.D. 1693, On the Art of Finding Springs, Mines, and Minerals by Means of the Hazel Rod. To Which Is Appended Researches, with Proofs of the Existence of a More Certain and Far Higher Faculty, with Clear and Ample Instructions for Using It*.

68. Solco Walle Tromp, *Psychical Physics: A Scientific Analysis of Dowsing, Radiesthesia and Kindred Divining Phenomena*, Elsevier, 1949, 325.

69. V.C. Reddish, *The Field of Rotating Masses*, Makkar Publishing, Edinburgh, 2010.

70. Z.V. Harvalik, *Physiological Chemistry and Physics* vol. 10, no. 6 (1978), 525, http://dowsing-research.net/dowsing/articles/Harvalik%20-%202%20articles%20-%20Anatomical%20localization%20of%20human%20detection%20of%20weak%20em%20radiation%20-%20and%20-%20A%20biophysical%20magnetometer-gradiometer.PDF.

71. Romex® is a registered trademark of the Southwire Company.

72. Sylvia Browne with Lindsay Harrison, *The Truth About Psychics: What's Real, What's Not and How to Tell the Difference*, Simon & Schuster, 2009, 131.

73. J.C. Maby and T.B. Franklin, *The Physics of the Divining Rod* (G. Bell and Sons, 1939); Evelyn M. Penrose, Chapter 3 in *Henry Gross and His Dowsing Rod*, Kenneth Roberts (Doubleday, 1951).

74. William Highcock, "Dowsing, An Applied Science? Two Experiments with the Dowsing Phenomenon," *Journal of the Merseyside Archaeological Society* vol. 10 (2000), 45, https://www.merseysidearchsoc.com/uploads/2/7/2/9/2729758/jmas_10_paper_4.pdf.

75. V.C. Reddish, *The Field of Rotating Masses* (Makkar, 2010), 21.

76. Henry Gee, "Cosmic Rays and Computers," *Nature* (30 July 1998), https://doi.org/10.1038/news980730-7.

Chapter 4

77. Letter from Dan Comstock to Kenneth Roberts, September 29, 1948, in Kenneth Roberts, *Henry Gross and His Dowsing Rod* (Doubleday, 1951).

78. William E. Whittaker, Ph.D., "Grave Dowsing Reconsidered," RPA Office of the State Archaeologist, University of Iowa, https://www.google.com/url?sa=t&rct=j&q=&esrc=s&source=web&cd=&ved=2ahUKEwjpsZfPhs7qAhVooHIEHSVkDqwQFjAOegQIBRAB&url=https%3A%2F%2Farchaeology.uiowa.edu%2Ffile%2F726%2Fdownload%3Ftoken%3DDqQdlDVi&usg=AOvVaw02IYTG_wN8b7KUqr-RocAM, accessed July 14, 2020.

79. Brendan McWilliams, "Scientific Theories To Explain Dowser's Art: Our Modern World Is Obsessed With Acronyms," *Irish Times*, February 16, 2000, https://www.irishtimes.com/news/scientific-theories-to-explain-dowser-s-art-1.245860; Keiron Allen, "Is There Any Scientific Evidence For Dowsing?" *BBC Science Focus* (no date available), https://www.sciencefocus.com/science/is-there-any-scientific-evidence-for-dowsing/; "Does divining actually work?" *UK Groundwater Forum* (no date available), http://www.groundwateruk.org/does_divining_work.aspx.

80. M.A. Wadsworth, "Mechanical Theory of the Divining Rod," *Nature* vol. 57, no. 1471 (January 6, 1898), 221.

81. "Professor Faraday on Table Turning, Letter from Michael Faraday to a contemporary," *The Courier* (10 October 1853), 3, https://trove.nla.gov.au/newspaper/article/2241156.

82. Michael Brooks, "Why Dowsing Makes Perfect Sense," *New Scientist*, July 29, 2009, https://www.newscientist.com/article/dn17532-why-dowsing-makes-perfect-sense/#ixzz6P0oeeLnK, accessed December 15, 2022; John Jackson, "The Ideomotor Effect, A Natural Explanation For Many Paranormal Experiences," *Critical Thinking* (2005), https://www.cbsd.org/site/handlers/filedownload.ashx?moduleinstanceid=80555&dataid=143557&FileName=Ideometer%20Effect_Magic%20Beads%20Follow%20up.pdf, accessed September 26, 2020.

83. Tom Stafford, "How The Ouija Board Really Moves," *BBC Future*, July 29, 2013, https://www.bbc.com/future/article/20130729-what-makes-the-ouija-board-move, accessed September 7, 2020.

84. Jason Blevins, "Divining Intervention: The Growing Popularity Of Dowsing," *Denver Post*, June 5, 2009, https://www.denverpost.com/2009/06/05/divining-intervention-the-growing-popularity-of-dowsing/.

85. James Randi, "Australian Skeptics Divining Test," https://www.skeptics.com.au/resources/articles/australian-skeptics-divining-test/, accessed August 22, 2020.

86. James Randi, "Australian Skeptics Divining Test," https://www.skeptics.com.au/resources/articles/australian-skeptics-divining-test/, accessed August 22, 2020.

87. William E. Whittaker, "Grave Dowsing Reconsidered," Office of the State Archaeologist, University of Iowa, https://www.yumpu.com/en/document/view/26192857/grave-dowsing-reconsidered-university-of-iowa, accessed December 16, 2022.

88. Jason Blevins, "Divining Intervention: The Growing Popularity of Dowsing," *Denver Post*, June 5, 2009, https://www.denverpost.com/2009/06/05/divining-intervention-the-growing-popularity-of-dowsing/.

89. Jason Blevins, "Divining Intervention: The Growing Popularity of Dowsing," *Denver Post*, June 5, 2009, https://www.denverpost.com/2009/06/05/divining-intervention-the-growing-popularity-of-dowsing/.

90. Richard Webster, *Dowsing for Beginners, the Art of Discovering: Water, Treasure, Gold, Oil, Artifacts* (Castle Books, 2001).

91. Guy Underwood, *The Pattern of the Past* (Abacus/Sphere Books, 1971); Dennis Wheatley, *The Essential Dowsing Guide* 3rd ed. (Ozark Mountain, 2012), 69.

92. Thomas Fiddick, *Dowsing with an Account of Some Original Experiments*, ed. Chris Bond (Cornovia Press, 2011), first published by the Cambourne Printing and Stationery Company, 1913.

93. Dennis Wheatley, *The Essential Dowsing Guide* 3rd ed. (Ozark Mountain, 2012), 11.

94. Kenneth Roberts, *Henry Gross and His Dowsing Rod* (Doubleday, 1951).

95. Richard Benishai, "Work and Protection Guidelines for Dowsers," (no date shown), https://www.geobiology.co.il/en_U.S./la-sante-du-radiesthesiste/, accessed December 16, 2022.

96. Richard Webster, *Dowsing for Beginners, the Art of Discovering: Water, Treasure, Gold, Oil, Artifacts* (Castle Books, 2001).

97. Nancy Malcom, "Dowser Can 'Witch' His Way to Unmarked Graves," *Nevada Daily Mail*, May 5, 2004, https://www.nevadadailymail.com/story/1067910.html.

98. Neal Du Shane, "Dowsing For Graves," *American Pioneer & Cemetery Research Project*, 2008, https://www.apcrp.org/DOWSING/DOWSING_TO_LOCATE_GRAVE.htm, accessed November 27, 2020.

99. Carol Brooks, "Grave Dowsing: Fact Or Fiction ... Or Just Fun?" *Yes Weekly*, updated June 9, 2021, https://www.yesweekly.com/news/jamestown_news/grave-dowsing-fact-or-fiction-or-just-fun/article_8382abee-c93a-11eb-a76e-737040d99177.html, accessed June 27, 2021.

100. Janet Reynolds, "Stamford Man Tracks Down Fossils, Time Capsules And More Through Dowsing," *CT Post*, May 16, 2021, https://www.ctpost.com/living/article/Stamford-man-tracks-down-fossils-time-capsules-16174396.php, accessed June 27, 2021.

101. Janet Reynolds, "Stamford Man Tracks Down Fossils, Time Capsules And More Through Dowsing," *CT Post*, May 16, 2021, https://www.ctpost.com/living/article/Stamford-man-tracks-down-fossils-time-capsules-16174396.php, accessed June 27, 2021.

102. Dan Schwartz, "Into The Mystical And Inexplicable World Of Dowsing," *Outside*, May 3, 2021, https://www.outsideonline.com/outdoor-adventure/exploration-survival/dowsing-water-magic-mystery/, accessed July 1, 2022.

103. Dan Schwartz, "Into the Mystical and Inexplicable World of Dowsing," *Outside*, May 3, 2021, https://www.outsideonline.com/outdoor-adventure/exploration-survival/dowsing-water-magic-mystery/, accessed July 1, 2022.

104. Michael Bass, "Professor Says It's Art of Obtaining Information: Dowser Will Find Anything, From Well Sites to President's Birthplace," *LA Times*, June 23, 1985, citing the *Associated Press*, https://www.latimes.com/archives/la-xpm-1985-06-23-mn-11883-story.html, accessed August 24, 2020.

105. Solco Walle Tromp, *Psychical Physics: A Scientific Analysis of Dowsing, Radiesthesia and Kindred Divining Phenomena* (Elsevier, 1949).

106. J.C. Maby and T.B. Franklin, *The Physics of the Divining Rod* (G. Bell and Sons, 1939).

107. Montague Keen, "Book Reviews Dowsing—An Outline Of Present Knowledge: 1994 By S. Scammell," *Journal of the Society for Psychical Research* vol. 61, no. 844 (1967), http://www.dowsing-research.net/dowsing/book_reviews/Scammell%20-%20review%20-%20Dowsing%20an%20outline%20of%20present%20knoweldge.pdf.

108. Tracy Devore, "Divining Rods In Paranormal Investigation," August 21, 2011, https://parallelrealmz.wordpress.com/2011/08/21/divining-rods-in-paranormal-investigation/, accessed November 27, 2020.

109. Maggie Percy, "How to Dowse Past Lives," https://www.discoveringdowsing.com/how-to-dowse-past-lives/, accessed November 27, 2020.

110. Charles Latimer, *The Divining Rod: Virgula Divina—Baculus Divinatorius (Water-Witching.)*, 1876, Project Gutenberg EBook #45020, February 26, 2014, https://www.gutenberg.org/files/45020/45020-h/45020-h.htm.

111. Charles Latimer, *The Divining Rod: Virgula Divina—Baculus Divinatorius (Water-Witching.)*, 1876, Project Gutenberg EBook #45020, February 26, 2014, https://www.gutenberg.org/files/45020/45020-h/45020-h.htm.

112. Thomas Saunders, *The Boiled Frog Syndrome: Your Health and the Built Environment* (Wiley, April 28, 2003).

113. Ivor Noël Hume, *Historical Archaeology: A Comprehensive Guide for Both Amateur, and Professions to the Techniques and Methods of Excavating Historical Sites* (Knopf, 1974).

114. Kathryn Eleanor Lillian Denning, "On Archaeology And Alterity," Doctor of Philosophy dissertation, Department of Archaeology and Prehistory, University of Sheffield, Submitted May 1999, https://core.ac.uk/download/pdf/42604401.pdf.

115. "The Detection Capability of the Sniffex Explosives Detector," *Naval Sea Systems Command Test Report*, 2005, https://s3.amazonaws.com/propublica/assets/docs/NavyReport.pdf.

116. Yuri Markov, "Apparatus and Method for the Detection of Materials," U.S. Patent 6344818B, February 5, 2002.

117. *Securities and Exchange Commission, Plaintiff V. Homeland Safety International, Inc. F/K/A Sniffex, Inc.; Mark B. Lindberg; Petar D. Mihaylov; Yuri P. Markov; Paul B. Johnson; Nicholas V. Klausgaard; and Ilona V. Klausgaard*, United States District for the Northern Dallas Division, Civil Action No.: 3–08CV1197-0, filed July 15, 2008, https://www.sec.gov/litigation/complaints/2008/comp20645_sniffex.pdf.

118. Johan Spanner, "Iraq Swears By Bomb Detector U.S. Sees as Useless," *The New York Times*, November 3, 2009, https://www.nytimes.com/2009/11/04/world/middleeast/04sensors.html?_r=2.

119. "GT200: The Dud Bomb Detector That Cost Thailand 1 Billion Baht—And More," *Thai PBS World*, March 17, 2023, https://www.thaipbsworld.com/gt200-the-dud-bomb-detector-that-cost-thailand-1-billion-baht-and-more/.

120. U.S. Department of Justice Office of Justice Programs, "Guide for the Selection of Commercial Explosives Detection Systems for Law Enforcement Applications, NIJ Guide 100–99," September 1999, https://www.ncjrs.gov/pdffiles1/nij/178913.pdf.

121. James Marchant, *Letter from Wallace to Prof. (later Sir) W.F. Barrett, December 24, 1900, Alfred Russel Wallace—Letters and Reminiscences, with Two Photogravures and Eight Half-tone Plates, in Two Volumes*, Volume II (Cassell and Company, 1916).

122. William Brown, "Science: The Physics Of A Dowsing Pendulum," *New Scientist* issue 1737, no. 6 (October 1990), https://www.newscientist.com/article/mg12817373-200-science-the-physics-of-a-dowsing-pendulum/, accessed August 3, 2020.

123. Venkatesh Rajender, Lavanya Kunduru, and S.C.R. Roshan, "A Review on Under Ground Water Dowsing Phenomenon," *International Journal of Emerging Trends in Science and Technology* vol. 3, issue 5 (May 2016), 3978–3981, https://www.google.com/url?sa=t&rct=j&q=&esrc=s&source=web&cd=&ved=2ahUKEwifq_iX2PPqAhUDhHIEHRvJDWoQFjAdegQICBAB&url=http%3A%2F%2Figmpublication.org%2Fijetst.in%2Findex.php%2Fijetst%2Farticle%2Fdownload%2F1077%2F881%2F&usg=AOvVaw14MXpYfqZyvJ6biKvq8ZqX.

124. William Highcock, "Dowsing, An Applied Science? Two Experiments With The Dowsing Phenomenon," *Journal of the Merseyside Archaeological Society* vol. 10 (2000), 45, https://www.merseysidearchsoc.com/uploads/2/7/2/9/2729758/jmas_10_paper_4.pdf.

Chapter 5

125. "Today in Science History," citing "Pierre Curie, with the Autobiographical Notes of Marie Curie," translated by Charlotte and Vernon Kellogg, 1923, 96, https://todayinsci.com/C/Curie_Marie/CurieMarie-Quotations.htm, accessed December 16, 2022.

126. Richard Heggen, *Underground Rivers: From the River Styx to the Rio San Buenaventura with Occasional Diversions* (Red Hen Press, January 16, 2015; July 20, 2018); John Wilcox, "The Use Of Dowsing For The Location Of Caves, With Some Results From The First Royal Forest Of Dean Caving Symposium," June 1994, http://www-sop.inria.fr/agos-sophia/sis/dowsing/dowsdean.html, accessed October 3, 2020; Richard Webster, *Dowsing for Beginners, the Art of Discovering: Water, Treasure, Gold, Oil, Artifacts* (Castle Books, 2001).

127. J.C. Maby and T.B. Franklin, *The Physics of the Divining Rod* (G. Bell and Sons, 1939).

128. Thomas Fiddick, *Dowsing with an Account of Some Original Experiments*, ed. Chris Bond (Cornovia Press, 2011), first published by the Cambourne Printing and Stationery Company, 1913.

129. Robert K. Willardson, Jerry W. Moody, and Harvey L. Goering, "The Electrical Properties of Uranium Oxides," Battelle Memorial Institute, Report No. BMI-1135, September 25, 1956. Originally confidential restricted data, now unclassified, https://www.osti.gov/servlets/purl/4339970.

130. "U.S. Nuclear Regulatory Commission, Radiation Basics," https://www.nrc.gov/about-nrc/radiation/health-effects/radiation-basics.html, accessed July 29, 2021.

131. "Harvard Natural Sciences Lecture Demonstrations," Note: Half value Thickness for Gamma Rays from Cobalt-60 is 13 cm, and from Caesium-137 it is 9.5 cm. https://sciencedemonstrations.fas.harvard.edu/presentations/%CE%B1-%CE%B2-%CE%B3-penetration-and-shielding, accessed December 28, 2020.

132. Richard Heggen, *Underground Rivers: From the River Styx to the Rio San Buenaventura with Occasional Diversions* (Red Hen Press, January 16, 2015).

133. J.C. Maby and T.B. Franklin, *The Physics of the Divining Rod* (G. Bell and Sons, 1939).

134. Phillip Hodgetts, *The Theory of Material Mind* (Xlibris, 2017), Sec. 12, Chapter 4. https://www.google.com/books/edition/The_Theory_of_Material_Mind/6WsTDgAAQBAJ?hl=en&gbpv=1&dq=%22neutrino%22+%22dowsing%22&pg=PT91&printsec=frontcover.

135. "Why And How Dowsing Works," posted July 12, 2005, *Treasure Net*, http://www.treasurenet.com/forums/dowsing/11339-why-how-dowsing-works.html, accessed November 22, 2020.

136. "Neutrino," *Wikipedia*, https://en.wikipedia.org/wiki/Neutrino, accessed March 19, 2023.

137. "All Things Neutrino, Fermi National Accelerator Laboratory," https://neutrinos.fnal.gov/sources/solar-neutrinos/, accessed September 23, 2020.

138. Gloria B. Lubkin, "Less Elusive Neutrinos To Look For Oil And Gas Deposits," *Physics Today* vol. 36, no. 8 (1983), 20, https://physicstoday.scitation.org/doi/abs/10.1063/1.2915793?journalCode=pto.

139. John Baines, "Fluid Transformation Using a Tachyon Beam," *British Patent Application*, GB2499254A, filed February 13, 2012, published August 14, 2013.

140. Gerry Wolke, "Tachyon Healing And The Physics Of Love," (1995), http://www.tachyon-aanbieding.eu/Documentation/TACHYON%20HEALING.pdf, accessed March 13, 2023.

141. John Baines, "Fluid Transformation Using

a Tachyon Beam," *British Patent Application*, GB2499254A, filed February 13, 2012, published August 14, 2013.

142. Jeff Jeffries, "The Higgs Boson: It Means More to You Than You Think!," Intelligent Energies, July 4, 2012, https://www.intelligentenergies.com/the-higgs-boson-and-healing-energies/, accessed November 23, 2020.

Chapter 6

143. John Dickinson, Richard Ellam, Manda Scott, Ann Newell, Jill Moss, Rev. Martin J. Smith, Roland Hill, and Miriam Farrell Shtaierman, "Letters: In Defence of Dowsing to Detect Water, Guardian Readers Share Their Stories on the Success of Dowsing," *Guardian*, November 27, 2017, https://www.theguardian.com/environment/2017/nov/27/in-defence-of-dowsing-to-detect-water, accessed June 10, 2020.

144. John Wilcox, "The Use Of Dowsing For The Location Of Caves, With Some Results From The First Royal Forest Of Dean Caving Symposium," June 1994, http://www-sop.inria.fr/agos-sophia/sis/dowsing/dowsdean.html, accessed October 3, 2020; Babasaheb Manik More, "An Experimental Study on Water Dowsing," *International Journal of Research and Innovations in Earth Science* vol. 1 (2014), 17–19, https://www.researchgate.net/publication/267022144_An_Experimental_Study_on_Water_Dowsing.

145. Leigh Dayton, "Incoming Australia Research Chief Touts Water Dowsing," *Science Magazine*, October 30, 2014, https://www.sciencemag.org/news/2014/10/incoming-australia-research-chief-touts-water-dowsing, accessed August 29, 2020.

146. U.S. Geological Survey, "Gravity Anomaly Map of the United States," https://mrdata.usgs.gov/gravity/map-us.html, accessed August 30, 2020.

147. Jamie Vovrosh, "Quantum Gravity Gradient Sensor Detects Outdoor Tunnel," *Laser Focus World* (May 2022), 33; B. Stray, A. Lamb, A. Kaushik, et al., "Quantum Sensing for Gravity Cartography," *Nature* vol. 602 (2022), 590–594, https://doi.org/10.1038/s41586-021-04315-3.

Chapter 7

148. V.C. Reddish, *The Field of Rotating Masses* (Makkar, 2010).

149. William Highcock, "Dowsing, An Applied Science? Two Experiments with The Dowsing Phenomenon," *Journal of the Merseyside Archaeological Society* vol. 10 (2000), 45, https://www.merseysidearchsoc.com/uploads/2/7/2/9/2729758/jmas_10_paper_4.pdf.

150. Charles Latimer, *The Divining Rod: Virgula Divina—Baculus Divinatorius (Water-Witching.)*, 1876, Project Gutenberg EBook #45020, February 26, 2014, https://www.gutenberg.org/files/45020/45020-h/45020-h.htm.

151. Anne Miller, "Dowsing: A Review," *The Scientific and Medical Network*, https://explore.scimednet.org/index.php/dowsing-a-review/, accessed October 6, 2020.

152. J.C. Maby and T.B. Franklin, *The Physics of the Divining Rod* (G. Bell and Sons, 1939).

153. Henry Gee, "Cosmic Rays and Computers," *Nature* published online (30 July 1998), doi:10.1038/news980730-7, available at https://www.nature.com/news/1998/980730/full/news980730-7.html.

154. M.G. Hogg, I.V. Timoshkin, S.J. MacGregor, M.P. Wilson, M.J. Given, and T. Wang, "Electrical Breakdown of Short Non-Uniform Air Gaps," *Digest of Technical Papers-IEEE International Pulsed Power Conference.* IEEE, GBR (2013), https://doi.org/10.1109/PPC.2013.6627482.

155. "Coherer," https://en.wikipedia.org/wiki/Coherer, accessed December 16, 2022.

156. Elena Abarca, Hanan Karam, Harold F. Hemond, and Charles F. Harvey, "Transient Groundwater Dynamics in a Coastal Aquifer: The Effects of Tides, The Lunar Cycle, and The Beach Profile," *Water Resources Research* vol. 49 (2013), 2473–2488, doi:10.1002/wrcr.20075, https://web.mit.edu/hemond/www/docs/transient_ground.pdf; Randall Cerveny, Bohumil M. Svoma, and Russell S. Vose, "Lunar Tidal Influence on Inland River Streamflow Across The Conterminous United States," *Geophysical Research Letters* vol. 37, issue 22 (November 2010), https://agupubs.onlinelibrary.wiley.com/doi/abs/10.1029/2010GL045564; Chelladurai Singaraja, Chidambaram Sabarathinam, and Jacob Noble. "A Study on the Influence of Tides on the Water Table Conditions of the Shallow Coastal Aquifers," *Appl Water Sci.* vol. 8 (2018), 11, https://doi.org/10.1007/s13201-018-0654-5.

157. Kristen Minogue, "Folklore Confirmed: The Moon's Phase Affects Rainfall," *Science*, October 6, 2010, https://www.sciencemag.org/news/2010/10/folklore-confirmed-moons-phase-affects-rainfall.

158. L.J. Turk, "Diurnal Fluctuations of Water Tables Induced by Atmospheric Pressure Changes," *Journal of Hydrology* vol. 26, issues 1–2 (1975), 1–16, https://doi.org/10.1016/0022-1694(75)90121-3; Zoltán Gribovszkia, József Szilágyib, and Péter Kalicz, "Diurnal Fluctuations in Shallow Groundwater Levels and Stream Flow Rates and Their Interpretation—A Review," *Journal of Hydrology* vol. 385 (2010), 371–383, http://snr.unl.edu/szilagyi/jh10.pdf.

Chapter 8

159. "Edward Mills Purcell," https://en.wikiquote.org/wiki/Edward_Mills_Purcell, accessed January 22, 2023.

160. T. Clynes, "Where Nobel Winners Get

Their Start," *Nature* 538 (2106), 152, https://doi.org/10.1038/nature.2016.20757.

161. "Precession," https://en.wikipedia.org/wiki/Precession, accessed January 7, 2023.

162. Y. Rocard, "Actions of a Very Weak Magnetic Gradient: The Reflex of the Dowser," Chapter 2 in *Biological Effects of Magnetic Fields*, Madeleine F. Barnothy, ed. (Plenum Press, 1964).

163. T. Parker, E. Limer, A.D. Watson, M. Defernez, D. Williamson, and E.K. Kemsley, "60 MHz 1H NMR Spectroscopy For The Analysis Of Edible Oils," *Trends Analyst Chem* 57, no. 100 (2014 May), 147–158, doi: 10.1016/j.trac.2014.02.006. PMID: 24850979; PMCID: PMC4024201.

164. "Dowsing with Magnetic Resonance," *Phys. Rev. Focus*, vol. 3, no. 27, (May 17, 1999), https://physics.aps.org/story/v3/st27, accessed July 19, 2020.

165. "New IP System," *Iris Instruments*, http://www.iris-instruments.com/numis-poly.html, accessed July 19, 2020.

Chapter 9

166. "Mysterious Quotes," *Goodreads*, https://www.goodreads.com/quotes/tag/mysterious, accessed August 2, 2021.

167. Tom Williamson, "Dowsing for Opals," *Canadian Society of Dowsers*, https://canadiandowsers.org/dowsing-for-opals/, accessed August 17, 2022.

168. Dean A. Keiswetter and Don W. Steeples, "A Field Investigation Of Source Parameters for the Sledgehammer," *Geophysics* vol. 60 (1995), 1051–1057, https://doi.org/10.1190/1.1443833.

169. Tom Williamson, "Dowsing for Opals," *Canadian Society of Dowsers*, https://canadiandowsers.org/dowsing-for-opals/, accessed August 17, 2022.

170. J.S. Lamancusa, "Noise Control, Noise Control Outdoor Sound Propagation 10.1," Penn State (July 20, 2009), Chapter 10, "Outdoor Sound Propagation," https://www.mne.psu.edu/lamancusa/me458/10_osp.pdf, accessed September 9, 2020.

171. Tom Williamson, "Dowsing for Opals," *Scientist*, vol. 81 (1979), 371–373.

172. Nicholas St. Fleur, "An Elephant's Silent Call," *Science* (August 2, 2012), doi: 10.1126/article.25790.

173. "Infrasound Toxicological Summary" (November 2001), https://ntp.niehs.nih.gov/ntp/htdocs/chem_background/exsumpdf/infrasound_508.pdf, accessed December 16, 2022.

174. "Properties of Seismic Waves," https://www.britannica.com/science/earthquake-geology/Properties-of-seismic-waves, accessed September 9, 2020.

175. "Seismic Noise," https://en.wikipedia.org/wiki/Seismic_noise, accessed December 16, 2022.

Chapter 10

176. "Today In Science History," https://todayinsci.com/QuotationsCategories/M_Cat/Mysterious-Quotations.htm, accessed August 1, 2021.

177. Allen Crabtree, "Maine Farmhouse Journal," July 10, 2002, citing American Society of Dowsers, https://www.crabcoll.com/journal/dowser.html, accessed December 30, 2020.

178. Ken Tylosky, "Finally New Scientific Evidence Behind Dowsing," http://www.waterdowsingindia.in/scientific_evidence.PDF, accessed December 31, 2022.

179. Paul Manger, Mike Calford, and Jack Pettigrew, "Properties Of Electrosensory Neurons In The Cortex Of The Platypus (Ornithorhynchus Anatinus): Implications For Processing Of Electrosensory Stimuli," *Proceedings of the Royal Society B: Biological Sciences* 263 (1996), 611–617.

180. "Electroreception and Electrogenesis," https://en.wikipedia.org/wiki/Electroreception, accessed December 31, 2022.

181. John Greenwood, "Locating Underground Features By Dowsing," *New Civil Engineer*, January 1, 2001, https://www.newcivilengineer.com/archive/locating-underground-features-by-dowsing-01-01-2001/, accessed October 3, 2020.

182. Brendan McWilliams, "Scientific Theories to Explain Dowser's Art," *Irish Times*, February 16, 2000, https://www.irishtimes.com/news/scientific-theories-to-explain-dowser-s-art-1.245860.

183. "Static Electricity Buildup in Plastic Pipe," OSHA Hazard Information Bulletins (September 30, 1988), https://www.osha.gov/dts/hib/hib_data/hib19880930.html, accessed August 28, 2020.

184. TheGoodVibrations, "The Physics Behind Water Witching," https://www.youtube.com/watch?v=xqWQBxhjcrs, accessed July 19, 2020.

185. Bo Nordell, "The Dowsing Reaction Originates From Piezoelectric Effect In Bone," Presented at the *6th International Svedala Symposium on Ecological Design*, May 19–21, 1988, Svedala, Sweden, https://www.ltu.se/cms_fs/1.5014!/dowsing.pdf.

186. Rene Ebersole, "He Teaches Police "Witching" To Find Corpses. Experts Are Alarmed," The Marshall Project, March 17, 2022, https://www.themarshallproject.org/2022/03/17/witching-dowsing-buried-bodies-police, accessed July 1, 2022.

187. M. Ikeya, "Earthquakes and Animals: From Folk Legends to Science," *World Scientific* (2004), 75.

188. "USGS—What are Earthquake Lights?" https://www.usgs.gov/faqs/what-are-earthquake-lights?qt-news_science_products=0#qt-news_science_products, accessed July 12, 2020.

189. Eiichi Fukada and Iwao Yasuda, "On the Piezoelectric Effect of Bone," *Journal of the Physical Society of Japan* 12 (1957), 1158–1162.

190. Bo Nordell, "The Dowsing Reaction Originates From Piezoelectric Effect In Bone," Presented at the *6th International Svedala Symposium*

on *Ecological Design*, May 19–21, 1988, Svedala, Sweden, https://www.ltu.se/cms_fs/1.5014!/dowsing.pdf.

191. Abhishek Kumar Mishra, Anurag Kumar, and Vikas Mishra, "The Variation of Atmospheric Electrical Conductivity as the Function of Altitude," *International Journal of Innovative Technology and Exploring Engineering* vol. 10, issue 2 (December 2020), 162, https://www.ijitee.org/wp-content/uploads/papers/v10i2/B83091210220.pdf.

192. K. Charan Kumar and Kamsali Nagaraja, "Electrical Conductivity of the Atmosphere over an Urban Location," *Atmospheric and Oceanic Optics* vol. 34, issue 6 (November 2021), 704–713, DOI: 10.1134/S1024856021060063.

193. Prasad Nagaraja Kamsali and Jayati Datta, "The Electrical Conductivity as an Index of Air Pollution in the Atmosphere," *Advanced Air Pollution* (August 17, 2011), DOI: 10.5772/17163, https://www.intechopen.com/chapters/17391.

194. B. Hariharan, A. Chandra, S.R. Dugad, S.K. Gupta, P. Jagadeesan, A. Jain, P.K. Mohanty, S.D. Morris, P.K. Nayak, P.S. Rakshe, K. Ramesh, B.S. Rao, L.V. Reddy, M. Zuberi, Y. Hayashi, S. Kawakami, S. Ahmad, H. Kojima, A. Oshima, S. Shibata, Y. Muraki, and K. Tanaka, "Measurement of the Electrical Properties of a Thundercloud Through Muon Imaging by the GRAPES-3 Experiment," *Phys. Rev. Lett.* 15, no. 122 (March 2019), 105101, DOI: https://doi.org/10.1103/PhysRevLett.122.105101.

195. Michael A. Gottlieb and Rudolf Pfeiffer, "Electricity in the Atmosphere," California Institute of Technology, https://www.feynmanlectures.caltech.edu/II_09.html, accessed February 15, 2021.

196. Anthony Hopwood, "Dowsing, Ley Lines and the Electromagnetic Link," *New Scientist* (20/27 December 1979), 948, available at https://books.google.com/books?id=3P5-7ZAAXsYC&pg=PA948&lpg=PA948&dq=%22anthony+hopwood%22+%22dowsing%22+%22new+scientist%22+948&source=bl&ots=o9PiLLKpPo&sig=ACfU3U1SQ-eHlyeSzjmZKb9fsrMWAmmvZTQ&hl=en&sa=X&ved=2ahUKEwif_aKn_OruAhWTFlkFHdYZAdkQ6AEwAXoECAMQAg#v=onepage&q=%22anthony%20hopwood%22%20%22dowsing%22%20%22new%20scientist%22%20948&f=false.

Chapter 11

197. "Quotes," YourDictionary, https://quotes.yourdictionary.com/ley, accessed August 5, 2021.

198. K. Vozoff, R.M. Ellis, M.D. Burke; "Telluric Currents and Their Use in Petroleum Exploration," *AAPG Bulletin* 48, no. 12 (1964), 1890–1901, doi: https://doi.org/10.1306/A66334D4-16C0-11D7-8645000102C1865D; Stephen Park, "Magnetotelluric Method," Presentation at University of California Riverside, http://web.gps.caltech.edu/classes/ge111/Docs/MT1_mtmeth.pdf, accessed September 27, 2020.

199. John S. Janks, "Dowsing Rods: Empirical Evidence and Applications for Charting the Subsurface," *Borderland Experimenter*, 2010, https://borderlandsciences.org/journal/vol/ie/Janks_Empirical_Evidence_for_Dowsing.html, accessed September 7, 2020.

200. J.S. Janks, "Utility and limits of dowsing rods to chart the subsurface," *Frontier Perspectives*, March 22, 2006, https://www.thefreelibrary.com/Utility+and+limits+of+dowsing+rods+to+chart+the+subsurface.-a0156136179.

201. A.A.R. Zohdy, "Electrical Methods," in *Techniques of Water-Resources, Investigations of the United States Geological Survey*, A.A.R. Zohdy, G.P. Eaton, and D.R. Mabey, Chapter Dl, "Application of Surface Geophysics to Ground-Water Investigations, Book 2 Collection of Environmental Data," https://pubs.usgs.gov/twri/twri2-d1/pdf/twri_2-D1_b.pdf, accessed December 31, 2022.

202. S. Thiel, "Chapter 1: Basics of the Magnetotelluric Method, in Modelling and Inversion of Magnetotelluric Data For 2-D And 3-D Lithospheric Structure, With Application to Obducted and Subducted Terranes," Ph.D. thesis, 2008, University of Adelaide, https://digital.library.adelaide.edu.au/dspace/handle/2440/48492, accessed September 27, 2020.

203. "Magnetotellurics, Geoscience Australia, "*Australian Government*, https://www.ga.gov.au/scientific-topics/disciplines/geophysics/magnetotellurics, accessed August 24, 2020.

204. "Electrical and Electromagnetic Methods," *Encyclopedia Britannica*, https://www.britannica.com/topic/Earth-exploration/Electrical-and-EM-methods#ref520570, accessed August 24, 2020.

205. Kimihiko Okamoto and Shichio Kawai, "Electrical Conduction and Phase Transition of Copper Sulfides," *Japanese Journal of Applied Physics* vol. 12, no. 8 (1973), 1130.

206. Roger C. Wells, "Electric Activity in Ore Deposits," *Department of the Interior United States Geological Survey*, Bulletin 548 (1914), https://pubs.usgs.gov/bul/0548/report.pdf.

207. Jong Doo Lee, "Detector of Water Current," PCT Patent Application WO2009028759A1, March 5, 2009.

208. Jong Doo Lee, "Detector of Water Current," PCT Patent Application WO2009028759A1, March 5, 2009.

209. Tim Sharp, "How Big is Earth?," Space.com, July 6, 2021, https://www.space.com/17638-how-big-is-earth.html, accessed December 31, 2020.

210. Ned Herrmann, "What Is the Function of the Various Brainwaves?" *Scientific American* (December 22, 1997), https://www.scientificamerican.com/article/what-is-the-function-of-t-1997-12-22/; "The Science of Brainwaves: Definitions," NeuroHealth Associate, https://nhahealth.com/brainwaves-the-language/, accessed July 12, 2020.

211. G.P. Hansen, "Dowsing: a Review of Experimental Research," *Journal of the Society for Psychical Research* vol. 51, no. 792 (1982), 343–367.

212. Iona Miller and Richard Alan Miller, "Schumann Resonance and Human Psychobiology (extended version)" Organization for the Advancement of Knowledge, 2003, https://nutesla.com/wp-content/uploads/2010/08/SCHUMANN-RESONANCE-AND-HUMAN-PSYCHOBIOLOGY.pdf, accessed January 5, 2020; "The Schumann Effect Part 1- How the Earth Influences Your Brain Waves," https://subtle.energy/the-schumann-effect-how-the-earth-influences-your-brain/, accessed January 5, 2021.

213. "Schumann Resonance, Glossary of Dowsing Terms S-Z," British Dowsing, https://britishdowsing.net/glossary-of-dowsing-terms-s-z/, accessed January 5, 2021.

214. Mark Krinker and Larry Pismenny, "What Stands Beyond Dowsing And Feng Shui?" ECO Dowsing LLC., 2006

215. Alexander P. Dubrov, "Modern Achievements of Dowsing, Brief review of scientific research, 1990–2000," for the Canadian Society of Dowsers https://canadiandowsers.org/modern-achievements-of-dowsing/, accessed July 18, 2020, citing: Yu.P. Kravchenko, "Indicator of Geophysical Anomalies," USSR author's certificate 1828268 (13/10/92), Patent of the Russian Federation 2119680 (27 Sept 1998), Method of geoEM reconnaissance and the device for its application (Russian); A.P. Dubrov, "The Ecology of the Human Dwelling and the Health Of Man," (Slovo [Russian], 1995); A.P. Dubrov, E.N. Akhmadeyeva, et al. "Geophysical Anomalies as an Ecological Factor In Traditional Medicine. Proceedings of the Congress "Traditional Medicine 2000." Research cum Practical Center of Traditional Medicine and Homeopathy (Ministry of Health of the Russian Federation. M. 498–502 [Russian] 2000).

Chapter 12

216. Thomas Welton, trans., *Jacob's Rod*, Translation from the French of *A Rare and Curious Work, A.D. 1693, On the Art of Finding Springs, Mines, and Minerals by Means of the Hazel Rod. To Which Is Appended Researches, with Proofs of the Existence of a More Certain and Far Higher Faculty, with Clear and Ample Instructions for Using It*.

217. J.C. Maby and T.B. Franklin, *The Physics of the Divining Rod* (G. Bell and Sons, 1939).

218. "Shortwave Radio," *Encyclopedia Britannica*, https://www.britannica.com/technology/shortwave-radio, accessed April 6, 2023.

219. Roger Jennison, "A Physicist Goes Dowsing Down Under," *Physics World* vol. 8, no. 6 (1995), https://iopscience.iop.org/article/10.1088/2058-7058/8/6/15; V.C Reddish, "The Field of Rotating Bodies," (Markar, 2010).

220. Alex Wilkins, "Strange Gamma Ray Flashes From Lightning Storms May Have Explanation," *New Scientist*, May 26, 2022, https://www.newscientist.com/article/2322043-strange-gamma-ray-flashes-from-lightning-storms-may-have-explanation/, accessed January 10, 2023.

221. Evelyn M. Penrose, Chapter 3 in *Henry Gross and His Dowsing Rod*, Kenneth Roberts (Doubleday, 1951).

222. Thomas Saunders, *The Boiled Frog Syndrome: Your Health and the Built Environment* (Wiley, 2003).

223. "Human Performance Laboratory," University of Calgary, Annual Report 1998, https://prism.ucalgary.ca/bitstream/handle/1880/110390/1998_w.pdf?sequence=1&isAllowed=y.

224. "Water Dowsing," *U.S. Department of the Interior/Geological Survey* (U.S. Government Printing Office, 1988), 218–668, https://pubs.usgs.gov/gip/water_dowsing/pdf/water_dowsing.pdf, accessed June 10, 2020.

225. "Science: Why Dowsing Works," *Time Magazine*, July 16, 1951.

226. Solco Walle Tromp, *Psychical Physics: A Scientific Analysis of Dowsing, Radiesthesia and Kindred Divining Phenomena* (Elsevier, 1949), 329.

227. Friedrich H. Balck, "Radiesthesia and Science, or Experiments to Determine the Orientational Ability of Lifeforms—Motivation for the Necessary Paradigm Change in the World View of Physics," Institut für Energieforschung, October 4, 2010, https://www.yumpu.com/en/document/read/10482512/prof-dr-friedrich-h-balck-wwwpetu-institut-fur-energieforschung-, accessed July 11, 2020.

228. F. Gray and J. Cruickshank, "Diamagnetism of Light and Heavy Water," *Nature* 135 (1935), 268–269.

229. Thomas Saunders, *The Boiled Frog Syndrome: Your Health and the Built Environment* (Wiley, 2003).

230. "Very Low Frequency (VLF)," https://fas.org/nuke/guide/usa/c3i/vlf.htm, last updated April 29, 1998, accessed February 2, 2021.

231. "Does Divining Actually Work?" *UK Groundwater Forum*, http://www.groundwateruk.org/does_divining_work.aspx, accessed December 31, 2022.

232. "Working With EMF/Microwaves," *University of Leeds*, https://wsh.leeds.ac.uk/emfrfmicrowaves/doc/working-emfmicrowaves, accessed August 7, 2021.

233. "Water Witching (Dowsing) Works!," http://sepwww.stanford.edu/data/media/public/sep/jon/dowsing.html, accessed July 19, 2020.

234. Paavo Huttunen, Ahti Niinimaa, Risto Myllylä, "Dowsing Can Be Interfered With By Radio Frequency Radiation," *Pathophysiology* vol. 19, issue 2 (April 2012), 89–94, https://www.sciencedirect.com/science/article/abs/pii/S0928468012000399.

235. Michael Fercik, *The Art of Dowsing, Separating Science from Superstition* (Page Publishing, 2020).

236. D. Kosarov, "The Reaction Time of Single Motor Units in the Human Muscle." *Agressologie* 20, no. 5 (1979), 279–85. PMID: 12679959; Erich

Luschei, Carol Saslow, and Mitchell Glickstein, "Muscle Potentials In Reaction Time," *Experimental Neurology* vol. 18, issue 4 (August 1967), 429–442, https://doi.org/10.1016/0014-4886(67)90060-X.

237. John S. Janks, "Voltage Changes in Hand-Held Dipoles ('Dowsing Rods') Resulting from Variable Electromagnetic Radiation," *Borderland Experimenter* (2012), available at https://borderlandsciences.org/journal/vol/ie/Janks_on_Dowsing_Rods_Voltage.html, accessed September 7, 2020.

238. The Hollies, "Introduction to the Art of Dowsing," May 13, 2019, https://www.thehollies.ie/2019/05/13/introduction-to-the-art-of-dowsing-2/, accessed November 7, 2020; Hartmut Lüdeling, *Handbuch Der H3-Antenne*, http://www.h3-shop.ch/docs/handbuch/handbu_en.pdf, accessed November 8, 2020.

239. Solco Walle Tromp, *Psychical Physics: A Scientific Analysis of Dowsing, Radiesthesia and Kindred Divining Phenomena* (Elsevier, 1949), 327.

240. Dudley H. Wheeler, "Mid-Atlantic Geomancy, Dowsing: A Technique," http://geomancy.org/index.php?option=com_content&view=article&id=201:dowsing-a-technique&catid=67:no-10-summer-solstice&Itemid=664, accessed July 18, 2020.

241. Dudley H. Wheeler, "Mid-Atlantic Geomancy, Dowsing: A Technique," http://geomancy.org/index.php?option=com_content&view=article&id=201:dowsing-a-technique&catid=67:no-10-summer-solstice&Itemid=664, accessed July 18, 2020.

242. Charles Latimer, *The Divining Rod: Virgula Divina—Baculus Divinatorius (Water-Witching.)*, 1876, Project Gutenberg EBook #45020, February 26, 2014, https://www.gutenberg.org/files/45020/45020-h/45020-h.htm.

243. David Robson, "The Mysterious Way Your Body Changes With The Weather," *BBC* (16 July 2015), https://www.bbc.com/future/article/20150716-the-mysterious-ways-the-weather-changes-the-body-and-mind, accessed August 7, 2021.

244. J.C. Maby and T.B. Franklin, *The Physics of the Divining Rod* (G. Bell and Sons, 1939).

245. Evelyn M. Penrose, Chapter 3 in *Henry Gross and His Dowsing Rod*, Kenneth Roberts (Doubleday, 1951).

246. Evelyn M. Penrose, Chapter 3 in *Henry Gross and His Dowsing Rod*, Kenneth Roberts (Doubleday, 1951).

247. Evelyn Penrose (Author), William Boissevain (Illustrator), "Adventure Unlimited: A Diviner Travels the World," (Neville Spearman, London, January 1, 1958).

248. Solco Walle Tromp, *Psychical Physics: A Scientific Analysis of Dowsing, Radiesthesia and Kindred Divining Phenomena* (Elsevier, 1949).

249. Y. Rocard, "Actions of a Very Weak Magnetic Gradient: The Reflex of the Dowser," Chapter 2 in *Biological Effects of Magnetic Fields*, Madeleine F. Barnothy, ed. (Plenum Press, 1964).

250. "Does Blood Conduct Electricity," Techie Scientist, https://techiescientist.com/does-blood-conduct-electricity/, accessed September 23, 2021.

251. G.P. Hansen, "Dowsing: A Review of Experimental Research," *Journal of the Society for Psychical Research* vol. 51, no. 792 (1982), 343–367.

252. Solco Walle Tromp, *Psychical Physics: A Scientific Analysis of Dowsing, Radiesthesia and Kindred Divining Phenomena* (Elsevier, 1949).

253. Solco Walle Tromp, *Psychical Physics: A Scientific Analysis of Dowsing, Radiesthesia and Kindred Divining Phenomena* (Elsevier, 1949).

254. Solco Walle Tromp, *Psychical Physics: A Scientific Analysis of Dowsing, Radiesthesia and Kindred Divining Phenomena* (Elsevier, 1949).

255. Solco Walle Tromp, *Psychical Physics: A Scientific Analysis of Dowsing, Radiesthesia and Kindred Divining Phenomena* (Elsevier, 1949).

256. Charles Latimer, *The Divining Rod: Virgula Divina—Baculus Divinatorius (Water-Witching.)*, 1876, Project Gutenberg EBook #45020, February 26, 2014, https://www.gutenberg.org/files/45020/45020-h/45020-h.htm.

257. "Material Matters: EVA foam," https://www.sneakerfreaker.com/features/material-matters/material-matters-eva-foam?page=0, accessed October 3, 2020.

258. Solco Walle Tromp, *Psychical Physics: A Scientific Analysis of Dowsing, Radiesthesia and Kindred Divining Phenomena* (Elsevier, 1949).

Chapter 13

259. "Senses Quote," Brainy Quote, https://www.brainyquote.com/quotes/frank_herbert_402112?src=t_senses, accessed January 14, 2023.

260. K.S. Chae, S.C. Kim, H.J. Kwon, et al., "Human Magnetic Sense Is Mediated by a Light and Magnetic Field Resonance-Dependent Mechanism," *Sci Rep* 12, 8997 (2022), https://doi.org/10.1038/s41598-022-12460-6; Connie X. Wang, Isaac A. Hilburn, Daw-An Wu, Yuki Mizuhara, Christopher P. Cousté, Jacob N.H. Abrahams, Sam E. Bernstein, Ayumu Matani, Shinsuke Shimojo, and Joseph L. Kirschvink, "Transduction Of The Geomagnetic Field As Evidenced From Alpha-Band Activity In The Human Brain," *eNeuro* vol. 6, no. 2 (March 18, 2019), https://doi.org/10.1523/ENEURO.0483-18.2019.

261. "TRPM8 Transient Receptor Potential Cation Channel Subfamily M Member 8 [Homo Sapiens (Human)] Gene ID: 79054," *National Library of Medicine*, updated on October 26, 2022, https://www.ncbi.nlm.nih.gov/gene/79054, accessed November 6, 2022.

262. "TRPV1 Transient Receptor Potential Cation Channel Subfamily V Member 1 [Homo Sapiens (Human)] Gene ID: 7442," *National Library of Medicine*, updated on October 23, 2022, https://www.ncbi.nlm.nih.gov/gene/7442, accessed November 6, 2022.

263. Thomas Saunders, *The Boiled Frog Syndrome: Your Health and the Built Environment* (Wiley, April 28, 2003).

264. "An Elephant Never Forgets The Way To The Watering Hole," Phys Org., https://phys.org/news/2015-03-elephant-hole.html, accessed July 12, 2020.

265. Evelyn M. Penrose, Ch. 3 in *Henry Gross and His Dowsing Rod*, Kenneth Roberts (Doubleday, 1951); Geer Haseman, "The Secret Lives Of Well-Digging Burros," Horsetalk.co.nz, June 5, 2016, https://www.horsetalk.co.nz/2016/06/05/-secret-lives-well-digging-burros/, accessed December 8, 2020.

266. "Why Do Animals Dig Waterholes?" *Science Daily*, November 4, 2015, citing Forschungsverbund Berlin e.V. (FVB), https://www.sciencedaily.com/releases/2015/11/151104125326.htm, accessed December 8, 2020.

267. J.B. Rhine, "Location of Hidden Objects By A Man-Dog Team," *Journal of Parapsychology* 35, no. 1 (1971), 18–33.

268. Solco Walle Tromp, *Psychical Physics: A Scientific Analysis of Dowsing, Radiesthesia and Kindred Divining Phenomena* (Elsevier, 1949), 301.

269. Jeffrey Keen, "The Physics of Dowsing and the Brain," British Dowsing, https://britishdowsing.net/the-physics-of-dowsing-and-the-brain/, accessed February 2, 2021.

270. Shelley Higgins, "The Effect of Magnetically Shielding A Dowser," *The Rose+Croix Journal* vol. 4, no. 45 (2007), https://citeseerx.ist.psu.edu/viewdoc/download?doi=10.1.1.496.2301&rep=rep1&type=pdf, accessed July 19, 2020.

271. Roger Jennison, "A Physicist Goes Dowsing Down Under," *Physics World* vol. 8, no. 6 (1995), https://iopscience.iop.org/article/10.1088/2058-7058/8/6/15.

272. Jeffrey Keen, "The Physics of Dowsing and the Brain," British Dowsing , 2001, https://britishdowsing.net/the-physics-of-dowsing-and-the-brain/, accessed December 7, 2020.

273. Anne Miller, "Dowsing: A Review," *The Scientific and Medical Network*, https://explore.scimednet.org/index.php/dowsing-a-review/, accessed October 6, 2020.

274. L.Q. Wu and J.D. Dickman, "Neural Correlates of a Magnetic Sense," *Science* 336, 6084 (May 25, 2012), 1054–7, doi: 10.1126/science.1216567.

275. "The Water in You: Water and the Human Body," Water Science School, May 22, 2019, https://www.usgs.gov/special-topic/water-science-school/science/water-you-water-and-human-body?qt-science_center_objects=0#qt-science_center_objects, accessed May 28, 2023.

276. Doug Proctor, "Dowsing and Divining the Direction of Debate," Tallbloke's Talkshop, September 4, 2013, https://tallbloke.wordpress.com/2013/09/04/doug-proctor-dowsing-and-divining-the-direction-of-debate/, accessed September 26, 2021.

277. Dudley Brown, "Experts Say Posture Matters: The Good … And The Bad," May 11, 2010, https://www.goupstate.com/story/news/2010/05/11/experts-say-posture-matters-the-good-and-the-bad/29824558007/, accessed July 22, 2020.

Chapter 14

278. Pliny, "The Magnet," Natural History XXXVI, *A Source Book in Greek Science*, Translation by Morris R. Cohen and I.E. Drabkin (Harvard University Press, 1945).

279. Thomas Saunders, *The Boiled Frog Syndrome: Your Health and the Built Environment* (Wiley, April 28, 2003).

280. Tom Williamson, "Dowsing Explained," *Nature*, April 17, vol. 320 (1986), 569.

281. Brendan McWilliams, "Scientific Theories to Explain Dowser's Art," *Irish Times*, February 16, 2000, https://www.irishtimes.com/news/scientific-theories-to-explain-dowser-s-art-1.245860.

282. Z.V. Harvalik, "Anatomical Localization of Human Detection of Weak Radiation: Experiments with Dowsers," *Physiological Chemistry and Physics* vol. 10, no. 6 (1978), 525, http://dowsing-research.net/dowsing/articles/Harvalik%20-%202%20articles%20-%20Anatomical%20localization%20of%20human%20detection%20of%20weak%20em%20radiation%20-%20and%20-%20A%20biophysical%20magnetometer-gradiometer.PDF.

283. Z.V. Harvalik, "A Biophysical Magnetometer Gradiometer," *Virginia Journal of Science* vol. 21. no. 2 (1970), 59, http://dowsing-research.net/dowsing/articles/Harvalik%20-%202%20articles%20-%20Anatomical%20localization%20of%20human%20detection%20of%20weak%20em%20radiation%20-%20and%20-%20A%20biophysical%20magnetometer-gradiometer.PDF.

284. The magnetometer is part of the Physics Toolbox Apps from *Vieyra Software* (the Apple Store) July 2020.

285. "A Cautionary Note on Magnetoreception in Dowsers," in *Magnetite Biomineralization and Magnetoreception in Organisms* Topics in Geobiology vol. 5, J.L. Kirschvink, D.S. Jones, and B.J. MacFadden (eds), (Springer, 1985), https://doi.org/10.1007/978-1-4613-0313-8_33.

286. R.A. Foulkes, "Dowsing Experiments," *Nature* 229 (1971), 163–168.

287. Solco Walle Tromp, *Psychical Physics: A Scientific Analysis of Dowsing, Radiesthesia and Kindred Divining Phenomena* (Elsevier, 1949), 311.

288. G.P. Hansen, "Dowsing: A Review of Experimental Research," *Journal of the Society for Psychical Research* vol. 51, no. 792 (1982), 343–367, http://www.tricksterbook.com/ArticlesOnline/Dowsing.htm, citing Tromp, 1968.

289. "ICNIRP Guidelines For Limiting Exposure To Electric Fields Induced By Movement of The Human Body In A Static Magnetic Field And By Time-Varying Magnetic Fields Below 1Hz," International Commission on Non-Ionizing

Radiation Protection, 2014, Available from https://www.icnirp.org/cms/upload/publications/ICNIRPmvtgdl_2014.pdf

290. R. Robin Baker, *Human Navigation and the Sixth Sense Hardcover* 1st ed. (Simon & Schuster, 1982).

291. G.W. Max Westby, Karen J. Partridge, "Human Homing: Still No Evidence Despite Geomagnetic Controls," *J. Exp. Biol.* vol. 120 (1986) 325–331.

292. "Can You Tap Into A Natural Sense Of Direction?" https://www.bbc.co.uk/programmes/articles/2QrT6nYwqhcntqQn4KGdkwk/can-you-tap-into-a-natural-sense-of-direction, accessed January 19, 2021. "A Sense of Direction," Out of the Ordinary Series 7, Episode 1 of 4, BBC Radio One aired February 24, 2020, https://www.bbc.co.uk/programmes/m000fpms.

293. Y. Rocard, "Actions of a Very Weak Magnetic Gradient: The Reflex of the Dowser," Chapter 2 in *Biological Effects of Magnetic Fields*, Madeleine F. Barnothy, ed. (Plenum Press, 1964).

294. R.A. Foulkes, "Dowsing Experiments," *Nature* 229 (1971), 163–168.

295. E. Balanovski and J.G. Taylor, "Can Electromagnetism Account for Extra-Sensory Phenomena?" *Nature* 276 (1978), 64–67.

296. J.L.Whitton and S.A. Cook, "Can Humans Detect Weak Magnetic Fields?" *New Horizons* 2, part 4, issue 9 (1978), 2–6.

297. Y. Rocard, "Actions of a Very Weak Magnetic Gradient: The Reflex of the Dowser," Chapter 2 in *Biological Effects of Magnetic Fields*, Madeleine F. Barnothy, ed. (Plenum Press, 1964).

298. Duane G. Chadwick and Larry Jensen,"The Detection of Magnetic Fields Caused by Groundwater," Reports, Paper 56, 1971, https://digitalcommons.usu.edu/water_rep/568, https://digitalcommons.usu.edu/cgi/viewcontent.cgi?article=1567&context=water_rep, accessed July 12, 2020.

299. "Permeability (electromagnetism)," https://en.wikipedia.org/wiki/Permeability_(electromagnetism), accessed January 1, 2023; Michael S. Zhdanov, *Foundations of Geophysical Electromagnetic Theory and Methods* 2nd edition (Elsevier, 2017).

300. Frederic G. Hirsch, E. Clinton Texter Jr., Lloyd A. Wood, William C. Ballard Jr., Francis E. Horan, Irving S. Wright, Constance Frey, and Dorothy Starr, "The Electrical Conductivity Of Blood: I. Relationship To Erythrocyte Concentration," *Blood* 5, no. 11 (1950), 1017–1035. https://doi.org/10.1182/blood.V5.11.1017.1017.

301. Y. Rocard, "Actions of a Very Weak Magnetic Gradient: The Reflex of the Dowser," Chapter 2 in *Biological Effects of Magnetic Fields*, Madeleine F. Barnothy, ed. (Plenum Press, 1964).

302. J.C. Maby and T.B. Franklin, *The Physics of the Divining Rod* (G. Bell and Sons, 1939).

303. "Magnetohydrodynamics," Wikipedia, https://en.wikipedia.org/wiki/Magnetohydrodynamics, accessed January 14, 2023.

304. Jan Mayman, "Water Diviners, Dowsers, May Have Special Sensitivity To Electromagnetism, When Jan Mayman Discovered She Could Divine Water, She Sought Advice From Some Old Masters," *The Sydney Morning Herald*, December 23, 2014, https://www.smh.com.au/national/water-diviners-dowsers-may-have-special-sensitivity-to-electromagnetism-20141223-12cpvm.html.

305. "Coin specifications," U.S. Mint, https://www.usmint.gov/learn/coin-and-medal-programs/coin-specifications, accessed July 11, 2020.

306. George P. Hansen, *Journal of the Society for Psychical Research* vol. 51, no. 792 (October 1982), 343–367, citing F.W. Cope, "Biological Sensitivity To Weak Magnetic Fields Due To Biological Superconductive Josephson Junctions?" *Physiological Chemistry and Physics* 5 (1973), 173–176. http://www.tricksterbook.com/ArticlesOnline/Dowsing.htm

307. "Causes and Effects of Microshocks Under Transmission Lines," *Electric Power Research Institute*, October 2013, https://www.epri.com/research/products/3002001150.

308. Yu. A. Kholodov, "Effects on the Central Nervous System," in *Biological Effects of Magnetic Fields*, Madeleine F. Barnothy, ed. (Plenum, 1964), citing N.A. Popov, *On the Physiological Action of Physical Agents*, Moscow (1940).

309. "MRI Safety Tutorial," Duke UNC Brain Imaging and Analysis Center, https://www.biac.duke.edu/research/safety/mri-safety-tutorial, accessed February 10, 2023.

310. "Safety Guidelines for Magnetic Resonance Imaging Equipment in Clinical Use, UK Medicines and Healthcare Regulatory Agency," November 2014, https://www.fdanews.com/ext/resources/files/11-14/11-14-MHRA-MRI.pdf?1503404206.

311. "Submission of Premarket Notifications for Magnetic Resonance Diagnostic Devices Guidance for Industry and Food and Drug Administration Staff," updated December 22, 2016, https://www.fda.gov/media/92921/download.

312. "MRI Safety Tutorial," Brain Imaging and Analysis Center, Duke University of North Carolina, https://www.biac.duke.edu/research/safety/tutorial.asp#USFDA-1998, accessed January 26, 2021.

313. Tamar Pashut, Shuki Wolfus, Alex Friedman, Michal Lavidor, Izhar Bar-Gad, Yosef Yeshurun, and Alon Korngreen, "Mechanisms of Magnetic Stimulation of Central Nervous System Neurons," *PLOS Computational Biology*, March 24, 2011, https://doi.org/10.1371/journal.pcbi.1002022.

314. J.C. Maby and T.B. Franklin, *The Physics of the Divining Rod* (G. Bell and Sons, 1939).

315. Solco Walle Tromp, *Psychical Physics: A Scientific Analysis of Dowsing, Radiesthesia and Kindred Divining Phenomena* (Elsevier, 1949), 135.

Chapter 15

316. "AZQuotes," https://www.azquotes.com/quote/92835?ref=electromagnetism, accessed January 21, 2023.

317. "Radiation: Electromagnetic Fields," World Health Organization, August 4, 2016, https://www.who.int/news-room/questions-and-answers/item/radiation-EM-fields, accessed January 15, 2023.

318. "Radiofrequency and Microwave Radiation," OSHA, https://www.osha.gov/radiofrequency-and-microwave-radiation, accessed January 15, 2023.

319. Z.V. Harvalik, "Dowsing Reactions to Electromagnetic Fields in the Frequency Range from 1 Hertz to 1 MegaHertz," *The American Dowser Quarterly Digest* vol. 13, no. 1 (1961), 90, http://dowsing-research.net/dowsing/articles/Harvalik%20-%20Dowsing%20reactions%20to%20EM%20fields%201Hz%20to%201MHz.pdf.

320. J.G. Taylor and E. Balanovski, "A Search for the Electromagnetic Concomitants Of ESP," *Psychoenergetic Systems* no. 3, 1979, 171–192.

321. "What Are The Cellular Frequencies Of Carriers In USA & Canada?" https://www.signalbooster.com/pages/what-are-the-cellular-frequencies-of-cell-phone-carriers-in-usa-canada, accessed October 26, 2021.

322. "iPhone 8 Plus—Technical Specifications," https://support.apple.com/kb/sp768?locale=en_U.S., accessed October 26, 2021.

323. "Potential Health Risks of Exposure to Noise From Personal Music Players and Mobile Phones Including a Music Playing Function," *Scientific Committee on Emerging and Newly Identified Health Risks, SCENIHR, European Commission*. The SCENIHR adopted this opinion at the 26th plenary on September 23, 2008, after public consultation. Available from https://ec.europa.eu/health/ph_risk/committees/04_scenihr/docs/scenihr_o_018.pdf

324. "Medical Management Guidelines for Hydrogen Sulfide," ATSDR, https://wwwn.cdc.gov/TSP/MMG/MMGDetails.aspx?mmgid=385&toxid=67, last reviewed October 21, 2014.

325. Jeffrey Keen, "The Physics of Dowsing and the Brain," British Dowsing, https://britishdowsing.net/the-physics-of-dowsing-and-the-brain/, accessed February 2, 2021; Z.V. Harvalik, "A Biophysical Magnetometer Gradiometer," *Virginia Journal of Science* vol. 21, no. 2 (1970), 59, http://dowsing-research.net/dowsing/articles/Harvalik%20-%202%20articles%20-%20Anatomical%20localization%20of%20human%20detection%20of%20weak%20em%20radiation%20-%20and%20-%20A%20biophysical%20magnetometer-gradiometer.PDF.

326. "Radio Frequency Safety," Federal Communications Commission, https://www.fcc.gov/general/radio-frequency-safety-0, accessed December 23, 2022.

Chapter 16

327. A.J. Ellison, "Reviews of J. Cecil Maby's *Physical Principles of Radiesthesia*; J. Cecil Maby, *Confessions of a Sensitive*; and J.C. Maby and T.B. Franklin, *The Physics of the Divining Rod*," http://www.dowsing-research.net/dowsing/book_reviews/Ellison%20-%20review%20-%20The%20Physics%20of%20the%20divining%20rod%20and%20Physical%20Principles%20of%20Radiesthesia.pdf, accessed July 29, 2020.

328. Roger Jennison, "A Physicist Goes Dowsing Down Under," *Physics World* vol. 8, no. 6 (1995), https://iopscience.iop.org/article/10.1088/2058-7058/8/6/15.

329. Anne Miller, "Dowsing: A Review," *The Scientific and Medical Network*, https://explore.scimednet.org/index.php/dowsing-a-review/, accessed October 6, 2020.

330. Anthony Hopwood, "Letter to the Editor," *New Scientist*, March 13, 1980, 862, https://books.google.com/books?id=axhPGjZT64wC&pg=PA862&lpg=PA862&dq=anthony+hopwood,+dowsing,+leylines+and+the+EM+link+new+scientist+1980&source=bl&ots=0c-GNMuIJT&sig=-ACfU3U0MTqzWqGQo5Q-uWXIBqJwINZ4ADg&hl=en&sa=X&ved=2ahUKEwjc59Kyjeru AhVDVTUKHRR0DdkQ6AEwBXoECCoQAg#v=onepage&q=anthony%20hopwood%2C%20dowsing%2C%20leylines%20and%20the%20EM%20link%20new%20scientist%201980&f=false.

331. Anthony Hopwood, "Dowsing, Ley Lines and the Electromagnetic Link," *New Scientist* 20/27 (December 1979), 948, https://books.google.com/books?id=3P5-7ZAAXsYC&pg=PA948&lpg=PA948&dq=%22anthony+hopwood%22+%22dowsing%22+%22new+scientist%22+948&source=bl&ots=o9PiLLKpPo&sig=ACfU3U1SQeHlyeSzjmZKb9fsrMWAmmvZTQ&hl=en&sa=X&ved=2ahUKEwif_aKn_OruAhWTFlkFHdYZAdkQ6AEwAXoECAMQAg#v=onepage&q=%22anthony%20hopwood%22%20%22dowsing%22%20%22new%20scientist%22%20948&f=false.

332. "Human Brain Facts," *Winston Medical Center*, https://www.winstonmedical.org/human-brain-facts/, accessed August 12, 2020, citing https://www.disabled-world.com/medical/human-body-facts.php; "Human Anatomy," https://www.dartmouth.edu/~humananatomy/part_7/chapter_41.html, accessed August 12, 2020, Link broken as of January 1, 2023; Tika Ram Lamichhane, Susheel Pangeni, Sharma Paudel, and Hari Prasad Lamichhane, "Age and Gender Related Variations of Pituitary Gland Size of Healthy Nepalese People Using Magnetic Resonance Imaging," *American Journal of Biomedical Engineering* 5, no. 4 (2015), 130–135, http://article.sapub.org/10.5923.j.ajbe.20150504.03.html; S. Ackerman, *Discovering the Brain* Ch. 2 (National Academies Press, 1992), available in part at https://www.ncbi.nlm.nih.gov/books/NBK234157/.

333. S. Kogame, S. Sawa, Y. Inoue, T. Fukuda, T. Tada, M. Shakudo, K. Yahata, H. Shimizu, and Y. Onayama. "MR Measurement of Normal Brainstem Cerebellum and Corpus Callosum on Midsagittal Section," *Rinsho Hoshasen* 34, no. 11 (Oct 1989), 1383–7.

334. H.H. Mitchell, T.S. Hamilton, F.R. Steggerda, and H. W. Bean, "The Chemical Composition

of the Adult Human Body and Its Bearing On the Biochemistry of Growth," *Journal of Biological Chemistry* 158 (1945), 625–637, https://www.jbc.org/content/158/3/625.full.pdf.

335. Ivor Noël Hume, *Historical Archaeology. a Comprehensive Guide for Both Amateur and Professions to the Techniques and Methods of Excavating Historical Sites* (Knopf, 1974).

336. "Microscopy," Wikipedia, https://en.wikipedia.org/wiki/Microscopy, accessed January 21, 2023.

337. "Sub-Diffraction Imaging," *Lewis Sigler Institute*, https://lsi.princeton.edu/facilities/-imaging-facility/sub-diffraction-imaging, accessed January 21, 2023.

338. "Scanning Electron Microscopy," *Nano Science Instruments*, https://www.nanoscience.com/techniques/scanning-electron-microscopy/, accessed September 21, 2021.

339. Roger Jennison, "A Physicist Goes Dowsing Down Under," *Physics World* vol. 8, no. 6 (1995), https://iopscience.iop.org/article/10.1088/2058-7058/8/6/15.

340. Roger Jennison, "A Physicist Goes Dowsing Down Under," *Physics World* vol. 8, no. 6 (1995), https://iopscience.iop.org/article/10.1088/2058-7058/8/6/15.

Chapter 17

341. Thomas Welton, trans., *Jacob's Rod*, Translation from the French of *A Rare and Curious Work, A.D. 1693, On the Art of Finding Springs, Mines, and Minerals by Means of the Hazel Rod. To Which Is Appended Researches, with Proofs of the Existence of a More Certain and Far Higher Faculty, with Clear and Ample Instructions for Using It*.

342. Solco Walle Tromp, *Psychical Physics: A Scientific Analysis of Dowsing, Radiesthesia and Kindred Divining Phenomena* (Elsevier, 1949), 356.

343. J.C. Maby and T.B. Franklin, *The Physics of the Divining Rod* (G. Bell and Sons, 1939).

344. "The Universe 101, Tests of Big Bang: The CMB," NASA, https://wmap.gsfc.nasa.gov/universe/bb_tests_cmb.html, accessed October 10, 2021.

345. "The Cosmic Microwave Background Radiation," https://ned.ipac.caltech.edu/level5/Birkinshaw/Birk1_1.html, accessed December 31, 2020.

346. G. Schiavon, P. Ferrazzoli, D. Solimini, P. de Maagt, and J.P.V. Poiares Baptlsta, "A Global High-Resolution Microwave Emission Model For The Earth," *Radio Science* vol. 33, no. 3 (May-June 1998), 753–766, https://agupubs.onlinelibrary.wiley.com/doi/pdf/10.1029/97RS02304; Catherine Prigent, Filipe Aires, and William B. Rossow, "Land Surface Microwave Emissivities over the Globe for a Decade," *Bulletin of the American Meteorological Society*, Online Publication vol. 87, issue 11 (November 1, 2006), 1573–1584, https://journals.ametsoc.org/doi/pdf/10.1175/BAMS-87-11-1573.

347. G.W.C. Kaye and T.H. Laby, *Table So Physical and Chemical Constants and Some Mathematical Functions* 14th ed. (Longman, 1973); "Ground Penetrating Radar," Wikipedia, https://en.wikipedia.org/wiki/Ground-penetrating_radar, accessed January 1, 2023.

348. Josef Cihlar and Fawwaz T. Ulaby, "Dielectric Properties of Soils as a Function of Moisture Content Remote Sensing Laboratory," RSL Technical Report 177-4 (NASA-CR-141868 [November, 1974]), Kansas Univ. Center for Research Inc., https://ntrs.nasa.gov/archive/nasa/casi.ntrs.nasa.gov/19750018483.pdf.

Chapter 18

349. "Today in Science," https://todayinsci.com/QuotationsCategories/T_Cat/Telescope-Quotations.htm, accessed August 1, 2021.

350. B. Opyd, K. Granat, and D. Nowak, "Determination of Electrical Properties of Materials Used In Microwave Heating of Foundry Moulds and Cores," *METALURGIJA* vol. 54, no. 2 (2015), 347–349, https://core.ac.uk/download/pdf/33269063.pdf.

351. "Dielectric Properties," Tissue Properties, https://itis.swiss/virtual-population/tissue-properties/database/dielectric-properties/ accessed May 28, 2023, citing C. Gabriel, "Compilation of the Dielectric Properties of Body Tissues at RF and Microwave Frequencies," Report N.AL/OE-TR-1996–0037, Occupational and Environmental Health Directorate, Radiofrequency Radiation Division, Brooks Air Force Base, Texas (1996).

352. "Version 1.51 23 April 2018," available for download from https://imagej.net/Fiji/Downloads.

353. S. Kralj, and S. Marchesan, "Bioinspired Magnetic Nanochains for Medicine," *Pharmaceutics* 13 (2021), 1262, https://doi.org/10.3390/pharmaceutics13081262.

354. M.M. Walker, T.P. Quinn, J.L. Kirschvink, and C. Groot, "Production Of Single-Domain Magnetite Throughout Life by Sockeye Salmon, Oncorhynchus nerka," *J Exp Biol.* 140, no. 1, (1988), 51–63, https://doi.org/10.1242/jeb.140.1.51.

Chapter 19

355. "Faint Memory Quotes," https://quotestats.com/topic/faint-memory-quotes/, accessed July 30, 2022.

356. Alexander P. Dubrov, "Modern Achievements of Dowsing (1990–2000)," https://canadiandowsers.org/modern-achievements-of-dowsing/, accessed August 18, 2020.

357. Dennis Wheatley, *The Essential Dowsing Guide* 3rd ed. (Ozark Mountain, 2012).

358. G.P. Hansen, "Dowsing: A Review of Experimental Research," *Journal of the Society for Psychical Research* vol. 51, no. 792 (1982), 343–367.

359. "Editorial," *Journal of the British Society of Dowsers* no. 1 (September 1922), 1, http://www.dowsing-research.net/dowsing/journals/VolI_No1_Sep_1933.pdf.

360. L.W. Codd, *Chemical Technology and Encyclopedic Treatment* vols. 2 & 5 (Rowman and Littlefield, 1975).

Chapter 20

361. "Josh Billings Quote," https://libquotes.com/josh-billings/quote/lbn0y1p, accessed December 6, 2021, citing *Josh Billings: His Works, Complete* (1873).

362. Heather Smith Thomas, "Water Dowsing Works (Even If We Don't Know Why)," Hobby Farms, September 8, 2020, https://www.hobbyfarms.com/water-dowsing-works-dont-know-why/, accessed August 7, 2021.

363. Swamp Fox, "The Disappearing Art of Dowsing," *The Free Library*, 2014, from *Countryside & Small Stock Journal,* Nov 1, 1997, accessed December 3, 2020, from https://www.thefreelibrary.com/The+disappearing+art+of+dowsing.-a020050042.

364. Kenneth Roberts, *Henry Gross and His Dowsing Rod* (Doubleday, 1951)

365. A.P. Tabraham, *Solar Energy & Dowsing in the Isles of Scilly: An Addendum* (E.V. Tabraham, St. Mary's, Isles of Scilly, 1992). This booklet is an addendum to *Solar Energy & Dowsing in the Isles of Scilly* (1982), and is published in memory of the author, who died November 1991. http://www.dowsing-research.net/dowsing/articles/Tabraham-solar_energy_and_dowsing_an_addendum.pdf.

366. Patricia Middleton and Newton Kansan, "Dowsing Finds What Lies Beneath, "*The Kansan*, September 8, 2017, https://www.thekansan.com/news/20170908/dowsing-finds-what-lies-beneath, accessed August 14, 2020.

367. Solco Walle Tromp, *Psychical Physics: A Scientific Analysis of Dowsing, Radiesthesia and Kindred Divining Phenomena* (Elsevier, 1949), 301.

368. Ian Pegler, "Bishop's Rule," British Dowsing Forum, November 1, 2010, http://britishdowsing.net/forum/viewtopic.php?t=2077, accessed July 26, 2020.

369. "Water Dowsing, Definition of Terms, Energy Dowsers," http://www.energydowsers.org/water-dowsing/, accessed July 26, 2020.

370. Dennis Wheatley, *The Essential Dowsing Guide* 3rd ed. (Ozark Mountain, 2012).

371. Letter from Donald S. Duncan to Kenneth Roberts in 1948, Kenneth Roberts, *Henry Gross and His Dowsing Rod* (Doubleday, 1951).

372. Charles Latimer, *The Divining Rod: Virgula Divina—Baculus Divinatorius (Water-Witching.),* 1876, Project Gutenberg EBook #45020, February 26, 2014, https://www.gutenberg.org/files/45020/45020-h/45020-h.htm.

373. Heather Smith Thomas, "Water Dowsing Works (Even If We Don't Know Why)," Hobby Farms (September 8, 2020), https://www.hobbyfarms.com/water-dowsing-works-dont-know-why/, accessed March 26, 2023.

374. Richard Webster, *Dowsing for Beginners, the Art of Discovering: Water, Treasure, Gold, Oil, Artifacts* (Castle Books, 2001).

375. "Ground Penetrating Radar," Contaminated Site Clean-Up Information, https://clu-in.org/characterization/technologies/gpr.cfm, accessed January 1, 2023; "Ground Penetrating Radar," Wikipedia, https://en.wikipedia.org/wiki/Ground-penetrating_radar, accessed January 1, 2023.

376. "How Deep Does GPR Go?," U.S. Radar Inc., https://usradar.com/how-deep-does-gpr-go/, accessed October 17, 2021.

377. Doyle A. Ellerbruch, "EM Attenuation Of Clay And Gravel Soils," *National Bureau of Standards* (1974), https://nvlpubs.nist.gov/nistpubs/Legacy/IR/nbsir74-381.pdf; S. Lv, Y. Zeng, J. Wen, H. Zhao, and Z. Su, "Estimation of Penetration Depth from Soil Effective Temperature in Microwave Radiometry," *Remote Sens.* 10 (2018), 519. https://doi.org/10.3390/rs10040519, https://www.mdpi.com/2072-4292/10/4/519/htm.

378. Heather Smith Thomas, "Water Dowsing Works (Even If We Don't Know Why)," Hobby Farms, September 8, 2020, https://www.hobbyfarms.com/water-dowsing-works-dont-know-why/, accessed March 26, 2023.

379. Paavo Huttunen, Osmo Hänninen, and Risto Myllyläh, "FM-Radio and TV Tower Signals Can Cause Spontaneous Hand Movements Near Moving RF Reflector," *Pathophysiology* 16, 2–3 (August 2009), 201–4, tps://pubmed.ncbi.nlm.nih.gov/19268549/; Paavo Huttunen, "Spontaneous Movements Of Hands in Gradients of Weak VHF Electromagnetic Fields," PhD dissertation (failed), 2012, University of Eastern Finland Department of Electrical Engineering, http://jultika.oulu.fi/files/isbn9789514297601.pdf.

380. Jonas Kavi, "Detection of Buried Non-Metallic (Plastic and FRP Composite) Pipes Using GPR and IRT," Ph.D. Thesis, 2018, West Virginia University, https://researchrepository.wvu.edu/etd/3724.

381. "Ground Penetrating Radar Cost," U.S. Radar Inc, https://usradar.com/ground-penetrating-radar-cost/, accessed January 1, 2023.

382. C. Prigent, W. B. Rossow, E. Matthews, and B. Marticorena, "Microwave Radiometer Signatures of Different Surface Types in Deserts," *J. Geophys. Res.*, vol. 104, no. D10 (1999), 147–12 158, https://agupubs.onlinelibrary.wiley.com/doi/abs/10.1029/1999JD900153; Haroon Stephen and David G. Long, "Modeling Microwave Emissions of Erg Surfaces in the Sahara Desert," *IEEE Transactions on Geoscience and Remote Sensing* vol. 43, no. 12 (December 2005), 2822–2830, https://digitalscholarship.unlv.edu/cgi/viewcontent.cgi?article=1019&context=sea_fac_articles.

383. B.U. Ungan and J.T Johnson, "A Study Of

Microwave Emission from a Subsurface Object," *Microwave and Optical Technology Letters*, March 12, 2002, http://people.ee.duke.edu/~lcarin/DeminingMURI/paper7.pdf.

384. Michael Brooks, "Why Dowsing Makes Perfect Sense," *New Scientist*, July 29, 2009, https://www.newscientist.com/article/dn17532-why-dowsing-makes-perfect-sense/.

385. T. Maeda and T. Takano, "Detection of Microwave Emission Associated with Earthquakes," *AGU Spring Meeting Abstracts* vol. 2007 (May 2006), S21A-03, https://ui.adsabs.harvard.edu/abs/2006AGUSM.S21A..03M/exportcitation.

386. Won-Ju Kim, Kee-Tae Kim and Kwang-Tae Kim, "Simultaneous 22 GHz Water and 44 GHz Methanol Maser Survey of Ultracompact H ii Regions," *ApJS*, 244 (2019), 2.

387. "LASER," Wikipedia, https://en.wikipedia.org/wiki/Laser, accessed August 15, 2022.

388. Yunwen Tao, Wenli Zou, Junteng Jia, Wei Li, and Dieter Cremer, "Different Ways of Hydrogen Bonding in Water—Why Does Warm Water Freeze Faster than Cold Water?" *Journal of Chemical Theory and Computation* 13, no. 1 (2017), 55–76, DOI: 10.1021/acs.jctc.6b00735.

389. "EM Absorption by Water," https://en.wikipedia.org/wiki/EM_absorption_by_water, accessed August 15, 2022.

390. Y.S. Djikaev and E. Ruckenstein, "Dependence of the Number of Hydrogen Bonds Per Water Molecule on its Distance to a Hydrophobic Surface and a Thereupon-Based Model for Hydrophobic Attraction," *J Chem Phys*. 133, no. 19 (November 21, 2010), 194105, doi: 10.1063/1.3499318.

391. Huanyu Yang, Anthony Boucly, Jérôme Philippe Gabathuler, Thorsten Bartels-Rausch, Luca Artiglia, and Markus Ammann, "Ordered Hydrogen Bonding Structure of Water Molecules Absorbed on Silver Iodide Particles Under Subsaturated Conditions," *The Journal of Physical Chemistry C* 125, no. 21 (2021), 11628–11635, doi: 10.1021/acs.jpcc.1c01767.

392. J. Bae, S.H. Park, D. Moon, et al., "Crystalline Hydrogen Bonding of Water Molecules Confined in a Metal-Organic Framework," *Commun Chem*. 5 (2022), 51, https://doi.org/10.1038/s42004-022-00666-8; H. Bartl, "Water of Crystallization and Its Hydrogen-Bonded Crosslinking In Vivianite $Fe_3(PO_4)_2 \cdot 8H_2O$; A Neutron Diffraction Investigation," *Z. Analytic Chem.*, 333 (1989), 401–403, https://doi.org/10.1007/BF00572335.

393. F. F. Wangaard, "The Hygroscopic Nature of Wood," Colorado State University Fort Collins, Defense Technical Information Center, October 29, 1979, Accession No. ADP003434, https://apps.dtic.mil/sti/citations/ADP003434.

394. Mukaila A, Ibrahim and René T. Boeré, "The Copper Sulfate Hydration Cycle. Crystal Structures of $CuSO_4$ (Chalcocyanite), $CuSO_4 \cdot H_2O$ (Poitevinite), $CuSO_4 \cdot 3H_2O$ (Bonattite) and $CuSO_4 \cdot 5H_2O$ (Chalcanthite) At Low Temperature Using Non-Spherical Atomic Scattering Factors," *New Journal of Chemistry*, issue 12 (2022).

395. G.E. Bacon and N.A. Curry, "The Water Molecules in $CuSO_4.5H_2O$," *Proceedings of the Royal Society A* vol. 266, issue 1324 (February 27, 1962), https://doi.org/10.1098/rspa.1962.0049.

396. Martin Ondrášik, "Thermodynamic Differences Between Adsorbed and Bulk Water in Rock Pores Under Microwave Radiation and Their Relationship to Rock Durability," 9th Congress of the International Association for Engineering Geology and the Environment (September 16–20, 2002), Durban, South Africa, https://www.researchgate.net/publication/289790815_Thermodynamic_differences_between_adsorbed_and_bulk_water_in_rock_pores_under_microwave_radiation_and_their_relationship_to_rock_durability.

397. N.D. Pavlov and Y.A. Baloshin, "EM Properties of Water on GHz Frequencies for Medicine Tasks and Metamaterial Applications," *J. Phys.: Conf. Ser*. 643, no. 012047 (2015); D.D. Turner, S. Kneifel, and M.P. Cadeddu, "An Improved Liquid Water Absorption Model at Microwave Frequencies for Supercooled Liquid Water Clouds," *Journal of Atmospheric and Oceanic Technology*, 33, no. 1 (2016), 33–44, https://journals.ametsoc.org/view/journals/atot/33/1/jtech-d-15-0074_1.xml.

Chapter 21

398. "Erik Brynjolfsson Quotes," Brainy Quotes, https://www.brainyquote.com/authors/erik-brynjolfsson-quotes, accessed September 23, 2021.

399. J.C. Maby and T.B. Franklin, *The Physics of the Divining Rod* (G. Bell and Sons, 1939).

400. A. Abromovich, N.S. Kopeika, and D. Rozban, "Glow Discharge Detector For Terahertz and Millimeter Wave Radiation Detection and Imaging," *Electro-Optical Remote Sensing, Detection, and Photonic Technologies and Their Applications; Proceedings* vol. 6739 (2007), 67390O. https://doi.org/10.1117/12.737767; L. Kahana, D. Rozban, M. Gihasi, A. Abramovich, Y. Yitzhaky, and N. Kopeika, "Inexpensive Millimeter-Wave Communication Channel Using Glow Discharge Detector and Satellite Dish Antenna," *Electronics* vol. 9 (2020), 677, https://doi.org/10.3390/electronics9040677; Alan D. White, "Gas Tube Microwave Detector," U.S. Patent 2877417A (Publ. March 10, 1959).

401. "Moving Mass Detector—Franklin and Maby (Research on Dowsing)—related to Louis Rota's work." Author not listed https://www.google.com/url?sa=t&rct=j&q=&esrc=s&source=web&cd=&cad=rja&uact=8&ved=2ahUKEwiZtb2k3v7uAhWUFVkFHbYvDeoQFjABegQIARAD&url=http%3A%2F%2Fwww.overunityresearch.com%2Findex.php%3Faction%3Ddlattach%3Btopic%3D272.0%3Battach%3D3859&usg=-AOvVaw0ugJHbILlvpk-bX0duiRbC, accessed February 23, 2021; Michael Watson, "Cecil Maby and Bedford Franklin," http://wikirota.org/en/Cecil_Maby_and_Bedford_Franklin, accessed February 23, 2021.

Chapter 22

402. William Highcock, "Dowsing, An Applied Science? Two Experiments with the Dowsing Phenomenon," *Journal of the Merseyside Archaeological Society* vol. 10 (2000), 45, https://www.merseysidearchsoc.com/uploads/2/7/2/9/2729758/jmas_10_paper_4.pdf.

403. Ivor Noël Hume, *Historical Archaeology: A Comprehensive Guide for Both Amateur and Professions to the Techniques and Methods of Excavating Historical Sites* (Knopf, 1974).

404. J.C. Maby and T.B. Franklin, *The Physics of the Divining Rod* (G. Bell and Sons, 1939).

405. "Sun, NASA, Space," Technology 5, https://www.jpl.nasa.gov/nmp/st5/SCIENCE/sun.html, accessed July 21, 2021.

406. "Using TechBASIC to Turn Your iPhone or iPad Into a Metal Detector," *Byteworks* (November 29, 2011). http://www.byteworks.us/Byte_Works/Blog/Entries/2011/11/30_Using_techBASIC_to_Turn_Your_iPhone_or_iPad_into_a_Metal_Detector.html#:~:text=The%20magnetometer%20in%20the%20iPhone,the%20strength%20of%20magnetic%20fields accessed September 21, 2021.

Chapter 23

407. Jacob Mathias Schlelden, "Grundzüge Der Wissenschaftlichen Botanik Nebst Einer Methodologischen Einleitung Als Anleitung Zum Studium Der Planze [Principles Of Scientific Botany]," *Today and Science*, https://todayinsci.com/QuotationsCategories/M_Cat/Magnetism-Quotations.htm, accessed December 3, 2021.

408. Joseph L. Kirschvink, Atsuko Kobayashi-Kirschvink, Juan C. Diaz-Ricci, and Steven J. Kirschvink, "Magnetite in Human Tissues: A Mechanism for the Biological Effects of Weak ELF Magnetic Fields," *BioEM S Supplement* 1 (1992), 101–113, http://web.gps.caltech.edu/~jkirschvink/pdfs/KirschvinkBEMS92.pdf.

409. Bryan A. Keller, Nathan F. Putman, R. Dean Grubbs, David S. Portnoy, and Timothy P. Murphy, "Map-Like Use of Earth's Magnetic Field in Sharks," *Current Biology* 31 (May 6, 2021), 1–6, https://doi.org/10.1016/j.cub.2021.03.103.

410. Lewis C. Naisbett-Jones, Nathan F. Putman, Michelle M. Scanlan, David L.G. Noakes, and Kenneth J. Lohmann, "Magnetoreception in Fishes: The Effect of Magnetic Pulses On Orientation of Juvenile Pacific Salmon," *J Exp Biol* 223, no. 10 (2020), https://doi.org/10.1242/jeb.222091.

411. Kenneth J. Lohmann, Catherine M.F. Lohmann, and Nathan F. Putman, "Magnetic Maps In Animals: Nature's GPS," *Journal of Experimental Biology* 210 (2007), 3697–3705.

412. Erik Stokstad, "Dogs May Use Earth's Magnetic Field to Take Shortcuts," *Science*, July 17, 2020, https://www.sciencemag.org/news/2020/07/dogs-may-use-earth-s-magnetic-field-take-shortcuts.

413. Kateřina Benediktová, Jana Adámková, Jan Svoboda, Michael Scott Painter, Luděk Bartoš, Petra Nováková, Lucie Vynikalová, Vlastimil Hart, John Phillips, and Hynek Burda, "Magnetic Alignment Enhances Homing Efficiency Of Hunting Dogs," *eLife*, 9 (2020), e55080, https://doi.org/10.7554/eLife.55080.

414. Max Yasgur, "Animal Magnetism: A Study of Captive Grey Wolves At Rest and Their Orientation Relative To Earth's Magnetic Field," John Jay High School, https://nywolf.org/wp-content/uploads/2020/05/MaxY-Wolf-Research-Paper.pdf, accessed February 11, 2023.

415. Vlastimil Hart, Petra Nováková, Erich Pascal Malkemper, Sabine Begall, Vladimír Hanzal, Miloš Ježek, Tomáš Kušta, Veronika Němcová, Jana Adámková, Kateřina Benediktová, Jaroslav Červený and Hynek Burda, "Dogs Are Sensitive To Small Variations of the Earth's Magnetic Field," *Frontiers in Zoology* 10, no. 80 (2013), https://frontiersinzoology.biomedcentral.com/track/pdf/10.1186/1742-9994-10-80.pdf.

416. S. Martini, S. Begall, T. Findeklee, M. Schmitt, E.P. Malkemper, and H. Burda, "Dogs Can Be Trained To Find a Bar Magnet," *PeerJ*. 6 (December 17, 2018), e6117, doi: 10.7717/peerj.6117.

417. S. Begall, J. Cerveny, J. Neef, O. Vojtech, and H. Burda, "Magnetic Alignment in Grazing and Resting Cattle and Deer," *Proc Natl Acad Sci USA* 105, no. 36 (Sepember 9, 2008), 13451–5, doi: 10.1073/pnas.0803650105.

418. Daniel Cressey, "The Mystery of the Magnetic Cows: Researchers Disagree Over Replication of Study Showing That Cows Line Up With Earth's Magnetic Field," *Nature* (November 11, 2011), https://www.nature.com/news/the-mystery-of-the-magnetic-cows-1.9350.

419. Thorsten Ritz, Salih Adem, and Klaus Schulten. "A Model for Photoreceptor-Based Magnetoreception in Birds," *Biophysical Journal*, 78 (2000), 707–718, https://www.ks.uiuc.edu/Publications/Papers/paper.cgi?tbcode=RITZ2000.

420. Miriam Liedvogel and Henrik Mouritsen, "Cryptochromes—A Potential Magnetoreceptor: What Do We Know and What Do We Want to Know?" *Journal of the Royal Society Interface* , November 11, 2009, https://doi.org/10.1098/rsif.2009.0411.focus.

421. Jo Marchant, "Plant Protein Responds to Radio Waves By Making Seedlings Grow Faster," *New Scientist*, August 2020, https://www.newscientist.com/article/2251835-plant-protein-responds-to-radio-waves-by-making-seedlings-grow-faster/#ixzz6VTPbm1D3.

422. Martin Vácha, Tereza Půžová, and Markéta Kvíčalová, "Radio Frequency Magnetic Fields Disrupt Magnetoreception In American Cockroach," *Journal of Experimental Biology* 212 (2009), 3473–3477, https://jeb.biologists.org/content/212/21/3473; Michael Le Page, "Radio Waves From Electric Devices May Affect The Body Clock of Insects," *New Scientist*, September 18, 2019, https://www.newscientist.com/article/2216690-radio-waves-

423. L. Foley, R. Gegear, and S. Reppert. "Human Cryptochrome Exhibits Light-Dependent Magneto sensitivity," *Nat Commun.* 2 (2011), 356, https://www.nature.com/articles/ncomms1364.

424. I.H. Kavakli and A. Sancar, "Circadian Photoreception In Humans And Mice," *Mol Interv.* 8 (December 2, 2002), 484–92, doi: 10.1124/mi.2.8.484.

425. Pete Wedderburn, "The Mystery of a Cat's Strong Sense Of Direction," *Independent*, August 19, 2017, https://www.independent.ie/regionals/goreyguardian/lifestyle/the-mystery-of-a-cats-strong-sense-of-direction-36031801.html, accessed November 8, 2021; Veronique Greenwood, "How a Kitty Walked 200 Miles Home: The Science of Your Cat's Inner Compass, A House Cat's Long-Distance Journey Raises New Questions About How Animals Navigate," *Time*, February 11, 2013, https://science.time.com/2013/02/11/the-mystery-of-the-geolocating-cat/, accessed November 28, 2021.

426. Christine Nießner, Susanne Denzau, Erich Pascal Malkemper, Julia Christina Gross, Hynek Burda, Michael Winklhofer, and Leo Peichl, "Cryptochrome 1 in Retinal Cone Photoreceptors Suggests a Novel Functional Role in Mammals," *Sci Rep* 6 (2016), 21848, https://doi.org/10.1038/srep21848.

427. E. Pascal Malkemper, Stephan H.K. Eder, Sabine Begall, John B. Phillips, Michael Winklhofer, Vlastimil Hart, and Hynek Burda, "Magnetoreception In the Wood Mouse (*Apodemus Sylvaticus*): Influence of Weak Frequency-Modulated Radio Frequency Fields," *Sci Rep* 5 (2015), 9917, https://doi.org/10.1038/srep09917.

428. Rachel M. Sherrard, Natalie Morellini, Nathalie Jourdan, Mohamed El-Esawi, Louis-David Arthaut, Christine Niessner, Francois Rouyer, Andre Klarsfeld, Mohamed Doulazmi, Jacques Witczak, Alain d'Harlingue, Jean Mariani, Ian Mclure, Carlos F. Martino, and Margaret Ahmad, "Low-Intensity Electromagnetic Fields Induce Human Cryptochrome to Modulate Intracellular Reactive Oxygen Species," *PLoS Biol* 16 (2018), 10, e2006229, https://journals.plos.org/plosbiology/article?id=10.1371/journal.pbio.2006229.

429. Jacques Vanderstraeten, Philippe Gailly, and E. Pascal Malkemper, "Low-Light Dependence of the Magnetic Field Effect on Cryptochromes: Possible Relevance to Plant Ecology," *Front. Plant Sci.* 14 (February 2018), https://www.frontiersin.org/articles/10.3389/fpls.2018.00121/full.

430. Kwon-Seok Chae, Soo-Chan Kim, Hye-Jin Kwon and Yongkuk Kim, "Human Magnetic Sense Is Mediated By a Light and Magnetic Field Resonance-Dependent Mechanism," *Nature Sci Rep* 12 (2022), 8997, https://doi.org/10.1038/s41598-022-12460-6.

431. Helen Matsos, "How Animals Sense Earth's Magnetic Field," *Astrobiology Magazine*, May 19, 2020, https://phys.org/news/2020-05-animals-earth-magnetic-field.html, accessed August 9, 2020.

432. James L. Gould, "The Case for Magnetic Sensitivity in Birds and Bees (Such As It Is): Surprising Concentrations of Magnetite in the Tissues of Some Animals May Explain Their Sensitivity to the Earth's Magnetic Field," *American Scientist*, vol. 68, no. 3 (1980), 256–267, https://www.jstor.org/stable/27849821?seq=1.

433. Stuart A. Gilder, Michael Wack, Leon Kaub, Sophie C. Roud, Nikolai Petersen, Helmut Heinsen, Peter Hillenbrand, Stefan Milz, and Christoph Schmitz, "Distribution Of Magnetic Remanence Carriers in the Human Brain," *Scientific Reports* 8 (2018), 11363, DOI:10.1038/s41598-018-29766-, https://www.nature.com/articles/s41598-018-29766-z.pdf.

434. Connie X. Wang, Isaac A. Hilburn, Daw-An Wu, Yuki Mizuhara, Christopher P. Cousté, Jacob N.H. Abrahams, Sam E. Bernstein, Ayumu Matani, Shinsuke Shimojo, and Joseph L. Kirschvink, "Transduction of the Geomagnetic Field as Evidenced From Alpha-Band Activity in the Human Brain," *eNeuro* 6, vol. 2 (March 18, 2019), https://www.eneuro.org/content/6/2/ENEURO.0483-18.2019.

435. Connie X. Wang, Isaac A. Hilburn, Daw-An Wu, Yuki Mizuhara, Christopher P. Cousté, Jacob N.H. Abrahams, Sam E. Bernstein, Ayumu Matani, Shinsuke Shimojo, and Joseph L. Kirschvink, "Transduction of the Geomagnetic Field as Evidenced From Alpha-Band Activity in the Human Brain," *eNeuro* 6, no. 2 (March 18, 2019), https://www.eneuro.org/content/6/2/ENEURO.0483-18.2019.

436. S. Nimpf, G.C. Nordmann, D. Kagerbauer, E.P. Malkemper, L. Landler, A. Papadaki-Anastasopoulou, L. Ushakova, A. Wenninger-Weinzierl, M. Novatchkova, P. Vincent, T. Lendl, M. Colombini, M.J. Mason, and D.A. Keays, "A Putative Mechanism for Magnetoreception by Electromagnetic Induction in the Pigeon Inner Ear," *Curr Biol.* 29, no. 23 (December 2, 2019), 4052–4059.e4, doi: 10.1016/j.cub.2019.09.048.

437. L.Q. Wu, and J.D. Dickman, "Magnetoreception in an Avian Brain in Part Mediated By Inner Ear Lagena," *Curr Biol.* 21, no. 5 (March 8, 2011), 418–23, doi: 10.1016/j.cub.2011.01.058.

438. E.P. Malkemper, D. Kagerbauer, L. Ushakova, S. Nimpf, P. Pichler, C.D. Treiber, M. de Jonge, J. Shaw, and D.A. Keays, "No Evidence for a Magnetite-Based Magnetoreceptor In the Lagena of Pigeons," *Curr Biol.* 29, no. 1 (January 7, 2019), R14-R15, doi: 10.1016/j.cub.2018.11.032.

439. Wolfgang Wiltschko, Roswitha Wiltschko, and Thorsten Ritz, "The Mechanism of the Avian Magnetic Compass," *Procedia Chemistry* vol. 3, issue 1 (2011), 276–284, https://doi.org/10.1016/j.proche.2011.08.035.

440. Hervé Cadiou and Peter A. McNaughton, "Avian Magnetite-Based Magnetoreception: A Physiologist's Perspective," *Journal of the Royal*

Society Interface (27 January 2010), https://doi.org/10.1098/rsif.2009.0423.focus.

441. Christian B. Billesbølle, Claire A. de March, Wijnand J.C. van der Velden, Ning Ma, Jeevan Tewari, Claudia Llinas del Torrent, Linus Li, Bryan Faust, Nagarajan Vaidehi, Hiroaki Matsunami, and Aashish Manglik, "Structural Basis of Odorant Recognition by a Human Odorant Receptor," *Nature* (2023), https://doi.org/10.1038/s41586-023-05798-y.

442. Kwon-Seok Chae, Soo-Chan Kim, Hye-Jin Kwon and Yongkuk Kim, "Human Magnetic Sense Is Mediated By a Light and Magnetic Field Resonance-Dependent Mechanism," *Nature Sci Rep* 12 (2022), 8997, https://doi.org/10.1038/s41598-022-12460-6.

Chapter 24

443. "Quotes About Radio Waves," Quotes Stats, https://quotestats.com/topic/quotes-about-radio-waves/, accessed October 30, 2021

444. "Active Denial System FAQs," Joint Intermediate Force Capabilities Office, U.S. Department of Defense Non-Lethal Weapons Program, https://jnlwp.defense.gov/About/Frequently-Asked-Questions/Active-Denial-System-FAQs/, accessed January 18, 2021.

445. "Non-Ionizing Radiation," U.S. OSHA standard 29 CFR 1910.97; Amir Raz, "Could Certain Frequencies of Electromagnetic Waves or Radiation Interfere with Brain Function?" *Scientific American*, April 24, 2006, https://www.scientificamerican.com/article/could-certain-frequencies/, accessed July 25, 2020.

446. Igor Belyaev, "Non-thermal Biological Effects of Microwaves," *Microwave Review*, November 2005, 13, http://www.mtt-serbia.org.rs/files/MWR/MWR2005nov/Vol11No2-03-IBelyaev.pdf; D. Kuzay1, C. Ozer, T. Goktas, B. Sirav, F. Senturk, G.T. Kaplanoglu, M. Seymen, "Effects Of 2100 Mhz Radio Frequency Radiation on the Viscosity of Blood and Oxidative Stress Parameters in Hypertensive and Normal," *International Journal of Radiation Research* vol. 16, no. 4 (October 2018), 431, http://ijrr.com/article-1-2397-en.pdf; C. Jonwal, R. Sisodia, V.K. Saxena, and K.K. Kesari, "Effect Of 2.45 Ghz Microwave Radiation on the Fertility Pattern in Male Mice," *Gen Physiol Biophys* vol. 37, no. 4 (July 2018), 453–460, doi: 10.4149/gpb_2017059; R. Meena, K. Kumari, J. Kumar, P. Rajamani, H.N. Verma, and K.K. Kesari, "Therapeutic Approaches of Melatonin in Microwave Radiations-Induced Oxidative Stress-Mediated Toxicity on Male Fertility Pattern of Wistar Rats," *Electromagn Biol Med* vol. 33, no. 2 (June 2014), 81–91, doi: 10.3109/15368378.2013.781; S. Verma, G.K. Keshri, S. Karmakar, K.V. Mani, S. Chauhan, A. Yadav, M. Sharma, and A. Gupta, "Effects of Microwave 10 Ghz Radiation Exposure in the Skin of Rats: An Insight on Molecular Responses," *Radiat Res.* vol. 196, no. 4 (October 1, 2021), 404–416, doi: 10.1667/RADE-20-00155.1.

447. "IARC Classifies Radio Frequency Electromagnetic Fields as Possibly Carcinogenic to Humans," International Agency for Research on Cancer Press Release 208, May 31, 2011, https://www.iarc.who.int/wp-content/uploads/2018/07/pr208_E.pdf; L. Hardell, "World Health Organization, Radiofrequency Radiation and Health—A Hard Nut to Crack (Review)," *Int J Oncol.* vol. 51, no. 2 (2017), 405–413, doi:10.3892/ijo.2017.4046; A. Aweda, O.K. Meindinyo, S.O. Gbenebitse, and A. Z. Ibitoye, "Microwave Radiation Exposures Affect Cardiovascular System and Antioxidants Modify the Effects," *Advances in Applied Science Research*, 2, no. 2 (2011), 246–251, https://www.imedpub.com/articles/microwave-radiation-exposures-affect-cardiovascular-system-and-antioxidants-modify-the-effects.pdf; Igor Belyaev, "Non-thermal Biological Effects of Microwaves," *Microwave Review* (November 2005), 13, http://www.mtt-serbia.org.rs/files/MWR/MWR2005nov/Vol11No2-03-IBelyaev.pdf.

448. "IARC Classifies Radio Frequency Electromagnetic Fields as Possibly Carcinogenic to Humans," International Agency for Research on Cancer Press Release 208, May 31, 2011, https://www.iarc.who.int/wp-content/uploads/2018/07/pr208_E.pdf

449. I. Sultangaliyeva, R. Beisenova, R. Tazitdinova, A. Abzhalelov, and M. Khanturin, "The Influence of Electromagnetic Radiation of Cell Phones on the Behavior of Animals," *Vet World* vol. 13, no. 3 (2020), 549–555, doi:10.14202/vetworld.2020.549-555.

450. T.M. Al-Khlaiwi, S.S. Habib, S.A. Meo, M.S. Alqhtani, and A.A. Ogailan, "The Association of Smart Mobile Phone Usage with Cognitive Function Impairment in Saudi Adult Population," *Pak J Med Sci.* vol. 36, no. 7 (November-December 2020), 1628–1633, https://www.ncbi.nlm.nih.gov/pmc/articles/PMC7674882/.

451. "Electromagnetic Fields and Public Health: Mobile Phones," World Health Organization, October 8, 2014, https://www.who.int/news-room/fact-sheets/detail/EM-fields-and-public-health-mobile-phones, accessed February 10, 2023.

452. W. Zhi, L. Wang, and X. Hu, "Recent Advances in the Effects of Microwave Radiation on Brains." *Military Med Res* 4 (2017), 29, https://mmrjournal.biomedcentral.com/articles/10.1186/s40779-017-0139-0.

453. Yanchun Zhang, Zhihui Li, Yan Gao, Chenggang Zhang, "Effects of Fetal Microwave Radiation Exposure on Offspring Behavior in Mice," *Journal of Radiation Research*, vol. 56, issue 2 (March 2015), 261–268, https://doi.org/10.1093/jrr/rru097.

454. John A. D'Andrea, Eleanor R. Adair, and John O. de Lorg, "Behavioral and Cognitive Effects of Microwave Exposure," *BioEM S Supplement* 6 (2003), S39-S62, https://onlinelibrary.wiley.com/doi/pdf/10.1002/bem.10169.

455. S. Qiu, S. Wang, W. Yi, C. Zhang, and H. He, "Changes of Resting-State EEG Microstates Induced By Low-Frequency Repetitive Transcranial Magnetic Stimulation," *Annu Int Conf IEEE Eng Med Biol Soc.* (July 2020), 3549–3552, doi: 10.1109/EMBC44109.2020.9176673; S. Qiu, S. Wang, W. Yi, C. Zhang, and H. He, "The Lasting Effects of 1Hz Repetitive Transcranial Magnetic Stimulation on Resting State EEG in Healthy Subjects," *Annu Int Conf IEEE Eng Med Biol Soc.* (July 2019), 5918–5922, doi: 10.1109/EMBC.2019.8857184.

456. Glenn B. Bell, Andrew A. Marino, Andrew L. Chesson, "Frequency-Specific Responses In The Human Brain Caused By Electromagnetic Fields," *Journal of the Neurological Sciences,* 123, 1–2 (June 1994), 26–32, DOI:10.1016/0022–510X(94)90199–6

457. H. Hinrikus, M. Bachmann, D. Karai, and J. Lass, "Mechanism of Low-Level Microwave Radiation Effect on Nervous System," *J. Electromagn Biol Med.* vol. 36, no. 2 (2017), 202–212, doi: 10.1080/15368378.2016.1251451.

458. A. Schienle, R. Stark, and D. Vaitl, "Sferics Provoke Changes in EEG Power," *Int J Neurosci* 107, no. 1–2 (March 2001), 87–102, doi: 10.3109/00207450109149759.

459. A. Schienle, R. Stark, and D. Vaitl, "Electrocortical Responses of Headache Patients to the Simulation of 10 Khz Sferics," *Int J Neurosci.* 97, no. 3–4 (April 1999), 211–24, doi: 10.3109/00207459909000661.

460. N. Perentos, R.J. Croft, R.J. McKenzie, D. Cvetkovic, and I. Cosic, "The Effect Of GSM-Like ELF Radiation on the Alpha Band Of The Human Resting EEG," *Annu Int Conf IEEE Eng Med Biol Soc.* (2008), 5680-3, doi: 10.1109/IEMBS.2008.4650503.

461. S.M. Bawin, R.J. Gavalas-Medici, and W.R. Adey, "Effects Of Modulated Very High Frequency Fields On Specific Brain Rhythms In Cats," *Brain Research* vol. 58, issue 2 (1973), 365–384, https://doi.org/10.1016/0006-8993(73)90008-5.

462. S.P. Loughran, A. Verrender, A. Dalecki, C.A. Burdon, K. Tagami, J. Park, N.A.S. Taylor, and R.J. Croft, "Radiofrequency Electromagnetic Field Exposure and the Resting EEG: Exploring the Thermal Mechanism Hypothesis," *Int J Environ Res Public Health.* 16, no. 9 (April 28, 2019), 1505, doi: 10.3390/ijerph16091505.

463. Bachmann M, Lass J, Kalda J, Säkki M, Tomson R, Tuulik V, Hinrikus H., "Integration Of Differences In EEG Analysis Reveals Changes In Human EEG Caused By Microwave," *Conf Proc IEEE Eng Med Biol Soc.* (2006), 1597–600, doi: 10.1109/IEMBS.2006.259234; M. Bachmann, J. Lass, A.A. Ioannides and H. Hinrikus, "Brain Stimulation By Modulated Microwave Radiation: A Feasibility Study," 2018 *EMF-Med 1st World Conference on Biomedical Applications of Electromagnetic Fields (EMF-Med), Split* (2018), 1–2, doi: 10.23919/EMF-MED.2018.8526055.

464. R.K. Sinha, Y. Aggarwal, P.K. Upadhyay, A. Dwivedi, A.K. Keshri, and B.N. Das, "Neural Network-Based Evaluation Of Chronic Non-Thermal Effects Of Modulated 2450 Mhz Microwave Radiation On Electroencephalogram," *Ann Biomed Eng.* 36, no. 5 (May 2008), 839–51, doi: 10.1007/s10439-008-9450-y.

465. H. Danker-Hopfe, A. Bueno-Lopez, H. Dorn, G. Schmid, R. Hirtl, and T. Eggert, "Spending the Night Next To A Router—Results From The First Human Experimental Study Investigating The Impact Of Wi-Fi Exposure On Sleep," *Int J Hyg Environ Health* 228 (July 2020), 113550, doi: 10.1016/j.ijheh.2020.113550.

466. W. Zhi, L. Wang, and X. Hu, "Recent Advances In the Effects Of Microwave Radiation On Brains," *Military Med Res.* 4 (2017), 29, https://mmrjournal.biomedcentral.com/articles/10.1186/s40779-017-0139-0.

467. W. Zhi, L. Wang, and X. Hu, "Recent Advances In the Effects Of Microwave Radiation On Brains," *Military Med Res.* 4 (2017), 29, https://mmrjournal.biomedcentral.com/articles/10.1186/s40779-017-0139-0.

468. Yu. A. Kholodov, "Effects on the Central Nervous System," in *Biological Effects of Magnetic Fields,* Madeleine F. Barnothy, ed. (Plenum Press, New York, 1964), citing N.A. Popov, *On the Physiological Action of Physical Agents*, Moscow 1940.

469. S. Ray and J. Behari, "Physiological Changes in Rats after Exposure to Low Levels of Microwaves," *Radiat Res* 123, no. 2 (1990), 199–202, https://doi.org/10.2307/3577545.

470. Baoming Wang and Henry Lai, "Acute Exposure to Pulsed 2450 MHz Microwaves Affects Water-Maze Performance of Rats," *BioEM S*, 21 (2000), 52–56, https://onlinelibrary.wiley.com/doi/pdf/10.1002/%28SICI%291521-186X%28200001%2921%3A1%3C52%3A%3AAID-BEM8%3E3.0.CO%3B2-6.

471. Hui Wang, Lequan Song, Li Zhao, Haoyu Wang, Xinping Xu, Ji Dong, Jing Zhang, Binwei Yao, Xuelong Zhao, and Ruiyun Peng, "The Dose-Dependent Effect Of 1.5-Ghz Microwave Exposure On Spatial Memory And The NMDAR Pathway In Wistar rats," *Environ Sci Pollut Res.* (2022), https://doi.org/10.1007/s11356-022-24850-4.

472. Z.V. Harvalik, "Dowsing Reactions to Electromagnetic Fields in the Frequency Ranges From 1 Hertz to 1 Megahertz," *The American Dowser Quarterly Digest* vol. 13, no. 3 (August 1973), 80, http://www.dowsing-research.net/dowsing/articles/Harvalik%20-%20Dowsing%20reactions%20to%20EM%20fields%201Hz%20to%201MHz.pdf.

473. J.A. Elder and C.K. Chou, "Auditory Response to Pulsed Radiofrequency Energy," *BioEM S Supplement* 6 (2003), S162-S173, https://onlinelibrary.wiley.com/doi/pdf/10.1002/bem.10163; Chung-Kwang Chou and Arthur W. Guy, "Auditory Perception Of Radio-Frequency Electromagnetic fields," *J. Acoust. Soc. Am.* 71, no. 6 (June 1982), 1321, http://www.stopthecrime.net/Chou-Auditory-perception-of-radio-frequency-EM-fields%20(1).pdf.

474. J.C. and Z. Wang, "Hearing Of Microwave Pulses By Humans And Animals: Effects, Mechanism, And Thresholds," *Health Phys*. vol. 92, no. 6 (June 2007), 621–8, doi: 10.1097/01.HP.0000250644.84530.e2.

475. "IEEE Standard for Safety Levels with Respect to Human Exposure to Electric, Magnetic, and Electromagnetic Fields, 0 Hz to 300 GHz." The current version of this standard is IEEE C95.1–2019, https://standards.ieee.org/ieee/C95.1/4940/.

476. I. Goychuk, "Sensing Magnetic Fields with Magnetosensitive Ion Channels," *Sensors (Basel).*, vol. 18, no. 3 (February 28, 2018), 728, doi: 10.3390/s18030728.

477. P. Huttunen, A. Savinainen, Osmo Hänninen, and R. Myllylä, "Involuntary Human Hand Movements Due to FM Radio Waves in a Moving Van," *Acta Physiol Hung.* vol. 98, no. 2 (June 2011), 157–64, doi: 10.1556/APhysiol.98.2011.2.7.

478. Paavo Huttunen, Osmo Hänninen, and Risto Myllylä, "Humans Sense the Standing Waves of 190 MHz Analogy TV Signals," *IFMBE Proceedings* 37 (January 2012), 1124–1127, 10.1007/978-3-642-23508-5_291.

479. Paavo Huttunen, Osmo Hänninen, and Risto Myllyläh, "FM-radio and TV Tower Signals Can Cause Spontaneous Hand Movements Near Moving RF Reflector," *Pathophysiology* 16, no. 2-3 (August 2009), 201–4, doi: 10.1016/j.pathophys.2009.01.00; Paavo Huttunen, "Spontaneous Movements Of Hands in Gradients of Weak VHF Electromagnetic Fields," PhD dissertation (failed), 2012, University of Eastern Finland Department of Electrical Engineering, http://jultika.oulu.fi/files/isbn9789514297601.pdf.

480. Z.V. Harvalik, "Dowsing Reactions to Electromagnetic Fields in the Frequency Range from 1 Hertz to 1 Mega Hertz," *American Dowser Quarterly Digest* vol. 13, no. 3 (August 1973), 90–91, https://dowsers.org/2016/v13.3_aug1973.pdf.

481. "The Water in You: Water and the Human Body Completed," by USGS Water Science School, May 22, 2019, https://www.usgs.gov/special-topics/water-science-school/science/water-you-water-and-human-body, accessed December 30, 2021.

482. "The Water in You: Water and the Human Body Completed," by USGS Water Science School, May 22, 2019, https://www.usgs.gov/special-topics/water-science-school/science/water-you-water-and-human-body, accessed December 30, 2021.

483. "Microwave Burn," Wikipedia, https://en.wikipedia.org/wiki/Microwave_burn, accessed January 1, 2023.

484. "Charles Richet," Chapter 2 in Kenneth Roberts, *Henry Gross and His Dowsing Rod* (Doubleday, 1951).

485. Dudley D'Auvergne Wright, "The Cause of the Phenomena of Dowsing," *Journal of the British Society of Dowsers* no. 1 (1933), 3, http://www.dowsing-research.net/dowsing/journals/VolI_No1_Sep_1933.pdf.

486. Luc J. Gentet, Greg J. Stuart, and John D. Clements, "Direct Measurement of Specific Membrane Capacitance in Neurons," *Biophysical Journal*, vol. 79, issue 1 (2000), 314–320, https://doi.org/10.1016/S0006-3495(00)76293-X.

487. Q.H. Hogan and M. Poroli, "Hyperpolarization-Activated Current (I(H)) Contributes To Excitability Of Primary Sensory Neurons In Rats," *Brain Res.* 1, no. 1207 (May 2008)102–10, doi: 10.1016/j.brainres.2008.02.066; J.C. Magee, "Dendritic Hyperpolarization-Activated Currents Modify The Integrative Properties Of Hippocampal CA1 Pyramidal Neurons." *J Neurosci.* vol. 18, no. 19 (October 1. 1998), 7613–24, doi: 10.1523/JNEUROSCI.18-19-07613.1998.

488. J.G. Jefferys, J. Deans, M. Bikson, and J. Fox, "Effects of Weak Electric Fields on the Activity of Neurons and Neuronal Networks," *Radiat Prot Dosimetry* 106, no. 4 (2003), 321–3, doi: 10.1093/oxfordjournals.rpd.a006367.

489. N. Radicheva, K. Mileva, T. Vukova, B. Georgieva, and I. Kristev, "Effect Of Microwave Electromagnetic Field On Skeletal Muscle Fibre Activity," *Arch Physiol Biochem.* 110, no. 3 (July 2002), 203–14, doi: 10.1076/apab.110.3.203.8290.

490. Justine Alford, "Dancing Frog Legs," *IFL Science* (June 25, 2014), https://www.iflscience.com/plants-and-animals/dancing-frog-legs/, accessed December 10, 2021.

491. Ehsan Hosseini, "Brain-To-Brain Communication: The Possible Role of Brain Electromagnetic Fields (As a Potential Hypothesis)," *Heliyon* vol. 7, no. 3 (March 1, 2021), e06363, doi: https://doi.org/10.1016/j.heliyon.2021.e06363.

492. Ehsan Hosseini, "Brain-To-Brain Communication: The Possible Role of Brain Electromagnetic Fields (As a Potential Hypothesis)," *Heliyon* vol. 7, no. 3 (March 1, 2021), e06363, doi: https://doi.org/10.1016/j.heliyon.2021.e06363.

493. J.C. Maby and T.B. Franklin, *The Physics of the Divining Rod* (G. Bell and Sons, 1939), citing *The Times* of August 27, 1938.

494. Joel Hruska, "New Research Confirms That Our Electronics And Radio Waves Disrupt Migratory Birds," *Extreme Tech*, May 8, 2014, https://www.extremetech.com/extreme/182077-new-research-confirms-that-our-electronics-and-radio-waves-disrupt-migratory-birds, accessed January 9, 2020.

495. Svenja Engels, Nils-Lasse Schneider, Nele Lefeldt, Christine Maira Hein, Manuela Zapka, Andreas Michalik, Dana Elbers, Achim Kittel, P.J. Hore and Henrik Mouritsen "Anthropogenic Electromagnetic Noise Disrupts Magnetic Compass Orientation In A Migratory Bird," *Nature* 509 (2014), 353–356, https://doi.org/10.1038/nature13290.

496. Zoë L. Hutchison, Andrew B. Gill, Peter Sigray, Haibo He and John W. King, "Anthropogenic Electromagnetic Fields (EMF) Influence the Behaviour Of Bottom-Dwelling Marine Species," *Nature Sci Rep* 10 (2020), 4219, https://doi.org/10.1038/s41598-020-60793-x.

497. Solco Walle Tromp, *Psychical Physics: A Scientific Analysis of Dowsing, Radiesthesia and Kindred Divining Phenomena* (Elsevier, 1949), 283.

498. M.L. Pall, "EM Fields Act Via Activation Of Voltage-Gated Calcium Channels To Produce Beneficial Or Adverse Effects," *J Cell Mol Med.* vol. 17, no. 8 (August 2013), 958–65, doi: 10.1111/jcmm.12088.

499. Simona D'Agostino, Chiara Della Monica, Eleonora Palizzi, Fabio Di Pietrantonio, Massimiliano Benetti, Domenico Cannatà, Marta Cavagnaro, Dariush Sardari, Pasquale Stano, and Alfonsina Ramundo-Orlando, "Extremely High Frequency Electromagnetic Fields Facilitate Electrical Signal Propagation by Increasing Transmembrane Potassium Efflux in an Artificial Axon Model," *Sci Rep.* 8 (2018), 9299, https://doi.org/10.1038/s41598-018-27630-8.

500. M.L. Pall, "Scientific Evidence Contradicts Findings and Assumptions Of Canadian Safety Panel 6: Microwaves Act Through Voltage-Gated Calcium Channel Activation To Induce Biological Impacts At Non-Thermal Levels, Supporting A Paradigm Shift For Microwave/Lower Frequency Electromagnetic Field Action," *Rev Environ Health* vol. 30, no. 2 (2015), 99–116, doi: 10.1515/reveh-2015-0001.

501. Martin L. Pall, "Wi-Fi Is An Important Threat To Human Health," *Environmental Research* vol. 164 (2018), 405–416, htttps://doi.org/10.1016/j.envres.2018.01.035; M.L. Pall, "Scientific Evidence Contradicts Findings And Assumptions Of Canadian Safety Panel 6: Microwaves Act Through Voltage-Gated Calcium Channel Activation To Induce Biological Impacts At Non-Thermal Levels, Supporting A Paradigm Shift For Microwave/Lower Frequency Electromagnetic Field Action," *Rev Environ Health* vol. 30, no. 2 (2015), 99–116, doi: 10.1515/reveh-2015–0001.

502. Andrew Wood and Ken Karipidis, "Radiofrequency Fields and Calcium Movements Into and Out of Cells," *Radiat Res* vol. 195, no. 1 (2021), 101–113, https://doi.org/10.1667/RADE-20-00101.1.

503. J.L. Kirschvink and J.L. Gould, "Biogenic Magnetite As A Basis For Magnetic Field Detection In Animals," *Biosystems* vol. 13, no. 3 (1981), 181–201, doi: 10.1016/0303-2647(81)90060-5.

504. Joseph L. Kirschvink, Atsuko Kobayashi-Kirschvink, Juan C. Diaz-Ricci, and Steven J. Kirschvink, "Magnetite in Human Tissues: A Mechanism for the Biological Effects of Weak ELF Magnetic Fields," *BioEM S Supplement* 1 (1992), 101–113, http://web.gps.caltech.edu/~jkirschvink/pdfs/KirschvinkBEMS92.pdf.

505. I. Goychuk, "Sensing Magnetic Fields with Magnetosensitive Ion Channels," *Sensors (Basel)* vol. 18, no. 3 (February 28, 2018), 728, doi: 10.3390/s18030728.

506. S.K. Dutta, A. Subramoniam, B. Ghosh, and R. Parshad, "Microwave Radiation-Induced Calcium Ion Efflux From Human Neuroblastoma Cells In Culture," *BioEM S* vol. 5, no. 1 (1984), 71–8, doi: 10.1002/bem.2250050108; I. Goychuk, "Sensing Magnetic Fields with Magnetosensitive Ion Channels," *Sensors (Basel)* vol. 18, no. 3 (February 28, 2018), 728, doi: 10.3390/s18030728.

507. G. Kletetschka, R. Bazala, M. Takáč, and E. Svecova, "Magnetic Domains Oscillation in the Brain with Neurodegenerative Disease," *Sci Rep.* 11 (2021), 714, https://doi.org/10.1038/s41598-020-80212-5.

508. Z.V. Harvalik, "Dowsing Reactions to Electromagnetic fields in the Frequency Range from 1 Hertz to 1 Mega Hertz," *American Dowser Quarterly Digest* vol. 13, no. 3 (August 1973), 90–91, https://dowsers.org/2016/v13.3_aug1973.pdf.

509. D.J. Panagopoulos, N. Messini, A. Karabarbounis, A.L. Philippetis, and L.H. Margaritis, "A Mechanism For Action Of Oscillating Electric Fields On Cells," *Biochem Biophys Res Commun.* 272, no. 3 (2000), 634–640, doi:10.1006/bbrc.2000.2746.

510. "Electrolytic Detector," Wikipedia, https://en.wikipedia.org/wiki/Electrolytic_detector, accessed January 2, 2023.

511. Peter Wust, Benedikt Kortüm, Ulf Strauss, Jacek Nadobny, Sebastian Zschaeck, Marcus Beck, Ulrike Stein, and Pirus Ghadjar, "Non-Thermal Effects Of Radiofrequency Electromagnetic Fields," *Sci Rep* 10 (2020), 13488 https://doi.org/10.1038/s41598-020-69561-3, https://www.nature.com/articles/s41598-020-69561-3.

512. A. Mathie, L.E. Kennard, E.L. Veale, "Neuronal Ion Channels and Their Sensitivity To Extremely Low Frequency Weak Electric Field Effects," *Radiat Prot Dosimetry* vol. 106, no. 4 (2003), 311–6, doi: 10.1093/oxfordjournals.rpd.a006365.

513. J. Wang, S.W. Ou, Y.J. Wang, "Distribution and Function Of Voltage-Gated Sodium Channels in the Nervous System," *Channels (Austin)* vol. 11, no. 6 (November 2, 2017), 534–554, doi: 10.1080/19336950.2017.1380758.

514. Bertil Hille, "Ion Channels," http://www.scholarpedia.org/article/Ion_channels, accessed February 7, 2021.

515. Radwan Al Faouri, Eric Krueger, Vivek Govind Kumar, Daniel Fologea, David Straub, Hanan Alismail, Qusay Alfaori, Alicia Kight, Jess Ray, Ralph Henry, Mahmoud Moradi and Gregory Salamo, "An Effective Electric Dipole Model for Voltage-induced Gating Mechanism of Lysenin," *Sci Rep.* 9 (2019), 11440, https://doi.org/10.1038/s41598-019-47725-0.

516. Francisco Bezanilla and Eduardo Perozo, "The Voltage Sensor and the Gate in Ion Channels," *Advances in Protein Chemistry* vol. 63 (2003), 211, http://nerve.bsd.uchicago.edu/FB/TheVsensorAndGate.pdf.

517. R.D. Saunders and J.G.R. Jefferys, "A Neurobiological Basis For ELF guidelines," *Health Phys.* 92 (2007), 596–603, https://journals.lww.com/health-physics/Abstract/2007/06000/A_Neurobiological_Basis_For_Elf_Guidelines.13.aspx.

518. David L. Chandler, "A Mechanical Way to Stimulate Neurons, Magnetic Nanodiscs Can Be Activated By An External Magnetic Field, Providing A Research Tool For Studying Neural Responses,"

MIT News Office, July 19, 2020, https://news.mit.edu/2020/neural-cell-stimulation-magnet-0720.

519. H. Hinrikus, M. Bachmann, and J. Lass, "Understanding Physical Mechanism of Low-Level Microwave Radiation Effect," *Int J Radiat Biol.* vol. 94, no. 10 (October 2018), 877–882, doi: 10.1080/09553002.2018.1478158.

520. H. Hinrikus, M. Bachmann, and J. Lass, "Parametric Mechanism Of Excitation Of The Electroencephalographic Rhythms By Modulated Microwave Radiation," *Int J Radiat Biol.* vol. 87, no. 11 (November 2011), 1077–85, doi: 10.3109/09553002.2011.620063.

Chapter 25

521. "Today in Science," https://todayinsci.com/QuotationsCategories/M_Cat/Mysterious-Quotations.htm, accessed August 1, 2021.

522. Carl Llewellyn Weschcke and Joe. H. Slate, "The New Science of the Paranormal, from the Research Lab to Real Life," (Llewellyn Publications, 2016), Chapter 7, 123.

523. Kate Kershner, "What are ley lines?" https://science.howstuffworks.com/science-vs-myth/unexplained-phenomena/ley-lines.htm, accessed August 18, 2020.

524. Guy Underwood, *The Pattern of the Past* (Abelard-Schuman, 1973).

525. Dennis Wheatley, *The Essential Dowsing Guide* 3rd ed. (Ozark Mountain, 2012).

526. "Geopathic Stress," The Guild of Energists, https://goe.ac/geopathic_stress.htm, accessed August 4, 2020.

527. "Geopathic Stress," The Guild of Energists, https://goe.ac/geopathic_stress.htm, accessed August 4, 2020.

528. A. Baerheim, and H. Sandvik, "Jordstråler—et underjordisk fenomen?" ["Earth Rays"—An Underground Phenomenon?] *Tidsskr Nor Laegefore* vol. 117, no. 17 (June 30, 1997), 2476-7, Article in Norwegian, English abstract https://pubmed.ncbi.nlm.nih.gov/9265308/.

529. B.H. Grandaunet, A. Baerheim, and S. Bondevik, "Barn Utsatt For "Jordstråler" Er Ikke Hyppigere Syke Enn Andre Barn [Children Exposed To "Earth Rays" Are Not More Frequently Ill Than Other Children]," *Tidsskr Nor Laegeforen* 119, no. 26 (October 30, 1999), 3896–8, Article in Norwegian, English abstract https://pubmed.ncbi.nlm.nih.gov/10592748/.

530. Jeffrey Keen, "The Power of Dowsable Energy Fields," *British Dowsing* , 2001, https://britishdowsing.net/the-power-of-dowsable-energy-fields/, accessed February 3, 2021.

531. Dudley H. Wheeler, "Dowsing: A Technique," *Mid Atlantic Geomancy* 9 (1998), http://geomancy.org/index.php?option=com_content&view=article&id=201:dowsing-a-technique&catid=67:no-10-summer-solstice&Itemid=664, accessed August 20, 2020.

532. William Highcock, "Dowsing, an applied science? Two experiments with the dowsing phenomenon," *Journal of the Merseyside Archaeological Society*, vol. 10 (2000) 45, https://www.merseysidearchsoc.com/uploads/2/7/2/9/2729758/jmas_10_paper_4.pdf.

533. Michael Fercik, *The Art of Dowsing, Separating Science from Superstition* (Page Publishing, 2020).

534. A.P. Tabraham, *Solar Energy & Dowsing in the Isles of Scilly: An Addendum* (E.V. Tabraham, St. Mary's, Isles of Scilly, 1992), http://www.dowsing-research.net/dowsing/articles/Tabraham-solar_energy_and_dowsing_an_ddendum.pdf. This booklet is an addendum to *Solar Energy & Dowsing in the Isles of Scilly* (1982), and is published in memory of the author, who died November 1991; A. P. Tabraham, *Solar Energy and Dowsing in the Isles of Scilly* (E.V. Tabraham, St. Mary's, Isles of Scilly, 1992), http://www.dowsing-research.net/dowsing/articles/Tabraham-solar_energy_and_dowsing.pdf.

535. Y. Rocard, "Actions of a Very Weak Magnetic Gradient: The Reflex of the Dowser," Chapter 2 in *Biological Effects of Magnetic Fields*, Madeleine F. Barnothy, ed. (Plenum Press, 1964).

536. C. Lin, R. Chiang, C. Chen, H. Lai, I. Lyubutin, and E. Alkaev, "Preparation of Magnetite Nanoparticles by Thermal Decomposition of Hematite Powder in the Presence of Organic Solvent," *MRS Proceedings* (2007), 998, 998-J08–05, doi:10.1557/PROC-998-J08–05.

537. Kenneth Roberts, *Henry Gross and His Dowsing Rod* (Doubleday, 1951).

538. Michael Fercik, *The Art of Dowsing, Separating Science from Superstition* (Page, 2020).

539. Thomas Welton, trans., *Jacob's Rod*, Translation from the French of *A Rare and Curious Work, A.D. 1693, On the Art of Finding Springs, Mines, and Minerals by Means of the Hazel Rod. To Which Is Appended Researches, with Proofs of the Existence of a More Certain and Far Higher Faculty, with Clear and Ample Instructions for Using It.*

540. Evelyn M. Penrose, Chapter 3 in *Henry Gross and His Dowsing Rod*, Kenneth Roberts (Doubleday, 1951).

541. Michael Fercik, *The Art of Dowsing, Separating Science from Superstit*ion (Page, 2020).

542. Kenneth Roberts, *Henry Gross and His Dowsing Rod* (Doubleday, 1951).

543. Evelyn M. Penrose, Chapter 3 in *Henry Gross and His Dowsing Rod*, Kenneth Roberts (Doubleday, 1951).

544. Kenneth Roberts, *Henry Gross and His Dowsing Rod* (Doubleday, 1951).

545. Dan Schwartz, "Into the Mystical and Inexplicable World of Dowsing," *Outside*, May 3, 2021, https://www.outsideonline.com/outdoor-adventure/exploration-survival/dowsing-water-magic-mystery/, accessed July 1, 2022.

546. "The Disappearing Art Of Dowsing," *The Free Library*, 2014, https://www.thefreelibrary.com/The+disappearing+art+of+dowsing.-a020050042, Accessed December 3, 2020.

547. Dave Tabler, "Divining for Water," Appalachian History, November 24, 2017, https://www.appalachianhistory.net/2017/11/divining-for-water.html, accessed December 30, 2020.

548. Richard Webster, *Dowsing for Beginners, the Art of Discovering: Water, Treasure, Gold, Oil, Artifacts* (Castle Books, 2001).

549. Kate Daloz, "The Dowser Dilemma: How A Town In Vermont Found Water It Desperately Needed And An Explanation That Was Harder To Swallow," *The American Scholar* vol. 78, issue 2 (Spring 2009), 87–100.

550. Psychic Hannah, "Dowsing Rods Help Locate Lost Items, Spirits And Measure Auras," Psychic Source, October 17, 2016, https://www.psychicsource.com/article/other-psychic-topics/dowsing-rods-help-locate-lost-items-spirits-and-measure-auras-by-psychic-hannah/15346, accessed February 3, 2021.

551. Penelope Quest, "Dowsing the Aura," International Center for Reiki Training, https://www.reiki.org/articles/dowsing-aura, accessed February 3, 2021.

552. Marcel Vogel, "British Dowsing Forum," https://britishdowsing.net/forum/search.php?keywords=aura&sid=07c2c4df13403d75455bbdbb8425e07e, accessed February 3, 2021.

553. Chris Connelly and Ia Robinson, "As Child, 'Psychic' Teen Included Auras in Drawings, Skeptical Neighbor Becomes True Believer After Teen 'Sees' Husband's Illness," *ABC News*, August 18, 2009, https://abcnews.go.com/2020/story?id=7916128, accessed February 4, 2021.

554. Dudley D'Auvergne Wright, "The Cause of the Phenomena of Dowsing," *Journal of the British Society of Dowsers*, no. 1 (1933), 3, http://www.dowsing-research.net/dowsing/journals/VolI_No1_Sep_1933.pdf.

555. Jeffrey S. Keen, "How Dowsing Works," https://vixra.org/pdf/1106.0015v2.pdf, accessed February 7, 2021.

Chapter 26

556. "Conclusions Quotes," *Brainy Quote*, https://www.brainyquote.com/topics/conclusions-quotes, accessed February 24, 2023.

Appendix

557. "Today in Science History," https://todayinsci.com/QuotationsCategories/W_Cat/Wave-Quotations.htm, accessed December 30th, 2024.

558. "Speed of Sound," Wikipedia, https://en.wikipedia.org/wiki/Speed_of_sound#Speed_of_sound_in_solids, accessed January 7, 2023.

559. "Refractive Index," *Encyclopedia Britannica*, https://www.britannica.com/science/refractive-index, accessed July 31, 2021.

Annex

560. "AZQuotes," https://www.azquotes.com/quote/619?ref=equipment, accessed January 22, 2023

Selected Bibliography

Barrett, Sir William, and Theodore Besterman. *The Divining Rod: An Experimental and Psychological Investigation*. New York: University Books, 1968.

Dowsing Research: A Comprehensive Library of Publications. www.dowsing-research.net.

Ellis, Arthur J. *The Divining Rod: A History of Water Witching, with a Bibliography*. Washington, D.C.: Government Printing Office, 1917.

Enright, J.T. "Water Dowsing: The Scheunen Experiments." *Naturwissenschaften*, vol. 82 (August 1995): pp. 360–369.

Hansen, George P. "Dowsing: A Review of Experimental Research." *Journal of the Society for Psychical Research*, vol. 51, no. 792 (October 1982): pp. 343–367.

Karmakar, Pranab Kumar. *Ground-Based Microwave Radiometry and Remote Sensing, Methods and Applications*. Boca Raton, FL: Taylor & Francis, 2013.

Kaufman, Alvin B. "Measuring the Phenomenon of Dowsing." *Parapsychology Review*, vol. 2, no. 1 (Jan.-Feb. 1971): pp. 10–12.

Kjørstad, Elise. "Is it Really Possible to Find Water with Dowsing Rods?" February 2, 2022, ScienceNorway.no. https://sciencenorway.no/natural-sciences-physics/is-it-really-possible-to-find-water-with-dowsing-rods/1965796.

Maby, J.C., and T.B. Franklin. *The Physics of the Divining Rod*. London: G. Bell and Sons, 1939.

Mager, Henri. *Water Diviners and Their Methods*. Translated by A.H. Bell. London: G. Bell & Sons, 1931.

Odenwald, Sten. "Experimenter's Guide to Smartphone Sensors." NASA, https://spacemath.gsfc.nasa.gov Version 6.0, May 2019.

Reddish, V.C. *The Field of Rotating Masses*. Edinburg: Makkar Publishing 2010.

Roberts, Kenneth. *Henry Gross and His Dowsing Rod*. Garden City, NJ: Doubleday & Company, 1951.

Rocard, Y. "Actions of a Very Weak Magnetic Gradient: The Reflex of the Dowser." In *Biological Effects of Magnetic Fields*, edited by Madeleine F. Barnothy, pp. 279–286. New York: Plenum Press, 1964.

Tromp, S.W. *Psychical Physics*. New York: Elsevier Publishing Company, 1949.

Underwood, Guy. *The Pattern of the Past*. New York: Abelard-Schuman, 1973.

Voet, Donald, and Judith G. Voet. *Biochemistry*. New York: John Wiley & Sons, 1990.

Ward, Jennabeth Louise. "Exploring the Shared Nondual Experience of Master Dowsers." Ph.D. dissertation, California Institute of Integral Studies, 2016.

Webster, Richard. Dowsing for Beginners: The Art of Discovering Water, Treasure, Gold, Oil, Artifacts. Edison, NJ: Castle Books, 2001.

Weschcke, Carl Llewellyn. *The New Science of the Paranormal, from the Research Lab to Real Life*. Woodbury, MN: Llewellyn Publications, 2016.

Wheatley, Dennis. *The Essential Dowsing Guide, 3d ed*. Huntsville, AR: Ozark Mountain Publishing, 2012.

Young, Hugh D., and Roger A. Freedman. *Sears and Zemansky's University Physics: With Modern Physics, 13th ed*. Boston: Pearson, 2013.

Index

Abell, Sam 261
active denial system 219
adverse symptoms 78
Agricola, Georgius 5
air bubbles in plastic 13, 235
alpha particles 33–35
alternating EM fields 99
aluminum foil 35, 37, 40–42, 48, 50, 67, 70, 77, 84–85, 87, 93, 101, 110, 113, 118, 120–123, 125, 134, 148, 154, 156, 157, 160, 163, 179–180, 184, 195, 197–198, 200–201, 203–204, 206, 236
American Society of Dowsers 51
Amperes's law 52
Angel_09 36
angle resolution 133
angular frequency 47, 252
animals 82–83
antenna 101–106, 108–111, 114–115, 127, 134, 141–143, 169, 178, 182, 193, 195, 218, 246
angular dependence 105; characterization 102; dipole 76, 114, 127, 141, 142, 194, 195; fractional bandwidth 127; gain 141, 142; horn 164, 165, 166, 168; isotropic 141; log-periodic 102, 105, 109; monopole 102–103, 141, 195; Oumefar 102, 105, 109, 110; parabolic dish 141, 195; polarization 105; reciprocity 103; wifi 114; Yagi 141, 195
archaeology 30
atoms 34
Aymar, Jacques 4

Baeck, Leo 235
Baker, Robin 91, 213
Balanovski, E. 93, 101
Barrett, Sir William 7
Basov, N. 185
bees 83, 210, 213, 239
Belinus Line 236
Bermuda 240
Besterman, Theodore 7
beta particles 33, 35
Betz, Hans Dieter 12, 27
Billings, Josh 170
Bishop of Grenoble 171
Bishop's Method *see* Depth:Bishop's Method

black body radiation 122, 124, 125, 128, 138, 207, 245
Bléton, Barthelemy 78
Blythe, Peter 12
Boltzmann, Ludwig 94, 188
Boston University 13
Bouly, Alexis-Timothée 11
Boyle, Robert 7
brain waves (alpha, beta, gamma, delta, theta) 65, 220
Brewster angle 258
Brooks, Carol 26
Brooks, Geoff 65
Brown, Elizabeth 4, 284
Brown, Sylvia 18
Brynjolfsson, Erik 191
Bull, Leroy 26, 27

Canary Islands 11
cardboard 23, 41, 67, 90, 101, 113, 121–122, 155, 157, 160–61, 163, 180, 195, 244
cattle 83, 242
cellular 101, 108, 179, 225, 230
Chadwick, Duane 8, 93, 94
Chevreul's Pendulum 23
chicken 83
Chinese Emperor Yu the Great 5
Chou, C.K. 222
circular objects 237
clairvoyance *see* psi effects
Clarkson, Jeremy 11
clearing the sticks 26
coconuts 5
coherer 44, 191, 192
Coleridge, Samuael Taylor 186
collective subconscious 27
collimation 38, 110, 133, 142–44, 148–151, 173, 179, 181, 246
comprehensive theory of dowsing 2
Comstock, Dan 22
conductivity 33, 55, 57, 59–60, 63–64, 79, 177–178, 232; skin 78, 79
confirmation bias 29–30
Cook, S.A. 93
copper tape 121, 179
cosmic radiation 20, 43–44, 57, 124
Critchley, Simon 218
critical angle 133–134, 137–139, 142–144, 148–149, 173

cryptochromes 211–212, 215, 219, 246
Curie, Marie 33
currents, Earth (telluric) 8, 59
Curry grid 236

D'Agosti, Simona 230
Daniel, Bernard 26
De Boer, Wilhelm 101, 223
Debye, Peter 177
defects in steel and plastic 13, 235
deltoid muscle 244
Denning, Karthyn 30
Dennis, Norma 26
depth 170; Bishop's method 170–174, 246
depth parallel: signal penetration 174–190; *see also* Bishop's method
Dharmadhikari, Nandkumar 8, 12
diamagnetic materials 72
Dickman, J.D. 86
dielectric constant *see* permittivity
dielectric loss 177
difference vs. differential response 67
diffraction 42, 116, 119, 122, 249–250, 256–257
diffusion, 226–227
dogs 83
donkeys 83
double slit experiment 118
dowsing: auras 242, 245; boat 237; dowser effectiveness 16; forked (Y) branch 3, 6–8, 17–19, 22–23, 28, 31, 43, 66, 172, 241; information dowsing 4, 5, 11, 27, 240; L-rod *see* L-Rods; linear structures 39–41, 61; low flying aircraft 61, 62; map dowsing 5, 11, 13, 27, 28, 30, 78, 240, 247; oil exploration 5, 27, 36, 67, 73, 78, 155, 174, 284; overhead 206; pendulum 4, 23, 27, 31, 89, 242; radio waves 222, 223; radon 241; resolution 181; rod material 17–18, 40, 66, 244; shadow 207; shared ability 241; spirits 241, 245; tongue position 148; vehicles 222, 240; visualization

291

25; water wells 5, 7, 23, 26, 70, 83, 240–241
dowsing sense organ 38, 82–85, 87, 110, 114–115, 118, 143–144, 148–149, 151, 210, 245, 246; base skull 84; brain 8–85, 138–139, 206, 245; brain stem 86, 144, 148–149, 215–217, 245–246; cerebellum 86, 115, 144, 147–149, 217, 245–246; crown 84; head 87; kidneys/adrenal glands 84–85; neck/upper back 84; pineal gland 84, 86, 116; thorax, T2-T4 vertebrae 84
dowsing signal path 87
dowsing test 14
Duke University (UNC) 98
Duncan, Donald 171
Dutta, S.K. 231

Earth energies 236
Earth rays *see* geopathic stress
École Normale Supérieure, Paris 47
Einstein, Albert 8, 36, 39, 49, 183
Elder, J.A. 88, 222
electric current 52, 63, 66, 92, 209, 232
electric field 32, 44, 51–58, 62, 67, 91–92, 98, 113, 141, 177, 180, 187, 215, 225, 228, 230–233, 244, 258; Earth 57, 60
electrocardiogram 18, 79, 80
electrochemical potential 62
electroencephalogram 18, 54, 65, 71, 98, 214, 220–221, 229
electrolytic rectifier 231
electromagnetic spectrum 112
electromyography 68, 69, 70, 80, 262
electrons 34–35, 52–53, 63, 71–72, 97, 100, 116, 186, 212, 219
electroreception 53, 215
elephants 83
Ellison, A.J. 113
Enright, J.T. 12

fading 108
Faraday, Michael 23, 41, 95, 100
fault line 8
Fercik, Michael 6, 73, 237, 240
Fiddick, Thomas 9, 25, 33
flowing water 13–14, 24, 32, 35–36, 40, 54–55, 66, 70–73, 78, 94–95
Foley, L. 211
footwear insulation 81
Fort, Charles 3
Foulkes, R.A. 13, 89, 92
Franklin, Bedford 8, 33, 42–45, 66, 95, 112, 124, 192, 207, 224, 229
frequency 112
friction 18, 24, 40, 74, 75, 244

Gader, Carol 17
Gallipoli campaign 10
gamma rays 33–35, 46, 64, 66–67, 100–101, 112–113, 244

geopathic stress 236
Gesellschaft zur wissenschaftlichen Untersuchung von Parawissenschaften 13, 14, 25
Gilder, Stuart A. 214
Global Technical Ltd. 31
glow discharge detector 192
Golde, Peggy 241
Gould, J.L. 214
Goychuk, I. 230–231
graves 2, 5, 14, 24, 26, 55, 93
gravitational constant 38
gravity 8, 32, 37–38, 40, 42, 52, 74, 75, 244–245, 254
Greene, Edith 241
Greenwood, John 12
grid 121, 122, 161, 163, 166, 179, 180, 184, 236
Gross, Henry 11, 25, 79, 170, 240–241
ground penetrating radar 5, 12, 15, 30, 178, 179
Guild of Energists 236
gyromagetic ratio 47

H3 Antenna 76
Hansen, George P. 8, 152
Harrison, Lindsay 18
Hartmann grid 236
Harvalik, Zaboj V. 9, 18, 84–86, 88–89, 93, 101, 116, 221, 223
Herbert, Frank 82
Herbert, Steve 27, 240, 241
Higgins, Shelley 84
Higgs bosons 36
Highcock, William 19, 207, 237
Hinkius, H. 234
Holmes, Oliver Wendell, Jr. 206
Homeland Safety International 31
Hopwood, Anthony 57, 58, 113
horses 83
HRB Singer Inc. 11
Hume, Ivor Noël 9, 30, 116, 207
Humphries, C.M. 42
Humphris, Robert 27
Hutchison, Zoë L. 229
Huttunen, Paavo 73, 222, 223
hydrogen bond 186–188

ideomotor effect 3, 17, 22–25, 29–31, 180, 242, 245
indicator of geophysical anomalies 65
infrared 36, 67, 100, 101, 112, 113, 125, 154, 157, 158, 161, 163, 200
infrasound 50
interference 39, 40, 113, 118–119, 195, 249–250, 257
internal reflection 133
International Agency for Research on Cancer 219
inverse piezoelectric effect 55–56
ion Channels 230
ionosphere 44, 59, 62, 64
Iris Instruments 48
isotope 34

Jackson, John 23
Janks, John 59–60, 62, 76
Jean, Nicholas 66, 124, 240
Jeffries, J.G.R. 233
Jena, Nicholas 17
Jennings, Philip 96
Jennison, Roger 7, 84, 113, 118, 122
Jensen, L. 94
Jensen, Larry 8, 93
Joel, Harry 73
Josephson junctions 97–98
Jung, Carl 27

Karipidis, Ken 230
Kassel dowsing experiments 14
Keen, Jeffrey 83–84, 236, 242
Keen, Montague 27
Kelly, Stephen 10
Kelvin water dropper experiment 54
Kholodov, Yu. A. 98
Kirschvink, J.L. 89, 213–214, 230
Klein, Étienne 51
Kletetschka, G. 231
Kniebes, Duane 24
Kravchenko, Yu. P. 65
Krinkler, Mark 65

L-rod 1, 3, 4, 5, 8, 9, 12, 17, 30, 75, 87, 243, 245, 247; friction 18, 18; insulated 18; material 17–18; quartz 12–13
Large Hadron Collider 36
Larmor frequency 47, 212
laser 118, 183–185, 257
Latimer, Charles 11, 27–28, 42, 78, 81, 172
Lawhead, Stephen R. 59
Lee, Jong Doo 64
ley lines 113, 235, 236
Lipid Bilayer 226
Loman, Joe 241
loop shaped rod 89
Lovegrove, Harry 84
low friction dowsing rods 6
low noise block detector 150, 195–198, 200–201, 203–205; C band 203–204; Ku Band 195, 200–201
Luther, Martin 1

Maby, Cecil 8, 13, 27, 33, 36, 42–45, 66, 78, 95, 99, 112, 124, 191–192, 207, 224, 229
Mager, Henri 4, 284
magnet neodymium 96, 121, 208, 209
magnetic field 8, 18–20, 32, 42–44, 46–47, 52, 60, 62, 71–73, 88–93, 95–96, 98–99, 121, 135, 145, 150–151, 154, 208–217, 229–231, 233–234, 244; Earth 32, 43, 46–48, 59, 71, 88, 90–91, 93–95, 208–212, 215, 229, 244, 246; effect of flowing water 94; FDA guidance 98; flowing water 32, 96; Induced EMF in dowser 95; magnetic induction 98

Index

magnetic field sense 82, 86, 89, 91, 99, 210, 211, 213–217, 231, 246; organ 86, 216, 246
magnetic flux density 47, 92, 94
magnetic induction 95
magnetic resonance imaging 98, 144–148
magnetism 71, 72
magnetite 72, 93–94, 150–151, 210–211, 213–217, 230–231, 233–234, 239, 241, 246; bees 213; birds 213; brain stem 214; cerebellum 214; hippocampus 213; human brain 213, 214; nerve 214; particle size 214; single domain 214
magnetohydrodynamic effects 95
magnetometer 8, 30, 43, 89, 90, 91, 96, 154, 208
Malkempter, E.P. 215
Marshall 171
Marshall, Larry 37
Martin, D. Abel 242
Martin, Michael 13
maser 183–185
Matthie, A. 232
Maxwell, James Clerk 177
membrane potential 229, 231–233
memory effect 152–158, 160–161, 163, 166, 168–169, 183–184, 189, 209, 246; activation 156–158, 169; creation 157, 160; detection 157, 163; dwell time 156; infrared 157, 169; pine 161, 166; skillet 153–157; temperature 157–158
Michael & Mary Line 236
microwaves 41, 46, 67, 97, 100–102, 10–106, 108, 109–116, 118, 121–122, 124–125, 127, 129–130, 132–135, 137–138, 140, 142–144, 146–150, 154, 157, 161, 163, 168–170, 173–175, 177–189, 191–193, 195, 200–201, 204, 206–209, 213, 217–219, 221–225, 229–231, 233–235, 238, 241, 244, 245–246; behavior 220; brain cancer 219; collimation 133; cosmic background 124–125; detector in head 110; EEG 220, 221; hearing 222, 230; penetration 115–116, 129, 144, 174–175, 177–181, 223–224; physiological effects 108; satellite 179; satellite measurements 129–130
Mikheenko, P. 97
Miller, Anne 8, 42, 84, 85, 113, 284
mineral exploration 5, 67
mines (weapon) see unexploded ordnance
molecular energy 94
Moses 5
Mouritson, Henrik 229
Mu metal 84
Murdoch University 96
muscle bicep 70
muscle deltoid 68–70
muscle tone 77

neon discharge tube 43–44, 192
nerve 246; antenna 225; dowsing 224; high intensity magnetic fields 98; local reflex 224; rectifier 231; resonant circuit 225; stimulation current 98; transcranial magnetic stimulation 98; triggering 225, 228
neutrinos 36
neutrons 34, 35
Newton, Sir Isaac 38
Nimpf, S. 214
Nordell, Bo 55, 56
Nottingham Trent University 12
nuclear magnetic resonance 46–48, 72, 144–145

Occupational Safety and Health Administration 54
Ohm's law 60
olfactory fatigue 110
Onnes, Heike Kamerlingh 97
Ouija board 23
overhead cables 40

Pall, M.L. 230
Panagopoulos, D.J. 231
parallel bands 42–45
past lives 27
Pearson-Anson oscillator 192
Pegler, Ian 171
Penetration of Microwaves 174–190
Penrose, Evelyn 19, 67, 78, 240
percent people can dowse 8–9, 87
permeability 52, 84, 92–94, 135, 177
permitivity 44, 115, 129–130, 135–137, 142, 144, 177, 223
photons 35, 46–47, 140, 183, 185, 189, 219, 257
piezoelectric effect 55; bone 55, 56; quartz 55, 56
pipes, PVC 19, 29–30, 35, 54–55, 58, 63, 93, 116, 142, 195, 200–201, 244
Pismenny, Larry 65
pitchblende 33
pituitary gland 144, 146–148
Planck, Max 36, 46, 125, 183, 245; Plank equation 46, 125, 183; Planck radiation 36; Planck's constant 46, 183
Plat, Gabriel 7
polarization 40–41, 56, 60, 105, 108, 149, 164, 178, 180, 228, 230, 244, 249–250, 258–259
positron 35
posture 76, 86
potential, skin 79
precession 47
Price, Robert 12
Prokhorov, A. 185
Proton Precession Magnetometer 12
protons 34, 46–48, 52, 144–145
psi effects 1, 3–5, 22, 26–30, 32, 62, 174, 240, 242, 247

Purcell, Edward Mills 46
PVC pipe see pipes, PVC

quackery and fraud 31
quantization of EM radiation 46
quantum gradient gravity device 37
quantum mechanical tunnelling 97
Quest, Penelope 242

Radicheva, N. 225
radio wave 20, 41, 43, 46–48, 64, 66–67, 73, 101, 112–114, 122, 124–125, 129, 133, 138, 140–141, 145, 154, 157, 161, 178–179, 193–194, 207–208, 213, 218–219, 222–223, 229–231, 235, 238, 244; birds 212, 229
radioactivity 33, 34, 35, 36, 101
radium 33, 35
radon 241
rain and snow 71
Randi, James 23
Rayleigh, Lord see Strutt, John William (Lord Rayleigh)
Reddish, Vincent 18, 19, 39, 40, 41, 42, 45
reflection 41, 113, 132, 138, 143, 144, 171, 173, 178, 249, 254
refraction 132, 134–135, 138–139, 142–143, 173, 246, 249, 250, 255–256
refractive index 134–138, 142, 144, 174, 256
Reid, Brian 174
Reiki 242
remote viewing 5
requirements for detection 19
resistivity 8, 60, 61; ground 8, 30
resolution 76, 92, 116–117, 122, 132–133, 139, 142–144, 154, 178–179, 205, 245; dowsing 118; optical 116
resonance 50, 64, 65, 71, 114–115, 145, 204, 212, 222–223, 234
response time 74, 81
Rhine, J.B. 83
Richet, Charles 10, 224, 225
Riddick, Thomas M. 70
Roberts, Kenneth 11, 22, 240
Rocard, Yves 47–48, 79, 89, 92--95, 239
Rota, Louis 192
rotating mass 42

Sagan, Carl 1, 152
Sangster, Harry 27, 28
Saunders, R.D. 233
Saunders, Thomas 67, 71, 284
Schlelden, Jacob Mathias 210
Schneider, Reinhard 76
Schulten, Klaus 212
Schultheiss-Grassi, P.P. 213
Schumann resonance 64–65
Schwartz, Dan 240
Shane, Neil Du 26

Shepard, Leslie 8
Sherrard, Rachel M. 212
shipping container 44, 207, 208, 209
Slate, Joe 12, 235
Smith. the Rev. Martin J. 37
Snell's law 133–134, 138, 140, 255
Sniffex 31
sodium potassium pump 227, 228, 229
software defined radio 193, 194, 203, 204, 205, 263
Solov'yov, Llia 212
Sommer, Robert 77
sound 42, 49, 50, 64, 73, 171, 193, 222, 244, 249, 250, 255
source of dowsing signal 19
spirits and spirit guides 27
spontaneous emission 183–186, 189
Stafford, Tom 23
standing waves 43,-45, 64, 121, 223
state of mind 24
static electricity 51–55, 63
stimulated emission 183–185, 186, 189, 233
Stone Henge 235
Storozuk, Greg 24
streams. underground 24, 78, 93, 96, 171
Strutt, John William (Lord Rayleigh) 116
sub-atomic particles 33
superconductors 97
superposition 39, 113
Suvla Bay 10

Tabraham, A.P. 170, 238–239
tachyons 36
Tassili Caves, Algeria 5
Taylor, Gordon Rattray 10
Taylor, J.G. 93, 101
telluric (Earth) currents 59, 62

Tesla, Nikola 112, 249
thermal emissions *see* blackbody radiation
thermal noise 48, 201
Thomas, Heather Smith 170
Thomson, William (Lord Kelvin) 55
Thouvenel, Pierre 78
torsion field 39
torsion radiation 39, 41, 42
transcranial magnetic stimulation 98, 220
transverse wave 40, 41, 180, 184, 244, 257
triboelectric effect 53
Tromp, Solco 8, 18, 27, 71, 77–79, 81, 83, 89–90, 99, 124, 171, 229
Turner, Barney 9

Ufa Aviation Engineering University 65
UHF band 221
UK Groundwater Forum 73
ultrasound 49
ultraviolet 19, 64, 66, 67, 100, 112, 219
Underwood, Guy 24, 25, 235
unexploded ordnance 11, 13, 31
University of Birmingham (UK) 37
University of Calgary 12, 68
University of California, Berkeley 14
University of Edinburgh 39
University of Giesen 77
University of Kent 7
University of Manchester 91
University of Sheffield 30
uraninite 33
US Geological Survey 59, 70
utility companies 5, 15, 247

Vass, Arpad 55
vehicles 73

visible light 67, 113, 129, 133–134, 154, 157, 207–208, 244
Vitruvius 1
Vogel, Marcel 242
Vogt, Evon Z. 241
Voids 142
voltage controlled ion gates 150, 215, 228, 230, 231, 233

Wadsworth, M.A. 22
Wang, Connie X. 214
water, adsorbed 169, 186, 188–189, 233
Weber, J. 185
Webster, Richard 4, 9, 284
Weschcke, Carl 12, 235
Wheatley, Dennis 4, 9, 24, 25, 152, 171, 284
Wheeler, Dudley 77, 237
Whittaker, William E. 22, 24
Whitton, J.L. 93
Wi-Fi 101, 108, 221
Wilcock, John 8, 9, 12
Williamson, Tom 88
Wood, Andrew 230
World Health Organization 100, 219
Wright, Dudley 225
Wu, J.Q. 86
Wu, L.Q. 215
Wűst, Joseph 49
Wust, Peter 232

x-rays 35, 66, 67, 100, 101, 112, 113, 244

yang energy 64
Yeosock, John John 13
Youngblood, Lloyd 5
Young's double slit experiment 113, 118, 119